Slave Society in the Danish West Indies

The

PRESS

University of the West Indies

Signed *Sophia Alexander*

Neville A. T. Hall

Slave Society in the Danish West Indies

St. Thomas, St. John, and St. Croix

Edited by B. W. Higman

With a Foreword by Kamau Brathwaite

The University of the West Indies Press
●JAMAICA ●BARBADOS ●TRINIDAD

The University of the West Indies Press
Mona, Jamaica
Cave Hill, Barbados
St. Augustine, Trinidad

Published for the Department of History of
The University of the West Indies at
Mona, Cave Hill and St. Augustine

99 98 97 95 94   5 4 3 2

NATIONAL LIBRARY OF JAMAICA CATALOGUING IN PUBLICATION DATA

HALL, NEVILLE A. T., 1936-1986
  Slave society in the Danish West Indies:
St. Thomas, St. John and St. Croix/
Neville A. T. Hall; edited by B. W. Higman.
  Bibliography: p.
  Includes index
  ISBN 976 41 0029 5
  1. Slavery – Virgin Islands, U.S.
  I. Title   II. Higman, B.W.
  305.5'67'0972972'2

Cover design by Prodesign Ltd., Kingston, Jamaica

Cover illustrations taken from Ingvar Zangenberg, *Dansk Vestindien for
250 år siden* (Copenhagen, 1981). Reproduced with permission of Dorte
Zangenberg.

Printed in the United States of America on acid-free paper

Contents

List of Tables

List of Figures

Abbreviations

AVS/FC   Akter vedkommende Slaveemancipation. Den ældre sag om de Frikulørte, 1826-34 (R/A)

CANS   Originale Forestillinger fra Kommmissionen angaaende Negrenes Stilling i Vestindien m.m., med Resolutioner, 1834-43 (R/A)

DVK   Dokumenter vedkommende Kommissionen vedrørende Negerhandelens bedre Indretning og Ophævelse samt Efterretninger om Negerhandelen og Slaveriet i Vestindien, 1783-1806 (R/A)

DVRA   *Dansk Vestindisk Regerings Avis*

FAN   Forslag og Anmærkninger til Negerloven med Genparter af Anordninger og Publikationer vedkommende Negervæsenet, 1785 (R/A)

Gtk   Generaltoldkammeret (R/A)

N/A   National Archives, Washington D.C.

NEER   Negeremancipationen efter Reskript af 28 Juli 1847 (R/A)

R/A   Rigsarkivet, Copenhagen (All references are to the Generaltoldkammeret papers unless otherwise specified)

RDAG   *Royal Danish American Gazette*

RG   Record Group (N/A)

SCG   *St. Croix Gazette*

STT   *St. Thomæ Tidende*

UBAN   Udkast og Betænkning agaaende Negerloven, 1783-89 (R/A)

VGRG   Vestindisk-guineisk Rent Samt (R/A)

VJ   Vestindiske Journaler (R/A)

VLA   Vestindiske Lokalarkiver (R/A)

n/d   not dated

n/p   not paginated

para.   paragraph

Rds.   Rigsdaler

Glossary

Articler	Articles, regulations
Bomba	Slave driver
Bosal	A slave recently brought from Africa
Byfoged	Judge
Conferenceraad	Jurist
Danske Cancelli	Danish Chancery
Etatsraad	Titular Counsellor of State
Generaltoldkammer	General Customs Office (often referred to by Danish West Indian officials as "det vestindiske Kammer," the West Indian office)
Landfoged	Country bailiff
Marronage	Running away, desertion of masters by slaves
Mulatinde	Mulatto (old Danish)
Patacoon	3 Rigsdaler or 6 Danish kroner (= $1)
Placat	Proclamation
Procurator	Attorney
Reglement	Regulations
Rigsdaler	Rix-dollar, standard Danish currency (10 Rigsdaler = £1 sterling)
Skilling	Shilling, an obsolete coin
Stænderforsamlinger	Assembly of the Estates of the Realm
Styver	Stiver, 4 pence sterling
Tønder	1.363 acres

Foreword

Neville Hall

THE SOFT-BRIM TAN SUN HAT, THE SHORTS, THE FIVE-SPEED cycle bell across the campus lawn, the loud clear mellow baritone, historian who sculptured radio ads even though his father named him Archibald & Theodore after some hopeful medieval Pope perhaps... Diana Ross sings *Tell me how the road turns* for her lost friend Marvin Gaye like Garcia Lorca for his Seville bullfighter... And in the late September dust, Nev's car in turning right towards the night of nearing home is crumpled into silence of all sound by a blind crowded heedless mini-van from August Town the speeding freedman's village he would write about hundred years before... *The victors all unvanquished* in the dusk...

For months we mourned the crashes, tinkle glass & metal falling, pondering with dumb pogo sticks among the ashes of the bad, confused handwriting of that "accident" while all the while a dark & mineral stain lay like his memory upon the growing lawn. Communities like ours cannot afford these losses, no? This candid raconteur who drew us all together, doyen among the Deans, imagination's lecturer, researcher, artist/actor, most admirable brother and a friend

Don't tell me don't tell me don't tell me why the road turns...

But when yr life produces love & family & sons, Mysser; and when yr care produces friends and caring colleagues who respond to you & what you are; and when your diligence & vision harvests history – Christiansted & Frederiksted, Charlotte Amalie & Buddoe & Tuit & Casimir von Scholten – as brought to lighted here by Barry Higman working patiently & lovingly from note & pasted page & manuscript & almost ts lost/so that we turn at last from shatter, silence, headless heedless chaos of the moment of the *turning turning turning road* to – *yes* – the future of the sun hat, fashionable ducks, brass voice & laughter of his tropical elation, the author of these elegant & rescued pages thinkeling his five-speed bike across the campus morning *tell me tell me tell me* lawn/our colleague gentleman & scholar & my friend

Kamau Brathwaite
Mona
15/1/90

Editor's Preface

NEVILLE A. T. HALL DIED IN SEPTEMBER 1986 AS A RESULT OF injuries sustained in a motor vehicle accident. A Jamaican, he was at the time of his death Senior Lecturer in the Department of History at the University of the West Indies, Mona campus. His first research was concerned with the political history of the British West Indies in the eighteenth century, but in the early 1970s he developed a particular interest in the slave society of the Danish colonies, those three islands – St. Thomas, St. John and St. Croix – which now form the Virgin Islands of the United States. This interest led him to mastery of the Danish language and of the archives of Copenhagen, and he began to publish articles on a variety of topics within the general field. His conception of the project was firmly located within the framework of the slave society model, viewing slaves and slavery as central to the entire colonial community and its metropolitan base rather than as objects easily abstracted from the larger history. As the project grew in Neville Hall's mind and on paper, it expanded beyond the bounds of a single book to a work of three or perhaps more volumes.

Shortly after Neville Hall's death I was asked by his widow Mysser to assist with bringing his work to publication. This I agreed to do and, following an initial sifting of his papers by Mysser and her sons Nikolas, Jonathan and Adam, I identified the materials central to his project on the history of slave society in the Danish West Indies. Although I had talked frequently with Neville Hall about the progress of his work and had participated in conferences and seminars at which he had presented papers, I was not aware of the details of the structure he proposed to create. Fragments among his papers enabled me to understand much better the organization of the project and the rethinking that was going on as research proceeded and writing continued. The summer of 1986 had been spent collecting further material in the Copenhagen archives, and chapters were in an active state of revision. A much revised outline of the project showed it to conceive a volume on the slaves, a second on freedmen during slavery tentatively titled " 'An Intermediate Sort of Class:' Freedmen in Danish West Indian Slave Society," and a third on the immediate post-emancipation period 1848-1878.

The present book consists chiefly of chapters planned for the first volume of the projected trilogy together with three which would have been placed in the second volume. Five of the twelve chapters have not been previously published. Only three projected chapters are missing: a study of slavery on a specific plantation to have followed chapter 4, an analysis of petit marronage to balance that of grand marronage found in chapter 7, and an account of amelioration and changes in the slave laws between 1800 and 1848 to have supplemented the material presented in chapter 11. But biographical papers on Anna Heegaard and Apollo Miller, destined for volume two, have not been included here. In editing the material I have made every effort to be faithful to Neville Hall's conception of the work in terms of structure, content and interpretation. It is clear however that some of the material was left in a state which the author himself regarded as unfinished and he had not revised the separately published papers to meet the requirements of a book; I have therefore taken certain liberties in order to complete the work and mold it into a coherent whole, while always attempting to preserve the stylistic character of the original. It has been necessary to introduce a paragraph from time to time, but generally my interventions have been limited to revisions on a smaller scale and I have used Neville Hall's own words whenever I could find appropriate material within the text.

Chapter 1 consists essentially of Neville Hall's monograph *The Danish West Indies: Empire Without Dominion, 1671-1848* (Division of Libraries, Museums and Archaeological Services, U.S. Virgin Islands, Occasional Paper No. 8, 1985), together with some introductory material taken from his papers "Maritime Maroons: *Grand Marronage* from the Danish West Indies," *William and Mary Quarterly* 42 (1985): 476-98, and "Slaves and the Law in the Towns of St. Croix 1802-1807," *Slavery and Abolition* 8 (1987): 147-65.

Chapter 2 was originally written as a seminar paper, titled "Public Opinion and Slavery in the Danish Virgin Islands in the Eighteenth and Nineteenth Centuries," presented to the Department of History, University of the West Indies, Mona, in March 1976. I have used Neville Hall's annotated copy of that paper, and a typescript revision he produced after the seminar. The notes had been revised but not typed, and those added after the seminar exist only in abbreviated manuscript. I have filled out the notes, and supplied the title and subheadings.

Chapter 3 is based on the published paper "Slave Laws of the Danish Virgin Islands in the Later Eighteenth Century," *Annals of the New York Academy of Sciences* 292 (1977): 174-86, with supplementary sections from "Slaves and the Law in the Towns of St. Croix." I have supplied the title and subheadings.

Chapter 4 is derived from a manuscript, probably written in the later 1970s, in two versions. There is also a typed version of the text but the notes are only in manuscript, very abbreviated and often incomplete. In most cases however the clues are sufficient to enable accurate reconstruction of the notes. I have included material from "Slave Laws of the Danish Virgin Islands" and introduced data on the slave trade from the papers of Svend Green-Pederson. I have also used material from C.G.A. Oldendorp's *History*, originally published in German, and appearing in English translation for the first time in 1987. All references to Oldendorp in this and other chapters have been keyed to the 1987 English edition.

Chapter 5 is taken from "Slavery in Three West Indian Towns: Christiansted, Fredericksted and Charlotte Amalie in the Late Eighteenth and Early Nineteenth Century" in *Trade, Government and Society in Caribbean History 1700-1920* edited by B.W. Higman (1983), and "Slaves and the Law in the Towns of St. Croix." I have added subheads.

Chapter 6 follows closely "Slaves Use of Their 'Free' Time in the Danish Virgin Islands in the Later Eighteenth and Early Nineteenth Century," *Journal of Caribbean History* 13 (1980): 21-43. I have supplied subheadings and a new title.

Chapter 7 is derived from the published paper "Maritime Maroons." I have moved some of the introductory material and added subheads.

Chapter 8 combines a seminar paper titled " 'An Intermediate Sort of Class:' Freedmen in the Slave Society of the Danish West Indies in the Later Eighteenth Century" presented at The Johns Hopkins University in 1985 with material published in "The 1816 Freedman Petition in the Danish West Indies: Its Background and Consequences," *Boletin de Estudios Latinoamericanos y del Caribe* 29 (1980): 55-73. Neville Hall explained in a note to his *Boletin* paper of 1980 that "Throughout this paper consistent use has been made of *freedman* as a generic term to describe free non-whites of both sexes. However, the term *freedwoman* is also used where the sexual distinction is important to the discussion. Like Jerome Handler, ... the present writer feels that this terminological usage avoids the ambiguities of the term *free coloured*." This usage has been retained in the book, the label *ex-slave* being used only to describe persons freed from 3 July 1848. I have supplied the subheads for chapter 8.

Chapter 9 comes from a typescript titled "The 1816 Petition and Its Antecedents" and dated 8 August 1985, with material from "The 1816 Freedman Petition" of 1980 added to the introduction and the conclusion. The notes for the typescript paper existed only in manuscript and in a very abbreviated form. I have supplied subheads and a new title.

Chapter 10 is a reduced version of a typescript titled " 'Strangers Within the Gate:' Émigré Freedmen in St. Thomas in the Nineteenth Century," with the introduction coming from a separate abstract. I have added subheads.

Chapter 11 derives from the published paper "Establishing a Public Elementary School System for Slaves in the Danish Virgin Islands, 1732-1846," *Caribbean Journal of Education* 6 (1979): 1-45. I have cut this by about one-third and readers with a special interest in education are referred to the original. I have provided a new title.

Chapter 12 derives from "The Victor Vanquished: Emancipation in St. Croix; Its Antecedents and Immediate Aftermath," *Nieuwe West-Indische Gids* 58 (1984): 3-36. The notes have been reorganized.

The bibliography has been constructed from items referenced in the notes. A number of references to recent publications have been added to the notes and these have also been included in the bibliography.

I thank the following copyright holders for permission to use material originally published by them: Centrum voor Studie en Documentatie van Latijns Amerika (Amsterdam), for material used in chapters 8 and 9; Division of Libraries, Museums and Archaeological Services, Department of Conservation and Cultural Affairs, U.S. Virgin Islands, for most of chapter 1; Faculty of Education, University of the West Indies, for chapter 11; Heinemann Publishers, Kingston, for parts of chapter 5; Institute of Early American History and Culture, Williamsburg, for material used in chapters 1 and 7; New York Academy of Sciences, for parts of chapters 3 and 4; and the Center for Caribbean and Latin American Studies (University of Utrecht) for chapter 12. Sections of chapters 1, 3 and 5 are reprinted by permission of Frank Cass and Co. Ltd., London.

Most of the translations from the Danish included in this book are by Neville Hall. For assistance with those he had not completed I am grateful to Karen Fog Olwig of the University of Copenhagen who also helped with the checking of references and commented on a draft of the manuscript. For his meticulous and extensive work in checking references in the Rigsarkivet and for organizing the archival section of the bibliography I am particularly indebted to archivist Poul Olsen. Assistance with the references was also given by George Tyson and the late Isaac Dookhan. I thank Merle Higman and Brian Moore for their comments on a draft, and Kamau Brathwaite for contributing the Foreword as well as for his reading of the manuscript. Roy Augier, Ralph Carnegie and Woodville Marshall supplied valued encouragement and advice at various stages of the work. For help in the production phase, I am grateful to Wycliffe Ho-Shing, Kathleen Miles and Donald Miller.

Publication of this book was made possible by the Research and Publications Fund Committee of the University of the West Indies, through the Departments of History at Mona, Cave Hill and St. Augustine.

The work involved in bringing the manuscript to publication was supported by a generous grant from Unesco. I thank Mervyn Claxton, Representative, and Alwin Bully, Sub-Regional Culture Adviser, for their cooperation and enthusiasm.

I wish particularly to thank Mysser Hall for trusting me with the work and for her continued interest in its progress.

No doubt Neville Hall would have wished to record his own acknowledgement of help received along the way. It is impossible for me to reconstruct his list, and I can only offer a general thanks to all those individuals and institutions that supported him and made available their archives, libraries and ideas.

B.W.H.

List of Publications of Neville A.T. Hall

"Governors and Generals: The Relationship of Civil and Military Commands in Barbados 1783-1815." *Caribbean Studies* 10 (1971):93-112.

"Public Office and Private Gain: A Note on Administration in Jamaica in the Later Eighteenth Century." *Caribbean Studies* 12 (1972): 5-20.

"Law and Society in Barbados at the turn of the Nineteenth Century." *Journal of Caribbean History* 5 (1972): 20-45.

"Some Aspects of the Deficiency Question in Jamaica in the Eighteenth Century." *Jamaica Journal* 7 (1/2) (1973): 36-41.

Review of Jerome S. Handler, *A Guide to Source Materials for the Study of Barbados History* in *Caribbean Studies* 14 (1975): 183-184.

"Anna Heegaard – Enigma." *Caribbean Quarterly* 22 (1976): 62-73.

Review of William Laws, *Distinction, Death and Disgrace* in *Social and Economic Studies* 26 (1977): 388-390.

"Slave Laws of the Danish Virgin Islands in the Later Eighteenth Century." *Annals of the New York Academy of Sciences* 292 (1977): 174-186.

"Establishing a Public Elementary School System for Slaves in the Danish Virgin Islands, 1732-1846." *Caribbean Journal of Education* 6 (1979): 1-45. Republished in *Education in the Caribbean: Historical Perspectives* edited by Ruby Hope King, special issue *Caribbean Journal of Education* 14 (1987): 1-44.

Translation with introduction and notes, *Forslag til Ordning af Vestindiske Forfatningsforhold Angaaende Negerne med Mere* (A Proposal for Regulating the Situation of Negroes in the West Indies, etc., Anon., 1826). St. Thomas: Bureau of Libraries, Museums and Archaeological Services: Department of Conservation and Cultural Affairs, Occasional Paper No. 5, 1979.

"The 1816 Freedman Petition in the Danish West Indies: Its Background and Consequences." *Boletin de Estudios Latinoamericanos y del Caribe* 29 (1980): 55-73.

"Slaves Use of Their 'Free' Time in the Danish Virgin Islands in the Later Eighteenth and Early Nineteenth Century." *Journal of Caribbean History* 13 (1980): 21-43.

"Surrogate Scribes: Review Article." *Caribbean Quarterly* 28 (1982): 53-57. (Review of Michael Craton, *Searching for the Invisible Man*, and Jerome S. Handler and Frederick W. Lange, *Plantation Slavery in Barbados*.)

Review of Richard Hart, *Slaves Who Abolished Slavery: Blacks in Bondage* in *Jamaican Historical Review* 13 (1982): 49-50.

"Slavery in Three West Indian Towns: Christiansted, Fredericksted and Charlotte Amalie in the Late Eighteenth and Early Nineteenth Century." In *Trade, Government and Society in Caribbean History 1700-1920*, edited by B.W. Higman. Kingston: Heinemann Educational Books, 1983.

Translation with an introduction, "Louis Rothe's 1846 Report on Education in Post-emancipation Antigua," *Caribbean Journal of Education* 10 (1983): 55-62. Republished in *Education in the Caribbean: Historical Perspectives* edited by Ruby Hope King, special issue of *Caribbean Journal of Education* 14 (1987): 46-53.

"The Victor Vanquished: Emancipation in St. Croix; Its Antecedents and Immediate Aftermath." *Nieuwe West-Indische Gids* 58 (1984): 3-36.

Review of David Eltis and James Walvin (eds.), *The Abolition of the Atlantic Slave Trade* in *Immigrants and Minorities* 3 (1984): 94-96.

Review of Roger D. Abrahams and John F. Szwed (eds.), *After Africa* in *Terrae Incognitae* 16 (1984): 97-100.

"Maritime Maroons: *Grand Marronage* from the Danish West Indies." *William and Mary Quarterly* 42 (1985): 476-498.

The Danish West Indies: Empire Without Dominion, 1671-1848. Division of Libraries, Museums and Archaeological Services, U.S. Virgin Islands, Occasional Paper No. 8, 1985.

Review of David Barry Gaspar, *Bondmen and Rebels* in *Journal of Economic History* 46 (1986): 1054-1056.

Le Processus d'Emancipation aux Antilles Danoises. Martinique: Foundation Schoelcher, Cahier No. 6, 1987.

Review of Karen Fog Olwig, *Cultural Adaptation and Resistance on St. John* in *Hispanic American Historical Review* 67 (1987): 147-48.

"Slaves and the Law in the Towns of St. Croix 1802-1807." *Slavery and Abolition* 8 (1987): 147-65.

"Apollo Miller, Freedman: His Life and Times." *Journal of Caribbean History* 23 (2) (1989): 196-213.

SLAVE SOCIETY
IN THE
DANISH WEST INDIES

1

Empire Without Dominion: The Danish West Indies, 1671-1848

CARIBBEAN HISTORY IS FULL OF IRONIES. NOT THE LEAST among them is the fact that the region's geological heritage of uncommonly arresting physical attributes is the product of tectonic activity many millenia ago that, while literally fragmenting a land mass, also set the stage for political atomization. The pearls, unstrung by nature, have defied each successive effort of political artifice, whether by Caribs, Spaniards, other European colonizers or post-colonial polities, to be re-strung on a single enduring chain and held together by some unifying informing principle. In the period of major European expansion, beginning at the end of the fifteenth century, some European colonizers did contrive to string together Caribbean empires of varying extent. Their size and longevity, however, were functions of power.

The kingdom of Denmark, with its satellite Norway, was one of the European powers that attempted to create and sustain a Caribbean empire beginning in the later seventeenth century. In comparative terms, Denmark was a relatively late entrant in the scramble for colonies and since it was not a European power of the first rank its authority as a colonizer was continuously compromised. Its colonization of St. Thomas, beginning in 1671, and of St. John in 1717, occurred at a time when England, France and Holland had long since broken, de facto and de jure, Spain's monopoly of the region and were consolidating their New World gains. Denmark's choice was limited in the extreme. Its acquisition of St. Thomas and St. John was determined not by choice but by lack of feasible alternatives. St. Croix, bought from France in 1733, completed Denmark's West Indian empire and the purchase had the dubious distinction of bringing to a close the first century of non-Hispanic colonization of the Caribbean. Apart from two British occupations during the Napoleonic Wars, in 1801 and again from 1807 to 1815, the islands remained in Denmark's possession until 1917. In that year all three islands – St. Thomas, St. John and St. Croix – were sold and came to comprise collectively the Virgin Islands of the United States.[1]

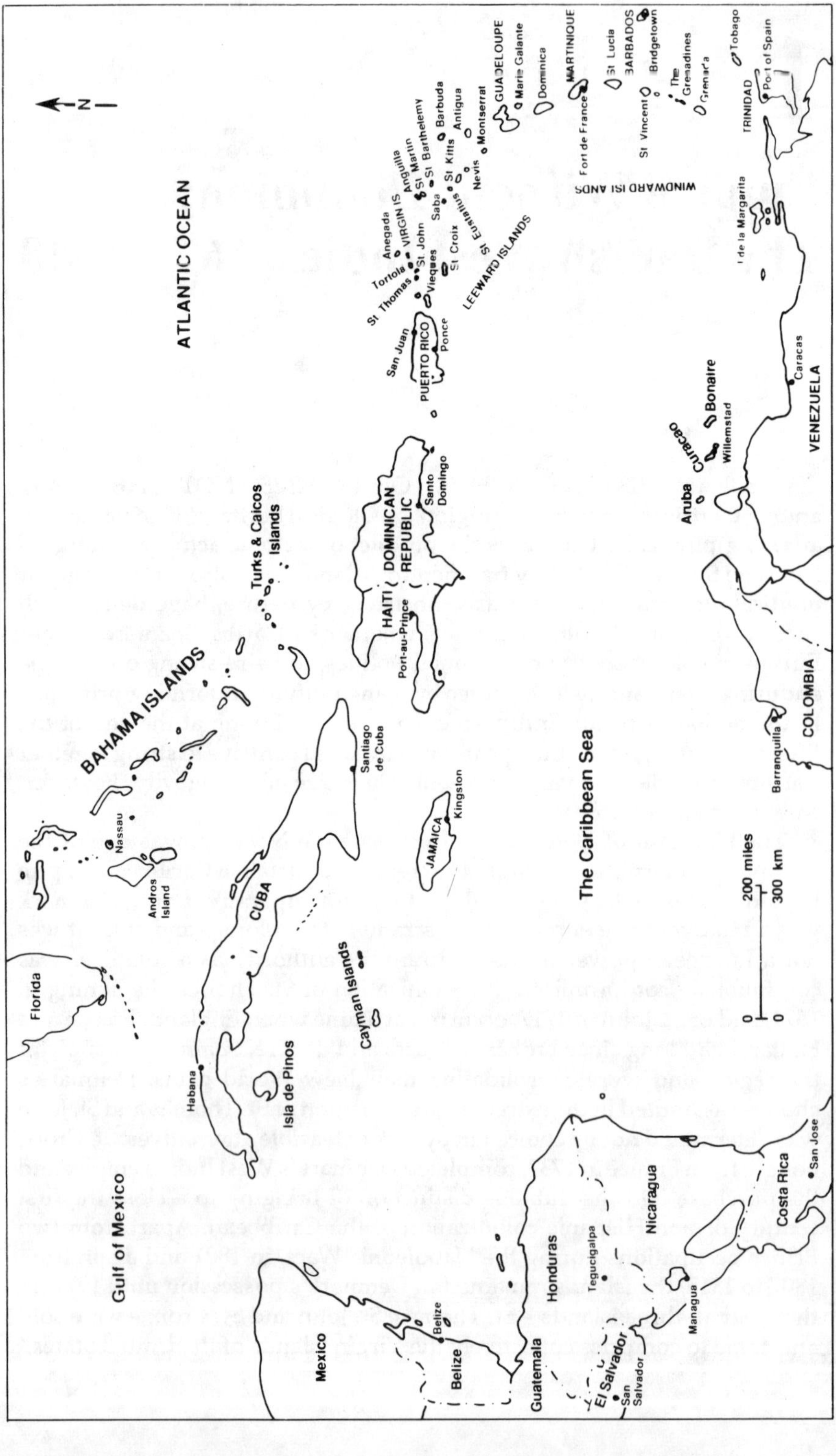

Figure 1. The Caribbean

The geological origins of the Lesser Antilles, the islands of the eastern Caribbean, fall between the Eocene and Pliocene epochs of the Tertiary Period, when the collision of the floors of the Atlantic Ocean and Caribbean Sea created an inner arc of volcanic islands to which the Danish West Indies belonged (Figure 1). These islands, unlike those of the outer arc such as Antigua or Barbuda, are characterized by serrated ridges and rugged peaks. St. Thomas and St. John rise respectively to 1,700 feet and 1,300 feet. St. Croix has a range of hills along its northern coast rising to 1,200 feet in its northwestern corner but contains in its center and south an area of flat and fairly well-watered land totaling about 39 square miles that is particularly well adapted to agriculture. This fact, combined with its greater area of 84 square miles, determined that neither St. Thomas, with an area of 28 square miles, nor St. John, with 20 square miles, ever rivaled St. Croix in sugar production (Figure 2).[2]

Sugar integrated these tropical islands into the economy of their metropolitan center, but the fate of the plantation economy and the slave system on which it rested was determined in large part by the interaction of political, demographic, economic, social and cultural factors over which Denmark did not always have control. Although the use of white indentured workers was attempted,[3] African slave labor soon became the exclusive basis of the monocrop culture of each of the Danish West Indian islands. The eighteenth century was a period of almost unvaryingly upward growth in the number of slaves, which peaked at the turn of the nineteenth century, coincident with Denmark's decision in 1792 to abolish the transatlantic slave trade in 1802 and with consequent feverish importations during the ten-year grace period (Table 1.1). Relatively and absolutely, the increments of growth were largest for St. Croix. As the nineteenth century progressed, however, all of the Danish islands experienced a gradual decline in their slave populations as rates of mortality exceeded those of fertility.[4] Even as their numbers dwindled, however, slaves remained in the majority, a position held almost from the outset of each island's exploitation. And even after 1835, when freedmen obtained their civil liberties and were enumerated with whites in the "free" category, slaves never lost their numerical superiority within the population as a whole until the termination of slavery in July 1848.

Notwithstanding a relatively late beginning, Denmark's efforts at West Indian empire were informed by the identical organizational strategies that had been applied by the other non-Hispanic colonizers of the Lesser Antilles in the gestational period of the early seventeenth century. The chartered and proprietary companies of that era were replicated in the Danish West India Company, whose chartering in 1671 confirms the view that in the Caribbean's colonial past symmetries of system, whether in the economic or other spheres, were not necessarily the product of coincident chronology.[5] Such company organizations of the earlier period were a sign of reluctance on the part of the crown to commit men, matériel and royal prestige in ventures for which success could not be guaranteed, and there

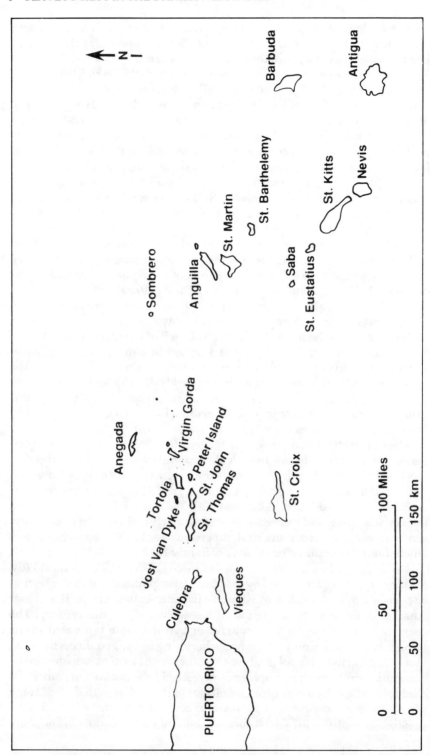

Figure 2. *The Virgin Islands*

Table 1.1: *Slave, White, and Freedman Populations of the Danish West Indies,
1688-1846*

	St. Croix			St. Thomas			St. John		
Year	Slaves	Whites	Freed-men	Slaves	Whites	Freed-men	Slaves	Whites	Freed-men
1688				422	317				
1691				547	389				
1715				3,042	555				
1733				**	**	**	1,087	208	**
1755	8,897	1,303*	*	3,949	325	138	2,031	213*	*
1770	18,884	1,515	**	4,338	428	67	2,302	118	**
1789	22,488	1,952	953	4,614	492	160	2,200	167	16
1797	25,452	2,223	1,164	4,769	726	239	1,992	113	15
1815	24,330	1,840	2,480	4,393	2,122	2,284	2,306	157	271
1835	19,876	6,805*	*	5,315	8,707*	*	1,943	532*	*
1846	16,706	7,359*	*	3,494	9,579*	*	1,790	660*	*

Sources: R/A, Diverse sager, Forskellige Oplysninger, VI; R/A, DVK, Oxholm's "Statistisk Tabelle over de danske Amerikanske Eilande St. Croix, St. Thomas og St. Jan,
1797;" R/A, Diverse sager, Visdomsbog I; R/A, Originale Forestillinger fra Kommissionen angaaende Negrenes Stilling; Waldemar Westergaard, *Danish West Indies*
(1917), p. 121; J. O. Bro-Jørgensen, *Dansk Vestindien indtil 1755*, vol. 1 *Vore Gamle
Tropekolonier* edited Johannes Brøndsted (1966), pp. 269-71; Hans West, "Beretning
om det danske Eilande St. Croix i Vestindien," *Iris* 3 (1791):13.
* These figures include freedmen as well as whites.
** No data.
Note: Between 1688 and 1715, neither St. John nor St. Croix had been acquired by the
Danes. St. John was acquired in 1718 and was Danish at the time of the slave uprising
there in 1733.

was the additional consideration to which Christian Degn has drawn
attention, that such organizations signified the inadequacy of public means
to promote overseas ventures.[6] These factors bore with special relevance
on late seventeenth-century Denmark. In so far as they acted as restraining
influences on overseas expansion, they were compounded by Denmark's
limited material resources and exiguous population base. That small
population, of less than half a million, was comparatively low in density.
England, France and the Low Countries, each with approximately 100 per
square mile, had populations twice as dense as Denmark in the late seventeenth century.[7]

Narrow resource bases and a comparatively late entry into the race for
colonies in the New World had a determining effect on the nature of
Denmark's West Indian empire. As the imperial construct developed over

time, the long-term national interests were forced into subordination by short-term expedients. For example "effective occupation," as understood in the seventeenth century, meant viable economic activity in colonies increasingly bound to their metropoles within the confines of autarchy; it meant, too, a deterrent military presence. Both required a sufficiency of able-bodied manpower. Unable, however, to provide this latter critical element, Denmark was forced to rely on a policy of "colonization by invitation" that introduced substantial numbers of foreign Europeans into the population. In the long run "strangers within the gate" had the potential to be Trojan horses. They bade fair to subvert the normative cultural values of the metropolitan power that, having gained currency in the colonies, should have become part of the mechanism of colonial domination and control. They also weakened the capabilities of colonies, already vulnerable to external attack by virtue of being small islands, to defend themselves. As a minor colonizing power, Denmark was unable to conduct its imperial affairs with the aggressive assurance of the British or the French, for example. The cumulative effect of the resultant structural weaknesses of such an imperial polity was to enfeeble that polity, as well as the economy and the society. In the latter regard, neither slavery as an institution nor the societal relationships it assumed remained unaffected. Slavery's ultimate collapse arose from the slaves' own revolutionary confrontation of their oppressors. They resolved the contradictions of their condition by exploiting another – an empire without dominion.

Early Colonization of St. Thomas

From the outset, Danish colonization in the West Indies was characterized by the paucity of a Danish colonizing population. In early Danish St. Thomas the official classes of soldiers, civil servants and clergy were overwhelmingly Danish, but foreign elements of Spaniards, Frenchmen, Englishmen and Dutchmen established a predominance in the planter and merchant cadres.[8] In the absence of a sufficiently large indigenous Amerindian population, Denmark sought to resolve the colonial manpower problem in the approved manner of the 1630s and 1640s. But Danish indentured servants, the "servinger" sent out to St. Thomas as plantation labor and militia footmen, suffered high mortality rates. Danish youth were reluctant, and when the prison populations were eventually called upon, that experiment had to be rapidly abandoned as prisoner discontent soon produced a mutiny.[9] As for the British and French, the Danish flirtation with indentured labor lasted well into the eighteenth century, but long before then the indenture system as a mechanism for affixing an imperial presence in the West Indies was a certifiable failure. J.L. Carstens, a contemporary, noted that indentureship differed from slavery only in name: servinger worked with slaves, ate the same food in the same place, wore the same clothes, shared slaves' quarters, were treated by the latter with condescension and by officials of the Company with arbitrary brutality.[10]

Few indentured servants lucky enough to survive the six years of physical and psychic abuse were likely to envision their future as empire-builders on Denmark's behalf.

In any event, that option was quickly removed by the rapid aggrandisement of the plantation system, the consolidation of estates and deployment of slaves into artisan and sea-faring trades (Figure 3).[11] By 1700 there were 122 plantations, by 1715 there were 160 with 32 operational sugar mills and more than 3,000 slaves. The white population of only 547, however, contained a minority of Danes.[12] The Company itself contributed significantly to such an attenuated imperial presence. Quite apart from its ill-treatment of indentures, it failed to capitalize on its monopoly. For the first two decades it was unable to declare dividends to its shareholders, doing so for the first time in 1690.[13] Indeed, well before that the Company's faltering fortunes obliged the crown to invite the Brandenburger Company to establish plantations and a commercial outpost on the island. The Danish West India Company's indifference to the qualifications of its personnel not only occasioned the contempt of other nationalities,[14] but more than likely also contributed to its indifferent showing. Its situation was sufficiently critical by 1685 for the crown to consider a generous lease to the Prussians – a cheap price to pay for revitalization of St. Thomas. Under the terms of the lease, the Brandenburgers were inter alia to remain for 30 years with an option of renewal; receive as much land as 200 slaves could cultivate; administer their own system of justice; trade freely with all nations; share the trade in slaves with the Danish Company and enjoy all their privileges in the event of war.[15]

The Brandenburgers exploited their opportunity. They felled the best trees to meet the lumber demands of those settled islands in the northern Leewards where the vanished forests put a premium on building material. They flooded the island with low-cost imports from Europe, and evaded whenever they could the stipulated tariffs for imports and exports.[16] In the War of the League of Augsburg, St. Thomas demonstrated for the first, but not for the last time, its considerable importance as an entrepot. Its commodious anchorage on the leeside of the island and Denmark's neutral status in that conflict resulted in a brisk traffic of ships and speculative merchants. But the traffic benefited mostly the Brandenburgers; and the merchants who profited, it would appear, were mostly non-Danes. In Nevis, the English Governor complained in 1688 of the indiscriminate grant of Burgher Briefs by the authorities in St. Thomas and of the Brandenburger's clandestine purchase of British Leeward Island's sugar. In the British Virgin Islands, the Prussians were able to supply slaves at a third below current costs, and in Antigua Governor Codrington noted with some asperity that they were accepting cotton in return for slaves at 30 percent above local prices. However much the court in Copenhagen had wished to curry favor with the Prussians, the experiment which began in 1685 produced only marginal benefits. The viability of St. Thomas as a colony was assured, but at a price. There was considerable local resentment

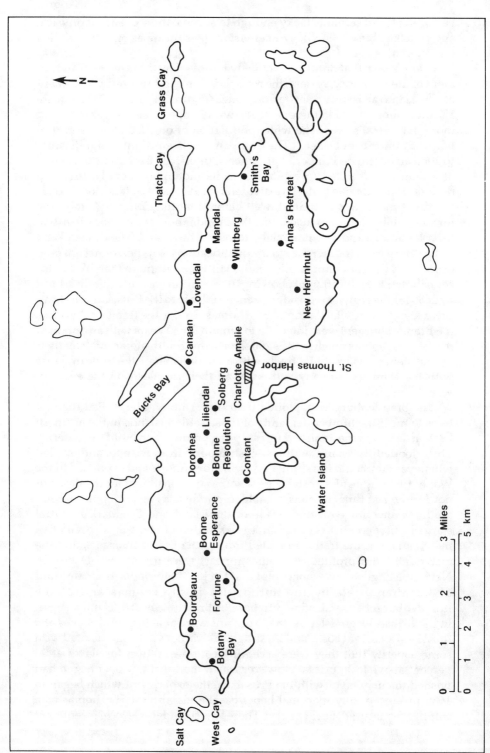

Figure 3. *St. Thomas, c.1840*

at the privileged enclave and representations to the crown in 1698-99 to curtail the agreement.[17] By the time it expired in 1715 there were no clamors for its renewal.

Dutch Cultural and Commercial Hegemony in St. Thomas and St. John

The Brandenburger episode was symptomatic of Denmark's early commitment to an accommodating mercantilism. But whereas agreements like that of 1685 could be terminated, other aspects of that accommodation, once introduced, were more difficult to remove. The first generation of settlement established a paradigm of development which left a lasting legacy of reign without rule. Even before the Prussians closed their establishments in 1715, St. Thomas was much more Dutch than Danish in character. Table 1.2 indicates the numerical preponderance of the Dutch by the end of the 1680s: already by 1686 they comprised 27.4 percent of the adult white population and by 1688 they comprised 44.6 percent of the free adult males. Although in 1691 there were only 36 Dutchmen in a free white population of 383, they nevertheless constituted a larger cohort than Danes.

When one bears in mind that creole Dutchmen from established settlements such as neighboring St. Eustatius or from Curaçao were numbered among the 174 non-Danish creoles in 1691, and that their children constituted a part of the category of "Danish" creoles, the size of the Dutch cohort looms larger still. Père Labat was of the view in 1701 that they controlled the islands' commerce.[18] Their numbers apart, the Dutch established an early cultural hegemony. Dutch was the lingua franca of commerce and social intercourse, Danish as a language was confined to the Danish enclave of the fort. Dutch also enjoyed some currency as the language of officialdom, being widely used for the issue of passes and proclamations.[19] Certainly, of the nine governors of St. Thomas between 1672 and 1727, the last six, beginning with Christopher Heins in 1688, issued proclamations in Dutch from time to time.[20] The Danish crown had apparently set no store by language as a tool of cultural imperialism, either because it lacked confidence in the cultural value of that language or more probably because it failed to perceive its imperial mission in exclusivist terms.

The deepening of Dutch cultural influence in early Danish St. Thomas was greatly helped by the presence of the Dutch Reformed Church. As a colonizing power, Denmark opted from the outset for a plurality of persuasions. It was perhaps a consequence less of deliberation than of the permissive political praxis which opened St. Thomas to virtually all comers. In any event, by the early years of the eighteenth century there were, apart from the state Lutheran Church, congregations of the Dutch and French Reformed Churches, the Church of England and Roman Catholics. All except the last had resident priests by 1717.[21] The Dutch Reformed Church,

Table 1.2: *St. Thomas' Adult White, Free Adult Male and Free White Populations by National Origin, 1686, 1688, 1691*

Nationality	1686 Adult White	1688 Free Adult Male	1691 Free White*
Creoles (non-Danish)	54	–	174**
Creoles (Danish)	–	–	94
Danes	13	17	24
Dutch	37	66	36
English	12	31	19
Flemish	1	4	7
French	10	17	14
Germans	5	3	7
Portuguese	1	1	1
Swedes	2	3	2
Other	–	6	5
Total	135	148	383
Danes as % of Total	9.6	11.5	30.8***

Sources: Calculated from Westergaard, *Danish West Indies*, p. 121; Bro-Jørgensen, *Dansk Vestindien indtil 1755*, pp. 170-71.

* These returns do not include personnel of the Danish West India Company.

** This number includes 109 Dutch West Indian creoles.

*** This percentage could be misleading, for it includes children born to other nationalities but registered as Danish creoles by virtue of their place of birth. Metropolitan Danes constituted only 6.2 per cent of the free white population in 1691.

which Labat described as one of two dominant confessions, the other being the Lutheran,[22] provided schools for the children of its own congregation; there were no Danish equivalents so that Danish children were obliged to make use of the Dutch facility. The Dutch priests also insisted that the issue of "mixed" marriages between Dutch women and Danish men should be brought up in the Dutch congregation. The marriage of leading officials of the Danish West India Company, such as Governor Holten, into prominent creole Dutch families, such as the Beverhoudts, gave an additional seal of legitimacy to Dutch culture and helped to perpetuate it.[23]

One consequence of early Danish West Indian policy was the creation of opportunities whereby the Dutch achieved a new lease of life in the Antillean theater. Checked by the exclusivist mercantilism of the English and French, defeated in three wars, and with their entrepreneurial edge blunted by the collapse of the first Dutch West India Company, the Dutch appeared to be a spent force in the Caribbean by the 1670s. The reality, however, differed substantially from the appearance. The chartering of the second Dutch West India Company in 1674, designed expressly as an instrument of trade, was an attempt to regain lost ground.[24] Interdicted access through the front door to the trade of the major maritime powers, the Dutch were able to find a convenient and accommodating rear entrance through the Danish West Indian colonies.[25] Unwittingly, Denmark played foster mother to this resurgence of commercial activity. The Dutch, once permitted to gain a foothold in St. Thomas, seized the opportunity to similarly insinuate themselves when St. John was occupied by the Danes in 1717 (Figure 4). By 1721, of the 39 planters in St. John 25 were Dutchmen and only nine Danes.

Half a century after the initial colonizing effort in St. Thomas, therefore, there had been no changes of direction in Danish West India policy. One constant of that policy had been the token deployment of the nation's resources on colonial defense. In the case of St. John this policy was particularly marked in its early years of settlement. Apart from an ineffective burgher militia, the effective military there in 1733 consisted of six infantrymen, one corporal and a lieutenant.[26] Even for a country resolutely committed to neutrality, this was less than a symbolic military detail. Its absurd inadequacy, even for purposes of internal security, was demonstrated by the course of the 1733 slave uprising. It took the intervention of the friendly French with troops from Martinique to suppress the revolt. Yet the experience forced no significant changes of direction from Copenhagen. Foreign elements in the colonial populations continued to play dominant roles in St. Thomas and St. John up to the middle of the eighteenth century and beyond. When Christian Martfeldt visited both St. Thomas and St. John in 1765, he observed that Danes numbered less than half the Dutch population.[27]

Danish Settlement and English Influences in St. Croix

The purchase of St. Croix from the French in 1733 represented the coping stone of Danish colonizing efforts in the northern Leewards. The island's topography lent itself in a way that neither St. Thomas nor St. John did to the promotion of plantation agriculture (Figure 5). For its exploitation, however, Denmark lacked not only a reservoir of population at home but also a sufficiency of personnel with plantation experience and expertise.[28] Faute de mieux, the country was obliged to fall back on a policy of open admission whatever its demonstrated inadequacies and inconveniences.

From the French it inherited some 50 English families to whom Governor Moth gave every encouragement to remain. The "masterless men" spun off by the centrifugal forces of the plantation system in the northern Leewards were welcomed in St. Croix, given small plots of land and expected to form a white yeomanry to protect it from the fate St. John had so narrowly escaped. As efforts to attract immigrants from Denmark showed meager results, the Danish West India Company unabashedly pursued an externally oriented policy. That policy continued to remain necessary, as the metropolitan poor, charges on the public purse since the depression of the 1720s, persisted in their perception of the West Indies as a graveyard. A few inmates from the poor houses were forced to go, but

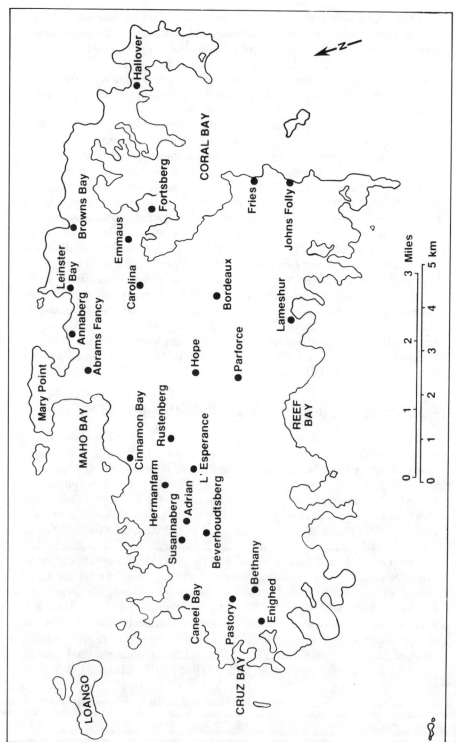

Figure 4. *St. John, c.1800*

precious few persons of means were attracted to St. Croix.[29] As a result the company from 1735 onwards made attractive offers of cheap land, generous loans and tax-free status to planters from nearby islands such as Antigua, St. Kitts and Virgin Gorda, and from islands as far away as Barbados. For such islands, already affected by soil exhaustion, St. Croix held out tempting prospects. There were also a number of Dutch immigrants from St. Eustatius, who under the leadership of Governor Pieter Heiliger sought refuge in St. Croix during the War of Jenkins' Ear in 1739.[30]

Overwhelmingly, however, the English comprised the most numerous and influential cohort of colonists at the beginning of the Danish development of St. Croix. English language and culture rapidly set their seal on St. Croix, paralleling Dutch cultural dominance in St. Thomas and St. John. By 1741 there were five times as many English in St. Croix as there were Danes, and it was the English more than any other national-cultural grouping that set St. Croix on its career as an important producer of sugar.[31] In this regard Nicholas Tuit bears particular mention. Born in Montserrat of Irish extraction and devoutly Catholic, Tuit was prevented by the English from practising his religion. A visit to St. Croix in 1749 elicited a promise from the authorities that he could bring a Capuchin monk and acquire burgher status. An influential planter of substance, he helped to finance the migration of his co-religionists and countrymen, who with their slaves numbered some 1,000, and he is commonly credited with securing royal approval for the free practice of Roman Catholicism.[32] Above all, he brought to St. Croix his knowledge of large-scale slave-based sugar culture, which formed the basis for the apotheosis of the plantation and the island's economic development. It was in perceptive anticipation of just such important contributions that the French as early as 1737 were moved to protest at the numbers of English who were being allowed to settle in St. Croix.[33]

Tuit and his heirs represent an outstanding, though not isolated, example of English-speaking planter class which dominated St. Croix in the period up to 1848. In the years between 1754 and 1804 the Tuits owned collectively more than 2,000 slaves and about 1,500 acres. There was also the McEvoy dynasty which by 1804, after about half a century in the island, owned over 1,000 slaves and 3,000 acres.[34] The dynasty's founder, Christopher McEvoy Sr., had become by 1776 one of St. Croix's most distinguished planters with one of the island's most gracious Georgian houses at his Whim estate. In Denmark his name was a byword for the wealth and extravagance of the West Indian planter class: he owned a palatial residence in Copenhagen; maintained a manor house in the country; privately financed the first experiments in gas lighting for his town residence and generously extended the facility to his near neighbors in the royal palace at Amalienborg Castle. Appointed Chamberlain to the Royal Household, he had elaborate equipage and livery rivaling that of the king himself, forcing a royal prohibition on the use of his six white chargers. With that touch of the whimsical which only the very rich can afford,

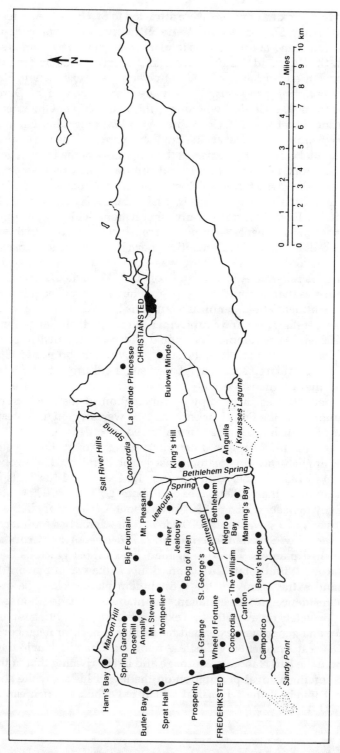

Figure 5. *St. Croix, c. 1848*

McEvoy went to the enormous trouble, time and expense of securing six white mules.[35]

The Anglo-Saxons were as quantitatively significant as they were qualitatively important as symbols of the new plantation gentry. Jørgen Bach Christensen has identified what he loosely describes as the "aristocracy" of St. Croix in the later eighteenth century. Using a criterion of ownership of 300 acres or more, he isolates 75 such families of whom 30 were English-speaking or from the British Isles. Most of the 17 Danish-owned or Danish-run estates meeting the acreage criterion were owned by Danish officials.[36] As Table 1.3 indicates, however, Danish estates represented only 22.7 percent of the total. The English-speaking gentry, on the other hand, comprised 40 percent and were a cohort larger than the Danes, Dutch and French combined. The size of the English-speaking element of this dominant planter group may have been even larger, however, for at least seven of those whose nationalities are not given had distinctly Anglo-Saxon/Gaelic family names. The polygot character of the leading element of the planter class in St. Croix, and the preponderance of English speakers within it, was a direct consequence of the deliberately outward orientation of Danish West India Company policy and the attractions of the islands' neutral status in the wars of the later eighteenth century. It is instructive to note that in Antigua, an island similar in size and productive capacity and frequently compared with St. Croix,[37] there were no more than two identifiably foreign families in a total of 65 owning more than 300 acres between 1730 and 1775.[38]

The most obvious earnest of English cultural hegemony in St. Croix was the language situation, and in that regard the newspapers serve as a very useful index. It is not without significance that the first regular newspaper *The Royal Danish American Gazette*, published with fair regularity between 1770 and 1802, was essentially English in tone. Its masthead was in English, so too were its advertisements, notices of impending auctions, creditors' demands, debtors' notices, obituaries, and foreign intelligence. It was only occasionally that any of these items appeared in Danish, although public proclamations and government announcements were invariably rendered in both languages.[39] Hans West, who spent the greater part of the last two decades of the eighteenth century as headmaster of a Christiansted school for white children, noted petulantly in 1791 that the newspaper was owned by an absentee English person who possessed no Danish type.[40] The language emphases of *The Royal Danish American Gazette* were continued by the *Dansk Ventindisk Regerings Avis*, notwithstanding its title, from 1802 to 1808 and again from 1815 to the end of the period. The publication of the *St. Croix Gazette* during the English occupation from 1802 to 1805 reinforced conclusively the tendencies in train from the later eighteenth century. What is true of these publications is equally true of their St. Thomas equivalent, the *St. Thomæ Tidende*, published from 1815 onwards.

Language apart, the newspapers provide important evidence of St. Croix's essential Englishness. In 1770, the year in which *The Royal Danish*

Table 1.3: *Ownership of Estates Larger than 300 Acres, by National Origin, St. Croix, 1742-1804*

National Origin	No. of Owners	% of Total
British	30	40
(English: 12)	–	–
(Irish: 13)	–	–
(Scots: 5)	–	–
Danish	17	23
Dutch	6	8
French	4	5
Other	18	24
Total	75	100

Source: Jørgen Bach Christensen, *Kolonisamfundet paa St. Croix i sidste halvdel af det 18. arhundrede, med særligt Henblik paa aristokratiet blandt plantageejerne* (Cand. mag. dissertation, Aarhus University, 1978).

American Gazette made its initial appearance, St. Croix was visited by the Leeward Island Company of Comedians. The players remained from July until the end of the year, performing under the direction of Linck Malone a series of Shakespearean offerings and popular contemporary farces and comedies of the English stage. They were sufficiently up-to-date with London theater to mount a production of one of Garrick's many unsuccessful comedies, *Lethe or Aesop in the Shades*.[41] After Malone's death early in 1771, the company ceased its performances but was to return for a limited engagement in 1776.[42] The outbreak of the American Revolutionary War presumably put an end to such itinerant thespian activity. Although there were brief revivals of enthusiasm, in 1814 for example,[43] the period of enduring interest in the theater appears to have passed with the 1770s.

Curiously, this "golden age" of sustained theatrical interest attracted no attention from the metropole, either officially or unofficially. The Kongelige Teater, Denmark's Royal Theater, was granted its charter in 1750 with a monopoly on the performance of serious drama and conventional plays.[44] But none of that theater fare was available in St. Croix or its sister islands in the years after 1750, if the newspapers constitute a reliable guide. These years, as it happens, overlap with the life, work and influence of Ludwig Holberg (1684-1754), Denmark's most distinguished dramatist of the eighteenth century and arguably of all time. Holberg was himself involved in the creation of the Kongelige Teater and authored a number of searingly satirical comedies which mocked the moeurs of his day. Prima facie there was no good reason why Holberg's plays were not performed in the Danish islands, nor can it be explained on the grounds of lack of audience interest. The problem lay, firstly, with an imperial directorate which did not place too serious a value on the promotion of metropolitan culture as part of the process of imperial control. In this connection, it is interesting to note that one of the Governors General in the late eighteenth century, Ernst von Walterstorff (1781-1796), became director of the Kongelige Teater on his return to Denmark.[45] The appointment would suggest an interest in theater and the esteem in which he was held at court but neither during his tenure as Governor General nor subsequently did his interest or influence result in Danicization of West Indian theater. Secondly, it should be borne in mind that there were other theaters apart from the Kongelige, not under royal patronage and confined by the terms of the latter's charter to the presentation of farces, musical comedies, operettas and similar light entertainment.[46] Their productions were never seen in the West Indies, however. Where the crown did not lead, its subjects were not encouraged to follow.

The drift towards cultural pluralism, or more accurately English cultural hegemony, was also marked by the development in St. Croix of an English-based creole lingua franca. Dutch dominance in St. Thomas had resulted in the evolution of a Dutch-based creole. The preponderance of English in St. Croix facilitated the development of a medium of communication in the towns, the market place, in the shops, warehouses and on the plantations, that reflected that preponderance. The expansion of the plantation economy after mid-century involved an ever-increasing influx of slave labor; its management, discipline and acculturation, particularly to the plantation regimen, required that English-speaking plantation owners, plantation help and merchants, had at their disposal an effective means of contact and control. Before the end of the eighteenth century, the emergence of a specifically English-based creole had been sufficiently well established for Hans West to make reference to its existence.[47]

Language, Amelioration and National Identity

This linguistic reality was an important consideration in the amelioration of slavery contemplated by Governor General von Scholten in the 1830s. When the Danish government determined to institute a primary-school system for slaves, it was decided that instruction would be in English.[48] The instructors in the proposed schools were however to be German Moravian missionaries, whose presence dated from the establishment of their initial mission in St.Thomas in 1732. Recourse to Moravian missionary instruction for the slave population was an admission of failure of the efforts of the Danish Lutheran missionaries, begun in any event some 25 years after the Moravians had entered the field. The choice of the Moravians was virtually automatic, given the size of their following, their past record and the dismal record of the Danish state church in proselytizing the slave population.[49]

Indeed the viability of Moravian missionary activity was the measure of the Danish government's unwillingness, inability, or both, to perceive of the presence of the state church as an important buttress for its imperial presence. It is true that in the British colonies the state church was no more enterprising in missionary work among slaves. But that situation was contextually different. Anglo-Saxon institutions were never, so to speak, under siege. Moreover there were the free church missionaries, increasingly and often abrasively active among the slave population. In any event, they shared many common values with the colonizing power, language among them, and were of the same national provenance. In the Danish West Indies, abandonment of the missionary field to the Moravians was both cause and effect of the faintness of the mother country's cultural imprint and it was not surprising that von Scholten in the 1830s accepted their influence among the slaves not so much with resignation as with guarded enthusiasm. It is of interest, in this connection, that the first voices of dissent against the slave school system and English, the language of instruction, were raised not so much against the Moravians as against their sponsor von Scholten.

Danish Liberals in the 1840s, distrustful of the court and of absolute monarchy, saw in the Governor General the colonial expression of arbitrary political authority to which they were opposed. Aided by a colonial faction of opposition in which the foreign plantocracy was influential, they opened the columns of the Liberal newspaper *Fædrelandet* to trenchant criticism of the Governor General and all his works. Under his leadership, the newspaper trumpeted in 1841, Moravians were being favored at the expense of missionaries of the state church.[50] These crudely chauvinist sentiments were inspired not so much by any sense of loss or concern for cultural nationalism in the colonies. Hard-headed considerations or economic advantage were very much at issue. By then the debate had been joined about the nature of the emancipation which was considered inevitable, questions of compensation and the eventual cost to the Danish treasury.[51] The Liberals were less than enthusiastic at the prospect of the Danish taxpayer eventually paying the piper. Orla Lehmann, a former co-publisher of *Fædrelandet* and a leading Liberal spokesman in the Stænderforsamlinger or Assembly of Estates of the Realm at Roskilde in 1846, was brutally candid: after more than 100 years of occupation, Denmark could not be said in any sense to own islands in which the planter class was, for all practical purposes, foreign.[52] In a similar vein Victor Prosch, the ship's surgeon who witnessed the sudden collapse of the slave regime in 1848, could subsequently associate that event with the internal weakness of colonial institutions. Prosch noted that foreigners had been given preferment over nationals; conscious attempts had been made to de-emphasize Danish as the language of commerce and the schools, and the resultant English tone and spirit with which the islands were infused was incompatible with their self-sustaining existence as Danish colonies.[53]

Liberals like Lehmann and others who expressed similar views were not only politically motivated, but were also attempting to close the barn door on the departed horse. The author of an 1840 *Fædrelandet* article on the Irish and Scots enclaves in St. Croix bitterly attacked the colonial political leadership of Peter von Scholten under whom those enclaves were alleged to have been encouraged.[54] Partisanship rendered the author oblivious to the fact that the composition of the planting community had been more or less determined even before the arrival of Nicholas Tuit a century earlier. Von Scholten was more accessory after the fact than perpetrator. The article is nevertheless important for a belated Danish formulation for what constituted self-interested colonization, and its assessment of Denmark's achievement in that context.

St. Croix, the writer observed, had never been colonized by the Danes and had never been Danish except in the narrowly political sense. If all it took to be Danish was the flag and the judicial system, then St. Croix was Danish. But colonization implied more than territorial claim and a body of laws. It called for a sufficient number of one's nationals, sharing one's customs and values and, above all, language. Without these, the objectives of colonization (establishing a place to relocate the metropole's surplus population, a market for its products, a source of raw material and a nursery for a national and merchant marine) could not be realized. This was a statement of the objectives of mercantilism as historically understood and practised. The fruitful symbiosis which it implied between mother country and colony, the author noted, was everywhere in evidence in the West Indies, except the Danish islands. A viable metropolitan-colonial nexus, he added, was a function of energy and patriotism – characteristics which, by implication, Danes lacked. The Danish flag flew over islands in the West Indies, but not over populations to which it was precious and sacrosanct. Whilst Irishmen and Scots flocked to the islands in their hundreds, Danes elected to remain at home, preferring destitution to migration. Whilst all the world's advanced nations established commercial houses in St. Thomas, and provided their nationals with opportunities for rapid mobility, Danish merchants lived a life of wretched toil at home. Herein lay the explanation, the author concluded, for the fact that, public servants apart, there were hardly any Danish families in St. Croix; that its Burgher Council, consisting of eight members, included only one Dane, and of the rest, only two spoke Danish; that the Irish proliferated as overseers and bookkeepers and that foreigners dominated estate ownership and management.

The Economics of Foreign Domination

This was good rhetoric but faulty history, particularly in its attribution of cause. In relation to estate ownership, another *Fædrelandet* article indicated in 1841 that St. Croix's 151 estates were distributed among 25 proprietors, partly resident and partly absentee, 60 foreign creditors, and the state which owned sixteen.[55] State ownership and the high proportion of estates in the hands of foreign creditors were new phenomena in the pattern of estate ownership. But they too arose out of policies consciously pursued by the crown in the past. The open colonization policy which had prevailed since the settlement of St. Thomas led eventually to open confrontation between foreign residents and the Danish West India Company in the 1740s, increasingly, if belatedly, insistent on its monopoly. The crown, called in to arbitrate the dispute, declared itself willing to consider taking over the colonies from the Company, to which the latter made no objection.[56] The crown's eventual assumption of control was not unrelated therefore to pressure from the foreign West Indian lobby. The irony was that in terminating Company rule in 1754, largely in response to pressure from the foreign colonial cadres, the crown itself laid the basis for further weakening of the imperial connection.

With the purchase of the Company's equity, the crown acquired also the legacy of the former's cheap-loans policy, a debt of 1,220,931 Rigsdaler.[57] The crown's immediate response was a heavy-handed collection of loans outstanding to the Company which forced the planters to turn to foreign creditors.[58] Dutch finance houses obligingly complied. For the second time in less than a century, the Danish West Indies were providing opportunities for Dutch entrepreneurship. Old debts apart, the escalating price of land in St. Croix as it developed agriculturally forced intending purchasers to look for credit, which Denmark could not provide.[59] The size of the "Dutch Loans" was increased from this second source. In just over two decades after 1754, upwards of 14 million guilders were lent to Danish plantation owners. More than half of that sum originated with the Amsterdam house of Abraham Ter Borch and Son, although there were other firms such as Gabriel Bourcourd and Son, or Bouwens and Van der Hoop which refinanced the old loans or backed new investment. By 1781 the loan portfolio stood at 16 million guilders, and Ter Borch, unable to get returns on their capital, were on the verge of ultimate bankruptcy.[60] As the "Dutch Loans" rose in the 1760s and 1770s, planters, in order to service their debts, were obliged to ship more and more sugar to Holland at the expense of Copenhagen refineries. To cauterize the haemorrhage the crown stepped in and bought the "Dutch Loans" in 1786,[61] adding thereby to the indebtedness acquired from the Danish West India Company.

Over time, the owners of the already heavily burdened estates contracted further debts, as productivity declined and the old "Dutch Loans," with unpaid accumulated interest, began to approach the value of the estates themselves.[62] It was in this way that foreign creditors achieved their lien on plantation property in St. Croix and the crown its ownership of 16 estates. Some of the crown's estates were leased to Danes, but an equal number were directed by foreign lessees, Irish or Scots for the most part. Foreign lessees had a natural preference for persons from their countries of origin in the employment of estate supervisory personnel.[63] In this way the crown's policy reinforced the tendency towards the domination of estate jobs by the Irish and Scots, a phenomenon which had elicited comment as early as 1787.[64] The floating of the "Dutch Loans," which Christensen believes was an index of Denmark's ignorance of the economics of empire,[65] opened the way for foreign infiltration and the circumstances of the late 1830s and early 1840s compounded this development. Governor General von Scholten's Labor Ordinance of 1838 contained a "deficiency" clause, requiring one free white person for every 50 slaves, or a deficiency complement of some 340 for the 17,000 slaves in St. Croix. The Ordinance provided the opportunity for further increments to the "tight phalanx" of Irish, many of whom were less acquainted with plantation routines than the slaves they were supposed to supervise. Some, by dint of frugality and hard work, became estate owners themselves before the 1840s had ended.[66] As owners, overseers or bookkeepers, such persons had life-styles and consumption patterns which further weakened the links with the official metropole.

In 1840 *Fædrelandet* observed bitterly that all businesses in St. Croix were foreign-owned.[67] That was exaggeration. But certainly since the 1760s and with regard to St. Thomas the crown had actively pursued policies which guaranteed that that island's commerce would be largely in foreign hands, as indeed it had been at the end of the previous century. Whilst St. Croix was made to adhere, however marginally, to the dictates of restrictionist mercantilism in the later eighteenth century, St. Thomas was developed as a free port. The Ordinance of 1764 which created St. Thomas as a Free Port breathed a spirit similar to the British West Indian Free Port legislation of 1766, in the sense that what was anticipated was the admission into the colonies of foreign staples and raw material not locally produced. The British legislation, however, was conceived of as an important adjunct to British restrictive mercantilism.[68] The Danish Ordinance of 9 April 1764 was not predicated on notions of exclusivism. Its essential difference from what the British attempted was illustrated in the preamble, where anyone was permitted to set up an enterprise in St. Thomas and engage in trade in either European or American goods.[69] A subsequent Ordinance of 1767 reconfirmed this concession to foreigners but unlike the earlier measure permitted such persons to send cargoes wherever they liked.[70] The 1764 Ordinance had confined return cargoes to Denmark and subsequent ordinances required that they be carried in Danish ships. However, by the end of the Napoleonic Wars, the regulations were again relaxed to permit foreign vessels to take European cargoes into St. Thomas and to return to any European port.[71] In a matter of some 50 years, Danish free-port legislation had not only laid the basis for enclaves of foreign merchants in St. Thomas but it had also thrown the port open to virtually all comers. By the 1820s, for example, much of the island's trade was in the hands of American factors.[72] In sum, the Dutch free port system was not, as in the British case, an adjunct of a well articulated mercantilist system. It cannot be said to have stimulated Danish shipping or to have acted as a conduit for metropolitan manufacturers to the markets of commodity-starved foreign possessions. Denmark's comparatively early implementation of colonial free trade in 1833 was less a matter of principled choice than expedient necessity.[73]

The permissiveness of the Danish free port system was not an isolated phenomenon. It was equally demonstrated in the operations of the

Kongelige Danske octroyerede Vestindiske Handelsselskab (The Royal Chartered Danish West Indian Trading Company) established in 1773. The intention behind its creation was to capitalize on the commercial opportunities for neutrals, such as Denmark, in the disturbances of the American Revolution. The Company was headquartered in Copenhagen with a branch office in St. Thomas and although privately funded, it had many high-ranking public figures on its directorate: a Prime Minister, a future Prime Minister, and the Crown Prince, to name but three. Indeed, the state was so closely connected to the directorate that company correspondence to government was signed by the same person who replied. The company's charter allowed it to take in goods from overseas in Danish or foreign ships and to trade in Europe as well as worldwide. So far as St. Thomas was concerned, the company's entrepot trade consisted partly in meat, cereals, bread, butter and salted herrings which the mother country produced; but there was a substantial list of trade goods originating outside Denmark. This would have been unthinkable for the merchants of London, Liverpool or Manchester consigning goods to the free ports of the British West Indies at any time in the later eighteenth century. Yet mill hardware, building material, coal, porcelain, cooking utensils, wine and spirits, and cotton goods of varied quality were purchased in Germany and Baltic countries for sale in St. Thomas.[74]

Denmark's economy showed substantial expansion in commerce and agriculture at the end of the eighteenth century but it had no tradition of factory industry and even the nation's best-connected entrepreneurs and statesmen failed to make the critical link between industrial revolution and empire. Unlike the British case, the many deviations from the mercantilist system permitted by the Danes resulted in little national advantage. The vulnerability of the enterprise was confirmed by the end of the American war, when Britain tightened its restrictions on trade, and falling prices, especially for dry goods, left large uncleared inventories in the company's St. Thomas warehouse.[75]

An important aspect of the entrepot trade in the free port of St. Thomas was the transit trade in slaves, in which British West Indian free ports such as Kingston, Bridgetown, St. George's and Nassau also engaged. But even here, as Svend Green-Pedersen has pointed out, that trade was conducted for the most part in foreign bottoms.[76] What was true of this transit trade was also true of the two other branches of the slave trade identified by Green-Pedersen: the trade which supplied St. Croix's labor needs and the triangular trade. For other European nations the trade in slaves was an important component of a mercantilist complex; it was a stimulus to other branches of trade; a nursery, however unhealthy, for seamen. The Dutch monopoly of the trade to British and French plantation colonies in the early seventeenth century had been untenable for precisely those reasons. Even the Spaniards, without access to the slaving coasts of West Africa, attempted a rationalization of slave supply through the Asientos. Denmark's triangular slave trade, however, and the trade by which St. Croix was supplied with its manpower, differed significantly from those of other leading European colonizers. In relation to the former, Green-Pedersen again observes that in the later eighteenth century the figures demonstrate "the high degree to which the Danish triangular slave trade was diluted by traffic with another nation in Africa," namely the French.[77] For the supply of St. Croix's slave manpower, foreign vessels were permitted for extended periods in the later eighteenth century to deliver slave cargoes and to take cargoes of sugar and cotton under licences. Of the 4,550 slaves imported into Frederiksted for the years 1767-1777, 1784, 1790, 1799-1800 and 1802 some 69 percent came from the foreign islands of the Leeward/Windward chain, with British islands providing 2,500.[78]

In the second half of the eighteenth century the Danish slave trade, in all its manifestations, was not confined within a closed mercantilist system, but was "based upon extensive co-operation with other slave trading nations both in Africa and the West Indies;"[79] and its principal plantation island, St. Croix, was not bound to the metropole and Danish Guinea in an exclusive nexus of commercial empire.[80] The dependence on other slave-trading nations, particularly Britain, was an important consideration in explaining Denmark's decision to abolish its own trade. By the autumn of 1791 Denmark was convinced of the imminence of a British abolition which would have created difficulties of supply particularly for St. Croix. In opting for abolition in 1792, therefore, it legislated a ten-year grace period within which it anticipated definitive British abolition.[81] The accompanying arrangement, which threw participation open to all comers in this final decade, was the terminal demonstration of a mercantilism manqué.

Foreign Domination and Internal Security

The crown was not unmindful of the likely consequences of a permissive trading policy for the composition of the islands' populations. What it did not anticipate and made scant provisions to guard against were the problems of security which large cadres of foreigners inevitably posed in the conditions of Caribbean revolution and virtually incessant war between the St. Domingue uprising of 1791 and 1815. The free port legislation of 1764 actively encouraged the residence of foreign merchants in St. Thomas. The extent of that encouragement can be gauged by Christian VII's instructions to Governor General Clausen on the occasion of the renewal of the Ordinance on 4 November 1782. Clausen was advised that the renewed Ordinance would probably bring more foreigners in search of their fortunes and that their presence would increase the population and bring beneficial prosperity to the islands. Accordingly, a series of accommodating regulations was established: once they had become burghers they were to be given equal treatment and exempted for two years from the duties of citizenship, presumably from militia duty.[82] If they decided to leave they were required only to pay a 4 percent tax on capital acquired locally. Personal property, slaves and trade goods with which they arrived were exempted from customs duties on departure. Incoming ships were to be dealt with expeditiously and extended every courtesy and consideration, including the waiving of the requirements for flags and pennants.[83]

The presence of foreigners in large numbers had important implications for the islands' internal security after the success of the St. Domingue revolution. For reasons related to economy and its philosophical view of empire, Denmark had chosen a system of colonial defense which put less emphasis on colonial garrisons than on local militias. A sufficient number of armed able-bodied colonists was seen as the front line of defense, and the professional soldiery hardly ever numbered more than was necessary for guard and ceremonial duty.[84] In the 1770s there was a token troop strength of some 320 distributed as follows: Christiansted 100, Frederiksted 100, St. Thomas 80, and St. John 40.[85] With the disturbances in St. Domingue and Grenada, there was an increase in the established troop strength in 1799 to 447: 373 infantry, 56 cavalry and 18 artillery. The increases notwithstanding, these troops were still seen as "an organized police to maintain internal peace, rather than a proper military force."[86] As P.L. Oxholm, consultant military engineer and subsequent Governor General, observed in 1798, Denmark had so few and such small islands compared to other European powers in the area that the latter could easily assemble and despatch an attacking force ten times the size of that which Denmark could with difficulty assemble for the islands' defense.[87]

The weakness of Denmark's military posture in the West Indies was compounded by high troop morbidity and mortality, inappropriate recruitment and deployment policies, and sheer neglect. The effective strength in 1801 was only 343: 222 in St. Croix and the remainder in St. Thomas and St. John.[88] The shortfall between effective and established strength was attributed to "the debilitating fever," which in the case of St. Thomas had a third of the troops in military hospital.[89] This problem of troop morbidity was never satisfactorily solved. In the period between 1830 and 1835, for example, an average complement of 420 was responsible for an annual average of 20, 428 man days lost through illness. This represented some 49 days in the year on which each soldier was incapacitated. Debility was even more severe among new recruits. In the period 1827-1832 new recruits averaged from 117 to 159 sick days per year. Among such soldiers the annual mortality rate reported in 1836-1837 was 140 per 1,000.[90]

As early as 1801 the Commandant at St. Thomas, Casimir von Scholten, regarded the current mortality rates among the troops, old and new, as unacceptable. There were the perennial problems of climatic adjustment, the unsuitable location of military hospitals, the inadequacy of the latter's accommodation and the deficiencies in medical care.[91] It would also appear that a significant element among new recruits had consisted for a long time of ex-prisoners or persons above 30 years.[92] Such soldiers on the West Indian station tended to do longer tours of duty than their counterparts in the British West Indies, who were rotated with greater frequency.[93] However, although longer residence ensured a greater degree of acclimatization, there was the countervailing consideration that extended periods of duty often led to incremental consumption of "new" rum with its resultant liver disorders. These complaints shared many symptoms with yellow fever and were as lethal.[94]

If Casimir von Scholten is to be believed, the levels of equipment supply and fort maintenance, in St. Thomas at least, were appallingly low at the beginning of the nineteenth century. Half of the redoubts at Frederiksfort were unable to take the weight of the cannon, there was a shortage of powder, and the carriages on which the artillery pieces were borne were so decayed that they would collapse if put to use.[95]

In the absence of a professional military of viable size, reliance had therefore to be placed on the militia. Contingency planning resolutely refused to address itself to the prospect of an invasion by foreign powers, as Denmark had remained a neutral in all of the major conflicts affecting the Caribbean since the end of the seventeenth century. The problem was not so much the enemy without as the perceived enemy within. The specter of St. Domingue lent urgency to these preoccupations. What was feared was not invasion by a hostile European power, but a slave uprising inspired by revolutionary agents. Governor General Walterstorff felt in 1798 that the greatest threat facing the islands was a slave uprising supported by a foreign power, and that such a rebellion was more imminent than his countrymen were given to believe.[96] The crown was under no such illusion and since the early 1790s had called on Walterstorff to exercise every precaution with the admission of slaves from other islands, who might bring the seeds of revolution with them. This fear of rebellion, imported from St. Domingue, Martinique, or Guadeloupe, was the basis of one contingency formulation for dealing with slave uprisings which persisted until the end of the era of slavery in 1848. The plan called for the establishment of close links with neighboring slaveholding colonies like Puerto Rico which shared a common interest in the suppression of rebellion, and could be expected to come to the assistance of the Danish islands if need be.[97]

But the first line of defense remained the militia. Its composition at the end of the eighteenth century reflected the years of officially sanctioned ease of access on the part of foreigners. The loyalty and reliability of such a force was suspect. Casimir von Scholten shrewdly observed in 1802 that the overwhelming foreign elements in the militia of St. Thomas could at least be expected to defend their own lives and property in the event of a slave uprising, but that there could be no such guarantee if a foreign invasion materialized. They were not likely to abandon their counting houses to enemy plunder, and risk their lives to defend a colony which they would sooner hand over to anyone, if they thereby preserved life and property.[98] Moreover, there were persistent doubts whether resident Frenchmen of republican sentiments or émigré gens de couleur from the French islands might not foment unrest among the slaves. It was this which inspired von Scholten to request from the French Consul, Citoyen Michel, detailed information on the number of Frenchmen and gens de couleur in St. Thomas in 1800: their ages and occupations, whether they were capable of bearing arms and owned any, and whether they had seen previous military service.[99] Citoyen Michel's return indicated 29 French émigrés and 114 gens de couleur capable of bearing arms, not already in the freedmen corps of militia.[100] But this contingent of affranchis, full of what von Scholten characterized as "pure revolutionaries," was an unacceptable Trojan horse and was forcibly deported.[101]

The feared slave uprising did not occur. It was the English invasion of 1801 which conclusively demonstrated the islands' vulnerability to attack. General Trigge and Admiral Duckworth forced a surrender and occupied all three islands, virtually without firing a shot, between 29 and 31 March 1801. Hans West, who was still in St. Croix and a member of the Council of War, advised against resistance because, as he drily observed, resistance was pure recklessness and that was no basis on which to make a stand for honor.[102] St Thomas' incapacity to withstand attack was graphically described by Casimir von Scholten in his report referred to earlier. His problems with a shortage of munitions and untrustworthy freedmen, especially the French, were complicated by a burgher militia consisting almost exclusively of Englishmen or English-sympathizers.[103] The Burgher Council of St. Thomas, dominated by English-speaking provision merchants, was itself hardly a model of patriotism. In both its private and public sessions on 13 March 1801, it was virtually advising capitulation before attack and hinted at an unwillingness to do duty as militia men. They were "not yet reconciled to the idea of being in an unprecedented manner posted in a Garrison where the duty allotted to them was of all others the most painful to their feelings and dishonorable to their public situation."[104] The statement forced the officials of the subsequent military investigation into the debacle of 1801 to ask whether the burghers felt no obligation to fight the English. This of course was vigorously denied.[105] In St. Croix the gravity of the situation made the Council of War consider the extreme step of raising a battalion of 1,000 slave artisans, a variation on the British West India regiments, detachments of which ironically took part in the reduction of the Danish islands in 1801. Opinion was sharply divided on the question and the proposal was shelved only on the practical grounds offered by the Council's military members: it would have been impossible in so short a period to train and discipline so many slaves even if there were sufficient arms and powder.[106]

The islands were returned to Denmark within a year. The military investigation which ensued merely helped to identify the weaknesses in the islands' defense capabilities without effecting any ameliorative changes. The outcome of the second English invasion of 1807 by General Bowyer and Admiral Cochrane was a foregone conclusion. None of the problems of 1801 had been resolved by 1807; if anything they had intensified. The size of the 3rd West India Infantry Company at 214 officers and men was below that of 1801, and many of the men were unfit for duty.[107] That difficulty was as nothing, however, compared with the discovery, on the very eve of the invasion, of a plot in St. Croix to overthrow Danish power and establish a republic under English protection. The author of the conspiracy was identified as Baron Friderich de Bretton, Jr., scion of one of the oldest émigré families in St. Croix. Free people of color were alleged to have been deeply implicated, but the centerpiece of the plan was the suborning of the officer corps, winning over the majority of the rank and file, capturing the rest and forcing the fort to surrender.[108] Considering that in Christiansted the 3rd West India Infantry Company's effective strength was 113, de Bretton's claim that he had 68 infantrymen on his side meant that he felt assured of the support of more than half the troops.[109] His appeal to the troops rested on promises of promotion, doubling or trebling of pay and improving conditions of service, which he said were appalling.[110] The Baron's incautious talk led to his arrest and an effective end to that conspiracy on 13 December 1807.[111]

Slaves and Internal Security

De Bretton had proudly boasted that "within a month the island would be strongly fortified, and since Denmark had no fleet there was nothing to be feared from that quarter."[112] The grounds for anticipating success, therefore, were not only the imperial power's weakness locally but its powerlessness internationally. The inability to mount any meaningful resistance to the invasions confirmed de Bretton's thesis. But disaffected émigrés, short on national sentiment; poorly treated soldiery, ripe subjects for mutiny; and oppressed free people of color, anxious to shed their yoke, did not exhaust the constituency of the potentially discontented.[113] There were the slaves, conspicuously absent from de Bretton's plans. The evidence of those crisis years of the early nineteenth century, however, suggests that they too were ready to exploit the situation's vulnerability; if not definitively to "test the chains," in Michael Craton's sense of the phrase, at least to probe their weak links.[114] But the documentation relating to slave unrest at the beginning of the nineteenth century must be approached with caution. Such evidence could have been given undue prominence by the authorities to emphasize their anxieties and the gravity of the crisis as they saw it, whilst the incidents to which such evidence referred were no more than routine. On the other hand, it is equally plausible that the anxieties were not unfounded. Slave unrest, worrisome at the best of times for the authorities, took on added significance when memories of St. Domingue were still fresh or a powerful British fleet was just over the horizon. For the slaves, there were opportunities here to heighten that anxiety.

Such might be the significance of an incident which occurred on the eve of the 1801 invasion. On 29 March, the day before the British fleet appeared off St. Croix, the Police Court at Frederiksted was convened by Governor General Lindemann to undertake "a thorough-going investigation" of a report that slaves at Jolly Hill estate intended to create a disturbance. The court heard that Mary Haycock, the overseer's wife, had given instructions that in case of emergency one white person should remain on the estate to prevent disorder. Dixy, her 12-year-old personal slave, posed a question, "what was one white man against so many when he could be easily despatched?" Mary Haycock attempted to protect Dixy by interpreting "so many " to refer not to the slaves, but to the English. Her husband entertained no suspicion of Jolly Hill slaves but he had heard from the overseer at neighboring Orange Grove that the artisan slaves had been behaving suspiciously. In recent times they had been away from the estate every night and he had no idea where they went or what they did. The most interesting deposition came from Dixy himself. A week previously he had overheard a discussion between two slaves in Frederiksted, one of whom said, "When this war begins I think the blacks will kill the whites on the plantations and plunder their houses." When the other expressed disbelief, his interlocutor said it was just a joke. Dixy made a further statement that a fortnight before, again in Frederiksted, he had heard one slave remarking to another, "When the English come, we will plunder and rob house slaves who will not reveal where their masters' money and treasure are hidden."[115] No slaves were charged on the basis of these investigations. What they suggest, however, is a slave boy's acute perception of the advantage of numbers, older slaves' recognition of that advantage, and its potential when married to the possibilities presented by the invasion emergency.

The anxieties did not end with the departure of the British in 1802. Governor General Walterstorff informed his superiors that year that it would be unreasonable to expect slaves to be unaffected by the developments in St. Domingue and the French islands. Moreover Walterstorff, who had served in a variety of West Indian posts for some two decades, concluded from his experience that slaves in 1802 were showing, if not outright contempt, certainly less respect for whites than previously. They were more defiant and refractory, and had even been known to set dogs on whites. He feared that the prophylactic boundaries between black and white, established by "prejudice and preference" more than by local legislation, stood in grave danger of being breached. By way of substantiation, he cited a number of cases. In March he had sentenced a slave to 150 lashes and transportation for striking a bookkeeper. Elsewhere slaves had used threats and force to prevent a bookkeeper from punishing a field slave. On another plantation, 30 slaves had run away in protest at the demotion of the driver; that same night the unharvested cane fields had been set alight and the fires put out with great difficulty. In May the bookkeeper on a fourth plantation had been abused in unmentionably descriptive terms and showered with a hail of stones from the slave quarters. When he sought refuge in his house, a slave named John came at the latch-window with an axe; the bookkeeper retaliated by putting his unloaded gun through the window, but another slave attempted to seize it. John and a third slave attempted to set fire to the stable roof with dried bagasse; they were chased away by the bookkeeper but only after the latter had been thoroughly beaten up. Walterstorff imposed a sentence of 100 to 150 lashes and transportation for the ringleaders, sentences which Col. Mühlenfels of the Regiment of Infantry thought inadequate. Hard labor in the fort, the latter argued, was a better deterrent for anyone similarly minded. Walterstorff, however, stuck to his sentences for a very significant reason: the garrison was weak, and in the absence of a sufficiently deterrent force such violent slaves might contemplate breaking out of their chains, with incalculable consequences.[116]

Walterstorff's report included several other recent incidents of threats to wound and kill. There was also, in July 1802, the violent murder of the bookkeeper at Mt. Misery by the slave Dick, resentful at the punishment ordered by the bookkeeper for the theft of sugar. On 14 June a letter addressed to freedman Thomas Towers was found in the street. Written in English, the letter read,

> Brothers all: When freedom at stake, ought free men and slaves to go hand in hand. We are ten against one white. In all this time they have treated us like dogs; now it was our time to show them we are men like they. God created us all, why shouldn't we be every bit as good as they and have the same rights. Let us demand our rights and them despite the whites. Long live the brave coloured people.[117]

The letter contained all the classic ingredients for apprehension: subversion by freedmen, their likely combination with the slaves, and the impotence of the latter's numbers in the event of confrontation. Walterstorff dismissed the letter as a forgery. His main concern was not to display fright or act out of panic, as this would weaken the government's authority. He intended to make use of every means at his disposal to exercise vigilance. But those resources, he concluded despairingly, were "very weak" – too weak indeed to give the slaves any idea of the mother country's power.

Adrian Bentzon, later Governor General but then in the colonial judicial service in St. Croix, had some interesting observations on the causes of the slave unrest of 1802 and the demonstrable impotence of the imperial power. He did not think the unrest was the work of creole slaves, who in his view were better equipped to organize and lead a general insurrection. Aware of the suppression of the Guadeloupe uprising, they had simply shown greater ability for restraint than bosals, recently imported slaves. But this did not mean that they did not harbor insurrectionary intentions. Bentzon also argued that the occupation of St. Croix "had awakened among the slaves an understanding of our weakness and by looking at themselves they came to appreciate their own strength."

General Fuller, the military governor during the occupation, had issued a proclamation in which he invited slaves to come forward with complaints, assuring them of a sympathetic audience and justice. This, Bentzon correctly concluded, provoked a perception of unjust treatment in the past. There was a broad hint on his part that there was justification for that perception; for although mistreatment of slaves was endemic in the sugar colonies, the case of the Danish West Indies, as he saw it, was distinguished from the rest by a very special circumstance – the exclusive control by foreigners of the day-to-day administration of the plantations. This "swarm" of foreigners, hailing "from the lowest classes of their country of origin," combined their perverse habits with "a high degree of ill-will towards and contempt for the country which gave them their daily bread." Because they made no attempt to conceal their sentiments from their slaves, they contributed in no small measure to the devaluation of public authority in the eyes of slaves "since it was unlikely that the latter could be insulated from the behavior of their immediate superiors."[118]

This situation analyzed by Bentzon is an interesting variation on that which prevailed at the South African Cape at the time. There, as George Fredrickson indicates, the substantial Boer slave-holders dominated neither the polity nor the society, before or after the British capture. The individual master-slave relationship, therefore, did not "have the kind of autonomy and power to shape the rest of the society in its image." At the Cape, "the masters themselves had masters, in the form of independent government officials, empowered to intervene in the owner-slave relationship."[119] In the St. Croix from which Bentzon wrote in 1802, the substantial slave-holders and plantation managerial class dominated the society, if not the polity; the slave master did indeed have a master in the representative of the colonizing power. But the credibility of the latter's hegemony was gravely compromised by the first, and perhaps shattered by the second, British invasion and this situation was aggravated by the contumely openly expressed by the largely expatriate planter class.

Deepened Difficulties and Challenges in the Nineteenth Century

For the remainder of the nineteenth century, Denmark suffered a series of reverses which considerably reduced its imperial standing. Having endured the indignity of two cataclysmic English assaults on Copenhagen in 1801 and 1807, the capture of the entire Danish fleet in the latter year, and the destruction of maritime trade, the Danish state went bankrupt in 1813. The final drop from this bitter cup of woe, before the Napoleonic wars ended, was the loss of Norway, which received an independent constitution in May 1814.[120] After 1815, Denmark, if not quite the genteel poor relation in the European family of nations, was clearly in reduced circumstances and the way forward was obscured by the uncertainty of the role. Certainly by the end of the 1820s proposals were being discussed for economies in colonial expenditure, particularly as they related to the military.[121]

By 1837 the Generaltoldkammer or General Customs Office, the office responsible for the oversight of Denmark's colonial affairs, supported a recommendation from Governor General von Scholten for the scaling-down of the colonial garrison by one company commander and 41 other ranks. A vital part of the motivation for the reform was that the interests of the free and unfree were so divergent that "in no circumstances would they combine against the political and administrative authority of the state." As before, great reliance was placed on the militia in the event of slave disturbances. What was instructive about the reform of 1837 was its predication on a number of incalculable contingencies: "crews from ships in harbor and the ready help that could be expected from the nearby islands of the English and French and warships." The Generaltoldkammer had no difficulty in concluding that any misgivings were groundless, "even if the reduction went so far that it was merely sufficient for maintaining normal guard duty."[122] Such a dependent mind-set was not new; it had continuities with 1793.[123] It arose not out of obtuseness, but as a response to reality. Seized of a similar reality, a Royal Commission in 1840 recommended a reduction of the colonial judicial establishment and the abolition of the appellate jurisdiction in St. Croix. The latter's utility was questionable, it argued, since the time of the homeward journey had been reduced by one-third.[124] The foreshortened journey was made possible by the introduction of the English Royal Mail Steamship service to Southampton. Copenhagen was reached only after that initial stop.

As with technology, so with ideology. Denmark's relationship with her West Indian colonies was increasingly affected after 1830 by currents of ideas over which she had no control. At the same time there were developments internally which complicated the context: the slow and painful redefinition of the nature of the monarchy and an attempt at the re-evaluation of the overseas empire. In the latter case, a study by Grethe Bentzen concludes that Denmark gave up on being a colonial power by 1842, accordingly sold out its East India possessions to Britain in 1845 and was being encouraged by the provincial legislature of Viborg to sell the West Indian islands as well as the Guinea colony.[125] In the former case, the absolute monarchy of many centuries was eventually replaced by the liberal constitution of 1849.[126] Externally, it was impossible to isolate the colonies from the British decision to emancipate or from the ferment of its effects.[127] British Tortola was practically within cannon shot of a poorly policed St. John and the narrows between could be swum by the intrepid, or negotiated by fishing boat and improvised raft. The British island held magnetic attractions for the slaves of St. John, particularly after 1840.[128] Nor was the deployment of a Danish frigate to stem the flow viewed with sympathy by the British, especially when it involved firing upon escapees in those ill-defined territorial waters.[129] By 1845 there were instances of slaves escaping from the more distant St. Croix to Tortola. In the same year the futility of attempts at prevention was demonstrated by the simultaneous escape of 37 slaves from St. John.[130]

The pressures brought about by British emancipation were proximate and explicit. To them could be added the more spatially remote but implicitly disruptive effects of Manifest Destiny, as it affected the Caribbean. The expansionist enthusiasms of Southern Democrats contained the potential catalyst for a series of chain reactions on Caribbean slavery from which the Danish West Indies might have found it difficult to escape. More perceptive public figures in Danish life were formulating a Domino Theory of the 1840s in which the Danish West Indies would be the last piece to fall. In 1847 a senior member of the Generaltoldkammer envisaged a scenario in which the United States' expansionist ambition to annex Cuba would elicit diplomatic resistance from Britain, whilst Spain, in order to consolidate such support and keep Cuba was likely to liberate her slaves there. Emancipation in Puerto Rico would follow automatically, and "in such a case, one is ashamed to say, it could be taken for granted that the Danish government would be obliged to follow suit."[131] Louis Rothe, a senior member of the colonial judiciary in 1847, was equally convinced of the vulnerability of Danish slavery to the pressure of international developments. Changes in the balance of the geopolitical equation, which caught Denmark on the wrong side would all too probably lead to the occupation of St. Thomas. Its large, easily fortified and defensible harbor would be of particular interest to a powerful maritime nation. Denmark could do nothing to prevent this, Rothe argued, nor the consequences if the occupying power were England. "The moment the English flag is raised on the colonies' forts, slavery would be abolished without regard to the consequences, and such questions as compensation for loss."[132] These were considerations of which the slave population would have been aware. They were equally aware of the developments towards emancipation in the French islands late in 1847 and early 1848; aware too of the growing public outcry against slavery in the mother country for a variety of pragmatic, economic, humanitarian and political reasons.[133]

The crown sought advice in the colonies as well as at home, and the consensus which emerged in the months of intense consultation early in 1847 was that emancipation should take place after a grace period of up to 15 years. There was less agreement on the question of compensation for the slaveowners. One compensation calculus by von Scholten called for a sliding scale of benefits diminishing as the years went by; but the calculus was informed by the assumption that at any time within the grace period the crown might be forced to a premature declaration because of "unforeseen circumstances."[134] As the State Commissioners for Debt, who were also consulted, remarked, the use of the phrase in von Scholten's widely known proposal was particularly unfortunate. Although they were not specified, everyone including the slaves knew precisely what those circumstances were. It was a public admission of national weakness that would not be lost on the enslaved:

> There is something inherently compromising in a government's publicly announcing its intention whilst acknowledging the possibility of being unable to see it through because it lacks the power to do so. Such an admission, besides, could give rise to turbulent ideas among the enslaved, ideas which otherwise might not have arisen. Indeed, it might well encourage shows of force to achieve what the government appears to be only waiting to bestow,

particularly when the prospects of an emancipation, only after 15 years, are not especially attractive for the enslaved.[135]

The Commissioners were right on all counts. The crown chose to declare for a 12-year grace period, beginning with the free birth of all slave children as of 28 July 1847 and, fortified by advice from the Chancellery, determined the compensation question by making no mention of it.[136] A grace period of whatever length was a species of apprenticeship *before* emancipation, with few attractions for slaves, as the Debt Commissioners correctly calculated. Parents were not readily reconciled to bondage with their children manumitted. Moreover, freedom had been conceded in principle. Within a year, they had created those "unforeseen circumstances" which forced a premature declaration of emancipation. It was a savage irony that the declaration was at von Scholten's own hands.

The demystification of whiteness as a mechanism of social control, a process facilitated by the disruptive presence of large numbers of Irish and Scots-Irish estate personnel, hastened the slaves' disposition to confront the structures that oppressed them.[137] Further, the slaves' decision to test conclusions with the polity arose from an acute awareness of its vulnerability. Victor Prosch was right.[138] An empire without dominion was an empire with inherent structural weaknesses. The Caribbean's second successful slave uprising conclusively demonstrated that fact.

2

"The Doom of the Almighty:" Slaveowning Ideology

TO SUSTAIN THE SYSTEM OF CHATTEL SLAVERY ON WHICH THE Danish West Indian plantation economy depended the minority European community had recourse to the mechanism of superior force. The ultimate manifestations of that force lay with the military and the power of the state to inflict pain on the bodies of the slaves. But the unholy matrimony of unwilling labor and productive land was effected not only by the musket's sanction or the tip of the whip. That union involved as well the creation, articulation, and elaboration of an ideology which had a double purpose. In the first place, it provided a comforting and justificatory theoretical foundation for man's inhumanity to fellow man. Secondly, the slaves' normative compliance would hopefully be achieved by an internalization of such ideas and acceptance of their bondage.

The Sanctions of Ancient Law

The principles of Roman Law formed an important part of the justification for slavery both in the eighteenth as well as the nineteenth century. There is a connecting continuum between the views of Etatsraad Lindemann expressed in St. Croix in 1783[1] and those of Procurator Fugl who as late as 1834 cited Roman Law as a basis for slavery which provided a definition of slaves as "inter res quia personam non habet."[2] Fortifying this appeal to Roman Law were others based on ancient Nordic law, which authorized slavery, and what A. S. Ørsted, the noted nineteenth-century jurist, called "the fundamental principles of legislation." Moreover, Ørsted argued, a view of slavery as contrary to law was a recent development in the history of Natural Law.[3] The "older" Natural Law system and that which applied when Denmark's major legal code, the code of King Christian V, was written in the later seventeenth century assumed servitude as a condition which Natural Law supported.[4]

These views of Ørsted's were expressed in connection with the 1802 litigation surrounding the slave Hans Jonathan, when the issue at stake was whether his presence in Denmark automatically made him free. These were the views which prevailed, although they did not go unchallenged. Hans Jonathan's counsel, Algreen-Ussing, submitted (a) that Danish law did not permit one person to be the property of another as a slave, (b) that the laws for the Danish West Indian islands in any case were only applicable there, and (c) that the Danish law could be used to support the *introduction* of slaves into the Danish West Indian islands, but not their birth into slavery in those islands.[5] This last submission represented perhaps the apogee of "enlightened" thought on the subject of slavery in early nineteenth century Denmark and its plantation colonies. If it was a significant discontinuity it was also a minority view. Nevertheless, it challenged in the most fundamental way the notion of perpetual servitude through which the servile status of the New World African became heritable. The central thesis of this position, although it was not expressly articulated, was that the Roman maxim "partus sequitur ventrem" was inapplicable to the situation of the Danish Virgin Islands. But Danish public opinion in 1802 was not receptive to such a radical proposition, basking as it was in moral self-congratulation at being the first European nation to abolish the transatlantic slave trade, in that same year. The prosecution's response, with which the court concurred, was that the ordinances governing slavery in the Danish West Indian islands presupposed that owners of slaves of both sexes acquired ownership rights over their children. Such a presupposition could in no way be sustained on the basis of positive law; the principle of "partus sequitur ventrem" so far as the court was concerned was validated by custom.[6]

"Eiendomsret," the right to property in slaves and their offspring, was a constituent part of Denmark's judicial traditions of the eighteenth and nineteenth centuries. Indeed that right was taken as given and the court before which Hans Jonathan appeared addressed itself simply to the question as to whether that right of ownership could be said to have been terminated by the fact of that slave having set foot on Danish soil. The irony was that, the Somerset case of 30 years before notwithstanding and the suspension of the Danish transatlantic slave trade in the very year that the case came before the court, it answered the question in the negative.[7]

Ørsted was of course familiar with the Somerset judgment. But in reacting to it he was quick to point out that Lord Blackstone in his *Commentaries* whilst conceding the slave's right to freedom in England had gone on to say that former slave owners continued to enjoy those personal services to which they were previously entitled. Such a relationship, Ørsted argued, was no more than the subordinate relationship of apprentice and master which could be perpetuated for a long term of years.[8] As further justification for his position, Ørsted pointed to the situation in the Prussian states. Slavery was not tolerated among their citizens but resident foreigners were allowed to exercise their rights over slaves they brought with them, although the authorities ensured that such rights would not be exercised to a point of abuse which endangered the slave's life.[9]

It is interesting to note that whilst Ørsted steadfastly maintained his position that residence in Denmark did not entitle the slave to freedom, he adopted an extremely unconventional position in relation to the master's power of jurisdiction and right to punish. Using the analogy of the serf, "the best example of arbitrary discretion under which anyone could be subjected" in Denmark, Ørsted asserted that the extensive rights to punishment exercised by West Indian slave owners were inadmissible under Danish law. King Christian V's Law, Cap. 6 Section 5 paragraph 5, and the Ordinance for the Good Order of Serfs 25 March 1791 paragraph 4, both limited the right to punishment and that limit could not be exceeded by private agreement.[10] In Denmark, therefore, there was no individual, including the serf, whose life and limb were not protected by due process. In the West Indies, on the other hand, any free person who killed a slave was not guilty of a capital offense. Ørsted therefore concluded that since Danish law did not permit the acquisition of such extensive private discretion over another's person, as in the case with West Indian slavery, the question resolved itself into whether and/or how the right acquired in the West Indies could be exercised in Europe:

> I can argue neither with that position which insists that the situation should remain unchanged, nor with those who see that servitude should end once the slave set foot in Europe ... [I]t would indeed be a disgrace if in a Christian European state such as Denmark so blatantly improper a power over any person could be exercised. On the other hand, the slave in coming to Denmark could clearly not be his own master, but his former master's rights must be confined to those limits which our laws make possible in the relationship of one subject with another.[11]

Slavery, then, according to the views of this influential nineteenth century jurist, was founded on the principles of ancient Roman and Nordic Law; Natural Law supported it; in Denmark no positive law forbade it; in the Danish Virgin Islands custom sanctified it; it was inheritable and in Denmark mollified only by the legal limitations of the arbitrary exercise of jurisdiction over another's person.

Martial Models

A further consideration which conditioned attitudes to slavery in the Danish West Indies was the parallel drawn, with frequency and facility, between the islands' situation and one in which Martial Law existed or War Articles were in force. As the eighteenth century advanced, as the plantations expanded and the slave trade kept pace with demand, the population disparity between ruler and ruled, black and white, slave and master, widened. This demographic imbalance was one of the bases of the military paradigm. The state-of-siege-psychosis is well illustrated in a comment by the soldier-administrator Major-General Schimmelmann in 1784. No slave, he remarked, should be punished less than a white man and a runaway slave no less severely than a deserting soldier. Blacks, said Schimmelmann, were a particularly stiff-necked race and could only be governed by the threat of severe punishment.[12] Discipline and the ultimate sanction of force were his watchwords, and they seemed all the more urgent and applicable for in the undeclared martial law and the perpetual state of siege characteristic of plantation slave society the enemy was not without but within.

Hans West, the priest who lived in St. Croix for a number of years in the 1780s, employed the martial allusion in one of his major works on the Danish West Indies, his *Bidrag til Beskrivelse over Ste. Croix* (Contribution to the Description of St. Croix) published in 1793. He enthusiastically endorsed beating as a form of punishment since it reinforced the differentiation between super- and sub-ordinate in the society, and saw corporal punishment as a particularly effective instrument for the maintenance of the stratified relationships of a slave society. It was not merely a question of the slave showing apprehension at being beaten or at the merest suggestion of it. West implied that forms of punishment appropriate for the Danish marine and military were equally appropriate for slaves. In any event, he argued, punishment by whip or birch-rod was far less hazardous to the slave than to a Danish soldier. The former was only beaten on his "fleshy parts" and consequently protected against internal damage and permanent impairment of health. No such nice discrimination, West concluded, was shown when soldiers or sailors were flogged.[13]

Neither Schimmelmann nor West elaborated the military parallel with the degree of detail found in Etatsraad Lindemann's draft slave code of 1783. Lindemann's draft began with two justificatory quotes from the Epistles: Ephesians 6:5-8 and 1 Peter 2:18-20. In both of these epistles Paul had called upon servants to be "obedient unto them that according to the flesh are your masters, with fear and trembling" and to "be in subjection to your masters with all fear; not only to the good and gentle, but also to the froward." But although Lindemann began with this Christian sanction of bondage, he did not sustain any argument for the specifics of his suggested code. Instead, in the very first article of the draft code, where slaves were called upon to show deference to whites, especially to their masters, Lindemann pointed out that current regulations for the Danish infantry required privates to show respect for their superiors in rank.[14]

A similar argument based on the rigid hierarchical structures of the military was used to justify the inclusion of Article 2 in Lindemann's draft slave code. It required the slave to step out of the way of any white and either with bared head to go slowly by or, when re-covered, to remain still until that white person had passed. If slaves were mounted they should dismount or else slowly ride out of the way, neither galloping nor hurrying nor, worse yet, to ride alongside.[15] Article 3 which specified that all slaves should respect and obey orders from all whites, regardless of whether the latter were their owners, was drawn from Article 595 of the Danish Naval

Articles. This was to apply with particular force when there was verbal or physical altercation between slaves, and whites intervened to put an end to them.[16]

Ordinary impoliteness or disobedience, under Lindemann's code, was to attract 20-50 lashes depending on circumstances.[17] If, however, disobedience was combined with rude and defamatory words, the penalty suggested was 150-200 strokes.[18] By the author's own admission the punishment was severe and considerably greater than the 40 strokes the New York assembly for example had prescribed in September 1708, to which he made reference:

> But in this connection it must be noted that the slaves in North America are not treated nearly as harshly as is the case on the islands, where much stricter discipline is a necessity considering the small number of whites in relation to the mass of slaves.[19]

Further provisions in the first section of Lindemann's draft code, governing such contingencies as wounding, riotous assembly, obstruction of justice, attempted suicide, marronage and abetting of marronage, were specifically based on paragraphs of the extant War Articles.[20] In all, eleven articles of a total of 43 in the first section of the code entitled "Slaves and Punishment for Misdeeds" had their inclusion justified on the grounds of similar provisions of the military code.[21]

Lindemann's preoccupation with deference, for which he found precedent enough in the military's standing orders, arose from a concern to enforce a pattern of social and class relationships current in contemporary Denmark. In the West Indies, with its added complication of a servile race, enforcement of deference was all the more important to hold that servile race in check. Such draconian discipline and exemplary punishment as he advocated, was necessary precisely because the numerical superiority of the slave population was too clearly a potentially decisive advantage. To neutralize that advantage and compensate for white numerical inferiority, the compliance of the blacks had to be achieved by an acknowledgement, forced if need be, of white social and, by extension, racial superiority.

Economic Expediency

In the literature on slavery in Denmark and the Danish West Indies arguments of economic expediency figured prominently, particularly in the nineteenth century. They appeared in their most ingenuous form in the Hans Jonathan case of 1802 already cited. Ørsted submitted then that both the plantations and plantation chattel slavery existed before the Virgin Islands became Danish, and there were "particular grounds which prompted our Lawgiver [Christian] to accept the situation in the West Indian Islands which existed before they fell under his rule, namely, the necessity of their continuance as sugar plantations and the extreme difficulty of discontinuing an already existing and complex institution."[22]

This view was quoted with approval by Fugl at the time of emancipation in the British West Indies. In a lengthy article Fugl counseled against any such measure for the Danish plantation possessions.[23] He found very little difficulty in expressing sympathy for Ørsted's opinions, for the slave in any event was "lazy, refractory, lying, dishonest and shiftless."[24] A less ethnocentric but equally expediency-oriented submission accompanied Lindemann's draft slave code of 1783. He objected with some vigor to the practice then current by which slaves were used as jobbers to bring weekly or monthly incomes to their masters. The practice was objectionable for the reason that it militated against plantation agriculture by depriving it of labor. Plantation enterprise, Lindemann emphasized, had not only given rise to plantation slavery but was the chief reason for its continued toleration.[25] An elaborated version of the same argument, expressed with more directness, came from the chief of police in St. John: slaves were necessary for the colonies' cultivation if for no other reason than that they were specially adapted by nature for tropical labor.[26] Whites ruled themselves out even if their numbers were adequate as a labor force for they could neither withstand the heat nor work in it. The case of creole poor whites, some of whom worked as hard as slaves, was invoked to substantiate the point: their enervated condition and chronic sickliness was taken as conclusive proof of the European's unsuitability for tropical labor.[27]

Hans West argued in much the same vein in both his major works, his *Bidrag* of 1793 and his "Beretning om det danske Eilande St. Croix" (Account of the Island of St. Croix) published in the journal *Iris* in 1791. Europeans, he said, could not cultivate the plantations because they were unable to withstand the climate;[28] without labor the plantations would die, the planters leave, and the islands be lost to Denmark.[29] In the immediate aftermath of the slave trade's abolition, the climatic argument was again pressed into service to reinforce the argument of economic necessity. As though conceding the loss of the battle for abolition of the trade but not the war to maintain slavery, Governor Mühlenfels wrote to the Slave Trade Commission in 1805 that "It is an irrefutable truth that only Negroes born in the same climate or in one even hotter than the West Indian are suited to sugar cultivation without their health suffering thereby."[30]

The literature of the late eighteenth and early nineteenth centuries, examples of which have been cited, provides abundant evidence of a continuing concern to maintain property in plantations. That material objective was paramount and in no way responsive to countervailing moral considerations on the subject of slavery itself. The right to property was a recurring theme among the Danish West Indian plantocracy of the period. Indeed, it is significant that four years after emancipation was a fait accompli the planters made their last anguished cry to the crown for compensation, resting their case on the implicit premise of the sacredness of property.[31] If that view prevailed among the plantocracy as late as 1852, it was an even profounder article of faith during the period of slavery.

In the formulation of attitudes to slavery in the eighteenth century, the concept of the slave as property and a factor of production perhaps received its earliest explicit articulation by Governor Philip Gardelin. His Placat of 5 September 1733, which was to remain for a century the only legal code affecting slaves in the Danish West Indies, was quick to point out in the preamble that slaves were the capital of their masters and mistresses, a circumstance which imposed an even greater obligation to servility than the disobedience which the slaves displayed.[32] Frederick V's "Reglement for Slaverne" of 3 February 1755 began by calling for religious instruction for slaves, and although its prescriptions for slave insubordination were considerably less harsh than anything found in the Gardelin code, it nevertheless elaborated the notion of property in a discrete paragraph, where Gardelin had disposed of it parenthetically: "Besides, the slaves are to be regarded as part and parcel of property. Their masters therefore have permission, following the content of the law, to dispose over the slaves much as they would their other assets or property."[33]

The development of the concept of the slave as property, and essentially a unit of production, was not unrelated to the development of the plantation system since the late seventeenth century and the expansion of capitalized agriculture. At the beginning of the nineteenth century, K. L. Rahbek, the pamphleteer, analyzed this correlation and argued inter alia that early slavery in the Danish West Indies had been patriarchal, the slave owner frugal and compassionate and agriculture limited in its objectives to self-sufficiency. Such modest goals neither necessitated large scale production nor called forth an expansive life-style.[34] No doubt Rahbek sharply overdrew his idyllic picture of the pater familias and the self-sufficient farm. For as a vigorous advocate of the anti-slave lobby at the end of the eighteenth century he had a particular purpose to serve.

On sounder ground Rahbek argued that the critical element which transformed the idyll into nightmare was the availability of capital for overseas investment in agriculture. Many planters borrowed more than they needed, deployed the surplus into luxury and altered their life style. This in turn required greater income, expanded cultivation, and an enlarged work force, increasingly dehumanized under a regimen of absenteeism and supervision by agents less concerned about overwork than with production. Such improvidence did not conduce to capital accumulation even with increased sugar prices.[35] In lean years – such as the notoriously bad harvests of 1789 and 1791 – there were no reserve funds on which to call and the cycle regenerated itself. New loans had to be sought at increased interest, cultivation had to be expanded to meet increased charges, more slaves had to be bought, which in turn required more loans.[36]

The slave, then, from Rahbek's point of view was caught in a tightening spiral of capitalist enterprise which exploited him as capital and degraded him as a person. The abolition of the slave trade was the first step in redeeming the slave's humanity, or as he said in conclusion:

There is the odd presumption that should the planters give better care to their Negroes, and should they improve their condition and give them the opportunity to feel the advantage of domestic well-being, then this would give cause for unrest. We might as well presume the contrary, and one hardly is mistaken, when one believes that even should an attempt to generate unrest be made from another quarter, this would have that much less effect, when the masters are more considerate so that the Negroes will regard them with more love and trust.[37]

In this affirmation, the slave's humanity had thus found powerful advocacy by the beginning of the nineteenth century. Indeed Christian VII in issuing the abolition proclamation in 1792 lay strong emphasis on promoting marriages and the advancement of education and "morals."

The Curse of Ham

Rahbek's conclusions and the crown's abolition of the slave trade constituted attempts to recall the African in the Antilles from a status of primarily property. The fact was, however, that European ethnocentricity and its corollary, negative attitudes towards Africans, were far too persistent to vanish by royal fiat or energetic pamphleteering. Svend Green-Pedersen has perceptively observed that a common feature of the literature on Danish Guinea – and the Danish West Indies – in the first 60 years of the eighteenth century, was the contempt for the religion of the Africans.[38] The missionary endeavor, moreover, was heavily tinged with depreciation of the culture of the pagan.[39] To this might be added a pervasive and continuing strain of racial pessimism.

It would be possible to argue, therefore, that the views of a Rahbek or a Christian VII represented aberrant terms in the series of ideas which prevailed on the subject of slaves and slavery. As early as 1739, Gardelin had announced that "our Negroes ... were made slaves by the Almighty Himself."[40] Governor Hansen was of similar persuasion when in August 1748 he issued a proclamation against runaways. Despite a general pardon in the previous July, maroons had continued to hold out in the bush and would not return to their masters' work "to which they nevertheless are tied by God and nature."[41]

This notion of the condemnation of God and nature, the curse of Ham as it were, found many echoes in the literature on slavery in both the eighteenth and the nineteenth centuries. Richard Haagensen, whose *Beskrivelse over Eylandet St. Croix* (Description of the island of St. Croix) appeared in 1758, was archetypical of this genre and stated his position with uncomprising clarity: "In my general opinion they are all evil by nature and little good is in them, yes, if I dare say so, I really believe that their black skin bears witness to their evil and they therefore are predestined to slavery and ought not to have any freedom."[42] The equation of blackness with evil, the mark of the literal beast, is repeated again and again throughout Haagensen's work. The skin of slaves was so thick that a whip had difficulty bruising or bringing blood from it. As an instance of the slave's animal hardihood he cited the case of two slaves who had been castrated; they were still alive but their masters were dead! Neither beating nor branding, he said, elicited the faintest show of pain.[43] The opinions expressed in the *Beskrivelse* bear suggestive resemblance to the views expressed in 1755 in an anonymous manuscript authored by "R. H." There the author stated that not only were blacks evil by nature but that whites could not live among them without fear and danger: "the evil of slaves is so great that were they not kept in the same fashion as dogs in chains, no one would dare nor be able to live with them."[44]

Hans West differed from Haagensen in the refinement of his style but not in the crudity of his racial views. In his *Bidrag* of 1793 West instanced a variety of circumstances to establish not only the physical difference but the moral inferiority of blacks. He cited, for example, the occasion on which he had seen a slave beat a horse, go away, come back, beat the horse a second time, and so on a third and fourth time. He had seen mothers beat their children, go away to do something else and come back to punish the very children with increased passion. It was possible, he suggested, that such behavior reflected their plantation upbringing and the treatment of their masters.[45] But, he continued to ask, if one accepted this thesis, how could one explain the sadism of the free, christened and confirmed black? West did not answer that question by pointing to the fact that violence was immanent in slave societies and left no one untouched, master, slave or free, black or white. Although he hinted that "this is no country for a liberal mind,"[46] the answer so far as he was concerned was that these children of the torrid zone had "other characteristics" which northerners did not have.[47]

Those characteristics included not merely the moral degeneracy which their improvidence suggested; for they merely ate, slept to wake up and eat again.[48] But there were also physical characteristics which for West singled out the blacks as inferior specimens of the human species. Woolly hair and heavily pigmented skin were protection against the sun, and therefore natural attributes in his assessment. But West felt differently about blacks' odor:

> The slaves' odor is of such a different kind compared with that of the Europeans and often stinks so abominably that this smell can leave a stench in a room for a long time. It is sometimes necessary to get out of the path of Negroes in order to avoid this nauseating unpleasantness. At the same time one must also do them the justice that they usually keep themselves clean and wash their bodies daily.[49]

The suffocating unpleasantness of odor was, for the fastidious West a mark of inferiority but he failed to say whether those slaves who washed on a daily basis were also open to his strictures. It is curious, to say the least, that West should have spent so much of his polished prose to make this point, without relating it in any way to the critical shortages of water which were chronic in St. Croix, and which he talks about elsewhere in the *Bidrag* as well as in his "Beretning" of 1791.[50]

West was convinced too that West Africans as a race were normally indolent, evil, proud and much given to theft, and offered as evidence six or seven occasions, one involving himself, of daring robberies in broad daylight.[51] In his general condemnation of slave immorality, West reflected very closely the opinions of the German Moravian missionary C. G. A. Oldendorp whose *Geschichte der Mission der Evangelischen Brüder auf den Caraibischen Inseln S. Thomas, S. Croix und S. Jan* (*History*) appeared in 1777. The moral character of the heathen African, Oldendorp believed, was seriously flawed. Africans were self-willed, deceitful and lying, given in a distressing degree to the lusts of the flesh and completely without understanding of the meaning of chastity or "pureness of heart." One could hardly expect otherwise, wrote Oldendorp, since from childhood they had been brought up simply to follow wherever the urges of passion led.[52]

Colonel, later Governor, Thomas de Malleville, a long-time resident of the islands and like Oldendorp a Moravian, began with the same premises and came to the identical conclusions as the missionary. Africans he argued in 1784 were corrupt by nature, that was the basic failing in their humanity. Left to develop by itself that failing conduced to the development of the worst evils. The upbringing of most blacks both in Guinea and the West Indies hardly helped matters. A regimen of forced servile labor which de Malleville supported, was therefore not merely a protective device for the white minority faced with this morally corrupt black majority.[53] The discipline of labor under the strongest sanction of force was, by inference, a moral cathartic. More explicitly, de Malleville argued that the severity of the extant law, Gardelin's draconian code of 1733, was necessary and expedient. If the crown could be persuaded to encourage and support missionary work among those "wretched heathens" maintenance of a severe code and forced labor would serve to remind the slaves of the state of corruption from which "by God's grace" they had been delivered.[54]

Views closely corresponding to de Malleville's are to be found in the submission made to a Christiansted court in 1784 by Crown Prosecutor Advocate Balling, in a case involving two slaves, Jochum and Sam, indicted for beating a white ship's captain, John Hart, at the request of their owner, ship's agent Lorentz Ebbesen. The petty sessions court or *Byting* handed down a judgment of a public beating and transportation for both. According to witnesses to the event, Hart was vigorously set about in a public street and from the cudgel blows to his head and elsewhere lost a great deal of blood. When the case came before the *Landsting* or magistrate's court, however, the presiding judge Colbiørnsen took cognizance of the slaves' circumscribed choice in obeying their master's orders. Their first duty, he said, was an unquestioning obedience to their master's commands. In confirming the sentence of the lower court Colbiørnsen was influenced by a notion of the slave's diminished responsibility and of the slave as primarily property, no different in fact from a well trained guard dog that was ever responsive to its immediate source of authority, its master.

In his presentation for the crown, Balling argued that the offense was one of the most dangerous and punishable a slave could commit. Assuming the unsuitability of white labor for the tropics, and the consequent necessity of a vast black labor force, the Crown Prosecutor advocated the most stringent control of that labor force. Absolute obedience and respect for the white population was called for; departures from that norm should be punished with the utmost severity. The alternatives were "Opror, Mord, og Odelæggelse." Rebellion, murder and destruction, Balling was saying, were all that could be expected from slaves unless they were restrained by the fear of punishment: "it is only fear of punishment and not religion or education that prevents the wild and ignorant Negro from committing a crime."[55]

The Civilizing Mission

Svend Green-Pedersen has noted that a distinguishing feature of the literature prior to 1760 was its acceptance of the slave system as given and an accompanying belief that "European material culture and Christian religion [were] far superior to Negro culture and religion."[56] The same observation holds true for the period from 1760 to emancipation. The assumed moral imperfection and cultural impoverishment of the African, the elevation of what was European and Christian above the African and pagan, explains not only missionary endeavor on both sides of the Atlantic. It explains as well the persistence of the view that plantation servitude had a redemptive function, and that this was a fundamental dimension of Denmark's "mission civilisatrice."

Hans West made the point strongly in his *Bidrag*:

> I must ... repeat that not only do most of the Negroes, who have become accustomed to the country, in no way wish to return to the Coast ... After having lived in the West Indies for a number of years, they even regard the Coast and the Coast Negroes with such contempt that it has become a word of abuse among the Negroes in the country to call one another busal or Guinea-Negro.[57]

Even if slaves who had lived for some time in the plantation system were contemptuous of new arrivals, and used the expression "Guinea Negro" or "Busal" as pejorative descriptions, West's conclusion that seasoned slaves had no desire to return to the coast was specious. One need not invoke Bruno Bettelheim's view of the captives' values becoming those of their captors in a situation of inverted reality, where the world "outside" was an abstraction.[58] To the extent that the plantation system induced psychological stress, much weight cannot be attached to West's observation. It is far more important to recognize that he attributed to the slaves attitudes which were certainly his own. Moreover, the specific example which he gives of slaves' unwillingness to return to the Coast does not bear examination. He tells the story of twelve slaves delivered to a planter on the south side of St. Croix by an American captain. A month later when the captain returned for payment and asked how the planter liked them, the slaves were sent for and asked if they were ready to go back with the captain. All unanimously answered no, held on to the planter's arms and clothing and would not let go until he told them it was a joke. Had West himself undergone the unpleasantness of the Middle Passage one month previously the likelihood is that he too would have been unwilling to return.[59]

This tradition of the mission civilisatrice died hard, particularly among those who were opposed to the abolition of the slave trade in 1802. One such opponent, Leinrich, submitted to the Slave Trade Commission in 1801 that although slavery was misfortune, the slave was better off in the West Indies than in Africa: "But if I must be a slave, I would rather be this on the West Indian islands than in Africa. I know slavery in both places, and with the utmost conviction I repeat that, provided the labor demanded of the slave is tolerable, he is happier as a slave in the West Indies than in Africa."[60] Governor Mühlenfels in St. Croix argued similarly in 1805. According to his reckoning, if slaves were protected by certain laws in the colonies, their situation would be considerably more advantageous than in their own country. Mühlenfels' view of Africa was a place where despots had their subjects beheaded for pleasure or for arcane religious purposes. Echoing West, he concluded that there were very few slaves who even in their present servitude wanted to return to their fatherland.[61]

As late as 1841, just seven years before emancipation, Etatsraad H. H. Berg, government official and planter in St. Thomas, was arguing along similar lines. In substance Berg's view was that the slaves were not to be considered unfortunate because they were someone else's property, having come from a race among whom slavery of the most loathsome kind was practiced; from a place where from birth they were familiar with the thought that they were someone else's property. What, asked Berg, made slavery "accepted law" in Africa where the strong sold the weak, fathers their sons and barbarism went as far as cannibalism? The answer was as facile as the assumptions were stereotypic: "It is because the Negro refuses to work that he refuses to follow God's law: 'In the sweat of thy brow shalt thou eat bread.' Do not accuse the European slave trade for this horrible condition which existed before the Europeans knew Africa."[62] In the West Indies, Berg was suggesting, the taint of Africa would be washed away in the copious sweat from the brow of coerced labor, the sin atoned by the penance of earning one's bread according to Divine Law.

Sin and Salvation

Berg and his predecessors in the latter half of the preceding century promoted a theory of secular salvation that was closely matched by the church's theology of redemption. The Danish Church and those denominations which also functioned in the Danish West Indies – the Moravians, the

Dutch Reformed Church, the Church of England and the Roman Catholics – shared that common inheritance of Christian thought which, according to David Brion Davis, accommodated slavery in a series of "balanced dualisms:" ideally undesirable but practically necessary. The slave, deemed chattel in things temporal, was accorded equality in things spiritual. This Christian tradition was also one in which slavery was perceived as a consequence of sin, of man's fall from grace. But by the same token, as Davis has pointed out, it was also "the starting point for a divine quest."[63] To extrapolate from that formulation, slavery was a form of necessary sacrifice which in the canons of Judeo-Christian thought preceded atonement. If absolution from the sin for which slavery was the punishment belonged to the spiritual realm, the penance or sacrifice was not only a matter for the here below but an essential part of the temporal order.

None of the denominations with congregations in the Danish Virgin Islands at any time inveighed against the social order in which they operated. Herman Lawaetz has observed in his study of the Moravians that they undertook a debate on slavery in the 1760s, but it made little difference in their acceptance of the institution up to the time of emancipation in 1848.[64] They kept slaves on all their establishments in the islands. The Lutheran and other clergy also had personal slaves.[65]

The church and its activities came to play an increasingly important part in the lives of Danish West Indian slaves, dominating their "free" time and facilitating their quest for status and respectability. Yet it is important to recognize, as Davis has in the case of British missionary effort,[66] that the church served to monitor those activities of the slaves which were not readily susceptible to the discipline of the plantation regime. Moreover, the Christian message of the dutiful bondservant promoted to a place of pre-eminence the virtues of obedience, patience, resignation and humility which singly or in combination were powerful instruments of social control.

The "balanced dualism" was nowhere more in evidence than in the attitude to baptism. In this regard, Davis has noted for the Americas generally what applies to the Danish islands specifically: "To make American slavery conform to the ancient Christian ideal of servitude ... meant that Negroes should be baptized and instructed in the faith, ... should be brought to internalize those precepts of humility, patience and willing obedience which would allow masters to rule by love instead of force."[67]

Inculcation by baptism into a denomination was therefore a form of social regulation and a reinforcement of the temporal order. Indeed, it is possible to argue that the singular absence of conspiracies and revolts, from the St. Croix conspiracy of 1759 down to 1848, was not unrelated to the significant increase in church affiliation.[68] That phenomenon's most arresting manifestation occurred in St. Croix, where by 1835 baptized slaves comprised 99 percent of the slave population.[69]

Baptism, however, was not regarded as a pathway to freedom. The fear that a positive correlation would be established between the two was an early preoccupation in British West Indian settlement and the matter was only finally laid to rest in the 1729 judgment of the English Attorney-General that baptism did not alter the slave's legal status.[70] That was a decision with which the Bishop of London heartily concurred. The Danish response, juridically and clerically was no different when the time came to adopt a position on the question. Frederik V's "Reglement for Slaverne" of 1755 coincided with the Danish crown's inauguration of a Lutheran mission in the Virgin Islands. Whilst the Reglement's preamble insisted on the need to preach Christianity to the slaves, it was quick to point out before that very paragraph ended that "The slaves were not to become free by virtue of becoming Christian, but to remain slaves no less obliged to owe their masters and owners obedience, diligence, fidelity and other duties."[71]

The church, for its part in the Danish West Indies, also accepted as given the moral imperfection and cultural impoverishment of the African, and saw no contradiction in the phenomenon of slavery. On the contrary, there developed in the eighteenth century particularly a strong tradition of theological defense of the institution. That tradition's most recent derivation was an aspect of Luther's social ideas, according to which equality in the spiritual kingdom had no validity for worldly society.[72]

By a separation of the spiritual and temporal realms, Danish theologians of the eighteenth century like the influential Erik Pontoppidan could reconcile bondage with Christianity. For Pontoppidan, Christian salvation concerned the soul and not the physical body, however much abused.[73] Matching echoes of this concept were to be found in Moravian theology. The missionary Oldendorp, who visited Moravian missions in the Danish West Indies in the 1760s, also argued for a view of Christian liberty which subordinated the physical reality of slavery to the ideal of the soul's redemption.[74]

Racial Arguments

The church's teaching formed part of the broad philosophical front on which slavery in the Danish possessions was justified, and by which, more particularly, the slaves' normative compliance with their place in the social order would be accomplished. However, as the eighteenth century drew to a close, and as the earlier decades of the nineteenth century passed, the grounds of emphasis for slavery's defense began to shift. More and more, supportive expressions of opinion about slavery addressed themselves to the presumed physical inferiority, animal characteristics and intellectual incapacity of the African. In part, in the Danish West Indies at least, it was a reaction or over-reaction to the revolution in St. Domingue and the founding of the black republic of Haiti. In Europe, as the progress of enlightened thought weakened the foundations of philosophical defenses of slavery, alternative strategies based on race were devised.[75] Indeed, the evidence suggests that there was greater rather than less hysteria as the years went by, fed by British emancipation and its aftermath – at the very doorstep of the Danish islands in British Tortola – and with the unrest and subsequent uprising in the French West Indies in the 1840s.

An early example of the trends which were developing towards the end of the eighteenth century is provided by an undated letter from the Chief of Police in St. John. The letter, which is among the Abolition Papers in the Rigsarchiv effectively dating it between 1788 and 1802, raised the anatomical question in as yet a neutral way. Blacks had no cartilage in the tips of their noses; apart from the "natural" differences between black and white, he argued, this was an essential difference.[76] The Vanderbourg Report to the Abolition Commission in 1798, however, made no pretense of neutrality. It stated: "Les observations de l'Anatomiste et du philosophe s'accorde en effet, a nous démontrer l'infériorité des Negres et la supériorité des blancs ..."[77] For Vanderbourg, therefore, there was no possibility of treating the enslaved population in the way that victors among the ancients treated the vanquished, by promoting marriage. Semi-rhetorically Vanderbourg posed an early version of the question, "Mais quand un Negre viendra vous demander votre fille en marriage, la lui accorderez-vous?" The only thing, he concluded, to be gained from such a "sacrifice" was the shame of the person with the temerity to attempt it.[78]

If the presumed inferiority of Africans eliminated them as prospects for civilization by absorption in Vanderbourg's calculus, he was, however, prepared to concede that the African was not naturally born to slavery: "ils sont nes, comme tous les peuples, pour être libres dans leur pays. Le grand mal est de les avoir transportés dans un autre, ou il est tres Donte ux qu'ils puissant être libres avec nous."[79] At best this was begrudging generosity. But even this, Adrian Bentzon, later Governor General, found impossible to achieve in a report to Count Schimmelmann and the Abolition Commission in 1802. The background to Bentzon's memorandum was the unrest, particularly among bosal slaves, in the early months of 1802. Bentzon advised the utmost despatch in dealing with the perpetrators of the events: the stoning of one overseer; the stabbing to death of another; knife threats to several whites and suspected cases of arson. It was Bentzon's unshakeable conviction that there was no branch of the human race so bestial and lacking in moral understanding as the African. If animality and moral obtuseness existed to some degree in all of humanity, in Bentzon's scale the African had them in more than ample measure. As long as their servitude was tolerable, as long as they were not overburdened physically, it would be very difficult, he argued, to tempt slaves, who had never known freedom and ease, to risk their lives to break their chains.[80] The implication was clear: like a patient but dumb beast of burden, the slave would continue to serve provided his animal wants were satisfied.

This report from Bentzon at the beginning of the nineteenth century typified the pro-slavery arguments of the period based on racial differentiation. They fell into temporary abeyance during the British occupation of

1807-15 and were of less urgency in the 1820s when the question of civil and legal equality for freedmen was attracting great attention. Once, however, emancipation had occurred in the British islands and Governor Peter von Scholten introduced a series of ameliorative reforms preparatory to an emancipation he saw as inevitable, the stage was set for a reactivation of the debate on the nature of the slave and slavery.

If there was innovation in argument, there was equally continuity in content. Bentzon's contention in 1802 that slavery would continue as long as it was tolerable, may be compared with a memorandum to von Scholten from a St. Croix resident in 1841. The memorialist could see no reason why the slave should not continue during his lifetime as servile plantation labor, "as we have no proof that his race is peculiarly fitted for any much more useful or noble career, or worthy of more consideration than we bestow on the poor of our own." What is of even greater interest, however, is that this argument for slavery's continuance differed little from those advanced by Gardelin a century before, and like Berg,[81] this memorialist saw slavery as part of an immutable and divine order: "That work is exacted of the black, is in strict conformity with the doom of the Almighty, which does and always will apply to the agriculturalist, 'that in the sweat of his brow he eat bread' and that 'the earth shall no longer bring forth her fruits without toil'."[82]

Procurator Sarauw, an implacable opponent of von Scholten's, was prepared to concede that Africans were more eager to learn and more retentive generally than Europeans, but the ease with which Africans learnt, was comparable with the difficulty experienced in profiting from what they had learnt.[83] The simian inference was elaborated, paradoxically, in the Liberal newspaper *Fædrelandet* early in 1841. Africa too had a civilization, it declared. But this was merely to damn with faint praise, for whilst the paper recognized that Africans belonged to the family of man, it also recognized validity in the view that their animal characteristics predominated.[84]

A contemporary daily *Kjøbenhavnsposten* was much less equivocal in stating its views: Africans had made no advance in the last 3,000 years of history; they had no capacity for memory and even less for reason. These were characteristics which in its view explained Africans' improvidence, disregard for the future, preoccupation with the pleasures of the present, ruling inclination to do nothing, and passion for dance and music, functions of that "imagination" which made them good raconteurs and prone to superstition.[85]

Perhaps the most sustained and elaborately presented views of the African's inferiority came at the very end of the period of slavery from the pen of Victor Prosch, formerly of the colonial medical service. In the autumn 1848 issue of *Dansk Tidsskrift*, a matter of months after emancipation, Prosch authored an article of enormous length which was the last anguished cry of the pro-slavery faction in Denmark and implied censure of emancipationists and all their works. Firstly, Prosch revived the notion of the mission civilisatrice. He observed that despite hundreds of years of contact with Europeans, Gold Coast Africans were still on "the lowest rungs of humanity," subsisting on fruit and fish, running around in their nakedness, bound by their fetishes and superstitions. For Prosch only what was recognizably European could be dignified by the description civilized. Even if by acculturation in the Danish West Indies the slave became the New World equivalent of the Danish peasant, this final term of the African's evolution to civilization under European tutelage was unrealizable. For Prosch, the moral and intellectual inferiority of Africans, and "characteristic" incapacity to grasp abstractions and a consequent inability to think in terms of the future, were insuperable obstacles. Even where the African showed a marked capacity to learn this was no more than an "inquisitive aping."[86]

Slavery, Prosch argued further, had been condemned only by association with the slave trade. All of its admirable effects as a consequence had been overlooked; not the least of which, he suggested, was that it rescued from certain death prisoners of war or surplus populations. To the triumph of the lesser of two evils, greed over gruesomeness, all Africans transported to slavery in the New World owed their lives. Prosch concluded his vigorous defense of slavery by choosing the example to which most writers of his persuasion in the nineteenth century had recourse. Like them, his reading of the history of Haiti since its independence was shot through with racial pessimism and, for him, provided ample evidence of the black man's need of the white man's tutelage.[87]

The Emergence of Anti-Slavery Ideology

Neither in terms of frequency nor persistency of articulation do the views of the less racially pessimistic match those on the other side. Such views, however, did find voice in Denmark itself, as instanced by Rahbek and Algreen-Ussing mentioned earlier, and in the Danish West Indies. It is possible to consider Frederik V's Reglement of 1755 in the spectrum of opinion on slavery which was less virulently antipathetic to Africans and more prepared to concede their humanity and the possibility of their perfectibility. It might appear inappropriate to regard the Reglement in this way, considering the explicitness with which it viewed the slave as property, but there are certain basic considerations which inform that document's initial paragraphs that invite attention. The crown made a commitment to introduce all slaves, including those yet to be imported, to Christian doctrine; to subject each slave to religious instruction long enough to make the decision to accept Christianity's precepts; to abstain from the use of force in such "a sacred undertaking," even where there were those who heard, understood, but would not embrace the gospel. Although this article's final paragraph carefully emphasized, as noted earlier, that baptism did not free, it should be read in conjunction with the second paragraph. The latter forbade all inhabitants of the Danish Virgin Islands, under pain of severe and exemplary punishment, to hinder in the slightest way the reception of the gospel or exercise of religion among slaves.[88]

To whatever degree, therefore, the 1755 Reglement elaborated the concept of the slave as property and addressed itself to police regulations, it assumed that the slave was a proper subject for religious instruction, and recognized and respected the slave's right not to be indoctrinated. A similar respect for the slave's individuality was expressed in 1759 by Byfoged Engebret Hesselberg in his account of the conspiracy in St. Croix that year. His account began with the remarkable admission from a police official in the colonial service that the slave had a legitimate aspiration to freedom. Such an aspiration, Hesselberg contended, was an inseparable part of the human condition; however imperfect the circumstances of one's birth, they were far more supportable than those imposed by random fate. Most of the slaves in a colony as recently exploited as St. Croix in 1759, he recognized, would have been Africans rather than West Indian born creoles, and as freeborn persons they had "as good a claim to their freedom, as we have to ours" ("ligesaa godt adkomst til deres Frihed som Vii til Vores"). But Hesselberg went further still in his insistence upon the slaves' humanity: "one unfortunate event or the other had brought them out of that natural equality which they otherwise shared with us from birth and made these persons our slaves, who, had the circumstances were different might very well have been our masters." Although such opinions did not prevent Hesselberg from handing down some exceedingly severe punishments, the internal logic of his argument suggests that he was more concerned with the maintenance of public order than with disciplining an "inferior" race. Indeed, at the very beginning of his account he conceded that it was not merely the slaves' legitimate aspiration to freedom but equally the "unreasonable behavior of some masters toward their slaves" which had occasioned rebellions in the past and would occasion them in the future.[89]

Some 25 years later, in the heat of the debate over the abolition of the slave trade in the 1780s, former governor Roepstorff, although arguing for slave labor on grounds of expediency and within the limitations of serfdom, expressed considerable doubt at the legitimacy of the trade or West Indian chattel slavery. The purchase of African prisoners of war did not confer rights of ownership, he argued, emphasizing that contemporary enlightened opinion did not regard prisoners of war as slaves. The grounds upon which the Africans' slavery in the New World was being justified, namely the color of their skins and their attachment to paganism, were for Roepstorff weak arguments. No one in his view, could be rightfully called "slave" who had neither committed a crime nor been sentenced. More appropriately, he submitted, the category of person called slave could be redesignated "unfree." It was no mere difference of nomenclature. Roepstorff contended finally that the rights and obligations of contemporary serfdom in Denmark should be made to apply in the West Indies: "And because of all that is mentioned above, I believe it is practicable to regard the unfree Negroes as serfs, their children belonging to the proprietors as their villeins, and their work for food and clothing as reasonable villeinage."[90] In view of the fact that serfdom was abolished only eight years after Roepstorff's submission, his views cannot be regarded as remarkably progressive. Yet, it was a significant step forward to recognize that the slave in the colonial context was a factor in a mode of agricultural production different in degree but not substantially in kind from the Danish manorial system of the eighteenth century.

Perhaps one of the most explicit of anti-slavery views appeared in a 1791 review of West's "Beretning" published the same year. The reviewer began by saying that West's account would be held dear by anyone who wished that nothing was done to better conditions for slaves or relieve them of their chattel status. The reviewer was hardly impressed with West's contention that slaves enjoyed far more comfortable circumstances than free servants in Europe. The true thrust of West's argument was that the slave was treated as well as a horse in Europe, simply out of self-interest, as both cost ready cash to replace when they fell down. It did not matter, the reviewer contended, that the coachman could ill-treat the horse, for it was mere property; in any case it was attended to when no longer up to the drudgery and had its stall full of fodder.[91]

The riposte was directed not only at West but also at Haagensen who in his *Beskrivelse* had spoken glowingly of the nutritive and fattening properties, for horses and slaves alike, of grated dried corn.[92] Nor was the reviewer any more impressed by the view, again Haagensen's rather than West's, that "Negerens Sjæl er saa sort som hans Hud" – the black man's soul is as black as his skin.[93] West's further contention that West Africans were universally indolent, evil, proud and given to theft, was dismissed by the reviewer as not proven, since that author had proffered as evidence only some six to seven incidents of breaking and entering and petty theft. With ironical wit, the reviewer made light of West's description of freedmen, whatever their color, as repositories of evil; of his counsels of caution against the extension of Christianity among slaves; of his contention "repeated a hundred times, but never proven" that the West Indian slave was better off in his bondage that as a free man in West Africa. The bird in its gilded cage was still a prisoner, and the reviewer's advice to West was to go to Abyssinia against his will, allow himself to be imprisoned and be provided with the "best" in food, drink and entertainment.[94]

The reviewer perceptively concluded that West's "Beretning" in its entirety had been calculated to blunt people's sensibilities to the gruesomeness of the slave trade, the abolition of which was then being actively canvassed at the Danish Court. One searched almost in vain, he commented, for the isolated places in the work where the slave trade and slavery were condemned as unchristian and evil. Such places were in any case masked by West's vigorous defense of the slave system. It was a matter of disbelief to the reviewer that West could find admirable a system in which 2,000 whites controlled 22,000 slaves, for that control rested wholly, in his view, on the deterrent effect of naked terror. There was nothing admirable for him about a law which prescribed the loss of a hand raised in anger against a white person; the loss of one's life for physical assault of a white; which proscribed communication in their own tongue among persons forcibly taken away from their country; which authorized the loss of a leg for a slave who sought humanity's first right, freedom. With laws like this the control of eleven blacks by one white was no problem as long as those blacks were unarmed and had not the least vestige of human rights.[95]

In a particular passage in his "Beretning" West had hit out at the critics of the slave system and the humanitarians of the 1790s as nothing more than narcissistic stylists of the spoken and written word, more concerned with drawing overemphatic pictures and producing "pretty periods" than with demonstrating the limitations of what they criticized.[96] No doubt, the reviewer observed, West would feel similarly about his views. But West, like those he berated, was interested in creating his own special effects: "that is to affirm the noble thought that these depraved black people, descendants of Ham, ought to remain in serfdom for eternity."[97]

This apostrophe of indignation, in reaction to West, marked one of the high points of anti-slavery sentiment in Denmark in the eighteenth century. It was no coincidence that it found expression roughly at the same time that the commission investigating the slave trade had recommended its abolition in another ten years. Nor was it a coincidence that within a year serfdom was abolished and its passing symbolically marked by the laying of the foundation stone of the commemorative obelisk, Frihedsstøtten, in Copenhagen's Vesterbro. Both were fruits of enlightened opinion which West's reviewer demonstrated to an unusually high degree.

The vigor of these enlightened and humanitarian initiatives was hardly sustained during the early nineteenth century and for much the same kind of reason that brought an abatement of pro-slavery stridency. In addition to the reasons mentioned earlier there was as well Denmark's bruising involvement in the Napoleonic conflict. When the humanitarian voice was raised with any vigor again, it was in support of the reforming Governor General Peter von Scholten, and as a counter to the renewed campaign of pro-slavery opinion.

The timing of von Scholten's initiative was significant, in relation to British West Indian emancipation, but his expressed motivation was also noteworthy. Von Scholten perceived that British emancipation had set in motion a process which would over time have a distinct bearing on the situation in other islands.[98] His Plan for Emancipation of 13 October 1834 was a recognition of this reality. If, as he confessed, he had been guided from the beginning of his term in office by a consideration that slaves' welfare was critical for the future of the Danish islands,[99] such pragmatism was colored by a conviction of the slaves' right to enfranchisement. This explains his series of ameliorative reforms over the next decade and half, a process of preparation for an emancipation which he deemed not only inevitable but desirable.

Von Scholten's enthusiasm and belief in the slave's essential humanity was shared by a number of foreign visitors to the Danish West Indies who produced accounts of their travels in the early 1840s. The American abolitionist James Smith and the British Quaker G. W. Alexander, for example, saw slavery as morally indefensible.[100] Alexander, whose work was published in Danish in 1843, contended that Denmark had lost the moral authority which it achieved by being first to abolish the slave trade and was now obliged to abolish the reprehensible system which it had once sustained. Immediate and full emancipation, he protested, was the only antidote for the brutality, immorality and irreligiosity characteristic of slavery as an institution though not of those shackled in it. Another foreigner who visited the Danish islands in 1840, the Frenchman Victor Schoelcher, argued the case for instant emancipation of the "captive black" as the most generous and least dangerous course to adopt.[101] Although Schoelcher expressed the greatest admiration for von Scholten and defended him against his calumniators, he regarded servitude no matter how mild as an abomination in the Danish no less than in the French islands. But slavery was to survive in the French Antilles until 1848, the year of the Danish emancipation, and in the United States until 1865.

Criticism of slavery became increasingly common in Denmark itself in the 1840s. Admiral Hans Dahlerup, after a visit to the Danish islands in 1841, opined that one needed only to begin with the premise of the Negro race's potential for improvement, and the means could be found to effect the necessary changes in the colonies' agricultural system. Like Smith and Alexander, Dahlerup argued that what were ascribed to slaves as inherent qualities were functions of that system in which they operated. Dahlerup argued further that even though sugar, involving a complicated manufacturing process, was different from other forms of agriculture, it was no more complicated than manufacturing processes in "civilised" countries worked by free labor.[102]

Dahlerup's implicit conclusion in favor of emancipation was elaborated explicitly in an emancipation plan. It called for general emancipation to be followed by a period of apprenticeship of one year, in which freedmen would be bound to a given plantation with wages fixed in relation to the nature of their work. Under such a plan, rights and obligations of ex-slaves and employers, rental for grounds and houses, deductions from wages for clothing, frequency of wage payments, health care, duration of the work week and the like, would be closely regulated by government. At the end of that period, Dahlerup envisaged yearly contracts with heads of families, where that was possible, such contracts subject to a maximum of six and a minimum of three months' notice.[103]

This attempt by Dahlerup to devise a system of transition to freedom, without disruption of plantation agriculture, reflected a current of opinion in Denmark at the beginning of the 1840s which held that emancipation was both necessary and imminent. The view was given its most articulate expression by the newspaper *Fædrelandet*, the voice of emergent Liberalism and energetic defender of the West India interest. In an unsigned article published in October 1840 it contended that British West Indian emancipation had foreclosed the issue for the entire West Indies:

> The Act of Parliament of August 28, 1833 had decided the question of the emancipation of the Negro slaves for the entire West Indies. This is because it had hereby not just provided ample proof of the possibility of enacting this major measure, and this, furthermore, without significant inconvenience, but it has also given the slave population on the islands, where their chains are not yet broken, such an energetic longing after freedom that it can no longer be restrained, let alone suppressed. The question which therefore must be addressed by the Danish government concerning its small West Indian islands is not *whether*, but when and *how* it will grant freedom to the resident slaves.[104]

This was a view shared in large measure by Denmark's Liberal spokesmen in the 1840s. Using the forum of the newly created Stænderforsamlinger, leading Liberals like Professor C. N. David, the educational and religious reformer N. F. S. Grundtvig, D. G. Monrad, Orla Lehmann and others, began to express their opposition to servitude and to question the economic utility or advantages of the colonial connection. At the 1846 session of the Roskilde Stænderforsamling, for example, Orla Lehmann was led to remark that a close examination of that connection would very likely reveal that its continuance was sustained only by national vanity. Lehmann pointedly added that, to the contrary he felt a sense of national humiliation; for after more than a century, Denmark still did not own its Virgin Islands, the majority of whose planters were in fact foreigners.[105]

It was in some measure in response to domestic opinion like this that Christian VIII on his birthday 18 September 1847 decreed the immediate emancipation of all children born to slave parents thereafter and the entire abolition of slavery at the end of a twelve year period. But, if humanitarianism had finally triumphed, its advocates were few if influential, and metropolitan rather than colonial, with the notable exception of von Scholten. In the islands themselves, it was the foreign element of the population which resisted with greatest vigor von Scholten's reforms of the 1830s and continued to rationalize slavery's continuance in the 1840s. In such circumstances, the prospects of translating legal equality into social reality were dim indeed. Royal edicts could not and did not alter overnight attitudes and prejudices born in slaveowning ideology and hallowed by time.

3

"Part and Parcel of Property:" Slaves and the Law in the Eighteenth Century

THE IDEOLOGICAL CONTENT OF SLAVE OWNING ATTITUDES IN the Danish West Indian empire found its most formal representation in the legal codes of the islands. The image of the black in the white mind was most explicitly expressed in the laws devised to control slave behavior, in which slaves were conceived primarily as pieces of property but also as individuals whose natural inclinations were depraved and inherently criminal. The slave codes leaned not merely towards a "legal" definition of what constituted crime, that is, a violation of a body of statutes that established normative order. They comprehended as well a sociological definition of criminal deviance in its emphasis on what was inimical to society's interests.[1] Those interests of course were apprehended from the perspective of the dominant class, the whites, whose hegemonic power put at their disposal resources to protect and preserve their universe. A contemporary parallel springs readily to mind, but there are equally arresting historical parallels with comparable use of the law as central legitimizing ideology. For instance, Douglas Hay has noted that in eighteenth century England the landed aristocracy used their virtually unbridled power to devise criminal codes that were "critically important in maintaining bonds of obedience and deference, [and] in legitimizing the status quo."[2] It follows that the slave codes are not only important in their own right but also have much to tell about actual slave behavior in the Danish West Indies and about the state's notions of "good order and government" as applied to the "ungovernable passions of blacks."[3]

Gardelin's Code of 1733

The slave laws of the Danish West Indies in the eighteenth century comprised the two seminal codes of 1733 and 1755, and a vast number of ad hoc proclamations. The code of 1733, the work of Governor Philip Gardelin, expressed the fears and paramount preoccupations of official-dom and planter alike, outnumbered by five to one and plagued incessantly by the recurring problem of marronage. Almost half of the proclamation's nineteen clauses dealt explicitly with the subject of marronage, and ex-pressed quantitatively the qualitative nature of the white community's major concern. All marronage, actual or contemplated, that involved leav-ing the country carried the death penalty for the ringleaders, after torture with red-hot pincers at three separate public locations. Those convicted of or caught in conspiracies to run away would have a leg removed in the event that their masters refused to pardon them. In such circumstances, 150 strokes and the loss of an ear in the presence of a justice of the peace was the prescribed penalty.[4] There were additional penalties, varying from death and the amputation of legs to branding and whipping, for, respec-tively, absences over six months, absences over three months, failure to inform of impending marronage, and absences over fourteen days.[5]

If marronage prejudiced the effectiveness of economic enterprise and threatened public order, failure to show deference to whites was perceived to be no less prejudicial to the social order. Menacing gestures or insulting words were, therefore, punishable by three applications of glowing pincers followed by hanging. If the insulted white so desired, however, the offend-ing slave's right hand could be amputated.[6] When slaves met whites on horseback or on foot, they were required to deferentially step aside until that person had passed, or else face the consequence of instantly ad-ministered corporal punishment.[7] Similarly, the proscription of iron-tipped sticks or knives worn at the side, in the towns, was directed not so much at the potential threat such weapons held for whites, but rather was concerned with imposing norms of dress and deportment that reinforced deference. Ironically, although the very raison d'être of sugar plantation slavery made the machete ubiquitous, it was never deemed the lethal weapon it could be. Obviously, confident of their levels of control in the countryside, whites regarded it as an agricultural tool and nothing more. In the towns, however, the concentration of deference-demanding whites made knives and cudgels weapons under the law. In the same way, slaves who "dared" to fight among themselves in town were each to get 150 strokes of the whip.[8]

Further concern for public order was evidenced in the provisions regarding stealing, the establishment of a curfew, and slave entertainments. Theft of property valuing more than five styvers (about 20 pence sterling) was punishable by hanging after torture; theft of goods of lesser value incurred branding on the forehead and upwards of 150 lashes, depending on the persistence of the offense.[9] Slaves receiving and concealing stolen goods were to be branded and similarly beaten.[10] No plantation black was to be found in town after the beating of the evening drum, and failure to observe this curfew entailed a thorough beating.[11] All dancing, merrymak-ing or funeral rites, which involved the use of "Negro instruments," were expressly forbidden on pain of corporal punishment since they had been the occasion of "serious disturbances" in the past. On those days when there was no work, however, "small diversions" were allowable with the permission of the master or overseer, or of the nearest owner where no whites were resident on the particular estate.[12]

If deviant behavior on the part of slaves was unacceptable in public, it was no less insupportable in those private areas of their lives not readily accessible to the regimen of plantation discipline and control. This was manifestly the case with the practice of obeah. Gardelin dismissed it as a lot of superstitious "tomfoolery involving feathers and nails, wrapped in rags by which they thought they could do each other harm." Yet he felt it necessary to prescribe a sound thrashing for its practice, on grounds that had less to do with saving slaves from the work of a devil – "reinforcing these dumb heathens the more in their blindness" – than with a more pragmatic objective. The article on obeah, significantly, is followed immediately by one dealing with poisoning. Those slaves about whom there was a firm conviction of their intent to poison were to be tortured with glowing pincers, broken on the wheel and then burnt alive.[13] Both articles taken together indicate a concern to discourage and suppress those aspects of African belief and practice that were beyond the comprehension of the beleaguered white community and that, in the case of the African's facility with poison, directly threatened that community's existence.

In the preamble to Gardelin's code, slaves were seen as essentially the property of their owners. As property, it was logically impossible for slaves to be possessed of anything. No slave, therefore, could offer goods for sale in country or town: neither chickens, turkeys, geese, sheep, pigs, potatoes, corn nor vegetable; nor could they be seen in clothing of any "consequence," unless they could produce a certificate from their master. Failure to produce such a certificate was to be punished "proportionately with the offence." Failure to return the goods at the end of the same day would attract an appropriate whipping for the forgetfulness.[14]

Gardelin's code, in view of the fact that it was not effectively replaced for another hundred years, is important not only for what it says, but also for what it does not say. The slave as property, consigned to servitude by the Almighty, and petrified in dumb superstition by ignorance, had only obligations. Slaves were not conceived as having rights even in respect of those essentials of food, clothing and shelter that made them more efficient units of production. The assumptions that informed Gardelin's code were perhaps implicitly expressive of the priorities of the Danish West India Company.[15] It is not without significance that until the assumption by the crown of the islands' ownership in 1755, none of the ad hoc proclamations addressed themselves to even those minimum essentials. Thus Governor Moth's "Articler for Negerne," published 11 December 1741, was devoted to an elaboration of Gardelin's provisions governing slaves' movements, public order and deference. Moth's articles attempted further to restrict, if not eliminate social and sexual congress between slave and free. Whites found gambling or drinking with slaves were subject to imprisonment on a bread and water diet. Slave women were not to be found in any white man's room at night unless they were doing household or other innocent chores.[16]

Governor Lindemark, Moth's successor, found it necessary to prohibit slave ownership of punch or ale houses, and the dispensation by them in any way of spirituous liquors.[17] The provision is of interest because it substantiates the earlier prohibitions on slaves' rights to the control of property. Given the basic assumptions of the society, slave enterprise of any sort was inadmissible; conformity, predictability and regimentation were the basic desiderata of the codes up to the middle of the eighteenth century. No detail was considered too insignificant, particularly if questions of public order were involved. This explains Lindemark's regulation forbidding slaves to be seen with dogs of whatever size outside their masters' estates, unless they were provided with an explanatory ticket. Even then the dogs had to be on a leash.[18]

Considerations of welfare, therefore, were almost totally absent from the slave laws of the Danish West Indies before the Reglement of 1755. A single gesture in this direction appeared in 1742, when Moth sought to regulate a situation that had arisen in St. Croix. Clearing the virgin forests of the island to facilitate sugar culture was work of a very demanding kind. It involved the back-breaking labor not only of felling the trees, but also of firing the stumps in insufferable heat and smoke.[19] Nine years after St. Croix's purchase in 1733, the work of clearing the forests was still in progress. Overseers and others, without permission from the owners concerned, were in the habit of hiring out slaves for this high-premium work on Saturdays and Sundays. Rewards for this high-risk activity were payable in rum. This practice robbed owners of the wages of the slaves' hire and had the added effect of leaving the slaves too affected by drink to perform effectively on Monday morning. Moth's placat forbade the continuance of further hiring out without owners' permission.[20]

Frederik V's Reglement of 1755

Between Moth's proclamation of 1742 and the Reglement of 1755, some owners had been in the habit of giving slaves unrefined rum, known locally as "kill devil," in place of proper rations. The Reglement, under the signature of Frederik V, forbade this practice, and laid down what the crown considered adequate weekly rations. For slaves ten or more years of age, two and a half quarts of cassava flour or corn meal, or three cassavas each at least two and a half pounds in weight, were deemed an adequate carbohydrate ration. To supplement this, the code prescribed two pounds of salt beef or three pounds of fish. Children under ten were entitled to half of these rations. No owner was exempted from these conditions, nor permitted to grant slaves a free day in the week in lieu of the prescribed rations. As to clothing, the Reglement called for two sets of clothing of coarse material annually, or in their stead eight alen (about five meters) of similar material.[21]

In laying down these requirements, the code of 1755 acknowledged for the first time that there were minimum rights to which the slave was entitled. It is interesting to note, however, that there were no stipulations in respect of housing, and that the sanctions for non-observance of these points of the code were not specific. Failure to comply would be punished "according to circumstances" and owners were merely "encouraged" to treat their slaves with humanity and justice. This essentially hortatory emphasis was dispensed with only for old and sick slaves. Their maintenance was made the explicit responsibility of their masters, who stood to lose such slaves to the crown in the event of non-compliance and be required to pay a daily sum for subsistence.[22]

The Reglement contained a number of other provisions that sought to protect slaves' rights and promote their welfare beyond considerations of food, clothing and shelter. Religious instruction without coercion was to be made available through a mission of the Danish Lutheran Church, with particular attention being paid to newly arrived "bosal" slaves. All slave children were to be baptized at birth and exposed to the catechism when old enough, at such times as planters deemed appropriate. The code carefully emphasized, however, that what was proposed was a grasp of "the essentials of faith and salvation," not the rudiments of knowledge for its own sake. Learning to write was unnecessary and a reading skill for slaves useful only in so far as it helped with learning the Bible. In any event, all instruction to slaves of whatever age or sex was to take place on the plantation premises. No slave was to be admitted to church unless attending a white as a domestic, although at death the baptized were entitled to Christian burial without condition.[23]

Anticipating a later paragraph in which the slave was described as essentially property, the Reglement in its initial paragraph stipulated with logical consistency that conversion did not diminish the powers of owners over their slaves; neither did it imply any alteration in the slave's material condition or legal status. On this point the Reglement could not have been more unequivocal. Christian slaves were obliged, despite their conversion, to show obedience and the same sense of duty and fidelity to their masters as before. The slave's right not to work on Sundays and the high holy days of the Danish Lutheran Church, namely Christmas, Epiphany, Good Friday, Ascension and Annunciation, was recognized. Other denominations were allowed a similar observance of days important in their religious calendars.[24]

Whereas previous regulations, such as Moth's of 1741, had concerned themselves only implicitly with the question of the sexual exploitation of slave women, the Reglement of 1755 explicitly condemned such "fornication and moral laxity." The crown considered such behavior no less punishable than it was in metropolitan Denmark. The white men involved were to be fined 2,000 pounds of sugar, and a fine of equal amount was to be paid by the owners of the slave women if they were aware of the offense but did nothing about it. An owner guilty of such illicit relations would pay a similar fine, and where there was issue lose both mother and child to the crown without recourse.[25]

Slaves were permitted to marry but only with their masters' permission; at the same time, they were not to be compelled into unions to which they were not agreeable.[26] All slaves about to marry were required to be Christian, but for those not so intending there was a blanket prohibition of polygamy. The status of marriage under the code automatically protected partners from separation by auction, other sale, attachment for debt or any similar transaction. Minors were not to be separated from their parents and any owner who by sale separated a slave family, was to incur the loss to the purchaser of those members retained, without compensation.[27]

While the 1755 code accepted the Roman principle of partus sequitur ventrem and regarded the slave as property over which an owner had the same discretion as with other forms of property, it nevertheless implicitly rejected the notion of perpetual servitude.[28] The principle of manumission as part of an owner's discretionary power was admitted. Such manumission could take place either during the owner's lifetime or after death by testamentary devise.[29] No institutional provisions comparable to the Hispanic-American coartación found themselves in the code. As minors and incompetents before the law, slaves could own nothing and could therefore not hope to achieve freedom by self-purchase.[30]

Despite its delineation of certain limited rights and privileges, the Reglement of 1755 was, in the final analysis, a regulatory code to ensure slaves' good behavior. As in 1742, the bearing of firearms was expressly forbidden, except where the master's permission existed in writing; large sticks were similarly prohibited. Under pain of whipping and branding for the first, and death for subsequent offenses, slaves belonging to different masters were forbidden under any pretext whatever, by day or night, to assemble at weddings or other festivities. Such assemblies in the public highways, in the fields, or in out-of-the-way places were looked upon by the code with special disfavor. The enforcement of this regulation was considered sufficiently important to empower any citizen not an officer of the law, to arrest any slave contravening it.[31] Owners who turned a blind eye to such activity were liable to heavy fines.

Sugar cane, fruit, foodstuffs, garden vegetables, firewood and small stock were not to be offered for sale by slaves either at home or in the public market. However, since such articles formed a part of the stock-in-trade of itinerant huckstering, in which many slaves were engaged on their owners' behalf, a ticket to that effect exempted them from arrest.[32] Indeed, the code indicates that at mid-century, a vigorous effort was being made to arrest the development of an internal marketing system dependent on the initiative of the slave. Unable to own anything, slaves were only to bring to market goods consigned to them for sale by their masters. Anything else was by definition stolen goods. The Reglement accordingly authorized the appointment of two persons as inspectors at every market to establish the legal possession of goods being offered; as with unlawful assemblies, every white inhabitant was vested with police powers and authorized to seize stolen goods for return to their legitimate owners.[33]

Neither in civil nor in criminal cases was evidence from a slave admissible, although statements could be taken to assist magistrates in determining the truth. Such statements, however, were not acceptable as proof. Likewise, slaves could not bring charges of civil or criminal nature, nor claim compensation for injury. At the same time, they were themselves indictable for offenses, without implicating their masters unless the latter had participated. Interestingly enough, although slaves had no access to the judicial apparatus of the state for offenses committed against them, there were no such obstacles where they were the offenders.[34]

Whereas Gardelin had prescribed the death penalty for theft, the Reglement of 1755 was content with branding and castration; and although it made no provisions for insulting words or threatening gestures, violence to or bodily assault against a white person was punishable by death.[35] On the other hand, the Reglement's provisions on marronage were undoubtedly harsher than those of 1733; there were no provisions for corporal punishment for short absences, nor alternatives to the death sentence, as under the Gardelin code. Punishment for marronage was prescribed on a sliding scale, computed on the basis of length of absence and frequency. For up to a month's absence in the first instance, offenders would lose both ears and be branded. For the second offense, they would pay with loss of both legs, and for the third they would be executed.[36]

The Reglement was, therefore, at once more humane and more draconian than the Gardelin code. It remained, however, a dead instrument. The Danish authorities permitted the first royal Governor, von Pröck, to make public such parts of the code, or none, as he thought politic. Von Pröck exercised this discretion by choosing to publish no part of the code, hoping thereby to gain the goodwill of a planter community which was opposed to the notion of slaves' rights.[37] This left the Gardelin code wholly intact in letter, and its spirit could still find energetic defenders. One such representative of this system of ideas was the contemporary planter and resident Richard Haagensen, in whose view all blacks were fundamentally evil. Servitude was the only condition they deserved, and the severe penalties entirely appropriate.[38]

Subsequent Concessions

The Danish islands, therefore, began their administration under crown rule with a code in which the slave had no right recognized in law. Even when custom sanctioned certain concessions, such as a free half-day on Saturday, those, too, came under restrictions in practice. Limitations on this customary privilege were not unrelated to the 1759 conspiracy in St. Croix.[39] Von Pröck took the view that the freedom and opportunity that slaves from different plantations had had up to that time for gathering in large numbers was one of the chief circumstances contributing to the plot. Accordingly, he issued a proclamation in which planters were instructed to arrange free time on their estates in a way that would be completely unpredictable.[40]

The extent of the concern caused by the conspiracy was reflected in several of the proclamation's provisions that addressed themselves to the maintenance of public order and supervision of the slaves under the strictest disciplinary regimen.[41] Activities that encouraged lax supervision were singled out for specific attention, their prohibition a further erosion of customary privilege. Itinerant Christmas minstrels were forbidden; random visiting from plantation to plantation was restricted even for slave partners; the sale of rum or punch to slaves by publicans or plantation personnel became an offense. Slaves playing dice or anything else for money, in town or elsewhere, would be instantly taken to the whipping post for 50 lashes. An earlier proclamation of Von Pröck's forbidding slaves to ride in the streets in town, was sharpened by including a fine for any master who refused to give up a slave who rode away from police apprehension.[42]

The explicit attenuation of privilege was no less marked in the 1760s and 1770s. Peter de Gunthelberg, Commandant in St. Thomas, framed ordinances for the town of Charlotte Amalie in 1765 which were later adopted as a model for the towns of St. Croix. Among other things, they provided that no urban slave could be on the street after 9 p.m. unless on a properly authenticated errand. Whereas the pass or ticket system was used systematically to control the movement of plantation slaves, day and night, it did not have general application in the towns. There, the criteria of selection were associated with areas of activity, temporal or spatial, considered prejudicial to optimal control. Thus, areas which automatically selected themselves for regulation included access to wharves, employment in any capacity on sailing or other vessels capable of long range voyages, and the use of fishing boats. De Gunthelberg's ordinances of 1765 forbade slaves' attendance at the Moravian Mission church after 8 p.m. and slaves leaving services were obliged to walk in groups not exceeding six, each with a leader.[43] Although slave dances in St. Thomas were permitted up to 10 p.m. and even beyond with police permission, the police were under the strictest injunction to prevent drumming on those occasions.[44]

De Gunthelberg saw slave wakes as nothing more than occasions for drunkenness and revelry and prohibited them under pain of severe corporal punishment.[45] Governor Clausen in 1774 raised the punishment for gambling on the streets from 50 to 150 lashes, since the former had proven inadequate to restrain the slaves' ungovernable passion to gamble.[46] Clausen also banned the Bangelar, a stick mounted with iron or copper rings and a metal point, which made it into a formidable weapon. The stick, however, was indispensable for the stick-fighting duels dearly cherished by slaves. The popularity of these duels, engaged in for sport, was obviously not confined to slaves alone. Whites had been seen to follow them and instead of arresting them, not only found pleasure in the spectacle, but had actively encouraged it. Clausen recognized a disruptive potential in those occasions, and was scandalized that any person of education or good breeding could find pleasure in such activity.[47]

It is interesting to note, however, that this proclamation of Clausen's began with the observation that many previous proclamations for the government of slaves had been honored largely in the breach. This suggested laxity in their enforcement by the 1770s, collusion in their evasion by some masters, and the slaves profiting by that laxity to enjoy in practice some concessions denied in theory. Such a conclusion is supported by a report of the St. Croix Burgher Council in 1778.[48] Independent huckstering by slaves was continuing despite several previous proclamations forbidding it, and it gave rise not only to the hawking of stolen goods but also to smuggled contraband. As for the sale of bread, salt beef, pork, herring and other fish, the Burgher Council found it prejudicial to the interests of both plantation slaves and their owners. Given the meagerness of their rations, the slaves could not resist the contents of the hawkers' trays. The owners suffered because when the slaves could not offer for barter maize, guinea corn, other provisions or small stock, they stole their masters' rum, sugar or whatever they could lay their hands on. Additionally such itinerant vending provided useful cover for runaways to appear in public. The Burgher Council also sought to inhibit the random assembly of slave porters in search of work, in the towns of St. Croix.[49]

The more general problem for the Burgher Council was that it believed the congregation of slaves in large numbers, except for Christian worship, an event to be discouraged. Even then, it sought to restrict mourners at Christian slave funerals in Christiansted to six pairs, apart from pall bearers. It was not uncommon to have up to 300 slaves in attendance on such occasions, all dressed in the finest, and although the Burgher Council conceded that most were members of Christian denominations with no evil intent, it nevertheless thought preventive measures necessary because "it was unwise to have so many Negroes assembled in one place" ("Det er imod god Politique at saa mange Negere paa et Stæed burde være forsamlede"). If assembly for religious purposes was viewed with such suspicion, it comes as no surprise that the authorities were even more vigilant towards purely secular celebrations, especially where refreshments included liquor.[50]

The extent to which masters contributed to the de facto relaxation of some restrictions, especially on the slaves' freedom of movement, is to be gathered from the Burgher Council's observations regarding tea and coffee parties organized by slaves and free blacks. The practice, it observed, was getting out of hand; some planters, as a way of favoring their slaves, turned a blind eye to it. Even if those planters were few in number, it added, there was still cause for concern, since rumor had it that many slaves paid from one to eight patacoons to get in, and were often becomingly decked out from head to toe in silk. The Burgher Council wanted the parties limited at worst and at best forbidden.[51]

Lindemann's Draft of 1783

By the beginning of the 1780s there was an awareness on the part of officialdom, metropolitan and colonial, that the provisions relating to public order in the only extant code, that of Gardelin, were far too brutal to be consistently enforced. Branding and the death sentence for several instances of breaking and entering, stealing, and long-term and habitual running away had been commuted by governors in the past to whippings, hard labor for life, and/or transportation.[52] In the case of the slaves Jochum and Sam, who had assaulted a white ship's captain at their master's bidding in 1785, both slaves were sentenced to whippings and transportation instead of the amputation or execution the law prescribed.[53]

The metropolitan government, for its part, inspired by the humanitarianism of Count Reventlow and others, thought that the slave law of 1733 was so harsh as to be unenforceable, and opened the way for the exercise of clemency on an ad hoc basis, which it thought undesirable. It considered, further, that the more severe punishments – execution, amputation, branding and the like – should be reserved for offenses that could lead to rebellion. Not only did the metropolitan government call on the colonial officials to prepare a new and less stringent code, but it made suggestions as well for the spread of religious and secular education; the creation of opportunities for eventual self-purchase; the encouragement of slave marriages and the regulation of punishments administered on the estates.[54]

The colonial government agreed that Gardelin's code was no longer appropriate. Governor Clausen pointed out that his administration had dispensed with mutilation as a punishment, and it would not be included in the new slave law about to be drafted.[55] The responsibility for drawing up the new consolidated slave law fell to Etatsraad Lindemann, who produced, with great speed, a draft by the end of 1783. The draft comprised four sections: a regulatory code for slaves; a section relating to free coloreds; whites' obligations to their slaves; and a final section on the judicial process as it ought to apply to slaves.

The first and most detailed section drew together the police provisions of Gardelin's time and after, and deleted the more objectionable punishments like castration and mutilation. Like murder of a slave, they now became criminal offenses, cognizable, however, before the metropolitan and not the colonial courts.[56] The draft was nevertheless emphatic in its insistence on deference and was protective of the minority white community from assault, rebellion, conspiracy, arson and poisoning, all of which carried the death sentence.[57] Desertion and marronage were to cease to be capital offenses but in extreme cases carried a sentence of 200 strokes, branding and work in chains for life.[58]

Provisions for the maintenance of public order in the draft concerned themselves in the main with prohibiting games of chance, fights, drunkenness, higglers without tickets, unauthorized dances, wakes and burial parties – all of which were assumed to be potentially disorderly and punishable. The unauthorized possession of dogs, metal-tipped sticks or large staves, hunting knives, daggers, light swords, firearms, powder and shot was likewise forbidden. Slaves were not to be permitted to run through the streets with open fires or glowing embers, to smoke lit pipes near rum stores, to possess flammable materials such as sulphur in dangerous quantities, nor to participate in the throwing of fireworks to mark public holiday.[59]

Amusements that were difficult to supervise, unlike the authorized dances, were singled out for proscription. Stone-throwing and kite-flying, two favorite slave diversions, fell into this category: the latter, not only because it was time-consuming and required cash for the decorative accessories, which gave rise to petty theft, but also because horses excited thereby had been known to part company with their white riders. The activities of itinerant minstrels at Christmas and New Year equally did not lend themselves to supervision and were to be forbidden.[60]

The 1733 provisions and all subsequent ones relating to curfews, were consolidated into four clauses. Significantly, Lindemann recommended that evil intent, if established, was to be more severely punished than an actual offense against public order.[61] The latter was a known quantity, and could be legislated against and punished. The former was beyond prediction, and could not as readily be provided for in every particular.

This largely explains why Lindemann considered it so necessary to vest every white person with powers to arrest; to insist on the gainful occupation of slaves at all times, in order to reduce the possibility of wrongdoing or its contemplation; to empower each plantation owner with a magistrate's discretion for non-criminal offenses; to legitimize the use of the cartwhip, and institutionalize the plantation whipping post. As further reinforcement, a fixed deficiency ratio of 5:1 was thought necessary.[62]

While Lindemann insisted on deference from blacks, he thought it equally important that whites should refrain from familiarity, supervising but not participating in slave dances and other festivities. Least of all should white men engage in sexual relations with slave women, and any white woman so indecently degrading herself was to be fined, imprisoned and subsequently deported.[63]

The judicial process Lindemann envisaged for slaves was simple and summary. Experience had shown, he said, that court actions involving slaves were time-consuming, the significance of the punishment decreased by time and the treasury burdened with the additional cost.[64] In cases of grave offenses, and it is clear Lindemann had conspiracies and rebellions in mind, he proposed court martial and an increase in numbers of, and responsibility for, the local police to deal with them. The court of first instance would serve for other cases where the death penalty was involved.

Petty criminal offenses were to fall within the competence of the police, with summary powers.[65] In none of these circumstances were slaves to be treated as competent witnesses against white persons, although if they were baptized they could give evidence against other slaves.[66]

Whites' minimum obligation to their slaves was to consist in the provision of housing; rations in good times and bad; grounds on which to cultivate and one free day at least per week in which to tend them; five meters of coarse cloth annually; a hat every other year and compulsory care of the ill.[67] Each estate was to keep a plantation journal in which punishments, rations, and sick and maroon slaves' names were to be entered.[68]

Lindemann expressed concern that the intention in the unpublished Reglement of 1755 to promote missionary work among the slaves remained largely unfulfilled. Priests had been reluctant to baptize slave children whose parents were heathen, and Roman Catholic estate owners had discouraged proselytization among their slaves. For the future, he recommended that although no adult slave should be forced into accepting Christianity, every slave child should be routinely baptized.[69]

The other significant ameliorative provision related to the slave's right to earn and own in specified circumstances. Lindemann's intention, in this regard, was that such money and property could provide the basis of a manumission fund through which slaves could eventually purchase their freedom.[70] Lindemann was also eager to establish a system resembling coartación. He proposed that the purchase price should be fixed by contract, and slaves with one third of that price could obtain freedom, although obliged to serve their former owners during their lifetime if the owners wished.[71] This was without doubt the most innovative of Lindemann's proposals, but neither it nor any of the other clauses in his voluminous draft was ever enacted. Nor did another attempt at a code worked out in Copenhagen, by a committee under van der Østen in 1785, fare any better.[72] Comments on the latter were being received as late as the autumn of 1787.[73] In any event, both drafts were overtaken by events relating to the abolition of the slave trade.

Abolition, Amelioration and the Law

The commission established by the crown in 1791 to consider the abolition of the transatlantic slave trade took the view that the amelioration question was inextricably bound up with that of abolition. The committees formerly concerned with working out a comprehensive consolidated code were therefore to confine themselves to the details of a criminal code. On amelioration itself, the commission was of the view that its benefits were self-evident; its alternative was insurrection, and for reasons of self-interest alone should recommend itself to the planter community whose cooperation it was confident in having.[74] The commission, in short, was not prepared to make any statutory inroads into the masters' discretion in matters relating to food, clothing, housing, pre- and post-natal care, or care of children and the sick. These were areas comprehended by the sacred right of property, which the commission had no intention of violating.[75] Indeed, as late as 1805, the secretary to the abolition commission, Kirstein, was reiterating its position that a comprehensive code noir was not an urgent priority; that its immediate concern was a police code which would reflect what was customary among better planters.[76]

By the beginning of the nineteenth century, therefore, there were no encoded provisions of any substance protecting the slave's welfare. While the law was non-existent in this regard, custom certainly did not favor the slave's interest, if the comments of contemporaries not noted for their humanitarianism are to be believed. The planters' spokesman, Peter Oxholm, clamored on their behalf for continuance of the trade, and received support from the Burgher Council of St. Croix.[77] Amelioration by cooperation was a dead letter.

The implementation of the definitive police code and the judicial system for slaves had no better success. The commission's policy had borne no results by 1769, when the missionary Peter Lund called from St. Thomas for a special court dealing exclusively with slave matters and comprised of "coloureds" under the supervision of the governor and other whites. The colonial government thought the proposal administratively impossible, socially impolitic, and premature in view of the new code yet to be worked out.[78] In 1802 Adrian Bentzon was lamenting the continuing absence of a proper civil and criminal code for slaves. The vast number of disparate placats, he urged, was a testament to the inadequacy of the civil and the brutality of the criminal code.[79] If the law was fragmentary, the difficulty was compounded by the near total absence of a proper magistracy and police. The latter by the end of the eighteenth century were not only small in number but also notorious as time servers.[80] Such a situation left unresolved a major problem relating to slave punishments, namely, the degree of discretionary authority a slave owner should have in administering punishment on his estate.

Lund gave an instance of an owner in St. Thomas who in 1796 burnt a slave child with a lit cigar on its ear and nose.[81] A comparable instance of arbitrary discretion to punish involved the slave Sally. With other slaves on the plantation to which she belonged, Sally was denied rations as punishment for the alleged theft of some guinea-fowl eggs. Sally complained to governor Lindemann, who ordered that the slaves be given their rations. But Sally, as chief complainant, was whipped and put in irons for her trouble by the overseer, Dr. Kenny, who took the view that on questions involving the right of private property, the governor had no competence. Kenny was heavily fined, but the symbolic deed had already been done.[82]

By 1801, the year of the first brief British occupation, the extant police code of Gardelin's was not being enforced in all its rigor. Custom had tempered its administration; but this by no means eradicated instances of rank brutality. Nor could they be removed until the metropolitan and colonial governments had the will and the energy to delimit with precision the boundaries of the slave master's discretion in relation to punishment and to devise appropriate machinery for the administration of a police code. None of this was to be achieved before the 1830s and the administration of Peter von Scholten.

4

The Rural Milieu:
Slavery on the Plantations

FROM ITS INCEPTION UNTIL ITS FORMAL TERMINATION IN 1802, the transatlantic slave trade supplied an estimated 75,000 slaves to the Danish colonies of St. Croix, St. Thomas and St. John.[1] A significant proportion of these slaves and their creole offspring were employed in the three major urban commercial centers of the colonies – Charlotte Amalie, Christiansted and Frederiksted – but the vast majority, as elsewhere in tropical America, saw out their days on large-scale rural holdings, most of them sugar plantations. As a result, from very early in the Danish settlement, the distribution of slaves between the islands reflected their relative advantages and disadvantages for plantation agriculture and the cultivation of sugar.

In 1755, immediately following the transfer of ownership from the Danish West Indian Company to the crown, the slave population of St. Croix numbered 8,897, that of St. Thomas 3,949, and that of St. John 2,031, a total of 14,877 (Table 1.1). The free population in the same year totaled 1,979, forming a distinct minority in the ratio of 8:1. The disproportion was considerably larger in the plantation zones, and it was in the rural milieu that African-born slaves dominated the population in the middle of the eighteenth century when the slave trade was at its peak.[2]

Roots

The substitution of black for white labor in the plantation fields of the Danish West Indies was facilitated by the establishment in 1659 of the Danish African Company, the erection of the trading forts Christiansborg and Frederiksborg on the Gold Coast, Denmark's active entry into the slave trade by the 1660s, and the founding of the Danish West India Guinea Company in 1674.[3] It should not be assumed, however, that the presence of Danish slave trading forts on the Gold Coast of Lower Guinea necessarily meant that a preponderance of the slaves brought to the Danish West Indies were drawn from the ethnic groups of that region. Svend Green-Pedersen has been at pains to point out the extent to which the Danish slave trade was penetrated by other European slave trading nations.[4] Similarly, Sidney Mintz and Richard Price have suggested, in the case of Suriname, that the conventional view that its slave population was dominated by slaves from Dutch occupied areas of the Guinea Coast needs to be re-examined. Indeed, they indicate that quantitative data point to a predominance of Loango/Angola slaves.[5]

The Moravian missionary C. G. A. Oldendorp, who visited the Danish islands between 1767 and 1769, claimed to have observed a large number of "tribes": Fulani, Mandingoes, Amina, Akims, Popos, Ibos and Yorubas, corresponding to a geographical area stretching from the Senegal River to the Bight of Benin. Although he provided no figures for the Danish West Indies, he maintained that the "Amina" were the most numerous.[6] Pauline Holman-Pope has sustained Oldendorp's observations by identifying large numbers of Akan-Amina speakers of Twi in St. Croix in the later eighteenth century, and a similar preponderance of this ethnic group in St. John. Their martial prowess and organizational skills were very much in evidence in the almost successful uprising in the latter island in 1733.[7] Similarly, the 1759 slave conspiracy in St. Croix can be attributed to their leadership.[8] There is no concrete evidence reflecting a preference for Akan slaves on the part of Danish West Indian planters, as was the case with their Jamaican counterparts.[9] However, given the interdigitation of the national transatlantic slave trades, the preponderance of English-speaking elements in the planter class, and the dislocations of Ashanti warfare in the second quarter of the eighteenth century, it would be entirely possible for large numbers of Akan to have found their way to the plantations of the Danish West Indies.[10] .

The dominance of the Gold Coast supply area appears to have undergone modification in the later decades of the eighteenth century, as a consequence of the shift of the main area of trade eastwards and southwards.[11] References to cargoes of Congo slaves newly arrived for sale, or to slaves of the Congo nation among runaways, particularly in St. Croix, are instructive in this regard.[12] This was also the period during which the slave population of St. Thomas remained more or less stationary, while that of St. Croix trebled to over 20,000 (Table 1.1). This development was accompanied by two parallel processes which had a bearing on the tribal provenance of the African population of the Danish West Indies: the increasing importation from the foreign islands of the Leewards into the port of Frederiksted to satisfy the labor needs of St. Croix, and the thriving transit trade in slaves in St. Thomas, from which some slaves were retained for the local labor force.[13] The rigor of formal mercantilist theory and practice was broken by the admission of slaves from such foreign sources of supply. But the breach opened the way to the further ethnic diversification of the African population of the Danish islands.

Modern scholars have argued for the broad sociocultural similarities shared by the peoples bordering on the Guinea Coast.[14] But in the Danish West Indies, the cultural homogeneity of the Africans who were brought by the slave trade cannot be assumed. The geographical spread of their points of departure embraced the entire area of Upper Guinea to Angola, between the Senegal and Cuanza Rivers. This heterogeneous aggregate nevertheless came to achieve coherence and a sense of community, and to build institutions. As the slaves' society matured, there evolved a discrete slave culture: shared patterns of behavior and ideology – and their material products – which were not only socially learned but transmitted.[15]

Plantation Labor

Although the slave population was involved in roles and specialties independent of plantation production and associated activities, the raison d'être of slave labor was the maximization of plantation output. On arrival, slaves in the Danish West Indies underwent the same routine: public auction, until its practice was abolished by Governor General von Scholten in the late 1830s, branding,[16] the march to the plantation, and seasoning. The plantation as a unit achieved a stable mean size by the end of the eighteenth century, consisting of 100 Danish Tønder, approximately 136 acres, subdivided into squares of 8-10 acres with a communicating way, or as was common, a border either planted with guinea grass or with slave provisions.[17] Many contemporary accounts made no attempt to mask the difficulty of the work routine at each stage of the sugar cycle. P. L. Oxholm, writing at the end of the eighteenth century, described holing and planting as work of the most arduous and disagreeable kind, especially for female slaves. To relieve its tedium, the slaves sang and swung their hoes in rhythm. Some planters, Oxholm noted, gave double rations of food and two or three daily issues of rum, sugar, and water, during the exacting planting season.[18]

Taking St. Croix as a whole in 1792, a total of 15,564 slaves out of a total of 18,121, or 86 percent, were engaged in field labor.[19] The strenuous nature of the work involved had serious consequences for the general health of the slave population, for the women in particular, and as is discussed below, for that population's capacity for reproducing itself. Table 4.1 indicates that more than 70 percent of St. Croix's 197 estates in 1792 had a work force of 100 or less. A great concentration of those estates existed in the East End of St. Croix, its least fertile quarter, where 36 of its 41 estates each had less than 100 slaves.[20] Indeed the mean size of plantation workforces in the East End in 1792 was 42.7 with complements ranging up to 147 on John Heyliger's Mt. Welcome estate.[21] Such estates in a relatively less fertile area were unable to enjoy the benefits of economies of scale, and more likely to drive their slaves harder and less able to make provisions for them. The spatial no less than occupational distribution of field slaves, therefore, had significant demographic implications for the slave population.

Table 4.1: *Size of the Workforce: Frequency Distribution of Field Slaves, St. Croix, 1792*

Slaves per Plantation	No. of Plantations	% of Plantations
0-5	70	35.5
51-100	71	36.1
101-150	37	18.8
151-200	13	6.6
201-300	4	2.0
300+	2	1.0
Total	197	100.0

Source: Calculated from R/A, DVK.

Until plantation hours were regulated by the reforms of von Scholten in the 1830s, the workday began at 4 a.m. with a summons from the Bomba, or driver, using either the plantation bell or more commonly the conch shell known in the islands as a tuttue. Like the bell, the tuttue was used as an emergency signal in the event of fire or an uprising. Writing in 1788, Schmidt described what by then had become the established routine after the four o'clock summons. Work proceeded until 8 or 9 a.m. with a half hour breakfast. There were slaves, however, who had nothing with them to eat. In crop time, such slaves would breakfast on a couple of canes. Schmidt did not say how they fared in the dead season (July to November).[22] Work continued until midday and was then interrupted by a break of one-and-a-half hours. Slaves without families took that break in the field but those with families tended to return home. If, however, there was no food at home, the midday meal was only possible after a trip to the provision grounds for yams or potatoes. The afternoon period continued until sundown, and the dead season workday ended when plantation animals had been provided with fodder in what was known as "grass throwing." The entire day's work was undertaken under the watchful eye of the Bomba whose business it was to ensure that there was no malingering, that the rows were kept straight and that the whip was in evidence and use. Nursing mothers commonly worked with children on their backs and took them aside for suckling. Other unweaned children, now on their mothers' backs, lay in the fields on sheep- or calf-skins.[23]

The work schedule of the crop season differed from the above in the lengthening of the workday after sunset. Hans West asserted that 11 hours were maximum in crop season.[24] Schmidt, however, was perhaps closer to the mark in his observation that work proceeded "from nine until late night."[25] Cane tops in bundles had to be transported to the cattle enclosures; dried cane stalks to the boiling house for fuel and water from wells or cisterns to the distillery. Schmidt also indicated that during crop time women did cane cutting as well as men and even the sickly were sometimes pressed into service to tie the cane into bundles. In the mills, the work was particularly demanding and dangerous. At wind-powered mills, the work detail usually consisted of ten slaves, two of whom fed the cane into the rollers. But there were hazards. Hands sometimes got caught in the rollers. For that reason, there was always an ax lying ready at mill-side to save any slave so caught.[26] At animal-powered mills, the work detail was somewhat smaller, requiring only four: two to feed the mill, one to extract the trash and another to attend the animal driving the mill.[27]

As the Barbadian planter Sir Philip Gibbes observed in 1797, "One of the most important parts of management is a judicious division of Negroes into gangs."[28] That axiom equally applied in the Danish West Indies. The work force, as indicated earlier, was under the supervision of the Bomba or driver, and if Schmidt is to be believed two drivers were not unusual.[29] Indeed, there are indications that the practice of having two drivers on some estates persisted until the very end of slavery.[30] Schmidt described drivers in the eighteenth century as "old," an observation borne out by plantation inventories. The capacity to command respect from their fellow slaves was an indispensable precondition of their appointment. Drivers' roles did not change significantly over time; if anything those roles were reinforced by the passage of time. In Governor General von Scholten's Labor Ordinance of 1838, their significance was unambiguously spelt out:

> The driver of every estate shall be appointed by the owner or ad-ministrator ... Such drivers shall be considered as appertaining to the police and to assist in the preservation of good order on the estate ...
> In order to give the driver greater respectability they ought to have and be furnished with a uniform and this uniform to consist of a red jacket with a green collar and further to inspire the driver with greater zeal and attention in the discharge of his duties he should be allowed by the estate $1 monthly independent of the usual rations.[31]

The leadership function of the driver in the plantation regimen is also borne out by the initial listing of his name on the plantation work force list. The work force inventories from La Grange and La Grande Princesse estates in 1759, are both cases in point.[32] How important ultimately the driver could be as a leader, can be gathered from the fact that the emancipation uprising of 2-3 July 1848 was commanded by Gotlieb Bordeaux, alias General Buddoe, formerly driver on La Grange estate.

The descriptive literary sources are not particularly forthcoming on the question of the division of the field labor force into gangs, but it is never-theless possible, extrapolating from the documentary sources, to reconstruct at least three and possibly four categories which comprised the greater part of any estate's slave population. The effective or first gang consisted of the grown men and women; a second gang of "half-grown" adults of both sexes, known sometimes as the Crooken or Little Gang, of 15-18 year olds; a third gang of children between 6 and 15 years; and a fourth gang of children under 6 years of age.[33] On large estates such as La Grange, with 450 of its 675 acres in sugar, some 90 percent of its 288 slaves

Table 4.2: *Deployment of Slaves, St. Croix, 1792*

Occupational Category	No. of Slaves	% of Slaves
Field Slaves	15,564	85.9
Artisans	1,222	6.7
House Slaves	1,335	7.4
Total	18,121	100.0

Source: Calculated from R/A, DVK.

were employed as field laborers in 1792. In the same year another large estate, La Grande Princesse, covering 726 acres, deployed 321 or 85 percent of its 379 slaves in field labor.[34]

On the plantations, house slaves occupied a position of privilege comparable to that of house slaves in the urban setting. The literary evidence, produced for the most part by persons familiar with slavery's urban manifestations, is not especially helpful on house slaves in the rural milieu. Nevertheless, there is a sufficiency of evidence to suggest that their numbers in individual plantation households were as large as they were in urban establishments. The Slave Trade Commission of 1792 was persuaded that their reduction and deployment in plantation field work would go a long way towards meeting the planters' demands for labor. Indeed it was for this reason the Commission saw to the institution of a differential poll tax on house slaves. The funds so derived were set aside as prize money for planters with a good record of population growth or large numbers of slave marriages on their estates.[35] As Table 4.2 indicates, there were less artisans than house slaves in St. Croix. A large and well organized estate like La Grande Princesse, had a large house slave population of 25, but this represented no more than 6.5 percent of its total workforce and its 33 artisans in any event constituted 8.7 percent of that workforce. But there were estates such as Diamond, located like La Grande Princesse in Company Quarter, with a total of 72 slaves on its 187 acres, where there were as many as 20 slaves or 27 percent employed in household work.[36] However, as Table 4.3 indicates, eleven estates with five or less household slaves represented more than half the number of estates in Company Quarter, followed by the next largest cohort of four plantations (20 percent) with between six and ten. In this sense neither La Grande Princesse nor Diamond was typical, although estates the size of Diamond predominated in the Quarter, and as a group had the highest proportion of house slaves (Table 4.4). Oxholm, a stout defender of the slave trade's continuance, was quick to deny any suggestion of the wasteful use of labor. If there were planters who took slaves from productive work in the field for domestic service, he submitted, it was a rare occurrence. The opposite was more often the case,

Table 4.3: *Distribution of House Slaves, Company Quarter, St. Croix, 1792*

No. of House Slaves per Plantation	No. of Plantations	No. of House Slaves*	% of Plantations
0-5	11	28	55.0
6-10	4	32	20.0
11-15	2	26	10.0
16-20	1	18	5.0
21-25	2	45	10.0
26-30	–	–	–
Total	20	149	100.0

Source: Calculated from R/A, DVK.
* Calculated on the basis of the mean of each cohort.

in his view, especially in crop time when they worked the mill compound, leading mules, drying bagasse and the like.[37]

Housing

Very little literary evidence exists providing information as to the size of plantation villages. Oldendorp said only that on the plantations "the Negro houses form a kind of village" and "often fifty, sixty, or even more of them are constructed in a row."[38] The best indicators in any event are contemporary estate maps and illustrations. Oxholm's "Groundplan for a plantation and its customary subdivisions," published in 1797, showed the layout of a presumably typical plantation village in three rows of seven houses each on an estate of about 100 tønder (136 acres). The village on Oxholm's map was situated in the immediate vicinity of the mill and boiling house, but separate quarters were identified for house slaves at the rear of the plantation house.[39] This imaginary layout corresponds with the actual arrangements deducible from extant maps. Judith's Fancy in St. Croix, containing about 400 acres with half under cane and about 150 slaves,[40] is shown by a map of 1779 to have had a plantation village layout which corresponds with Oxholm's idealized plan. There are 44 identifiable houses arranged in three rows of ten, with the fourteen remaining houses in rows of unequal numbers.[41] An undated map of de Windt's estate, Bethlehem, also drawn by Oxholm shows the same general locational pattern, and was unusual only to the degree that it identified two slave villages; the expected one in the vicinity of the works comprising four rows of ten houses each; the other, more distant, a similar number of rows with the same number of houses.[42] The only explanation for the double village seems to be that Bethlehem was particularly large: 1,125 acres with 700 under sugar and 356 slaves.[43]

Table 4.4: *House Slaves by Size of Estate, Company Quarter, St. Croix, 1792*

Estate Size in Acres	No. of Estates	% of Estates	No. of House Slaves	Total No. of Slaves	House Slaves as % of Total
0-100	3	15	–	24	–
101-200	8	40	66	681	9.6
201-300	5	25	29	449	6.4
301-400	–	–	–	–	–
401-500	1	5	7	102	6.8
501+	3	15	40	726	5.5
Total	20	100	142	1,982	7.1

Source: Calculated from R/A, DVK.

The evidence for St. Thomas suggests that there were no significant divergences from the practices which prevailed in St. Croix. Certainly on the Moravian estates, judging from the illustrations in Oldendorp's *History* depicting New Herrnhut estate, a presumably more humane clerical ownership, followed the established pattern used by the lay planter class. Nevertheless the general principle of locations and layout suggested by the cartographical-pictorial evidence is an arrangement of regular rows, closely grouped to facilitate order and supervision and proximity to the plantation works. The mean occupancy also appears to have been three or four slaves per hut.[44]

At the period of the transfer from the Company to the Crown in 1754, slave houses were constructed of wattle and daub walls and thatch roofing. Even Richard Haagensen, no friend of emancipationists, was forced to admit that slaves' houses were worse than those of the meanest serfs in Denmark. Their doors, he said, were so low that it was impossible to go in or come out without bending, and as for interior appointments there was only bare earth or a board in lieu of a bed.[45] Oldendorp, a decade later, described the construction of such dwellings:

> The layout and the foundation of their houses rest on four stakes, which are driven into the ground. Fork-shaped at the top end and spaced in such a manner as to form a square, these stakes are linked together at the top by an equal number of horizontal boards. On these rest the rafters of the roof which come together in a crest. A few more vertical stakes are placed between the four corner posts, and pliable branches are woven among these. The latter are covered with quicklime and plastered with cow dung. Once the roof rafters have been covered with sugarcane leaves, the entire house is complete. The entry-way is so low that a man cannot pass through it without bending down. This doorway and a few small openings in the walls

allow only a little light to flow into the dwelling during the day. The floor is the bare earth, and the two inclined sides of the roof, which extend almost down to the ground on the outside, make up the ceiling. An interior wall divides the house into two rooms of unequal size, the smaller one serving as a bedroom.[46]

Although Oldendorp argued that the "dwellings of the civilized, Christian Negroes are more orderly and present a better appearance than those of the coarse and not yet trained Negroes," the only architectural improvements he mentioned were the covering of the walls with a coat of lime and the addition of a separate cookhouse for the storage of utensils and victuals. But the furnishings of such slave houses, he said, were more elaborate and included tables, chairs and chests. The slave's mattress however consisted only of a "kavanne" or mat made from reeds. West, in his *Bidrag* of 1793, also mentioned the use of banana bedding.[47] A refinement added before the end of the eighteenth century was the use of sheep- or calf-skins. Schmidt noted their use by nursing mothers in the field for unweaned children to lie on, and described these skins as "Negerindernes visseste møbler" – slave women's most important item of furniture.[48]

According to West, the slave huts were divided into two rooms and each hut had its own fence around it. However, his assertion that each slave had a separate room must be considered an exaggeration.[49] The two room structure which he described would simply have facilitated a variety of household types: man, woman, their children; two women, their children; two couples without children, and so on. But the occupancy of one room per slave could hardly have been the norm. Oldendorp reported that "where sleeping accommodations are concerned, matters of order and decency are observed by the better part of the Negroes," parents occupying the inner bedroom and the children the front room of the dwelling.[50]

The literary evidence is silent on the precise overall dimensions of these huts. A useful guide, however, would be van der Østen's suggested dimensions of 30 Danish square feet (approximately 40 English square feet) as the standard dimensions for a single free person of color, unless specific permission was granted for a larger structure.[51] It would not be an unreasonable assumption that the two room slave hut was double this dimension, or approximately 60 Danish square feet. Even this cannot be regarded as commodious accommodation.

These conditions of size, type and interior appointments were generally applicable for the later eighteenth century. By the 1840s, the decade of emancipation, they had hardly undergone widespread modification. Victor Schoelcher remarked that even among the Moravians at their Friedensthal estate in St. Croix, he was shocked at the slave housing he saw; the board planks instead of beds were still in evidence, and the meanness of the cabins contrasted markedly with the large, spacious and airy houses of the missionaries. It was worse too than the slave houses of the contemporary French West Indies.[52] By and large, noted Schoelcher, the slave cabins were dark and airless as in the French islands and so low, as

Haagensen and Oldendorp had observed earlier, that you had to bend double to get out or in.[53] Some owners claimed that slaves preferred to sleep in the burning sun.[54] The persuasiveness of this opinion was very difficult to resist, Schoelcher remarked, until one saw slaves resting just like whites in shade along the roadside. It was mostly on the sixteen estates belonging to the crown, the "Kongelige Forpagtede Plantager" or Royally Leased Estates, that housing conditions were markedly better. For them the crown laid down stringent regulations relating to housing which lessees were obliged to meet: houses were to be high, airy, wooden floored with masonry walls, shingled or tiled, partitioned in two, with minimum measurements of 18 feet by 12 feet and with a separate kitchen.[55]

Notwithstanding von Scholten's call for improved housing in 1838,[56] therefore, slave housing in the decades of emancipation had made no great advances over what it had been a century earlier. Apart from the estates in crown ownership, wattle and daub walls and cane-trash roofing prevailed. Such houses were draughty and damp, and the consequences for the slaves' health, fertility and general well-being were very severe. But the plantocracy seemed neither to know nor to care.

Food and Clothing

Since few slave houses had separate outside kitchens before the 1840s, meal preparation was done most often on open fires outside the cabins in good weather or on the earthen floors inside in the rainy season. The weekly plantation allowance consisted of salted herring, and imported flour or corn meal. With the latter the slave made a roasted "johnny" cake or boiled dumplings in their calaloo-pepperpot or pulse broth. Observers like West and Schmidt noted the extensive use of green vegetables in a kind of pottage spiced with red or Spanish peppers.[57] The green vegetable content of the slaves' diet was entirely of their own production as were the carbohydrate fibres like yams, cassavas or potatoes. The same might be said of the sources of second class protein such as black peas or "bandubønner" which Schmidt mentioned.[58]

Overwhelmingly the diet was deficient in fresh meat as a source of first class protein, a fact which even the pro-slavery West was forced to admit.[59] Other writers did not consider this lack to be critical. Haagensen, for example, considered cornmeal to be nutritive and fattening, and when mixed with salt and water and boiled (turned) to make "fungee," a great "delicacy".[60] According to Haagensen, the breakfast eaten in the field by plantation slaves generally consisted of roasted sweet potatoes and brackish water, while fungee was more for leisure times. But Schmidt, in the 1780s, claimed the standard breakfast fare was fungee and a bit of salted meat or fish. The midday meal included roasted yams or potatoes eaten with salted herring.

By the 1790s custom had legitimized a practice by which slaves mostly fended for their own food with uncertain supplemental rations of flour, salted meat or fish provided by the plantation. This dependence on slave initiative for the provision of their own basic food supplies had its origins in the early eighteenth century. Oldendorp in the middle of the century said that each slave family was given a piece of land by the planter on which they were required "to produce their own means of sustenance." His view of the system was optimistic:

> The yield is generally great enough that it provides the diligent cultivator with a surplus beyond his basic needs, and from this he can provide himself with other commodities. This arrangement relieves the master of any further cares concerning the upkeep of this slaves, and it is much more agreeable and advantageous to the slaves than when the essentials for their sustenance are handed to them in kind, as is the case on several English plantations on St. Croix. The Negro, therefore, enjoys a kind of freedom on his little plantation, wherein he cultivates the soil according to his own free choice. ... As a result, the Negro is all the more bound to the plantation of his master insofar as he has a stake, so to speak, in the master's holding.[61]

In St. Thomas and St. John, by the end of the eighteenth century, dependence on the slaves' initiative to feed themselves was even greater than in St. Croix.[62] And by 1802 Adrian Bentzon was proposing that owners of slaves who could neither feed nor clothe them adequately should be forced to sell them.[63]

In general, the clothing of plantation slaves was even more deficient than their food. According to Haagensen, most wore nothing and many had no more than a rag to cover them. Apologist for slavery that he was, Haagensen was quick to point out that field slaves were in fact content with their nakedness and that house slaves were in any case properly clothed.[64] Similarly, Oldendorp argued that the slaves were simply continuing the practice of Africa. Here the civilizing impact of the Moravian mission was particularly striking, he said; once "the Gospel found an entry into the hearts of the Negroes there, they were soon convinced of the impropriety of a predominantly naked church meeting" and the custom spread to secular life. Male field slaves while working, reported Oldendorp, wore long trousers of rough linen and, occasionally, a short shirt. Women wore a skirt "and possibly a shirt and jacket." But they all went barefooted, even when they dressed in "festive attire" for Sunday services, funerals and other rites.[65]

The World the Slaves Made

It was in the slave villages that the behavioral and ideological patterns that were shared, learnt and transmitted among the slaves as a group enjoyed the best opportunities of survival either as African retentions or Afro-West Indian syncretisms. The Danish West Indies shared with the rest of the New World plantation community the indulgence of those magico-religious practices, imperfectly understood and negatively perceived by

Europeans as obeah. But as Edward Kamau Brathwaite has observed in this regard, "the obeah man was doctor, philosopher, and priest. Healing was, in a sense, an act of faith, as it was in the early Christian church, and the fetish (*suman*) had come to mediate (in many instances to replace and obscure the connection) between man and god."[66] The obeah man's healing function in the Danish West Indies is best illustrated by Schmidt's account of a salivation cure for a variety of illnesses, including skin infections and venereal diseases, based on a diet of raw lizard meat.[67] The cure was the work of a slave who "practised his art with the greatest success and became the best doctor for venereally infected slaves." The lizard's head and legs were first removed and the rest cut up into small bits which were rolled in batter the size of small pills, concealing the contents. All attempts to persuade the slave to reveal his secret were fruitless until he was granted his freedom, some money and a bit of land from which to live.[68]

It is interesting to notice that where the role of the obeah man as healer was positively perceived, the white community gave it encouragement and support. Many slaves, old women in particular, thus had special status on their plantations for their knowledge of the healing properties of plants and trees for sores and other illnesses. West, for example, considered them indispensable to their owners and undoubtedly they would have been viewed with similar esteem by their peers.[69] There was a different response, however, to those aspects of the magico-religious complex which were beyond the whites' comprehension. The earliest slave codes of the eighteenth century made the practice of magic and the use of fetishes: nails, feathers, hair, animal and human teeth, egg shells, punishable offenses.[70] Whilst it derided such practices it was nevertheless clear that white official-dom associated them with the use of poison for harmful purposes. It is interesting in this regard that prohibitions against the use of poison in the slave codes of the eighteenth century invariably preceded or followed immediately the provisions relating to obeah. Both carried the death sentence.[71]

Those who were practitioners of sympathetic magic or had knowledge of poisons were most likely to have leadership potential and were for that reason standing threats to the personal security of the white minority and their property. Other slaves could be poisoned and stock animals had been known to have died from the administration of the juice of the bitter cassava.[72] West also gives us to understand that the incidence of induced abortions among slave women was widespread and draws attention to the skill, particularly of the old women, in isolating abortifacients from nature's pharmacopoeia. The effects of the herbs "Ram Goat Bush," *tagara tragodes*, and *Adelia Rincinella Linnaei* were well known to such women. In this regard they were no different from their counterparts in Demerara who used the root of the Mimosa Sensitiva, or those in Barbados who used "Gully Root" for the same purpose.[73]

Where pregnancies were allowed to come to term, there is some evidence, although it is not abundant, that by the middle eighteenth century there were certain ritual observances to mark the occasion. One of the few references relating to beliefs surrounding birth derives from Schmidt who made his observations at La Grande Princesse estate in St. Croix. According to his account, the first eight days after birth were critical. It was then the usual practice when a slave woman delivered for her to receive a quantity of wine, rice and candles. The two former were obviously intended as dietary supplements and the latter as gifts. Schmidt leaves us in no doubt, however, as to the ritual uses to which the candles were put. They were left burning every night of the first eight days of the new born child's life; on the eighth night the child was carefully guarded by more than twenty persons: to prevent it being stolen or eaten by evil spirits. This belief in spirits, Schmidt remarked, was so deep rooted that it was particularly resistant to Christian indoctrination. According to Schmidt, the belief was that when, during this period an evil spirit was able to look the new born child in the eye, it would absorb the child's spirit and it would die. With the passage of the first eight days the spirit's power no longer prevailed. The spirits were given human attribution from time to time. In Schmidt's experience, Lehna, an old crone at La Grande Princesse had the misfortune to be taken for a witch who ate children. Whenever a new born child died, therefore, she had to endure severe beatings, to avoid which she was obliged to go into hiding for a few days.[74] In so behaving the slaves of the Danish West Indies were no more or less developed than the serfs of contemporary Denmark, said Schmidt. The only difference was that the "hexes" of Northern Jutland and elsewhere were treated deferentially as oracles, overwhelmed with honors of all sorts and were not the objects of humiliating beatings.

The midwives officiating at deliveries were more often than not older slave women like old Martha, who headed the list of female slaves at La Grande Princesse in 1759.[75] Some post-partum mothers rejoined their gangs or returned to their duties in the house in a fortnight; others took longer.[76] But not until von Scholten's ameliorative labor ordinance of 1838 was there a stipulated work-free post-natal period.[77] Haagensen, for his part, simply attributed the early return to work to the slave woman's natural hardiness and indifference to discomfort. He has nothing to say about the importunities of a system that demanded the earliest possible resumption. His statement therefore that "they think nothing of giving birth to a child" is to be taken for no more than the subjective evaluation that it was.[78]

The evidence does not indicate significant differences between creoles and Africans in their neo-natal practices. The same does not apply, however, to mortuary beliefs and practices. In this regard there were behavioral differences not only between bosal and creole, but also between plantation and town, Christian and non-Christian. Among "coast negroes," as Judge Edvard Colbiørnsen referred to them in 1788, there prevailed a belief that suicide was a certain way of returning to their homeland, provided that their bodies had not been touched by fire. This belief was especially prevalent among the Ibo. Bosal slaves in general, Colbiørnsen observed, displayed a remarkable indifference to death: "fear of death can have no effect on a slave who had nothing to lose but a life of wretchedness."[79]

At slave funerals, said Schmidt, bosals interred their fellows according to "the custom of the coast" and performed "a heathen dance with curious gestures."[80] Haagensen wrote in the 1750s that bosals were cast into a little hole in the ground "without the least ceremony." Clearly he did not categorize as ceremony the drumming and singing around the grave to which he also referred. Burials among house slaves were different only in that such slaves were given four boards with which to make a coffin.[81] Haagensen does not say, however, whether such house slaves were baptized or unbaptized, creole or bosal. Schmidt, on the other hand, inferred a correspondence between creole and Christian and mentioned the use by them of coffins, and of candles for pallbearers and mourners.[82] By law, burials of slaves who were unbaptized took place at night in unconsecrated ground and required silence. Christians, however, were allowed day time burials according to the rites of the church to which they belonged.[83] Among the latter it had become established practice by the 1780s to hold some kind of pre-interment treat at the house of the deceased involving coffee, tea, strong drink and food. Those occasions went on well into the night.[84] Although not described as such, this has all the appearance of a wake, but whites tended to be suspicious of them, viewed them and indeed all slave funerals as unlawful assemblies and anticipated the worst.[85]

Family, Kinship and Demographic Survival

Though the evidence is scanty, it is nevertheless possible to piece together some picture of family structure and kinship networks among the rural slave population of the Danish West Indies. The slave law of 1755 recognized only Christian marriage and the nuclear family based on it, and offered protection against separation only to the partners and dependent children of such unions.[86] The law relating to the separation of families was never enforced until the decade before emancipation. The effect was that the nuclear family – a woman, her children and current spouse living in a Christian union or non-Christian concubinage – came under severe pressure to maintain continuity or stability in such circumstances. Despite these pressures, however, where informal unions existed they were often noted for the degree of their mutual affection and loving care.[87] Indeed, in many instances one or other partner ran away to be with a mate who lived on another estate, or spent a great deal of time braving the cold and damp evening air to share each other's company. Such consensual unions were widespread. In 1792 there were 2,338 such unions in St. Croix out of an adult (20-and-over) slave population numbering 8,568. Married couples, on the other hand, numbered only 371.[88] Comparable statistics for the period are not available for St. Thomas and St. John. However, data for 1805 suggest that by that year unions of this type in all three islands constituted over 30 percent of the adult slave population, while Christian marriages in none of the three islands reached 10 percent.[89]

Notwithstanding the high incidence of consensual unions, it needs to be recognized that the nuclear family's prospects for survival were exceedingly slender, since it was protected neither by law nor convention. The only significant resistance to the tendency to instability came from the Christian missionaries, and notably from the Moravians. They had an ideological interest in suppressing the informal alternatives to marriage: concubinage, polygamy and polyandry, since all were inimical to their teaching. Among the denominations, the Moravians were the best circumstanced to protect the vulnerable nuclear family unit, since they owned their own estates and were in more direct contact with the objects of their proselytization.[90]

In such unfavorable circumstances, significant genealogical ties were virtually impossible. The matri-central cell of mother and child "would often have constituted the practical limits of an individual's kinship network."[91] The instability of family and the limitations of the kinship network could have been counteracted to some degree by the relative smallness of the islands, their relative contiguity, and the deliberate interposition of creative institutional substitutes. Oldendorp, for example, offered some basis for believing that during the middle years of the eighteenth century there existed important ties of fictive kinship. He mentioned a practice, tantamount to an initiation rite, to which newly arrived bosals were subjected. They were beaten to atone for "sins" committed in Africa; but the object, Oldendorp assures us, was to give the bosal new kin and tribesmen, god-parents in a new world with its trials and tribulations.[92]

The possibilities of establishing family and kinship networks within the context of plantation slavery were powerfully influenced by the unnatural sex ratios created by the system. Throughout the eighteenth century, the proportion of male slaves to female was deliberately skewed in favor of the former. The ratio was a function of the conviction, common in the plantation Americas, that males were more appropriate for plantation labor and that it was better to "buy rather than to breed." Data on sex ratios are not forthcoming for the period prior to the 1790s, but it is a reasonable assumption that the pattern in that decade was not atypical. When the abolition of the slave trade by 1802 was announced in 1792, a stated objective of Danish policy was to redress the balance in favor of females, so that the slave population could at least maintain itself by natural increase.[93] But that policy had no immediate effect. Figures provided by Oxholm for St. Croix in 1792 demonstrate that the field slave population of that island had a sex ratio of 106 males per 100 females. By 1799 the situation had if anything worsened, in that for a total field slave population of 22,530 the sex ratio stood at 118. St. Thomas in 1792 was better circumstanced with 95 males for every 100 females, but these figures comprehended the population at large rather than the field force exclusively. In 1802, by way of comparison, St. Thomas had reached neither parity nor a preponderance of females in

Table 4.5: *Plantation Slaves, St. Croix, St. Thomas, St. John, 1805*

	St. Croix	St. Thomas	St. John	Total
Males	11,601	1,720	1,285	14,606
Females	10,475	1,624	1,132	13,231
Creoles	11,530	2,096	1,521	15,147
Africans	10,546	1,248	896	12,690
Total	22,076	3,344	2,417	27,837
% Creole	52.2	62.6	62.9	54.4
Males as a % of Total	52.5	51.4	53.2	52.5
Females as a % of Total	47.4	48.6	46.8	47.5
Males per 100 Females	110	106	113	110

Source: Calculated from R/A, DVK, 1783-1806; R/A, Diverse sager, Forskellige Oplysninger V.
Note: The table includes house and artisan slaves.

the field labor force. Of the total 2,942 slaves in the field, including old, infirm and runaways, there were 103 males for every 100 females. Indeed, as late as 1805, notwithstanding massive importations, such as the 3,132 new slaves landed in 1799 alone, the balance in favor of males still prevailed (Table 4.5). Gradually, beginning in the second decade of the nineteenth century, the proportions began to be reversed, so that by 1840 in the case of St. Croix females exceeded males by 4.5 percent and the sex ratio stood at 92 for the total slave population (Table 4.6).

The progressive decline of the slave population, derived in part from the high death rate among the newly imported. Despite the substantial importations and improvements in the sex ratio between 1792 and 1802, mortality among bosals was high. One third of all bosals were reckoned to die during the seasoning period. In the decade 1780-1790, the crude death rate for the slave population was calculated at 35.7 per thousand. Despite the improvements in sex ratios, disease still wasted the slave population and excess mortality persisted into the 1840s. The slave population of St. Croix, having shown a significant growth of 12 percent between 1805 and 1815 (Tables 4.5 and 4.6), not only failed to sustain itself as hoped but declined significantly as the nineteenth century progressed. Deaths persistently exceeded births. This failure to achieve a position of natural demographic growth or even stability is all the more noteworthy in view of the increasingly creolized nature of the population.

Medical attention was of the most rudimentary sort. The practice was to have one doctor serve eight to ten plantations, not necessarily contiguous. He was assured of his fee of $1 per slave per annum whether he

Table 4.6: *Slave Population by Sex, St. Croix, 1815-1840*

Year	Total Slaves	Males	% Males	Females	% Females
1815	24,723	12,198	49.3	12,525	50.6
1820	23,754	11,611	48.8	12,143	51.1
1825	22,120	10,640	48.1	11,480	51.8
1830	20,693	9,955	48.1	10,738	51.8
1835	19,876	9,453	47.5	10,423	52.4
1840	18,605	8,891	47.7	9,714	52.2

Source: West, "Beretning," p. 13; P. L. Oxholm, "Statistisk Tabelle" in *De Danske Vestindiske öers Tilstand* (1797); R/A, DVK; H. B. Dahlerup, "Skizzer fra et kort Besøg paa vore vestindiske Øer," *Nyt Archiv for Søvæsenet* 1 (1842):28-35; G. W. Alexander, "Om den moralske Forpligtelse," *Dansk Ugeskrift* 2 (76) (1843);376.

attended or not, but preferred to practice in town where he was better paid. The doctors moreover were of doubtful professional competence and highly motivated by considerations of gain, as was exemplified in their operation of their own pharmacies.[94] Apart from the introduction of smallpox vaccination in 1818, medical science made little contribution to arresting the decline of the slave population.[95] More important in explaining the decline was the inadequate housing of the slaves, and the poor quality of their food and clothing. Those slaves who had the compounded misfortune to be owned by poor whites, some of whom could scarcely feed themselves, were overworked that much more to meet creditors' demands and often faced by severe shortages of food.[96]

5

The Urban Milieu:
Slavery in Christiansted,
Frederiksted and Charlotte Amalie

URBAN SLAVERY WAS FIRMLY ESTABLISHED IN DENMARK'S West Indian colonies by the middle of the eighteenth century. In St. Croix, slaves accounted for more than 60 percent of the populations of Christiansted and Frederiksted in 1758, and at no time for the rest of the century did they comprise less than half of the population of either town (Tables 5.1 and 5.2). Between 1758 and 1803 the island's urban slave population grew from 1,454 to 3,879. This represented a relative decline from 65.2 to 56.0 percent of the total urban population. But that decline has to be seen in the context of a rapidly growing urban freedman population that increased, almost five-fold in the case of Christiansted and more than three-fold in the case of Frederiksted, between 1775 and 1800. This largely explains the relative decline of some 10 percent in Christiansted's slave population in that period. Frederiksted, on the other hand, with less rapid growth in its freedman population and an absolute decline in its white population from 1786, shows a slight relative increase of almost 2 percent.

Data for Charlotte Amalie, St. Thomas, in the eighteenth and nineteenth centuries indicate that there too the urban slave presence was substantial. In 1797 two-thirds of the town's population were slaves but despite absolute growth since 1789 there had been a relative decrease of some 6 percent (Table 5.3). This absolute growth had been offset by the near doubling of the white population and an increase by half as much again of the freedman population. Nevertheless in Charlotte Amalie as in Christiansted and Frederiksted, the urban slave population outnumbered whites and freedmen combined at the end of the eighteenth century.

By the 1830s, however, the situation was different. The progressive urbanization of St. Thomas was reflected by Charlotte Amalie accounting for more than three-quarters of the island's population in 1838. The relative

Table 5.1: *Growth of the Urban Population, Christiansted, St. Croix, 1758-1803*

Year	Slaves	Freedmen	Whites	Total Urban	Island Total Free & Slave	Urban as % of Island Total	Slaves as % of Urban Total
1758	1,422	–	753	2,175	13,497	16.1	65.3
1766	1,342	–	861	2,203	19,043	11.5	60.9
1775	2,364	290	944	3,598	15,873	13.9	65.7
1786	2,850	730	1,207	4,787	25,102	19.0	59.5
1789	2,977	797	1,055	4,829	25,377	19.0	61.6
1792	2,488	797	961	4,246	24,663	17.2	58.5
1797	2,998	973	1,085	5,056	28,803	17.5	59.2
1803	3,038	1,407	1,065	5,510	30,155	18.2	55.1

Sources: Oxholm, "Statistisk Tabelle" in *De Danske Vestindiske Oers Tilstand* (1797); Jens Vibæk, *Dansk Vestindien 1755-1848*, vol. 2 *Vore Gamle Tropekolonier* edited Johannes Brøndsted (1966), pp. 102-103; West, "Beretning," p. 13.

size of the urban slave population had declined pari passu. A corresponding development can be observed for St. Croix in the 1830s and in both islands the development is largely to be explained by the introduction of the free port system in 1782, the importance of Charlotte Amalie in that system and the opportunities offered by it to whites and freedmen.

The preponderance of slaves in these towns in the late eighteenth century was the direct result of their expansion as service ports for the prospering plantations and of their role as free ports and centers of distribution and exchange. As the white community responded to the commercial opportunities, it generated a demand for labor in service areas related to commerce, such as porters, stevedores and wainmen, in the production and distribution of goods to meet the everyday needs of the white community, in the provision of personal service. In all of these areas slave labor occupied a position of cardinal importance.

Domestics, Hucksters, Artisans

The provision of personal service heavily skewed the urban sex ratio in favor of female slaves. In 1797 there were only 83 males per 100 females in Christiansted and Frederiksted, and 68 in Charlotte Amalie (Table 5.4). This pattern was in marked contrast to that on the plantations. The balance in favor of female slaves did not alter over time in St. Croix (Table 5.5), and the same was probably true of St. Thomas.

The domestic staff of the Lutheran priest Ohm was not atypical. In 1792 it consisted of a cook, a washer, her two female children, and a seamstress.[1] It was female slaves such as these who cooked, baked, laundered, made and repaired clothes, waited at tables, attended their masters and mistresses in public, carried messages, fetched water from Christiansted's

Table 5.2: *Growth of the Urban Population, Frederiksted, St. Croix, 1758-1803*

Year	Slaves	Freedmen	Whites	Total Urban	Island Total Free & Slave	Urban as % of Island Total	Slaves as % of Urban Total
1758	32	–	20	52	13,497	0.3	61.5
1766	209	–	132	341	19,043	1.7	61.2
1775	405	71	236	712	25,873	2.7	56.8
1786	487	133	302	922	25,102	3.6	52.8
1789	597	156	298	1,06	25,377	4.1	56.2
1792	649	174	270	1,093*	24,663	4.4	59.3
1797	712	191	267	1,170	28,803	4.0	60.8
1803	841	249	237	1,327	30,155	4.4	63.3

Sources: As for Table 5.1.
* Vibæk, through an error in aggregating, gives this figure as 1,087.

well in the case of poorer whites, or from private wells in the case of the more well-to-do, and performed myriad other chores. If Ohm's slave retinue was more or less average size, there were others whose staffs were even larger. Carl Holten, adjutant to the Governor General, who arrived in 1799, recorded in his memoirs that he had a staff of fourteen including five children: "A mulatto servant; 2 black boys; a cook; an assistant cook; a washer; two chamber maids and an old biddy who supervised the women and looked after the children."[2]

Hans West, Rector of Christiansted's school for white children and, like Ohm and Holten, part of the town's Danish official classes, nevertheless disapproved heartily of the numbers and efficiency of these establishments. Compared to their European counterparts, he observed, what such slaves did was more pastime than work.[3] This comment, however, must be seen in the context of West's Negrophobic views. West complained further that so far as the size of the establishments went, the white women, particularly the creoles, were largely to blame. They were so possessed by vanity that they could not see an attractive female slave without wanting her in their entourage as a servant.[4] Many years later, Governor General Bentzon similarly criticized what he described as a form of idleness supporting a creole tendency to luxury, and called for a reduction in the number of household slaves.[5]

In 1792, Governor General Walterstorff, in attempting to explain the inflated numbers of household servants, pointed out that for one thing townsfolk tended to have a less spartan lifestyle than planters; that for another, the open doors and windows of West Indian houses invited more dust and more cleaning and polishing than houses in Europe; and that West Indian children were not confined to a nursery, as in Europe, where a single

Table 5.3: *Growth of the Urban Population, Charlotte Amalie, St. Thomas, 1789-1838*

Year	Slaves	Freedmen	Whites	Total Urban	Island Total Free & Slave	Urban as % of Island Total	Slaves as % of Urban Total
1789	1,527	260	398	2,085	5,266	39.5	73.2
1791	1,527	160	400	2,087	7,353	28.3	73.1
1797*	1,943	239	726	2,908	5,734	50.7	66.8
1831	2,894	8,177**	–	11,071	13,492	82.0	26.1
1838	2,093	5,024	1,770	8,887	11,433	77.7	23.5

Sources: P. L. Oxholm, *De Dansk Vestindiske öers Tilstand;* Hans West, "Beretning;" Hans West, *Bidrag til Beskrivelse over St. Croix* (1793), p. 329; J. P. Nissen, *Reminiscences of a 46 Years' Residence in the Island of St. Thomas in the West Indies* (1838).

* I have taken Oxholm's figures for "house negroes" to refer to those in Charlotte Amalie, on the assumption that since he does not give separate figures for house slaves among his figures for plantation slaves in St. Thomas or St. Croix, but confines the term "house negro" to Christiansted and Frederiksted, his "house negro" was an urban slave.

** This figure includes the total for whites as well.

servant could oversee them. In explaining the practice, Walterstorff was not attempting its justification. Like West and Bentzon, he identified vanity as an operative factor among several families in Christiansted, but added that it had also become hallowed practice to have a particularly large retinue of servants, whose numbers were increased over time by reproduction. In one decade, he claimed, the household slave staff could double its number by natural increase; and no master in Walterstorff's view would sell the children of slaves who had been in his service for some time. There was also the factor of over-specialization of functions, whereby a cook could be used to do nothing else but cooking. The end result was that one became surrounded by "a large army of useless persons who cost more than a little to feed and clothe."[6]

Domestics represented but a fraction of the wide range of occupational skills found in the towns. Slaves also made important contributions to urban life and economic activity through the production of goods and services and their distribution, and the generation of income for white townsfolk. Nowhere was this more applicable than in the itinerant retail trade, an important generator of income. White townsfolk, poor and better-off alike, had their slaves take to the streets hawking a variety of goods. These slaves, mostly women, armed with their passes and trays on their heads, pictures of grace if West is to be believed,[7] were a constant feature of the landscape in town and country. The stock in trade consisted of such

Table 5.4: *Sex of Urban and Rural Slaves, St. Croix and St. Thomas, 1797*

Location	Males	Females	Males per 100 Females
St. Croix Rural	11,670	10,036	116.3
Christiansted	1,361	1,637	83.1
Frederiksted	323	389	83.0
St. Thomas Rural	1,472	1,354	108.7
Charlotte Amalie	791	1,152	68.7

Source: Oxholm, *De Danske Vestindiske öers Tilstand.*

items as bread, butter, coffee beans, fruit, meat, vegetables, candles, cushions and haberdashery notions. Plying their trade on behalf of their masters and mistresses, they were the lifeline of an internal marketing system, complementing the Sunday market of the country slaves. Huckstering was an ideal outlet for stolen goods, but neither the concern of the Burgher Council at Christiansted nor the police as late as 1812, seemed to have made any appreciable difference to the use of higglers as "fences."[8]

Hucksters were particularly important as sources of income for poor whites. The same was true for freedmen, who by 1802 owned an estimated 30 percent of the slaves in Charlotte Amalie.[9] In Christiansted in 1792 most slaveowning households held a maximum of four slaves (Table 5.6). The same was true for Frederiksted. If it is assumed that the ownership of a large number of slaves was a measure of substance in eighteenth century Christiansted and Frederiksted, it would be reasonable to conclude from the data in Table 5.6 that the great majority of households in those two towns were peopled by the less well to do. This has important implications for the quality of shelter and food provided by such households, and raises doubts of the authenticity of West's claim that each slave in Christiansted was comfortably housed and adequately fed.[10]

In relation to the pattern observed in Table 5.6, the comment of the Burgher Council of St. Croix in 1792 is very instructive. Many persons, it informed the Danish West Indian government, had no other property than a few slaves and nothing to live on apart from what these slaves brought in. Such persons were reduced to the necessity of sending out their slaves to earn whatever they could to ensure their support.[11] The Danish West Indian government in turn commented that "It should be noted that the apparent superfluity of house slaves can in many instances be justified having regard to the fact that such slaves are their owners' sole means of support, either as craftsmen or help hired out to others."[12]

Skilled craftsmen, particularly carpenters, and other skilled slaves like seamen, were as important as itinerant vendors as "sole means of support" for some of the towns' whites and freedmen. Hired out, such slaves could

Table 5.5: *Urban Slaves by Sex, St. Croix, 1831-1839*

Year	Females	Males	Total Urban Slaves	Urban Total Free & Slaves*	Island Total Free & Slaves	Urban as % of Island Total	Slaves as % of Urban Total	Female % of Urban Slaves
1831	1,613	1,103	2,677	7,905**	25,208	31.3	33.9	59.4
1835	1,463	911	2,374	8,154	25,087	32.5	29.1	61.6
1839	1,196	713	1,909	7,322	23,826	30.7	26.1	62.7

Source: G. W. Alexander, "Om den moralske Forpligtelse," *Dansk Ugeskrift* 2 (76) (1843): 374-96.

* These totals are probably inflated as Alexander does not separate country whites from town whites. The urban free total is thus probably inflated by 300.

** Alexander gives a figure of 1,589 for the freedman and white population in 1832. This was a transposition of the two initial digits. His figure would be less than the known total of the free urban population of 2,472 in 1803 (Table 5.1). The figure of 5,189 used in this calculation accords with what is known of the growth of the freedman and white populations in St. Croix at the end of the 1820s.

bring in the not inconsiderable sums of $2-3 per week at the start of the nineteenth century.[13] In the dry docks carpenters were always in demand, and in the boats which put into port, slaves on hire as crew were indispensable.[14] In Charlotte Amalie in particular, this was an important consideration as more and more after 1782 it became the free port crossroads of the Caribbean.

The range of artisan skills commanded by slaves in the towns covered an impressive spectrum. A random sample will suffice. J. B. Moreton, a Christiansted butcher, claimed in 1808 to have one slave "the most active butcher in the West Indies" and another a "nimble segar-maker" capable of rolling up to 100 per day.[15] To such well promoted individuals and skills, one can add others; silversmiths like Creole Jimmy; saddlers like Jasper; Major de Nully's Osmond, who was a tailor; masons such as Nathaniel; jockeys like John Jones, alias Anguilla Johnny; slaves who combined more than one skill like Benjamin who "tripled" as barber, hairdresser and fiddler; Lewis, who was both tailor and barber; Mulatto, carpenter as well as wheelwright; and Commodore Morgenstern's Cuffy who was a tailor and also played the violin.[16] Even the Negrophobic West was forced to the grudging admission that there were no artisan skills which slaves found difficulty in acquiring, and the range of skills seems to have been matched by excellence in execution. West had nothing but the highest praise for the women's needlework and his comments on the men bordered on the rapturous: "Some of them acquire artisan skills which they bring to such a point of refinement, that I would be prepared to wager that no fully accomplished journeyman in any of Copenhagen's many famous guilds

Table 5.6: *Distribution of Slaves by Size of Households, in Christiansted and Frederiksted, 1792*

Town	Slaves per Household	No. of Households	Estimated No. of Slaves*	% of Households	% of Slaves
Christiansted	1-4	238	476	59.5	19.6
	5-9	93	651	23.2	26.8
	10-14	30	360	7.5	14.8
	15-19	18	306	4.5	12.6
	20+	21	630	5.2	26.0
	Total	400	2,423	99.9	99.8
Frederiksted	1-4	53	106	49.0	15.7
	5-9	33	231	30.5	34.2
	10-14	15	180	13.8	26.6
	15-19	4	68	3.7	10.0
	20+	3	90	2.7	13.3
	Total	108	675	99.7	99.9

Source: R/A, VJ, 1793, no. 911.
* Estimated number of slaves derived from the assumed mean of each size-group: 2, 7, 12, 17 and 30.

could stitch a pair of shoes, a garment or a button hole with the fit and finesse of a creole black."[17] The cash incomes generated by these slaves on their masters' behalf was estimated in 1784 at about 100,000 Rigsdaler,[18] a not inconsiderable sum.

Conditions of Life

Differences in the occupational and ownership structure of slave society in town and country were reflected strongly in the material conditions of life of the slaves. In some respects the urban slaves had a clear advantage. Housing was a case in point. It has been shown that in the slave cantonments on the plantations the quality of housing was notoriously indifferent throughout the eighteenth and early nineteenth centuries until it became the subject of ameliorative reform by Governor General von Scholten.[19] There is little or no data on housing for urban slaves. Bearing in mind, however, the extent of ownership by freedmen and poor whites, a substantial proportion of the towns' slaves could not have enjoyed housing considerably superior to the plantation quarters. Notwithstanding, one would hazard the guess that most urban slaves were assured of rain-proof and draught-free accommodation. In relation to food, the data are equally sketchy. West's claim of universal plenty in Christiansted is not to be treated with seriousness. But the urban setting would have provided the possibility, at least, of more frequent access to a wider variety of nourishing food than was possible on the plantation. There was a daily market in the towns on weekdays, conducted by the town slaves themselves, and slaves with purchasing power to take advantage of this facility.[20]

What probably holds true for housing and food can be demonstrated with more certainty for clothing. For slaves resident in the towns, contact with white society was more sustained, intimate and frequent than was the case on the estates. Indeed, Oxholm's use of the term, "house negro" to apply exclusively to urban slaves, was perhaps influenced by that consideration. In the circumstances, there was an almost automatic assumption on the part of white society that slaves in their households should wear clothes of better quality than field slaves, an assumption for which the reported vanity of white creole women would have served as reinforcement. It was this assumption which informed Schimmelmann's sumptuary ordinance which dealt with household slaves and artisans. Plantation field slaves were allowed coarse cotton or linen for daily use and, as a concession for Sundays and public holidays, cast-offs of little value. On the other hand, household slaves and artisans were permitted shoes, coarse stockings and items of cheap jewelry in addition to coarse cotton for daily use, and on Sundays clothes of better quality cotton or linen. Schimmelmann added that in any case, slaves in personal service could use whatever livery their owners provided, as well as cast-offs of whatever description. He pointedly concluded with the hope that no owner, in clothing household slaves, would overstep those boundaries defined by the slaves' station and status nor encourage them in extravagance, even if the latter of their own resources could buy clothing more costly than the ordinance permitted.[21]

There were other aspects in which the constraining regimen of the plantation by its absence in the towns, favored the urban slave. As West cryptically observed, no household slave could be made to do anything he or she had set his or her face against. How far this was true is difficult to determine. However, both West and Holten independently remarked that urban house slaves were not normally sold by public auction except when the owner's estate came under the jurisdiction of the probate court. According to Holten, "The usual practice when a house slave is to be sold is to give him a ticket which says he is to be sold and at what price. He then goes about looking for another owner and if he is known to be a good-natured sort, he can count on finding a good master or mistress."[22]

What this implies is that until von Scholten's reforms of the 1830s which abolished the sale of slaves by public auction as inhuman and degrading, it was the exception for urban slaves to be sold publicly. The convention of allowing urban slaves to seek new masters can be substantiated by two examples. When 14 year old Jane, described as the mustee and "somewhat freckled" child of Rachel Malcolm, ran away from 15 Company Street, Christiansted, in August 1817, her owner indicated that should she come home voluntarily "she shall have the choice of an owner."[23] There was also

Anthony Houseman who belonged to a Charlotte Amalie baker; at the time Houseman ran away in May 1821 he had a permit to seek a new owner.[24]

Such comparatively favorable conditions relating to food, shelter, clothing and relationships with authority would suggest a lower mortality rate for urban than for plantation slaves. Oxholm, in the debate on Abolition in 1792, made the explicit claim that slaves in the urban milieu were materially better off than their rural counterparts. In support of that position, he produced a rare but important statistic: the death rate among slaves in Christiansted during the influenza epidemic of 1789 was 1:77, while the mean for the rest of the island exclusive of Frederiksted was 1:16. Frederiksted registered a death rate of 1:45, but this poor showing by the West End was explained, in Oxholm's view, by the presence of "an evil smelling lagoon behind Fredericksted town."[25] Such data support the view that the material conditions of life of urban slaves were in general better than those of their rural counterparts.

Urban-Rural Interaction

Town and country did not however constitute a sharply defined dichotomy. Plantation slaves made important contributions to the urban economies and in some cases formed part of the towns' populations even though they belonged to contiguous estates. For example, the proximity of La Grande Princesse to Christiansted and of La Grange to Frederiksted made these plantations peculiarly well placed to supply skills and services to the towns. The opportunities in Frederiksted were of lesser magnitude than those in Christiansted and related largely to the presence of the fort there. In 1759, only three of La Grange's work force of 104 were hired out in the town, all at the fort; a water carrier, a barber and a baker.[26] For La Grande Princesse the attractions of Christiansted were more compelling. The estate's inventory for 1759 shows the importance qualitatively and quantitatively of the support services it provided for the town. Seven men of a total work force of 193 were engaged in the towns: two permanently in Christiansted; four on a daily basis and one permanently in Frederiksted. In addition there were fourteen boys who went on a daily basis to provide fodder for the governor general's stables. Apart from supplying fodder the other services included that of a stable boy, an apprentice mason and a drummer with the garrison in Frederiksted.

This 1759 inventory also illustrates the bias in favor of females for service in the towns, and the high degree to which white officialdom made use of their services. In 1759 La Grande Princesse had a total of 103 women and girls, nineteen of whom were employed in some capacity in Christiansted; seven on a daily basis and twelve permanently. Their occupations ranged from fodder-carrier, to baker, to cook and washer, and they were employed variously at the governor general's, the fort, the priest's, the police prefecture, the Regimental Quarter Master's. Of the estate's overall workforce of 194 in 1759, a total of 42 or some 22.8 percent were employed in activities related to the urban milieu. The inventory list, if nothing else, conveys the important symbiotic relationship which bound the estate to Christiansted.[27]

In addition there were the country slaves who lived and worked on plantations but maintained continuous contact with the towns. The towns were provisioned largely through the slave Sunday market.[28] Apart from this major activity, it was common practice for country slaves, especially those from the nearby estates, to come to town every evening, selling fodder in the form of grass, corn stalks and leaves for the towns' horses, and firewood. Without this service, said von Roepstorff in the 1780s, the towns would have been unable to function effectively.[29]

The marketing of grass and firewood was responsible for a significant cash flow among the country slaves who supplied the towns. The cash income earned by these slaves was about one-half of the income generated by urban artisans for their owners in St. Croix in the late eighteenth century. West attempted to measure this cash flow in the early 1790s. On the basis of an estimate of 250 horses for Christiansted and 50 for Frederiksted, each of which cost 24 skillings per day for fodder, West calculated that the gross annual intake was 22,813 Rigsdaler from Christiansted and 4,562 Rigsdaler from Frederiksted, or a total of 27,375 Rigsdaler from both towns.[30] The income from the sale of firewood was of a similar order of magnitude. West calculated that providing the 664 houses in Christiansted with firewood at 8 skillings per day represented a yearly expenditure of 20,141 Rigsdaler. In the case of Frederiksted with 190 houses, the yearly cost was calculated at 5,972 Rigsdaler, making a total for both towns of 26,113 Rigsdaler.[31] The sale of fodder and firewood therefore grossed 53,488 Rigsdaler annually. Slaves in this kind of contact with the urban milieu, were collectively earning incomes that were probably the near equivalent of the cost of maintaining the Danish West Indian garrison, estimated in 1826 at 68,000 Rigsdaler.[32]

The income derived from marketing activity and earned by urban artisans working on their own account, gave such slaves independent purchasing power. This in turn enabled them to establish bases of interaction with urban whites: patronage of the punch and beer houses and grog shops. Mutual interest ensured a degree of collusion between slaves and spirit retailers in the towns, to defeat the laws or ordinances governing the sale of alcohol. The sale of spirits was not permitted on the plantations, but in the towns no such prohibition applied. Access to the "værtshus" or tavern was one of the small areas of freedom which urban slaves and their country counterparts could enjoy. Despite the fact that drunkenness was not a widespread phenomenon in the islands, at least not in the nineteenth century,[33] the conditions of spirit sales to slaves were rigidly prescribed for reasons of public order: none on Sundays or feast and fast days of the Church, or after sundown drum. By and large, however, publicans seem to have treated the stipulations none too seriously.[34] Further infractions are suggested by Governor General Clausen's proclamation in 1766 which emphasized that slaves were to be sent on their way after buying one drink, and in any event were to be served outside the tavern.[35]

The publicans for their part, had every interest in encouraging loiterers and in offering service to their slave clientele inside their establishments. But the værtshus was also identified by white officialdom in the later eighteenth century as the center of a traffic in stolen goods. The law deemed the reception and handling of stolen goods as criminal as the theft itself.[36] The goods stolen were usually of moderate value and readily vendable in the comparative privacy of the taverns. Sometimes too, they were of greater bulk than the latter but of no less value: items such as fence posts and lumber for carriage wheels, or even the traditional staples, rum, sugar and cotton.[37] Bulk does not appear to have been any obstacle to the disposal of stolen goods. The Burgher Council of St. Croix, expressing great alarm at the traffic in 1787, pointed to the channel of procurement of the staples and a method of disposal that implicated the towns' free population, white as well as non-white:

> Particularly during crop time, itinerant Negro hucksters betake themselves to the estates, encouraging the slaves there to theft. They themselves offer a pittance in exchange for what rum, sugar or cotton they can get, and finally consign them to good-for-nothing whites and freedmen in the towns. Greater quantities can be disposed of in this way and in complete security.[38]

Communal Interaction

This urban demi-monde of slaves, "good-for-nothing whites and freedmen" shared, as marginal groups, a community of interest expressed in a variety of ways, all of which were in violation of the law. In St. Croix, it appears that whilst the 1766 ordinance to serve slaves outside the grog shops was being observed in the 1780s, an earlier ordinance prohibiting sale on Sundays was being flagrantly ignored. The Burgher Council noted that sales in the back of premises on Sundays and holidays gave rise to gambling with cards and dice, which the owners of such premises found it advantageous to encourage and permit.[39]

Colbiørnsen, a judge in the colonial service, also expressed unease about the operation of the grog shops: the rum puncheons were located inside the shops and could easily be set alight by an overturned candle, if they remained open after sunset. Such indeed had been the origin of one Christiansted fire. More importantly, however, Colbiørnsen independently confirmed the Burgher Council's observation about gambling and the comparative security of the backyards for this purpose. He also reinforced the view that they constituted ideal locations for the disposal of illegal merchandise.[40] The two activities were not of course unconnected, or as Governor General Clausen remarked in 1774, gambling was the father of "theft, swindles and roguery."[41] Whites in this urban demi-monde were not mere spectators at these sessions of gambling and drinking. As early as

1741, an ordinance forbade whites to sit and drink or gamble with slaves. The severity of the punishment, which was eight days imprisonment on bread and water, is indicative of the seriousness with which the offense was viewed.[42]

The other important basis of communal interaction was undoubtedly the dance. Clausen's ordinance of 1774 prohibited whites from attending any dances at which slaves were present, or to drink and dance with them, on pain of a fine of 100 Rigsdaler or imprisonment on bread and water for fourteen days.[43] The dances to which whites ventured for enjoyment rather than as monitors of law and order were not, however, exclusively slave dances. They were as likely to be revels put on by freedmen at which slaves were consistent but illegal participants. Persistent attempts were made to prevent this form of social intercourse between freedmen and urban slaves. Such attempts were aimed at disrupting important links in the stolen goods trade, and at preventing, as was tried in the cities of the United States South, the forging of common links between slaves and freedmen. On neither of these counts did official policy enjoy noteworthy success. It was difficult to legislate against the natural affinities of kin and, where these did not exist, of ethnic affiliation and marginality. This helps to explain also the enthusiasm with which the freedmen of the towns patronized the frequent tea and coffee party treats that town slaves held in the later eighteenth century.[44]

The communal interaction of urban slaves and freedmen is to be seen not merely as pleasurable inter-ethnic social commerce. In an important sense it existed also as a defense against the whites' hegemonic power; in another sense, as an offensive instrument aimed at containing that power's effectiveness or, under proper auspices, of defeating it. It is of interest that both contemporary literary and archival sources carry the conviction that the traffic in stolen goods was an important point of contact between slave and urban freedman. West, for example, excoriated Christiansted's Free Gut – the freedmen's ghetto – not only as a den of carnal iniquity but also as a storehouse of every conceivable stolen good.[45]

The Burgher Council of St. Croix, as mentioned earlier, was convinced of such collusion in illegal trafficking. On another occasion it described with grave disquiet "the Free Negroes' connection and too great familiarity" with slaves, hinting darkly that no good would come of it.[46] Governor de Malleville, writing from St. Thomas in the 1780s, was far more explicit. He deplored equally the trade in stolen goods and the games of chance in which slaves became involved with freedmen. His concerns were colored by the austere morality of the good Moravian convert that he was. However, he was as determined to undermine the forging of any sense of community through "too great familiarity." Such a determination, shared by many of his contemporaries, was a form of insurance against the recurrence of the St. John uprising of 1733 and, after 1791, prophylaxis against infection from St. Domingue. In St. Thomas, de Malleville had recorded instances where "the close connections" between slaves and freedmen in Charlotte Amalie had resulted in slaves receiving assistance by gift or loan to obtain freedom.[47] For him this was no matter for celebration, praying as he frequently did for a reduction in the numbers of freedmen whom he perceived more as "a burden and a plague than an advantage." What was worse, he asserted, was that the freedmen in the town were a source of encouragement for marronage, as they were known to provide refuge for slaves on the run.[48]

Some contemporary whites, then, were convinced that urban slaves found among the freedmen of the towns companions in crime and spiritual succor. This is not to say, however, that the relationship between urban non-whites, free and unfree, was void of tension, contradiction and conflict. Certainly slaves were no less prone to run away from freedmen owners.[49] Contemporary whites would no doubt have explained such slaves' escape by attributing to freedmen as slave owners, a capacity for cruelty which was a form of over-compensation for their lowliness in the societal scale. Writing about the situation in Jamaica, Bryan Edwards commented quite unfavorably on the treatment freedmen meted out to the slaves they owned.[50] An anonymous memorialist in the Danish West Indies at the beginning of the nineteenth century, believed that the worst tyrants over their slaves were not only vain creole white women – when not in their overindulgent mood – and Jews, but also the "emancipated colored." This memorialist claimed that such owners seldom handed over their slaves to the public authorities for punishment, preferring the limitless correction which domestic privacy permitted. It was not uncommon, he observed, to have several hundred lashes administered with a riding crop. Examples were supposed to abound of such owners taking it upon themselves to punish the weak and pregnant when the police had refused.[51] And yet, there are indications of charity and humanity to belie the lurid tales of sadism portrayed above. In St. Thomas in 1822, for example, two freedwomen Nancy Westphall and Petronella Möller secreted their slaves to avoid public punishment for offenses unspecified.[52]

In the final analysis, the relationship between urban slaves and freedmen appears to have been one of some ambivalence. On the one hand, there are indications of co-operation; in the traffic in stolen goods, the use of the Guts as havens for runaways, in assistance to achieve manumission, in protection from the law. On the other hand, there is evidence of marronage from freedmen and suggestions of extreme cruelty on their part. The ambiguities were further reinforced by the developments of the early nineteenth century which stratified freedmen on the basis of wealth, social standing and freeborn or manumitted status.[53] Urban slaves were not unaffected by these developments, for they provided the basis of conflict between the two groups. Governor General Bentzon submitted in 1818 a detailed memorandum to the Danish government in which he gave a plausible explanation of the grounds for conflict, or its absence, between slaves and freedmen in the towns. It was his view that the "lower classes" of freedmen, those manumitted rather than freeborn, formed a "transitional class" and regarded slaves with a suspicion and deep hatred which was reciprocated. Many a worthy and intelligent bondsman, he observed, worked for the most contemptible freedman, and the slaves themselves had taken notice that the fact of being in their ownership and employ was a guarantee of the worst treatment. The slaves' negative perception of such owners had been expressed in several uncomplimentary proverbs of which he was aware.[54]

Urban slaves and the poorer freedmen were in daily contact and, given the undercurrent of tension, it was little wonder that they were in perpetual collision and conflict. Bentzon noted that whilst the slaves' relationship with the poorer freedmen was marked by uneasiness, the same could not be said of their relationship with freeborn and better off freedmen. He suggested that the urban bondsman regarded light complexioned freedmen with favor because the latter approached the whites in phenotype.[55] But in as much as he also admitted that even noticeably black freedmen who were freeborn were also held in high regard by town slaves, it would appear that the respect was not exclusively a function of color, nor necessarily mediated by it.

As the freedman population in the towns expanded, it appears, the less privileged among them came in direct competition with urban slaves for economic opportunity. That was the circumstance which kept the town slave and the more privileged freedman apart, and explains Bentzon's remark that "the opportunities for confrontation which arise from too close association do not exist with this class [of freedmen], who keep a marked degree of distance between themselves and slaves." There is no direct evidence of economic competition in the towns between slaves and freedmen, but it must be assumed, from the range of occupation skills which the former possessed, that those skills coincided at many points with those listed for the latter by contemporary authors such as West.[56] There is evidence of competition between slave artisans and whites of similar skills.[57] Poorer freedmen, for their part, might have had neither enough means nor sufficient self-confidence and literary skills to air grievances of this kind for public consumption and posterity.

Social Control

As in Brazil and the American South,[58] urban slavery in the Danish West Indies posed the problem of enforcing white authority in circumstances where the institution of servitude was its most flexible. That being the case, the presumption of the slave's potential criminality was even greater in the towns than in the plantation countryside. The continuing concern with the maintenance of public order in the towns is well illustrated in the case of Charlotte Amalie in the later decades of the eighteenth century. As the town grew in economic importance as a result of the free port system, there was an increasing demand for labor associated with the port and warehouses. This was an area of occupation for those slaves whose owners depended on their hireage for livelihood. But it was clear from contemporary comment that the supply was sometimes in excess of demand. De Malleville and Lillienschiold, the administrators of St. Thomas, commented in 1792 that it was as difficult in the West Indies to keep slaves with no fixed employment out of the towns, as it was to keep "Strand Cadetter" or Shore Cadets out of Copenhagen.[59] Work in the West Indian customs houses where porters were mostly engaged was seasonal; in between times they tended to congregate on the street. This was a source of annoyance and alarm to officialdom. De Malleville and Lillienschiold, for example, thought that their numbers should be controlled, that they should be made to carry passes and assemble for hire only in the customs house.[60]

Walterstorff, the governor general at the time, was similarly concerned about the porters as a potential public nuisance. Their threat to public order was made all the worse in his mind by an indolent and inefficient constabulary.[61] The Burgher Council of St. Croix, with whom he consulted, was as apprehensive, although they hesitated to prescribe a remedy that was worse than the disease. The Council recognized that many white townsfolk had no other property, no other source of income than the few slaves and the cash which these brought in. They recognized further that the convenience of having porters on hand for hire came at a price: runaway slaves from the country districts often passed themselves off in town as porters. The only solution the Burgher Council envisaged was the slave porters should have a readily distinguishable badge – like the huckster's ticket – with their owner's name on it; that, as a general principle, all slaves hiring themselves out in town should have a ticket of authorization and that stricter police measures should be taken against urban vagrancy.[62]

The problem of accommodating slavery to the environment of the towns, and the effect of urban slavery on the laws affecting servitude, were graphically illustrated by the case of Jochum and Sam.[63] That case elicited a proclamation from Governor General Schimmelmann, in the following year, stating that like events were in the future to be investigated to establish whether the assault was justifiable, using as a criterion the necessity to save a master's life or property. If proven otherwise, the slave would be suitably punished.[64] The proclamation, however, failed to differentiate between town and country. It prescribed the same law for both, on the assumption presumably that the town's problem of public order was larger than the countryside's and that the lesser would be comprehended by the greater. But writing from St. Thomas two years after Schimmelmann's ordinance, de Malleville was strongly in favor of differentiating the contexts. In the country parts the slave's help was virtually an unavoidable necessity. The situation in Charlotte Amalie, he argued, was entirely different. It was very seldom the case that in an emergency in that town one could not do without the assistance of slaves since there were always whites about.[65]

In recognizing that the different circumstances of town and country called for different prescriptions, de Malleville was responding, in a way that Schimmelmann was not, to the legal tradition of half a century. As early as 1733 the use of iron-tipped sticks or knives as sidearms in Charlotte Amalie had been forbidden, and the presence of plantation slaves in town after sundown prohibited.[66] The importance of the curfew generally and its specific application to dances was emphasized in ordinances in 1741, 1765 and 1774.[67] In a series of ordinances proclaimed between 1756 and 1759 Governor General von Pröck required patterns of public behavior that were to be at once deferential and free from suspicion; no galloping in the streets; no gambling on pavements; no throwing of firecrackers during the celebrations of Christmas or the New Year.[68] In St. Thomas in the 1760s, de Gunthelberg made it an offense for slaves to ride horses through the town when they were to be watered. Nor was he overjoyed at the scant respect which slaves showed for police patrols, nor at the loud noises and derisive laughter which sometimes characterized their behavior on the streets.[69] Indeed, any occasion on which slaves assembled in numbers in the towns was a source of misgiving whether it involved casual loitering or organized activities like dances, funerals or tea and coffee party treats.[70]

Crime and Punishment

The laws specific to the urban slave merely delineate prescribed areas of unacceptable conduct without any helpful indication of frequency. In the case of grand marronage, however, the abundant evidence provided by contemporary newspaper advertisements makes it possible to study in detail its frequency and persistence over time, and the way in which the flexible milieu of the towns facilitated running away from or to them. The insularity and commercial structure of the Danish West Indian colonies meant that grand marronage was overwhelmingly maritime marronage, a movement from one urban center to another, and this process is analyzed in chapter 7. A wider range of urban slave offenses can be illustrated from the extant police journals, available for Christiansted and Frederiksted for the five years of the British occupation 1802-1807. These journals record a total of 1,130 slave violations in the two towns, and shed important light on the urban slaves' response to the elaborate efforts to secure their compliance with certain patterns of conduct.[71]

Of the total number of incidents colony-wide, more than twice as many had been committed by men as by women, and the proportion was similar in each town. Men were apprehended for 730 of the 1,068 incidents in Christiansted and 42 of the 62 in Frederiksted (Table 5.7). Despite their preponderance, women were therefore greatly under-represented in the statistics of urban "crime" in early nineteenth century St. Croix. This prompts the conclusion that they were more reconciled to their status. On the other hand, however, it may well be that the nature of their employment, in which domestic service figured very prominently, kept many of them off the streets in the day and reduced the possibility of breaches of the law. But women were responsible for 42 percent of 267 curfew

Table 5.7: *Violations of the Slave Law: Christiansted and Frederiksted, 1802-1807*

Violation	Christiansted		Frederiksted		Total	
	Male	Female	Male	Female	Male	Female
Drunk & Disorderly Behavior	96	24	8	2	104	26
Fights	101	45	1	5	102	50
Curfew/Pass Violations	149	108	7	3	156	111
Insults / Assaults	16	10	2	1	18	11
Theft	94	26	9	4	103	30
Gambling	9	–	–	–	9	–
Sugar Sales	10	19	–	–	10	19
Torches etc.	1	6	2	–	3	6
Galloping	26	–	–	–	26	–
Weapons/Arson	2	–	2	2	4	2
Maroon	220	91	7	3	227	94
Miscellaneous	6	9	4	–	10	9
Total	730	338	42	20	772	358
Total Male & Female	1,068		62		1,130	

Source: Calculated from N/A, RG 55, Boxes 485-487: Udskrift af Christiansteds Jurisdictions Politi Journaler; ibid., 496: Udskrift af Frederiksteds Jurisdictions Politi Journaler.

violations reported. Once the towns were in darkness, slave women showed that they were only a little less prone than the men to be abroad "without pass, lantern or lawful errand."

There was one activity in which women were altogether unrepresented and for which they were consequently never arrested. No women were grooms or stable boys as these were gender specific occupations. None of the 26 slaves apprehended for hard riding through the streets of Christiansted was therefore a woman. Similarly, there were no women gamblers, at least not on the streets. All the slaves caught at dice or card games were males. On the other hand twice as many women as men were arrested for the dangerous use of fire, particularly of open torches. In part this reflects their dominance of market vending at the daily weekday markets in the towns, where after dark and before the curfew they sometimes hawked their wares by torch light instead of the safer lantern. A comparable proportion of arrests for "economic crimes" such as the sale of sugar, sugar cane and cotton is also explained by the female domination of the huckstering trades.

Twice as many men as women were involved in fights on the streets, at the provision market or fish market. "Insulting behavior," impertinence towards or physical assault on whites, the police or freedmen was again twice as prevalent among male slaves.[72] Eighty percent of the 130 slaves drawn before the courts for drunken and disorderly behavior were males. Urban slave women were frequently disorderly, but there were no incidents of women slaves apprehended for drunkenness. The consumption of alcohol in quantity therefore does not seem to have been a preferred diversion of urban slave women. This is further borne out by the fact that no female slave was ever taken up for illegal presence in a grog shop or punch house. In whatever ways women sought diversion or companionship in the towns, the established convention appears to have put public houses out of bounds. That was exclusively a male world.

Where disorderly conduct involved stone throwing, however, male slaves did not have it all to themselves. Of the eight incidents reported for Christiansted in 1806, women were responsible for two.[73] Most of the incidents of stone-throwing concerned altercations with other slaves. On one occasion the object of the stoning was a shop owned by a Jewish merchant. Mekal, the slave responsible, was the property of free mulatto Catherine Oxholm.[74] Whether the incident has significance as an index of anti-semitism on the part of the slave himself or as surrogate for his owner would be difficult to tell. But covert anti-semitism was not unknown in contemporary St. Croix.[75] Nor was lampooning of whites by slaves. Here urban slave women made up in inventiveness and creativity what they might have lacked in predilection for fisticuffs or inclination for liquor. In August 1806, Juliana, the property of free mulatto Susanna Campbell was detained for singing "pasquiller" on the streets and received 30 lashes on the same day.[76] On Christmas day that year, Hanna, a mulatto slave owned by a white man, was arrested with two freedwomen, Elisa Messer and Fillis, for singing satirical songs. She received 50 lashes.[77]

The comparative anonymity of the towns conduced to both petit and grand marronage on a scale which the countryside of St. Croix did not make possible. Fully 28 percent of the arrests recorded in the police journals were of slaves on the run (Table 5.7). The majority by far, some 71 percent, were men. As elsewhere, male slaves were more likely candidates for running away, irrespective of the sex ratio or stage of creolization of the workforce.[78] As the arrest records do not consistently specify which slaves taken up as runaway belonged to the towns or to rural estates, it has not been possible to quantify urban marronage with precision. However, the rich possibilities of the towns for escape from servitude are well illustrated by three arrests in Christiansted in 1807. John was removed from an American sailing vessel in February 1807 since he had no pass to work as a seaman.[79] Even those urban slave seamen who were authorized to work on sailing vessels often used this access to a wider world to desert. This therefore made John's intentions legitimately suspect. The second instructive incident involved Susanna, owned by Christiansted's printer Hennings. Susanna had been at large for four months when she was taken up in February 1807.[80] Her absence was insignificant compared with Carty's Nancy. At her arrest in August 1807 by the Christiansted police Nancy explained that Carty had long since been dead and that she had been out for 15 to 16 years.[81]

Male dominance of the crime statistics is also demonstrated by the arrests for theft. Of the 133 arrests for larceny 77 percent were attributed to male slaves. This constitutes an even higher percentage than males as a proportion of reported incidents of marronage. Viewed in their totality, however, as activity involving both sexes, these incidents of larceny point in another significant direction. Marronage, fights and curfew violations lead the tables in the statistics. But the first did not always clearly involve slaves of identifiable urban provenance; the second and third no infraction of property rights. Thus although larceny and attempted larceny rank only fourth in the statistics on urban slave crime, they perhaps represented one of the most important categories of deviance. Short of being attacked by a slave, which did not happen often, white townsfolk were most put upon by the loss of personal property, which happened with frequency. The absence of a petit maron was inconvenient but the probability of recovery was high. The loss of effects or goods, some of them valuable, that could vanish in the demi-monde of slaves, freedmen and poorer whites, was more likely to be permanent; poultry, clothing, cooking utensils, saddles and harnesses, watches and gold coins were readily saleable.

The most valuable good by far, and the raison d'être of the plantation economy was sugar. By its theft from time to time the slaves, consciously or unconsciously, displayed a proper sense of irony; for they were engaged in the re-appropriation of surplus value which they themselves had produced. Sugar stealing was not an aberration taken lightly by the authorities, and it was the sort of activity therefore that only the boldest slave would contemplate. One such was Mads, attached to the fort in Christiansted and the property of the crown. There are seven entries in the journals on this slave beginning with Boxing Day 1805, when he ran away for a third time. In between, Mads had been arrested and punished for drunken and disorderly behavior, as well as for creating a disturbance in the market. Mads, not exactly a contented slave, also displayed leadership potential and an awareness of the importance of cooperation in probing the defenses of urban slavery. He and two other crown slaves, Carolina and Peter, were caught stealing sugar from a hogshead on the wharf on 19 November 1806. It is perhaps worth recording that on 23 April 1807, the day after Mads had run away for the seventh time, Christiansted's Chief of Police Mouritzen was in search of persons "of that Plot who (sic) breaks open the sugar hogsheads on the wharf."[82]

For their caper on the wharf, Mads and Carolina each received 100 lashes, Peter 60. The whip was the instrument of correction most commonly in use in early nineteenth century St. Croix. It symbolized in equal measures the "discipline, deterrence and degradation" so dear to the ante-bellum South.[83] It emphasized too in the most literally painful way white authority and black subordination. The quantum of lashes was a measure of the seriousness of the offense. The punishments of Mads and Carolina were towards the upper end of the continuum; at the other, 25 lashes for a straightforward curfew violation were not uncommon.[84] If, however, the violation was compounded by misleading information about address or ownership, the offense could attract as much as 75 lashes.[85] Rude remarks to the police were treated as a major offense and were punishable by up to 100 strokes.[86] Interestingly enough, physical assaults on whites were no longer punished as capital offenses in the early nineteenth century.[87] Such acts, uncommon enough, attracted no more than 100 lashes, although not less than 50. The likely explanation inheres not so much in the greater "enlightenment" to which one administrator attributed this development. More plausibly, St. Croix's whites may have become more confident in their capacity to control, having successfully dealt with the conspiracy of 1759.[88]

The whip in question was often the cartwhip, also referred to in contemporary parlance as the cowskin. A graphic description of its deadly potential was given by Governor General Walterstorff in 1803. He claimed that, administered in anger on bare flesh, it left marks more indelible than branding, with long term consequences no one could calculate.[89] Routine applications of the whip for the more minor offenses took place within the prison. In matters of greater seriousness the sentence was administered at the public beating post, the "Justitsstøte," located in a prominent place in each town. The most disgraceful whipping of all took place under the gallows. So considerable was the opprobrium attached to it, and the comparable disgrace of branding as punishment, that both were considered to render a slave ineligible for manumission.[90] Only one such whipping and branding is recorded in the journal entries for 1802-1807. It took place in Frederiksted and the nature of the offense was not disclosed. Simon, described cryptically as "the criminal negro," received 150 lashes and was branded on the forehead.[91]

Irons are not mentioned in the journals and perhaps the periods of detention, ranging from a day to a fortnight, did not necessitate their use. But some urban slaveowners still employed chains in their domestic correctional regimen.[92] Governor General Peter Oxholm's ordinance of 1815 governing prison-slave labor use for road maintenance and public works, indicated that it was normal practice to chain such slaves together. It should be noted also that Oxholm exempted children, mustee (the children of mulatto and white parents) and castice (of mustee and white parents), from such public degradation.[93] Silent on the subject of irons, the journals do however hint at differential and perhaps deferential treatment of slaves, mustee and lighter, in the administration of punishment. For example on 8 December 1806 three slaves were arrested in Christiansted for curfew violations. Thomas and Christian, described by owner and not by color, and presumably black, received respectively 25 and 50 lashes. Another Thomas, described not only by owner but also by color as mustice, received no lashes.[94]

The prisons themselves had no discrete existence, for in each town the military fort did double duty as municipal prison. Indeed, St. Croix's first prison was not built until the early 1840s, when emancipation was actively being canvassed, by the island's most reformist administrator Peter von

Scholten.[95] Incarceration in the forts, for however brief a period, placed the offending slave face to face with the ultimate sanction of white military power. The fort-prison had no treadmill, for that infernal machine had not yet, and never appears to have, reached the Danish West Indies. It did, however, have a dungeon, known as "det Sorte Hul," the Black Hole, into which refractory slaves regardless of sex were placed in solitary confinement for up to 48 hours.[96] The jails and their facilities, the jailors and other prison personnel, were thus part of the state apparatus, not of some subordinate jurisdiction of county or municipality.

The judge in the proceedings was invariably the Chief of Police in each town. His writ ran not alone in cases that came formally to his notice in court, where he was sole arbiter. There were occasions when, outside the formal proceedings of the court, he used his authority to have slaves detained and even placed in the dungeon. Sometimes in his lay capacity as private owner he would order his own slave to jail.[97] In doing so he was resorting to the public agency of discipline and punishment. Such action had its own peculiar logic. Wade has reported for the ante-bellum South that many masters there preferred to use the public system because of its convenience, and because it saved them from having to use the whip and developing reputations for harshness.[98] Private use of the public correctional facility of the fort-prisons of St. Croix, was also encouraged by the authorities. Governor General Walterstorff for example declared in 1803 that he had no wish to deprive individual masters of their due right to punish their slaves in a manner appropriate to the offense. He did think, however, that when the latter called for serious punishment, the fort was a more suitable place for its administration. The public system had the further advantage, in his view, that it was unlikely to err on the side of leniency.[99] Many owners of slaves in Christiansted, but from all appearances not in Frederiksted, availed themselves of the convenience of the public system. Susanna, house servant to C. C. Hennings the Christiansted printer, ran away thrice between 1804 and 1807 to join either her family or her husband on rural plantations; for her four months of petit marronage she was punished with 100 lashes at the public whipping post, at the end of which she was detained in the fort for another six days at her owner's request.[100] A further refinement in the use of the public system occurred when third parties intervened to secure the punishment of other persons' slaves.[101] This did not occur with regularity but when it did, it approximated a form of citizen's arrest, serving to remind the offending slave that the power of apprehension was the province of every white and not just the official police.

This was just as well. The police patrols at the start of the nineteenth century were not such as to inspire respect. Indeed the open contempt in which they were held by town slaves in St. Thomas was doubtless equally true of St. Croix.[102] Mostly but not exclusively freedmen, they were not particularly numerous. In 1802 they numbered five in Christiansted, with a slave population approaching 3,000.[103] Since they could not all be on duty

24 hours per day, the patrol:slave ratio of 1:600 that their absolute numbers suggest might therefore be misleading. Nor were they always particularly efficient. There were numerous occasions reported in the police journals when slaves taken into custody escaped, and others ran away before being apprehended.[104] It is not to be assumed therefore that the 1,130 cases reported in the police blotters of the towns represented the totality of incidents on the days of which they constitute the record. Unrelentingly, the efficacy of the system of discipline and control, whose public agents-of-first-instance were the police, was being put to the test.

The slaves of St. Croix's towns show every sign of having developed, by the early nineteenth century, a clear enough perception of their interests. The proof lies in their grasping at opportunities to manipulate, in the direction of amelioration, the powers of private punishment enjoyed by their masters. It is worthy of notice that Governor General Lindemann saw fit to remark on his assumption of office in July 1799 that slaves, singly and in large groups, streamed into town with complaints about their owners.[105] In the towns, this recourse to an appellate jurisdiction of a kind, was also developing at the turn of the century. For example, Polly, the property of Christiansted freedman Thomas Armstrong, felt sufficiently aggrieved and, more importantly, confident enough to complain about her master to the Chief of Police. She did not receive a sympathetic hearing and was detained.[106] A few months later, Hennings' Susanna, already resentful of her owner from whom she had previously run away, lodged a complaint to the police about ill-treatment. She too got no redress and was detained for two days.[107]

Neither Polly nor Susanna was as successful in their appeals as another of Hennings' slaves, old Johannes who was on hire. In July 1805 he reported to the police Chief that he had been "barbarously abused" by Hennings' wife who had plied him with a measuring rod. She had seen him talking to some slaves in front of the printery where he guarded clothing she had put out for sale on the street gallery. He was given a hearing, in the course of which two white witnesses deposed that Johannes had been beaten from time to time with a cowskin. The physician who examined Johannes found welts consistent with a severe beating and certified that although his life was not in danger his left arm was badly swollen, one finger apparently dislocated and Johannes himself incapacitated for work for some time. Johannes' own view of his situation carried a ring of desperation: the Hennings were so impossible that he was actively contemplating suicide.[108] The case was referred to the Governor General. The Hennings were ordered to pay Johannes 5 Rigsdaler damages "for pain and suffering" and the costs of his medical attention. An obviously satisfied Johannes told the court on the day of the final hearing that he was now prepared to continue working at the printery since both Henningses had promised to treat him well in future.[109]

Johannes' case was a small but significant victory. An appeal to the authorities had resulted in their intervention between master and slave, limiting the former's power of discretionary punishment and placing judicial sanctions on its abuse. The slaves in the three cases cited had shown that they were capable of resisting, although with varied degrees of success, levels of punishment they defined as intolerable. In the process they demonstrated their grasp of a fundamental fact: their masters had other masters who represented a higher jurisdiction that could be invoked to their advantage.

The police journals for Christiansted and Frederiksted, therefore, portray urban slave populations that consisted of bondsmen anything but docile and deferential. In the more elastic environment of the towns, they proved willing to test conclusions with their masters, and with regularity challenged in all their particulars the laws for their "good order and government." They got drunk and created disturbances in the streets and markets where they often fought, they insulted and occasionally assaulted whites, showed the police to be ineffectual by escaping from arrest or evading it, constantly violated the curfew, stole a variety of personal effects, gambled, were incautious with fire and took many unauthorized absences as petits marrons. This was a record of slaves, more often men than women, daily and nightly in conflict with the law. If whites felt sufficient confidence no longer to impose the mandatory death sentence for assaulting a white, the origins of that confidence may have been tinged with a touch of irony. It is certainly arguable that slaves, located in towns where white power was concentrated, and making rational calculations of their circumstances and interests, had rejected violent confrontation at the individual or societal levels, as a worthwhile course. Rather, they saw greater virtue in seeking to curb the discretionary powers of punishment of individual masters and, on the macro scale, to exploit the flexible ambience of the towns to place the laws governing public order under continuous stress. It was a strategy of survival that could be deemed accommodationist. The word, however, with its possible pejorative connotations, hardly does justice to behavior which in the white universe was criminal deviance but in the slave's conscious defiance.

6

An Oasis of Humanity: Independent Slave Activity

DESPITE THE ALL-ENCOMPASSING NATURE OF SLAVERY IN town and country, in the Danish colonies as elsewhere in the Caribbean, the slaves' occupational spread and the nature of the work routine allowed many slaves to have discretionary time. Those slaves, for example, who were involved in roles and specialities independent of plantation production and associated activities, such as urban jobbers and artisans, wharf and warehouse porters and seamen, were in no way bound by the sunrise to sunset regimen of the plantations. Even on the plantations themselves, custom not to mention self-interest came to dictate that one day in the week, namely Sunday, was to be allowed to the slaves to rest from their labors. There were moreover individual planters who, in addition to Sunday, were in the habit of giving slaves an extra day for purposes of cultivating their provision grounds in lieu of plantation rations.[1] Long before 1843, when Saturday was legally created into a "free" day and Sunday, the feast days of the Lutheran Church and royal birthdays, likewise, there was ample opportunity for slaves in the towns and on the plantations to have discretionary leisure. Analysis of the ways in which the slaves used this "free" time provides a deeper understanding of the slave society and important indicators of the process of cultural change associated with the construction of that society.

The process of cultural change characteristic of slave societies has from time to time been described as "acculturation," but the use of that word conceals a value judgment, a presumption of a terminus ad quem, and the accommodation by the enslaved majority to the normative values of the white minority. Conceptualized in this way, the interaction of Europe and Africa in the New World locates the African exclusively as object, never as subject; and by a kind of hubristic Eurocentrism, ignores the double process of "transculturation" in which each cultural legacy is stimulated by and responds to the other.

Bronislaw Malinowski observed in this regard that, "the two races exist[ed] upon elements taken from Europe as well as from Africa ... from both stores of culture. In so doing both races transform[ed] the borrowed elements and incorporate[d] them into a completely new and independent cultural reality."[2] Edward Kamau Brathwaite, in examining this cultural process which he describes as "creolization" not only concurs implicitly with Malinowski's basic propositions, but also goes further to identify this process as "the single most important factor in the development of Jamaica," affecting whites no less than slaves.[3] Further, in situations of cross-cultural contact, as Serghei Arutuniev has concluded, "the dissimilarities, the morphological heterogeneities and the polymorphism existing even within the same population will ... serve man as a means to cultural adaptation. The fact is that the plurality of cultures and of cultural variants ... constitutes the adaptation mechanism which enables man to develop by selection of the best elements and renewal of his cultural heritage."[4]

The cultural cross-currents of the Danish Virgin Islands flowed from a variety of sources, and involved the intermingling of several cultural influences of the Danish official classes, Dutch and German missionaries, Jewish and French traders and craftsmen, English and Irish plantation owners and Scots-Irish overseers with an African cultural input that was itself by no means monolithic. Following Arutuniev's analysis, the foundations for the adaptation mechanism would have been well established by the middle of the eighteenth century, when the maximal exploitation of the Danish Virgin Islands began under crown rule. It is argued here that the heterogeneous aggregate of Danish West Indian slaves – more than 20,000 by the beginning of the nineteenth century – originating in an area that extended from Upper Guinea to Angola, came to comprise a community, achieve coherence, and evolve a discrete slave culture, involving, to precis Handler and Lange, behavioral patterns that were shared by the slaves as a group, and socially learned and transmitted.[5] These patterns were molded as much by the slaves' creative use of discretionary time for independent activities as by their experience of daily toil.

God

Both before and after 1843, a significant proportion of the work-free Sunday was spent in religious observance. The slaves responded with fair enthusiasm to the stimulus of missionary proselytizing. Although the state Lutheran church was not itself a vigorous campaigner for slaves' souls, there were other denominations that entered the field with official concurrence and with varying degrees of success. The Moravians who were earliest in the field had by far the largest number of slave adherents followed by the Roman Catholics, the Anglicans, the Dutch Reformed Church and the Methodists in that order. Among slaves who became Moravians it was not uncommon to spend part of a week-day evening

Table 6.1: *Christian Slaves in the Danish West Indies, 1805*

Island	Baptized Slaves	Total Slave Population	Baptized Slaves as % of Total
St John	1,294	2,417	53.5
St. Thomas	2,103	3,344	62.8
St. Croix	14,603	22,076	66.1
Total	18,000	27,837	64.6

Source: R/A, DVK.

receiving instruction from a Moravian brother on the plantation, or walking to the nearest mission station.[6] Attendance at church on Sunday had also assumed significance before the end of the eighteenth century. One observer noted in 1788 as many as 200 slaves from a single estate on their way to church on Sunday. His description of the phenomenon, moreover, suggests strongly that those occasions had also been seized as opportunities for group activity and social interaction, for the display by some of "chintz and other finery, such that a stranger would not think they were slaves."[7]

By the beginning of the nineteenth century, church affiliation among slaves had achieved significant levels. The first complete figures indicate that in all three islands church affiliation exceeded 50 percent of the total slave population (Table 6.1). As the century grew older, despite the fact that the slave population was declining in all the islands except St. Thomas the numbers of church affiliated slaves had grown not only relatively but also absolutely (Table 6.2). In the island of St. Croix, those numbers had reached an astonishing 99 percent by 1835.

It is therefore surprising, given this significant response to the religion of the Europeans, that the slaves of the Danish West Indies showed no inclination whatever to graft their African religious beliefs and practices onto Christianity, to produce a syncretic religion of their own or to indigenize Christianity. There were no Moses Bakers or George Leiles, nor the emergence of any sect like the "native" Baptists, as in Jamaica.[8] The explanation probably relates, firstly, to the fact that the missionary penetration was thorough, particularly on the part of the Moravians. Secondly, that penetration was a function of the islands' relatively small size, and their topography. None of these islands exceeded 85 square miles in area, and it was possible for a denomination as indefatigable as the Moravians, or as zealous as the Roman Catholics, to saturate the communities with Christian teaching. It is worthy of note that the missionaries' efforts met relatively less success in St. John, an island of notoriously difficult terrain. The lower percentages of converts from that island indicated in Tables 6.1 and 6.2 have a direct correlation with this geophysical fact. Thirdly, as the slave population became more and more creole after the Slave Trade's Abolition in 1802 it was distanced with each passing year from aspects of its African roots.

Table 6.2: *Christian Slaves in the Danish West Indies, 1835*

Island	Baptized Slaves	Total Slave Population	Baptized Slaves as % of Total
St. John	1,636	1,943	84.1
St. Thomas	5,064	5,315	85.2
St. Croix	19,692	19,876	99.0
Total	26,392	27,134	87.2

Source: R/A, CANS, (5), Governor General von Scholten's Report 2 January 1839, Bilag 16B.

Missionary endeavor, it would seem, had pre-empted the population's leadership cadres, lessening the possibility thereby of cultural continuities, at least so far as religion went. Such a co-opted leadership could also help to explain why, between the aborted conspiracy of 1759 in St. Croix[9] and the uprising of 1848 which brought emancipation, there was neither conspiracy nor uprising. As that process of pre-emption and co-option took place, African magico-religious practices pari passu fell into abeyance. Whereas in the eighteenth century, proscriptions against obeah figure very prominently in the slave codes and the proposed drafts for codes,[10] in the nineteenth century neither regulatory ordinances nor the accounts of contemporary travelers have anything to say on the subject of obeah.

It is not to be assumed, however, that the culture contact between European and African which religion provided was unidirectional. The flow in the other direction was equally noteworthy. The slaves' adoption of Christianity compelled the acquisition and more widespread use by the Europeans of the slaves' lingua franca, "creolsk."[11] At a time when "the art of writing a book was so seldom practised in Denmark,"[12] two ABC creole books, a creole grammar, a hymnal and a catechism had been produced by 1770; a creole translation of the New Testament in 1779; a translation of the Old Testament, unpublished, in 1781; and in the remaining years before emancipation an impressive run of readers (1798, 1827); hymnals (1799, 1823); children's Bibles (1822); and catechisms (1827). By invention and cross-breeding a new element was created in creole and the de facto domination of Malinowski's "new and independent cultural reality" remained basically unchanged, until the introduction by Governor General von Scholten of a Lancastrian school system for slaves in 1838, with English as the official medium of instruction.[13]

At its introduction von Scholten's school system catered for younger children aged four to eight on Monday to Friday mornings, and older children, up to age fourteen, on Saturday mornings and Sunday afternoons. When the school system was finally formalized in 1846, instruction to the older children was confined to three morning hours of the "free" day, Saturday, established in 1843.[14] In St. Croix, where eight of the eleven schools were located, all the contemporary accounts bear witness to the children's enthusiasm. According to one account, they were attentive and responsive and showed a quicker grasp than white children in general. Their parents were no less enthusiastic about what they had missed and obviously made special efforts to send their children to school clean and well dressed.[15]

This positive response on the part of the slaves to increased leisure and its opportunities, bears a direct causal relationship with the uprising of 1848. The availability of education at state expense, the adjustments to plantation routine which it necessitated, between them heightened the slaves' perception of their own worth. The Law of Free Birth of 28 July 1847 simply reinforced that perception and acted as a catalyst on the impatience which had slowly emerged in the previous decade with the introduction of education and the "free" day associated with it.[16]

Mammon

The declaration of that "free" day in 1843 also introduced Saturday as market day, rescheduling it from Sunday on which it was traditionally held. By the middle of the eighteenth century the markets were well established in the islands' towns. They represented an important contribution on the slaves' part to the internal distribution system, no less important than what Mintz and Hall have identified for Jamaica in the eighteenth century.[17] The markets moreover provided an important opportunity for social interaction among the slaves from different plantations, an opportunity further to supplement their rations by barter or purchase, and to earn cash.

The market in Christiansted was usually open until 8 p.m., but as it got dark by 7 p.m., the slaves lit their stalls with candles. A variety of products was offered for sale: vegetables such as cabbages, green pulses and tomatoes; peas; poultry, pigeons, eggs, yams, potatoes, maize, guinea corn and cassava, known collectively as Indian provisions; pumpkins; melons, oranges, wild plums and berries from the hills on St. Croix's north side; rope tobacco; cassava bread, which many whites particularly creoles, were especially fond of; fish; firewood and fodder.[18]

Market regulations were first codified as part of the Slave Reglement of 1755, and they called for two white market supervisors and the permission of slaves' owners, as a deterrent to the sale of stolen goods.[19] The convention was also established in the course of the eighteenth century that slaves could not offer for sale any of the export staples such as cotton and sugar or rum.[20] The Reglement was never enforced and in practice supervision appears to have been lax. Nevertheless there is little evidence to suggest that goods sold in the market provided an outlet for illegal trafficking in the way that itinerant vending did. The available market produce were, overwhelmingly, the result of the slaves' creative initiative in the use of their "free" time, particularly in the cultivation of their provision grounds. Literary evidence from the eighteenth century certainly identified the same kind of goods for sale in the market as were grown on the provision grounds.[21] This creative initiative was particularly evident in the slaves' identifying and satisfying the urban market for grass and firewood. Hans West testified to the extent of this activity in St. Croix in the 1780s,[22] and Thurlow Weed who wrote in the 1840s supplied evidence for the continuing vigor of this traffic.[23] Equally interesting, it appears that there was a rationalization of this activity, and a sex-specific distribution of the work involved at least by the 1840s. Like itinerant huckstering, market vending was largely a female monopoly; work on the provision grounds was largely the province of males.[24] For West Indian purposes, the slaves had adopted the prevalent practice of the Gold Coast, from which many of them had originated.

Dances and Other Diversions

The cultivation of provision grounds and the Sunday, subsequently Saturday, market apart, a major portion of slaves' discretionary time was spent in dancing. As early as the first codified slave laws of 1733, there were indications that "fetes, balls, dances and divertissements with Negro instruments" were sufficiently established to warrant the imposition of conditions under which they could be held.[25] In the 1740s Governor Moth's "Articuler for Negerne" stipulated that such revelries should end at sundown or at 8 p.m. on moonlight nights.[26] In St. Thomas in the 1760s a proclamation of Governor de Gunthelberg extended the time limit to 10 p.m.; thereafter police permission was required, but in no circumstances was the use of Goombay drums permitted.[27]

Understandably, dancing or the opportunity and energy to engage in it, was a greater likelihood for urban slaves. In St. Croix in the 1770s, Governor General Clausen permitted dances in town but not beyond the 8 p.m. curfew. The same proclamation allowed free people of color to hold dances until 10 p.m. but both slaves and whites were prohibited, on pain of severe punishment in the one case, and fines and imprisonment in the other, from either attending or participating.[28] The prohibition would suggest that in the towns at least the inflexible lines of slavery were being both bent and breached by the compelling attractions of the dance. That suggestion is reinforced by other similar provisions such as that contained in Lindemann's draft slave code for 1783.[29] There are, therefore, strong presumptive grounds for believing that some slaves and some whites by deliberate choice shared, in the eighteenth century at least, one common social activity, albeit illegally and under the cover of darkness.

Such violence to the society's implicit premises was not the only remarkable feature of the slaves' preoccupation with the dance. In 1791 Hans West reported that dances were held several times per week, with an entrance fee as much as three Rigsdaler per couple. It was this frequency, he concluded, that was a prime consideration in the limitation of the activity.[30] Carl Holten, brother of Christian, the Commandant of St. Thomas in 1815, was another contemporary observer who shed some light on the subject of slave dances. With a good eye for detail, Holten noted that formal styles of address were often in use at these occasions: Mister, Mrs., Councillor, Captain and the like. Holten put this down to mere mimicry. But that hardly exhausts the possibilities. It might just as probably have been ridicule, and there is the third alternative that the slaves could have been investing the occasion with special significance by the adaptation of European styles of address and the usage in contemporary "society." At any rate the adaptations were subject to the slaves' own sobering sense of the appropriate, an eye for the absurd, and a capacity to poke fun at each other. The point is well borne out by one of Holten's numerous anecdotes: "I recall among other things a barber who got himself a pair of spectacles to waltz in, because he had seen Walterstorff's secretary Capt. Manthey doing so and when the other coloreds found this entirely ridiculous, replied surlily: 'You are a bunch of fools if you don't know that this is the style at court'."[31]

Non-dancing parties, at which tea and coffee were served was another favorite diversion of slaves. The evidence, however, points to this being a particularly urban activity. They had become popular enough by the 1770s to attract the notice of officialdom, and the Burgher Council of St. Croix gave it their attention in 1778, declaring that those entertainments had got completely out of hand. Some slave owners not only turned a blind eye to these occurrences, but also used permission to attend them as a means of granting favors to some slaves. An entrance fee was charged, as with the dances on which West reported. The payments involved were more than likely one use to which the proceeds of marketeering or own-account jobbing were put. Like the dances too, these tea and coffee parties were opportunities for social intercourse among legally segregated strata of the society. The parties were attended by free people of color, whose "connections and too great familiarity" with slaves were, in the Burgher Council's opinion, a cause for concern. They thought these revelries should be either limited or forbidden altogether.[32]

Above all, the parties gave the slaves a chance to bring out their finery, finery of the sort that was the subject of a detailed sumptuary ordinance in 1786. The Ordinance mentions accessories of gold and silver and precious stones, silk, lace and other expensive fabrics as items all prohibited to field and house slaves alike, although the latter were allowed a silver clasp of simple design.[33] The implication was that the silks and jewelry were, if not cast-offs, stolen. The slave law tended to view the slave as above all a potential criminal. However, Governor General Schimmelmann, who drew up the Ordinance, did not calculate for the slaves' insistence on carving out of the wilderness of servitude the oasis of their own humanity by individual idiosyncracies of dress or dressing up when they had unencumbered time. How effective the 1786 Ordinance was is difficult to judge, but in 1814 the police chief of St. Croix, Gjellerup, issued a notice referring to "wearing apparel, jewellery and beads too numerous to specify found at a slave ball," and inviting their "owners" to claim them.[34] Despite Schimmelmann, the slaves had clearly not ceased to wear their best to balls, whether that best was the end product of their own sweat or borrowed surreptitiously from the masters' or mistresses' wardrobes as the police chief broadly implied.

By convention and latterly by royal instructions of 1 May 1840, slaves were allowed all the recognized feast days and high holy days of the state Lutheran church, as well as the monarch's birthday. No special significance appears to have been attached to these by the slave population, although it can be assumed that where appropriate they would have gone to church. Of the public holidays, the two days of Christmas and the New Year stand in a category by themselves. According to Weed, in the week that intervened "they contrive ... to do very little work ... And on these occasions the slaves' cup of enjoyment fills to the brim."[35] These days produced their own kinds of diversion and dynamics. The European practice of throwing firecrackers and letting off fireworks was a particularly pervasive practice among slaves in this holiday period; indeed, before – during the "several weeks preceding" in which they were "busied with preparations for their festivities" – and after.[36] Proclamations over several decades, particularly in St. Thomas, failed to arrest the practice.[37]

A colonial law officer commenting in 1783 blamed it on the indolence of the police. But in part the explanation also lay in the fact that "the throwing of fire-crackers was reckoned to be one of those innocent pleasures wherewith one distinguished special from ordinary days, and *even whites themselves participated.*"[38] Annual ordinances, issued by the police prefects just before Christmas, continued into the nineteenth century.[39] Their very issuance, however, are grounds for believing that this was one "innocent pleasure" in which whites and slaves found common enjoyment.

Itinerant minstrelsy at Christmas and New Year was well enough established by 1759 for Governor General von Pröck to issue a proclamation against it. It involved the use of violins, "other instruments" which von Pröck did not specify, and begging for money as minstrels everywhere did and still do. It was also the practice among some slave owners to have these slaves playing for them, and it can be inferred from the proclamation that they were sent to, or were hired by, other owners to perform.[40] Lindemann's draft slave laws of 1783 and van der Østen's of 1785 repeat the prohibitory paragraph of 1759, and indicate that the practice could not be legislated away.[41] It seems hardly likely that these slave musicians were performing African music on the violin for an audience of Europeans. It can safely be assumed therefore that the music was, if not European, at the very least a creolized variant of it.

In connection with the New Year festivities, Johann Nissen who lived in St. Thomas for 46 years from 1792, noted in 1832 that "It is the custom here, especially among the coloured persons to celebrate old year's night with music, dancing, singing and in short, making a great noise. They commenced this uproar as early as 4 o'clock in the afternoon, passing in great crowds through all the streets, crying out in their creole tongue, 'Old

Year's night'."[42] These street processions to which Nissen calls attention were probably not new in 1832. Some eighty years before, von Pröck in condemning the minstrels with their violins, makes mention of "de andre Negere som omløber" – the other Negroes who go about.[43] This is hardly conclusive, although tantalizingly suggestive. Nissen further remarked: "At 9 o'clock they pass through all the streets with music and continue to do so through the whole night. Some of them have a certain place, where they have put up a tent of coconut leaves, and dance there during the night. Many of them again dance in their own rooms, which are certainly very small, and are so full that the dancers have scarcely room to move."[44] In St. Thomas then the dance took over at the New Year's festivities, and the Goombay did duty here as with other dances. Nissen did not think a great deal of the slaves' dancing. Their free-form improvisatory style contrasted sharply in his mind with the then prescribed European measures of his day. Dancing was something which "well-educated" people learnt and performed. On the other hand, "the dances of the negroes are of one sort; turning and moving about – they have no *regular* dances."[45]

In St. Croix, nominally more Christian by far, the situation described by Weed at the beginning of 1845 was not very different. Indeed, he described dancing as the slaves' "only festive resource" and notes that for the New Year frolic, there was "turban, calico, ribbon, gewgaw and trinket" in abundance. Estate slaves elected Kings and Queens, Princes and Princesses, Maids of Honor and Pages; a somewhat more formalized structure than anything reported for St. Thomas. The dance was opened with "much gravity" by the King and Queen, to the accompaniment of ballads led by a "Prima Donna" supported by a chorus, and the ubiquitous Goombay "discours[ing] most eloquent music." As the dance progressed, the enthusiasm rose, as did the Prima Donna's voice, the chorus swelled, the drummer was carried away and the Queen eventually swooned, to be revived by her attendants sprinkling Bay Rum and plying their fans. But once recovered she joined the dance with renewed energy, having called upon the Princess to replace her as leader; she in her turn, and the King and Princes in theirs, calling on those of "inferior rank" when exhausted. The chorus accompaniment did not actually join the dance; indeed they constituted, according to Weed, the greater proportion of those present. "Towards the close of the festivities, however, all join in the dance, all, at the same time, singing most vociferously."[46]

Weed enables us to see not only the all-consuming nature of the event for the slave population. His information enables us equally to see the event's all-encompassing character for the entire population: "The first privilege (or duty as they esteem it) of the slaves on Christmas day and New Year's day, is to pay their respects, in a body, to their master, before whom they dance for an hour or more, paying tribute, in their songs to his liberality, generosity &c., after which they are regaled with cakes, cordial &c., and generally receive presents from their mistress."[47] While plantation whites were touched in this way, the free coloreds confined to the towns residentially, were in their turn touched by the celebrations of the urban slave population. Both groups, we are told, "form their parties, elect their Kings, Queens &c., and dance in like manner."[48]

The renditions of the Prima Donna and chorus were not mere accompaniments to the dance. They were sometimes complimentary – to greet, impromptu, some passer-by; or congratulatory – to the King, Queen Victoria or the Americans. In this regard the slaves were displaying in song a good grasp of current events. But nowhere was this grasp put to better use than in the songs of incisive social comment, indeed of social protest:

> All we girls must keep heads together; King Christian have sent to free us all; Governor SHOLTEN had a vote for us; King Christian have sent to grant us all; we have signed for liberty; our Crown Prince had a vote in it; our Gracious Queen had the highest vote; King Christian have sent to say he will crown us all.
> Oh yes! oh, yes! hurra! hurra!
> All we girls must keep head together.[49]

Some sixty years before Schmidt had warned that slaves sang songs for the courage to rebel; that if Europeans paid more attention to them than they did the possibilities of uprising would be considerably lessened.[50] Weed, an outsider visiting from North America, may very well have recorded without realising it, the first audible rumble of the eruption which took place three years later.

There are no explicit references in the literature to end of year mummery of the John Canoe type, which Brathwaite has argued was an African retention in Jamaica.[51] However, the Jamaican procession of "Set Girls" had an inexact equivalent in the organized processions from some estates that went into town on New Year's morning. The rivalry between the women of different estates was certainly as intense as that between the "Set Girls." They abused each other roundly for the poverty or parsimoniousness of their masters, cast slurs on the color of mistresses, and did not cavil to use that most opprobrious of epithets, "Guinea Bird."[52]

At least one slave diversion could be classified under the heading of the martial arts. Particularly among plantation or country slaves who had long distances to travel, it was not unusual for them, to walk with a stick for support. Indeed, the surviving newspapers of the eighteenth century bear this out. On the longest journey the slave could contemplate, namely when he ran away, the advertisements almost invariably represented him with a stick. The sticks were obviously large enough to be considered cudgels, and could be gnarled, pointed, metal-tipped or banded with metal. The slave's staff had the potential for becoming a murderous weapon, and was so regarded by white authority, which proceeded to ban it.[53] But the ban of the Bangelar, as it was known, was never very successful. It was difficult to suppress like Goombay drumming, and perhaps for the same reason: probable ritual significance, definite entertainment value and a high degree of skill required, in the case of the Bangelar, for its effective use. At the same time, white encouragement is also to be accounted a causal factor in its survival. According to Clausen, whites not only found pleasure in the spectacle of these stick-fighting contests but attended to egg on the contestants.[54] Stick-fighting, like cock-fighting which survived into the nineteenth century and was favored among whites no less than slaves,[55] was a blood sport; a brutal business for a brutal time. Whites and slaves could both find pleasure in the structured violence the contest involved, for co-existing in a society based upon an identical premise, neither could escape its logic.

One other pastime which served a second function as defense in situations of conflict, was the use of stones with and without slingshots. In 1783, a colonial law officer deemed stone-throwing a habit dangerous enough to merit 20 lashes. The habit, he said, was acquired in childhood: the slave child's first amusement as soon as it began to creep being stone throwing. It persisted into adult life, and stones were used not only for chasing dogs, pigs, goats and other animals but were also employed against each other in moments of irritation or during disputes: "One does not often see a Negro on the street without a stone in his hand. It has gone so far that one can no longer be secure in one's house or gallery from such careless stone-throwing. Already they have hit upon using slingshots. If such a practice became common, it could be a dangerous pastime."[56] These remarks which apply to St. Croix, could equally have applied to St. Thomas. That island's commandant in the 1780s, de Malleville, reported with concern the growing proportions that stone-throwing had assumed. In the years 1774, 1775, 1776, for several nights at a particular time of the year which de Malleville did not specify, stones rained down upon the houses and galleries of Charlotte Amalie from the sea and from the hills above. Those stones were large enough to kill and made it unsafe to sit outside after dark.[57] If one rules out a poltergeist theory, the only likely explanations with which one is left are gestures of defiance towards whites – a not uncommon phenomenon in the urban setting of Charlotte Amalie[58] – or a stone "war" between individual slaves or groups of slaves under the cover of darkness.

If the facility with stones for diversion and defense was African in origin, there is evidence of cultural cross-breeding in the West Indies. Lindemann suggested in his draft slave code that slaves should not be allowed to play "Kag."[59] But that game was almost certainly metropolitan Danish, for it is described in Verner Dahlerup's *Ordbog over det Danske Sprog* (Dictionary of the Danish Language) not as a game of African origin, but simply as: "Name of a children's game, the object of which is to hit down with a stonethrow, the uppermost stone in a pyramid-formed stone-heap; or to knock over a ninepin or a forked stick." Borrowing from a European children's game, the slaves had made it theirs, transformed it into an adult's game and used it as target practice to sharpen their stone-throwing skills.

Gaming was an important social activity among whites in Virgin Island slave society. Card games such as *L'Hombre*, Whist and Boston with 300 piastre stakes were an important part of official entertaining, at least under

Governor General von Scholten; among the haute monde in the elegant public salons of Charlotte Amalie in the 1840s or among the less respectable and in secret in St. Croix.[60] Slaves no less than their masters were given to games of chance, especially to cards and dice. However, none of the official proclamations from Gardelin's time in the 1730s takes any notice of the practice before the 1770s. Since it is unlikely that slaves could have played without attracting attention to themselves, one possible conclusion is that gambling as "leisure" time activity became popular after mid-century, and is probably one index of the creolization process. Clausen, in prohibiting all forms of gambling among slaves in 1774, claimed that "daily experience had taught that slaves had an insatiable lust for gambling" which had gone completely out of control. It was taking place, it would appear, not only in houses and on galleries, but also on the streets.[61] This suggests a largely urban manifestation. Lindemann's draft code of 1783 on the other hand is not specific as to place in recommending prohibition of "dice, cards ... or any such games,"[62] but van der Østen's did speak of gambling in the towns.[63] However, the St. Croix Burgher Council indicated in 1787 that there was gambling on the plantations as well: during the religious feast days of Christmas and the New Year.[64] De Malleville writing in the same year from St. Thomas, also expressed concern about the extent of card playing and all forms of gambling among the slave population, and the participation of free coloreds in these games of chance.[65]

Gambling was associated in the minds of some whites with other "vices" such as rum drinking, which officialdom did its best to discourage if it could not stop.[66] Some publicans apparently allowed slaves to sit in their rum shops when they were open on weekdays, Sundays and holidays. Some officials thought slaves should only be served from the back yards of the shops and not permitted to loiter; others that such loitering and the gambling to which it gave rise was allowed and encouraged by the publicans for pecuniary advantage or for trafficking in stolen goods.[67] Rum, traditionally, was never sold on the plantations so that a slave "on his own time," wanting to acquire his own liquor without stealing, or to buy himself a drink had to wait until there was an opportunity to be in town and have cash: an opportunity which the market provided. The market's attraction as an opportunity for release from the boredom and brutality of plantation life, was enormously enhanced, therefore, by the prospect of a few drams of "kill-devil."

A similar kind of release was found in horseback riding. The imperatives of the society, however, with its high premiums on discipline and deference, made such use of slaves' time in an essentially individualistic activity problematic in the extreme, particularly if slaves were given to hard riding. For both whites and slaves, it was as if the physical act of mounting a horse had a corresponding metaphysical significance, lessening the status gap between both groups. Lindemann in drafting his slave code in 1783, emphasized white concern in this regard. Any mounted slave was required to either dismount or ride slowly out of the way for approaching whites, but in no circumstances to gallop past nor ride side by side with whites.[68] This was in the spirit of Gardelin's earlier code of 1733, which had insisted on similar shows of public submissiveness, even when the situations were reversed and slave was on foot.[69] In van der Østen's draft code of 1785, we again meet with this concern with the slave on horseback. In his view, slaves' use of horses without permission was to be regarded as theft and punished accordingly.[70]

The abandon with which slaves apparently rode, as they savored these brief moments of glory, was the occasion of adverse white comment from time to time, for as a group whites were as much concerned about "public order" as they were about deference. Indeed, in their minds the two were closely related, if not synonymous. Governor General von Pröck noted in 1756 that hard riding in the streets of Christiansted had become a daily and dangerous practice on the part of slaves, and proceeded to prohibit it.[71] Lindemann too would have prohibited slaves riding in streets of towns or their immediate environs, unless there were evidence of some urgent errand. He remarked further that more often than not, the offenders were small boys,[72] who obviously rode with no less enthusiasm than their elders.

If there were constraints on this method of release in the towns and their vicinity, the country roads offered better opportunity. Estate slaves organized their own equestrian diversions. The following public notice in 1815 signed by the St. Croix Chief of Police, Mouritzen, suggests a well established practice involving, as in dancing and stick-fighting, whites no less than slaves and conducted in such a way as to avoid official attention: "It has been reported to this office that it had been customary even among slaves to run Horse Races on the high-roads in the Country: This being contrary to the Laws and good order, each and every one is admonished to desist from such bad practice; and, it is requested, that any one who might know of such races give information to this office, where the offended will be treated as the Law directs."[73] Horse racing as a sport did not have any currency before the first two decades of the nineteenth century. This was the period, at any rate, during which it was considered important enough to be advertised in the public prints.[74] The slaves had not only co-opted the sport among themselves for pleasure and, where possible, profit; they had also played a clear part in their role as jockeys in establishing the sport for whites.

Cultural Creation

In the last hundred years or so of slavery in the Danish Virgin Islands, the slaves by the use of the discretionary time legally and illegally at their disposal created certain modes of being and behavior that were distinctly theirs. The use of "free" time was far more conducive to this purpose, having regard to the demanding nature of the routines and discipline associated with plantation production. By the time of emancipation they had created a culture, neither wholly African nor yet European, retaining, adapting, borrowing and adopting. The transition from disaggregation to community necessarily involved a process of cultural change. As Mintz and Price have observed, "in order for slave communities to take shape, normative patterns of behavior had to be established, and these patterns could be created only on the basis of particular forms of social interaction."[75]

The creation was taking place not in a vacuum but in a dynamic context: of interaction among themselves and contact, sometimes intimate, with the other dominant cultural elements which were European. Masters as well as slaves were caught up in the process of cultural inter-change. The whites enjoyed or learnt to enjoy foods like cassava bread, and some, at any rate, slaves' sports like stick-fighting. Donors of their religions, they became recipients of the slaves' language and in several respects provide empirical justification for the conclusion that "the role of the powerless in affecting, and even controlling important parts of the lives of the masters was also typical of slave colonies."[76]

7

Maritime Maroons: Grand Marronage

THE CREATION IN THE DANISH WEST INDIES OF A SLAVE community and creole culture, shared in some measure with the whites and freedmen, occurred concurrently with the slaves' continuous resistance to enslavement. Their resistance took a variety of forms, shaped by the particularities of occupational patterns, changes in the composition of the population, and the geophysical facts of life in the islands. The determining influence of these factors meant that, short of the supreme act of rebellion, the most viable of alternatives to servitude was grand marronage – the permanent desertion of slaveowners – and that in those circumstances grand marronage tended to mean maritime marronage.

Under Danish administration, the three islands of St. Thomas, St. Croix and St. John constituted a wedge, as it were, between Spanish Puerto Rico with its dependencies to the west and Britain's Virgin Islands to the east. Many of these islands were within sight of one another. This factor of insular proximity in a patchwork of national properties had an important bearing on how grand marronage from the Danish West Indies developed. There were significant differences from the pattern in the rest of the hemisphere, where aggregates of single fugitives sometimes created discrete communities that threatened the plantation system militarily and economically. Irrespective of their location, the viability of such communities, as Richard Price has noted, was a function of topography.[1] Natural barriers such as jungle, swamp, and hardly penetrable mountain fastnesses enabled maroon communities to develop in isolation and successfully defend themselves against attack. Slaves on the Danish islands enjoyed none of these advantages. The extensive cutting of forests to make way for sugar plantations removed nature's only benefaction from which maroons could profit.

The relatively great concentration of the slave population in the busy seaports of the Danish West Indies, however, provided opportunities for escape to other islands. These opportunities were generally exploited most

Table 7.1: *Slaves by Sex, St. Croix, 1792–1840*

Year	Females	Males	Total	Females per 100 Males
1792*	7,364	8,579	15,943	85.8
1804	10,475	11,601	22,076	90.2
1815	12,250	12,080	24,330	101.4
1835	10,423	9,453	19,876	110.3
1840	9,714	8,891	18,605	109.3

Sources: R/A, DVK, Oxholm's "General Tabelle for St. Croix, 1792," R/A, Diverse sager, Forskellige Oplysninger, VI; R/A, CANS, "Extract af General Tabellerne over Folkmængden paa de danske vestindiske Øer, den 1ste Oktober 1835," G. W. Alexander, "Om den moralske Forpligtelse," *Danske Ugeskrift* 2 (76) (1843):374-96.
*Figures do not include disabled and runaway slaves, numbering 96 and 2,082 respectively.

effectively by individuals rather than groups of slaves, and more often by males than females. Although women were a majority of the urban slave population in the Danish West Indies, they were employed mostly as domestics and thus lacked access to the male world of the wharves and the sea. The data for male slaves do not permit quantification of their employment, but it is a fair assumption that most were occupied in maritime work – loading and unloading vessels, driving the wains that delivered or removed cargo, and laboring in warehouses or as crew in interisland or other seagoing traffic. As market centers the towns also drew slaves from the countryside to sell fruit, vegetables, poultry, grass, and firewood.[2] At least in St. Thomas and St. Croix, almost the entire slave population was in constant contact with the port towns. These towns not only provided the best opportunities for access to transport across the sea, but also contained rapidly growing and, by the nineteenth century, substantial communities of freedmen within which the fugitive slave could more easily become invisible.

Maroons from the Danish West Indies, as from Jamaica, Surinam, and Brazil, were preponderantly male.[3] The reason was not that women were physically less resilient or robust than men but, more probably, that men were more likely to have acquired skills needed to survive in forests, swamps, or at sea, while in addition women were rendered less mobile by pregnancy or the responsibilities of maternity. Thus the dramatic increase in the proportion of females in the slave population which took place after 1792 (Table 7.1) does not appear to have resulted in larger numbers of females than males among the slaves who escaped from the islands. In the Danish West Indies, moreover, women began to predominate in the slave population at a time when the creolization of that population was well advanced (Table 7.2). By the nineteenth century, creole slave women were arguably further deterred from deserting by attachments of family, sentiment, or a sense of place.

Table 7.2: *Creoles and Africans in the Slave Population of the Danish West Indies, 1804-1805*

Island	Creoles	Africans	Total	% Creoles
St Croix	11,530	10,546	22,076	52.2
St. Thomas	2,096	1,248	3,344	62.7
St. John	1,521	896	2,417	62.9
Total	15,147	12,690	27,837	54.4

Source: R/A, Diverse sager, Forskellige Oplysninger, V.

From the beginning of Danish colonization to the time of emancipation in 1848, grand marronage was a continuous form of resistance, indicating that its incidence was not significantly affected by the degree of acculturation or creolization of the slave population or by the changing proportions of male and female slaves. The numbers involved were never very great, though proportionately they were more significant than in many of the plantation societies of the Caribbean. Hans West, the Danish pedagogue, reported 1,340 slaves at large in 1789, when the slave population stood at 22,448 – 5.9 percent of the total.[4] P. L. Oxholm, the military engineer, identified 96 deserters in 1792, only 0.5 percent of St. Croix's 18,121 slaves.[5] In St. Thomas the 86 known deserters in 1802 constituted 2.7 percent of the slave population of 3,150.[6]

Early Patterns

Grand marronage commenced shortly after the settlement of St. Thomas and the beginnings of that island's development as a plantation colony, which Waldemar Westergaard dates at 1688.[7] During the governorship of Johan Lorentz in the 1690s, proclamations were issued on the subject of runaways,[8] and the Privy Council of St. Thomas resolved early in 1706 to take action against grand marronage. Accordingly, it was ordered on October 2 that all trees on the island from which slaves could make canoes were to be cut down; a proclamation of December 30 offered a reward of fifty Rigsdaler for the return of any slave dead or alive who had escaped to Puerto Rico.[9]

The proclamations of 1706 demonstrate two factors that had an important bearing on the phenomenon of marronage immediately and over time: environment and geography. In the early years of settlement, before the apotheosis of sugar, the primeval forest provided superb cover and supplied wood for canoes in which slaves could seek freedom in nearby islands. The "marine underground" to Puerto Rico and Vieques (Crab

Island), and farther afield to islands in the northern Leewards and elsewhere, ultimately became a major route of escape.

When the expansion of the plantations removed the forest cover, in St. Thomas and St. John by the 1730s and a generation or so later in St. Croix,[10] the best chances for permanent escape lay overseas, although, as we shall see, the islands' towns, as their populations grew, also provided havens. J. L. Carstens, who was born in St. Thomas in 1705 and died in Denmark in 1747, noted in his memoirs that in those early years runaways occupied the island's coastal cliffs, where they sheltered in almost inaccessible caves. Those first maroons chose well, with a keen strategic eye, for the cliffs could not be scaled from the seaward side and vegetation obstructed the landward approaches. Such refugees went naked and subsisted on fish, fruit, small game such as land turtles, or stolen provender. Slave hunts, organized three times a year, could neither loosen their grip on freedom nor dislodge them from the cliffs.[11]

Regrettably, Carstens recorded nothing of the size and social organization of this early community or its relationship with plantation slaves. It was the only such community that St. Thomas ever had, and it did not last long. The Danish authorities could ill afford to stand idly by, especially when St. Thomas was not yet self-sustaining.[12] During the war of the Spanish Succession they began to organize the "maronjagt" or maroon hunt more effectively, using planters, soldiers, free coloreds, and trusty slaves.[13] The forests then became less safe, while at the same time the agricultural exploitation of St. Thomas, peaking in the 1720s, reduced the vegetational cover.[14] As a result, slaves turned to the sea. Their line of escape led west, with favorable northeast trade winds and currents, towards Puerto Rico and other islands, none of which lay more than 40 miles from St. Thomas. Slaves had opportunities to become familiar with the surrounding waters on fishing expeditions for sea turtles around Vieques, and the same boats they manned on their masters' behalf could be used to make a break for Puerto Rico.[15] In 1747, nineteen slaves deserted from St. Croix, and the following year 42 seized a sloop there and sailed to comparative freedom among the Spaniards.[16]

Puerto Rico, which became their preferred destination, was sparsely populated before the Cédula de Gracias of 1815 and its authorities, perhaps for this very reason, looked leniently if not encouragingly on runaways from the Danish islands. As early as 1714, Governor Don Juan de Rivera organized 80 deserters from Danish and other islands into a community at San Mateo de Cangrejos east of San Juan, gave them public land, and required them to function as an auxiliary militia.[17] The Spanish government ratified these arrangements in cédulas of 1738 and 1750, and in the latter decreed freedom for runaways who embraced Catholicism.[18] Eugenio Fernández Méndez has argued that the Spanish acted largely from religious motives.[19] But there was also an element of calculating realpolitik: in addition to providing manpower, maroons were potential sources of useful intelligence in the event of hostilities. It is instructive to note that slaves from South Carolina found an equally agreeable haven in Spanish Florida in the early eighteenth century and were used by the Spaniards in border incursions that kept the British colony in a state of apprehension.[20]

Early legislative prescriptions against grand marronage authorized such physical deterrents as leg amputations, hamstring attenuation, and leg irons or neck collars.[21] Such measures hampered but did not prevent escape by water. Later laws elaborated rules for access to and use of boats. Even before 1750, legislation limited the size of canoes and barges that whites could keep and specified conditions of ownership.[22] Although mutilations and hardware such as neck irons fell out of use pari passu with the disappearance of the forests, regulation of boats persisted until the very end of the era of slavery.[23] The ordinance of 2 October 1706 was the forerunner of many, the necessity for which was proof of the problem they sought to eradicate. But despite a flurry of laws in the 1740s and 1750s, probably inspired by the beginning of the agricultural exploitation of St. Croix, grand marronage could not be suppressed.

Richard Haagensen, who lived in St. Croix in the 1750s, noted in an account of that island that planter families were being ruined by the running away of slaves in groups of as many as 20-25 in a single night. He instanced occasions when slaves seized boats by surprise attack and forced their crews to sail to Puerto Rico. Many plantation owners, Haagensen complained, had "capital staaende iblandt de Spanske hvoraf dog ingen Interesse svares" – capital deposited with the Spaniards that yields no interest.[24] It was commonly supposed in the Danish islands that a year in the service of the Spanish crown brought freedom. This Haagensen said he could neither confirm nor deny, but he had personal knowledge of slaves who had escaped to Spanish territory, lived well and in freedom, and sent back messages of greeting to their former masters and slave companions.[25] Similarly, C. G. A. Oldendorp noted that Maronbjerg – Maroon Mountain, in the northwestern corner of St. Croix – was no longer a secure retreat and that as a result the proximity of Puerto Rico and the promise of freedom there acted as powerful stimulants. The still large African-born slave population demonstrated the same levels of inventiveness and daring that Haagensen observed in the previous decade. Slaves secretly built canoes large enough to accommodate whole families, commandeered when they could not build, forced sailors to take them to Puerto Rico, and when all else failed, bravely swam out to sea in hope of accomplishing the same objective.[26]

Legislation and Diplomacy

Legislation dealing with marronage at the end of the eighteenth century and in the early years of the nineteenth showed a continuing preoccupation with the problem. Governor General Walterstorff attempted to introduce a boat registry in St. Croix in 1791 and insisted that all canoes have bungs that were to be put away, along with oars and sails, when the canoes were not in use. All craft were to be stamped with the royal arms and bear a registration number as well as the owner's name; none was to be sold or rented outside the towns' harbors.[27] In 1811 the police chief of Christiansted announced a fine of ten pistoles for employing slaves on the wharves or on boats in the harbor without a police permit.[28] The Danish West Indian government in 1816 expressed concern at the persistence of escapes by boat and contemplated introducing regulatory measures such as prohibition of boat ownership except in towns.[29] Finally, as late as 1845, three years before emancipation, Adam Søbøtker, the acting Governor General, promulgated a decree permitting plantations to keep only flat-bottomed boats, as slaves were unlikely to try to escape in such craft.[30] By then, however, the marine underground had other destinations than Puerto Rico, as will be shown below.

Over time, legislation to cauterize the haemorrhage proved only minimally effective. The failure of preventative measures prompted a search for other solutions. The absence of a formal extradition convention had enabled runaways to Puerto Rico to cock their snook at former owners, a form of salutation that Haagensen for one found less than amusing.[31] The establishment of such a convention, it was thought, would resolve the difficulty. Accordingly, a series of cartels between Spain and Denmark in 1742, 1765, 1767 and 1776 established that deserters would have to be claimed within one year by their owners; that the latter would pay the expenses of their slaves' maintenance for that period; that reclaimed fugitives would not be punished; that those who embraced Catholicism would be allowed to remain in Puerto Rico; and, finally, that a Catholic church and residence for its priest would be built in St. Thomas at Denmark's expense.[32]

These diplomatic initiatives, however, proved disappointing. The cartels applied to future deserters but not to slaves already in Puerto Rico. The Spanish authorities, moreover, were less than expeditious in dealing with claims. The Danish West India Company filed a claim in 1745 for the return of some 300 deserters known to be in San Mateo de Cangrejos, but 21 years passed before it was adjusted.[33] Less than a decade after the 1767 convention, Governor General Clausen was engaged in a brisk correspondence with Don Miguel de Muesos, Captain General of Puerto Rico. Several slaves had decamped from St. Thomas early in 1775, but the envoy sent to claim them was met by Spanish professions of ignorance of their whereabouts.[34] Grosso modo, the Spaniards showed little inclination to cooperate in the matter of runaways. Occupation of the Danish West Indies in the early years of the nineteenth century by Spain's wartime ally England appears to have made little difference. The British Lieutenant Governor of St. Croix in 1811, Brigadier G. W. Harcourt, issued a proclamation asserting that slaves had been carried off in Puerto Rican boats and declared that such boats found illegally four weeks thereafter in any harbor except Christiansted and Frederiksted would be seized and confiscated.[35] Two months later, the British authorities invited persons who had recently lost slaves and believed them to be in Puerto Rico to submit information on the slaves' age, sex, appearance, and time of desertion.[36]

As late as 1841, the "long-standing difficulties" with Puerto Rico were the subject of exchanges between the Danish West Indian Governor General and King Christian VIII, each hoping that the new Puerto Rican Captain General, Mendez Vigo, would be more disposed to "friendly conclusions" than some of his predecessors had been.[37] An incident reported by van Dockum in the early 1840s reveals the nature of the difficulties. Acting on information that two slaves had been spirited away to Vieques in boats from that island, the authorities in St. Croix sent the frigate on patrol duty in the West Indies to reclaim them. When the frigate arrived at Isabel Segunda, the main town of Vieques, that island's Governor, though full of conviviality and consideration, would admit only that a boat had in fact taken slaves from St. Croix to Vieques.[38] It appears that the shortage of labor in the Spanish islands after the legal suspension of the slave trade in the 1820s bred illegal trafficking, often with the collusion of Spanish authorities.[39] The episode to which van Dockum referred seems to have been an instance of labor piracy willingly embraced by the slaves of St. Croix as an avenue of grand marronage.

New Routes to Freedom

Taking refuge in forested hills and fleeing to Puerto Rico or Vieques were the most dramatic early acts of grand marronage. While slaves continued to escape by water, the disappearance of primeval vegetation prompted others to find ways of deserting without leaving the islands. Sugar served their need in turn. Harvesting began in late December or early January when the canes approached maturity and had grown high enough to conceal even the tallest person. Until the end of the crop season in July, therefore, each unreaped field provided an artificial forest in which slaves could continue to conceal themselves over a six-month period. The work of these months of harvest made the most strenuous and exacting demands on slaves' endurance. This was also the dry season, before high summer brought the heavy showers associated with the movement of the intertropical convergence zone. Slaves thus had multiple inducements: they could find cover, escape the period of hardest labor, and keep dry. A Danish official in the late eighteenth century noted that the expansion of plantations on St. Croix made it difficult for runaway slaves to find shelter in forests that were disappearing or in fields that no longer contained scrub. The alternative, he observed, rendered them secure but posed a constant fire hazard: "Fleeing to the cane fields in which cane and leaves can exceed a man's height, they put down poles of about a meter and a half and make a bower over these with the leaves of the nearest canes plaited together. In this way they form a little hut about four and a half feet high by six to seven feet around. Having cleared the ground in the hut of dry leaves and left an opening, they then use the place to lie up, to store whatever ground provisions they can, and as a fireplace."[40] The existence of maroon hideouts in the cane fields was authenticated by discoveries of corner posts, ashes, and coal. A causal link between such hideouts and cane fires was also established by remnants of pork and other meat abandoned to and partially consumed by fires out of control.[41]

Another variant of grand marronage was desertion to the coastal towns. Christiansted and Frederiksted in St. Croix, and Charlotte Amalie in St. Thomas, grew in population and commercial importance in the prosperous years of the late eighteenth century: plantations flourished, trade expanded, and Charlotte Amalie was established as a free port. For slaves on islands as small as the Danish West Indies, towns offered advantages of comparative anonymity; a prospect of work on the wharves, in warehouses, and aboard coastal or other vessels; the likelihood of finding a sympathetic reception and succor in the areas of these towns designated by law for free persons of color; concealment, incongruously enough, by whites; and the chance of using the town as a staging post in what might become a step-migration to freedom.

Anonymity was enormously enhanced when a slave on the run shipped from one Danish island to another. One cannot quantify this type of marronage, but it was known to have taken place, and as the bustle of free-port commerce in Charlotte Amalie arguably rendered that town a more impersonal place than either Christiansted or Frederiksted, it must be presumed that the tendency would have been toward St. Thomas. Newspaper advertisements appear to support such a hypothesis, although there is also evidence of marronage from Charlotte Amalie to St. John and St. Croix. Most notorious was the case of Jane George, who in an advanced state of pregnancy escaped from St. Thomas in a canoe with a white man early in September 1815 paddling for St. John or St. Croix.[42] Another runaway, James Dougharty, an artisan apprentice, headed for St. John in 1822. A reward of $20 was offered for information, "as it [was] not likely [he] walked all the way."[43] By and large, however, advertisements for maroons in St. Thomas over the first fifteen years of the publication of *St. Thomæ Tidende* (1815-1830) show approximately twice as many desertions to St. Thomas as to St. Croix or St. John from St. Thomas.

The variety of employment in the growing towns facilitated grand marronage into them, and the anonymity they offered was compounded by the notorious laxity of the Danish West Indian police, so that it was possible for runaways to sustain a livelihood in wharf-related work or itinerant vending without too great a risk of discovery. Fugitives enjoyed the normally supportive presence of freedmen in their legally prescribed areas of residence, the Free Guts. With freedmen, urban slaves, and poor whites, deserters composed a demi-monde of the marginalized. Governor General Clausen in St. Croix in the 1770s and Lieutenant Governor Thomas de Malleville in St. Thomas in the 1780s expressed only more explicitly than most the sense of community that prevailed among runaways and freedmen in the Guts.[44] Poor whites involved in petty retail trading or artisan trades were known to consort with and provide shelter for runaways. The latter were potential sources of stolen goods and, if they had an artisanal skill, could be hired out to earn an income for their protectors. Throughout the late eighteenth and early nineteenth centuries, therefore, one finds legislation aimed at curtailing the mutually reinforcing liaison of fugitives and their patrons, especially in the towns. An ordinance issued by Governor General Adrian Bentzon in 1817 spoke of the long history of this liaison and prescribed severe penalties for whites and free persons of color who either hired or hid slaves on the run.[45] As late as 1831, Adam Søbøtker, acting as Governor General, was still vainly attempting to curb that sort of collusion.[46]

For runaways, the coastal towns were above all a porthole of opportunity to a wider world. Marronage overseas to foreign destinations, before the significant growth of the towns, had been limited to Vieques and Puerto Rico. However, as towns grew, they attracted an increasing number of vessels from distant ports, widening the escape hatch for slaves. The schooners, brigs, sloops, yawls, and snows that called at these towns, especially Charlotte Amalie as it became a Caribbean entrepot, brought St. Dominigue/Haiti and Jamaica in the Greater Antilles, the islands of the Leewards and Windwards, the North American continent, and even Europe within reach, though after 1802 Denmark ruled itself out as a haven for escapees. An Upper Court decision that year in the case of the slave Hans Jonathan decreed that the free soil of the mother country did not confer freedom on the enslaved.[47]

Access to avenues of flight depended in some measure on the collusion of masters of vessels. Service at sea in the eighteenth and early nineteenth centuries was such as to suggest a parallel between masters of vessels and slave masters, between ships and regimented slave plantations, between crews and enslaved estate labor. Ship masters, not surprisingly, had their own problems of marronage in the form of desertion. It was not unusual for crewmen, singly or in numbers, to jump ship in West Indian waters. One Swedish sloop, the *William*, Captain Joseph Almeida, lost five hands in St. Thomas harbor on 5 February 1827.[48] Such incidents meant that additional or substitute crews were often needed, and since the white population of Caribbean coastal towns was too small to meet the need, it was unlikely that runaway slaves who offered themselves would be interrogated closely, if at all, about their status. Black crewmen were therefore commonplace. Many of Almeida's men were Africans of unspecified status, and slave shiphands were by no means extraordinary. One such, Jan Maloney, deserted from a vessel of British registry in St. Thomas in 1819.[49]

In 1778 regulations were adopted to obstruct this avenue of grand marronage by forbidding shipboard employment of any slave without a sailor's pass and written permission from his owner. Significantly, it was considered necessary to reissue these regulations in 1806.[50] The 1833 royal proclamation of Frederik VII, by offering the extravagant reward of 1,500 pistoles for information on masters of vessels secretly exporting slaves, suggests that the problem still persisted even at that late date.[51] The size of the reward indicated the seriousness with which the problem was viewed, particularly at a time when the slave population of the Danish islands was steadily declining.[52]

Some ship captains were free persons of color. One such was Nicholas Manuel whose ship, the *Trimmer*, plied between St. Thomas and Jeremie, St. Domingue, in 1796.[53] In such a vessel, arguably, a slave could find the maritime equivalent of a house of safety in a Free Gut. The legislation directed at captains thus took into account a potential collaborator, the colored shipmaster, while it also expressed the paranoia prevailing after the revolution in St. Domingue and accompanying disturbances in the French West Indies. Vulnerability to revolutionary contamination from these trouble spots was a recurring concern of Danish West Indian authorities, who lived in constant fear that their slaves would emulate the St. Domingue example. The years from 1791 to about 1807 were therefore punctuated by measures to establish a cordon sanitaire against St. Domingue. These included the confiscation of any boats arriving from St. Domingue/Haiti and the imposition of a fine of 1,000 Rigsdaler.[54] Yet there is evidence to suggest that such prophylaxis achieved only indifferent results. The traffic to St. Domingue/Haiti, especially from St. Thomas, continued and in the early 1840s Governor General von Scholten felt moved to remark on the "significant" number of "unavoidable" desertions to that island.[55]

Legislation could not prevent desertions, for the movement of interisland maritime traffic depended to a degree on slave crews, and the law permitted slaves with seamen's passes to be so engaged, making a pragmatic virtue out of necessity, considering the shallowness of the white labor pool.[56] Engaged as crews in their island of origin, slaves embraced the opportunity to escape on reaching a foreign port. Jamaica was one such destination in the western Caribbean at which goods from the emporium that was St. Thomas were arriving well before the end of the eighteenth century. Both the *Royal Gazette* and the *Jamaica Courant* carried information that confirms that slaves considered any port a station in the maritime underground. The St. Thomas sloop *Martha* arrived in Kingston in August 1788 and promptly lost Jack, a sailor aged 25, and Tony, 23 years, described as a "waiting man and occasional fiddler." Another St. Thomas sloop the *Hope*, lost George, aged 19.[57] Joe, 25, jumped ship in Kingston from the schooner *Eagle* registered in St. Croix, in May 1806.[58] Not all the deserting slave seamen from the Danish West Indies appear to have made it to freedom. Some like Sam, a St. Thomas creole who arrived in Kingston on a sloop in 1797, were apprehended.[59] No doubt a reasonable competence in an English creole tongue must have helped a slave negotiate the narrows of early freedom in a strange English-speaking island and in this regard slaves from St. Croix may have enjoyed an advantage. Having an employable skill also helped. Another Sam, for example, who deserted from a Danish island schooner in Kingston late in 1793, was a hairdresser by trade.

Since he was American-born and spoke good English, he stood a doubly good chance of getting past the exit turnstiles of this station in the maritime underground.[60]

In the Caribbean, the same flows of trade that took vessels to St. Domingue/Haiti or farther away to Jamaica also took Danish West Indian vessels to the Lesser Antilles in the opposite direction. These flows presented like opportunities to slaves for employment as crew, and such employment, legitimate or illegitimate, created chances for desertion to the Leewards, Windwards and elsewhere. That traffic, moreover, complemented the trade originating to leeward of St. Thomas and St. Croix, thereby widening the possibilities for maritime marronage. This branch of eastern Caribbean intercourse in the early nineteenth century was part of the expanding seaborne commerce into St. Thomas[61] and opened a major escape route for runaways to St. Thomas from islands in the northern Leewards and from as far away as Curaçao and Barbados.[62] Danish slaves were not slow to exploit the situation. One reported example from St. Thomas in 1819 indicates that eight slaves – seven men and one woman – probably crew on the 17-ton interisland schooner *Waterloo*, stole the ship when it arrived in St. Vincent in the British Windwards.[63]

This episode is remarkable for its daring and also for the fact that it is the only incident of running away to the non-Danish islands of the eastern Caribbean, excluding Tortola, that the newspapers report. Though one of the best sources for the study of all forms of marronage, the Danish West Indian newspapers are in fact less helpful than one would like on maritime marronage to the foreign islands of the eastern Caribbean – perhaps understandably so, for the logical place in which to advertise for deserters was the terminus a quo or point of escape. The Danish West Indian papers therefore report desertions from other islands more fully than desertions from the Danish islands. The local advertisement placed in the *St. Thomæ Tidende* by James Hazel, owner of the *Waterloo*, was thus unusual. Recovery of his lost schooner and slaves would have been better served by insertions in the foreign press. But perhaps the size of his loss – schooner, cargo, and eight slaves – obliged him to issue, in modern police parlance, an all points bulletin.[64]

From the inception of Danish colonization, slaves showed their capacity for creating possibilities for grand marronage overseas from each new set of circumstances. They responded ingeniously to the opening presented by the islands' ecology, the proximity of the Spanish islands, and the growing volume of traffic to and from the Danish ports. But of all the circumstances affecting grand marronage, none appears to have had a more quickening effect than emancipation in the neighboring British Leeward Islands, particularly Tortola. Desertions to Tortola began to increase from 1839, the year after the post-emancipation period of apprenticeship ended in the British West Indies.[65] Especially in St. John, no more than a cannon shot's distance away, the urge to desert became irresistible.

Slaves were well aware that once they set foot on Tortola their freedom was secure, for the effect of the British Emancipation Act of 1833 was to confer on them on arrival the free status that the West Indian slave James Somerset had acquired in England in 1772 only after litigation at the highest level. For example, in reporting the incident of the early 1840s involving the two slaves from St. Croix, van Dockum noted that before proceeding to Vieques they had requested to be taken to Tortola, where they went ashore. The authorities in Vieques used this fact to explain why they could not return persons who were in law free men.[66] The difficulties that British West Indian emancipation posed for the Danish authorities were practically insurmountable. Louis Rothe noted that desertions from St. John were almost impossible to control – and not only because of the proximity of Tortola. Overlooked by precipitous cliffs, St. John's innumerable bays made coastal patrols for the most part ineffective. Moreover, the patrols were too few to police bays that, even when contiguous, did not permit observation of one from another. Deserters crossed the straits by boats and improvised rafts from St. John. Boats also originated from Tortola; some even came by appointment to fetch a slave or group of slaves. In Tortola, Rothe observed, "all classes receive them with open arms and emissaries await with tempting offers of money and free transportation to larger islands, and promises of high wages and little work." For the years 1840–46 he reported desertion by 70 slaves.[67] Though the total seems insignificant, it was more than double the number of runaways from St. Thomas over the same period.[68] If Rothe was correct – and he admitted that no official records were kept – an important fact emerges. St. John's slave population declined from 1,970 in 1840 to 1,790 in 1846.[69] The 70 slaves therefore represented nearly 40 percent of the decline over that period.[70]

As the 1840s began, the Danish West Indian government sought to close this route to freedom by using frigates on the naval station. Governor General von Scholten's orders were apparently to shoot to kill, although his long-term objective, as expressed in a letter to Christian VIII, was to reduce the attractions of desertion by progressive amelioration of conditions for slaves.[71] In 1840, a slave woman attempting to reach Tortola by canoe was killed by naval fire. Two others in the party, a mother and a child were apprehended, but two escaped by swimming.[72] In Denmark, *Fædrelandet* observed in righteous indignation that "blood ought not to be shed to compensate for an inability to reconcile the slaves to their existence" and found a sinister significance in the recent erection of "an enormous prison" in St. Croix.[73] Von Scholten and the authorities were for the moment impervious to such voices of humanitarian protest, but it was another matter when pursuit of slaves involved firing upon them in ill-defined territorial waters claimed by the British. An ensuing British protest led to an investigation in 1841 by a senior Danish naval officer, Hans Birch Dahlerup. Formal charges were brought against a Lieutenant Hedemann for the killing of the woman and violation of British waters. The investigation ended in a court martial in Copenhagen and two months' imprisonment for Hedemann – "more to satisfy England and its then powerful abolitionist lobby," Dahlerup concluded, "than for the offense with which he was charged."[74]

The year 1845 was a particularly successful one for slaves bidding for freedom in Tortola. The administration's preoccupation, if not panic, was by then plain. Acting Governor General Søbøtker reported to the crown in tones of anguish a sequence of escapes. In October, six slaves – five men and a woman – from plantations on St. Croix's north side, got hold of a fishing canoe and made it to Tortola, although police and fire corps went in immediate pursuit.[75] The Tortolan authorities returned the boat but not the people. Of particular interest is the fact that the leadership of this escape was attributed to a seasoned maritime maroon who some years previously had deserted from Dutch Saba and had been recaptured and resold in St. Croix.[76]

Less than a month after this incident the most spectacular episode of grand marronage from St. John to Tortola occurred. On the night of 15 November, 37 slaves including six from one plantation deserted from southside St. John in two English boats sent from Tortola for that purpose. The maroon patrol, such as it was, was based on the island's north side, closest to Tortola, leaving the south side unguarded. For some time planters in St. John had been allowed to get their supplies of salt from Tortola in boats from that island, but they were less than vigilant in this instance. No satisfaction was to be expected, Søbøtker felt, as the government of the British Leeward Islands was unlikely to make reparations and would take no action against the two Tortolan boatmen who were accessories. "The established principle since emancipation," he pointed out, "was that no one who had helped an unfree person to gain freedom could be punished for it." The best the frustrated Søbøtker could do was to issue stern warnings to plantation owners, increase night patrols by his inadequate militia, and make new regulations respecting planters' ownership of boats.[77]

Strategies

Grand marronage by Danish West Indian slaves lasted from the beginning of colonization, when the slave population was exclusively African-born, until slavery's end in 1848, when it was largely creole. In the decade or so before that date, emancipation in the British West Indies, particularly in neighboring Tortola, stimulated desertions on a scale that, especially in St. John, threatened to destabilize the slave system. In the 1840s such desertions, though they may have robbed the slave population of its potentially most revolutionary leadership, nevertheless prefigured and arguably acted as a catalyst for the successful rebellion of 1848.

Later commentators, like earlier observers, rationalized grand marronage in a variety of ways, some self-serving, others perceptive. These included depravity, overwork, fear of punishment or impending trial, arbitrary owners, the attractions of a work-free Sunday on other islands, and scarcity of food.[78] Whenever the occasion arose, officials were given to asserting, in an access of obtuseness or arrogant self-satisfaction, that fugitives would willingly return if only they would enjoy more discretionary time.[79] One of the 37 who fled to Tortola in 1845 seized a boat and did indeed return to St. John early in 1846. The records do not disclose his reasons but report him as having said that others were equally ready to return, "which was not improbable," the authorities smugly concluded, "having regard to the prevailing destitution in Tortola."[80] But there is no evidence that these escapees came back to St. John nor did this one swallow make a summer. On the occasion of the 1759 slave conspiracy in St. Croix, the examining magistrate, Engebret Hesselberg, made the surprisingly enlightened observation that "the desire for freedom is an inseparable part of the human condition."[81] Oldendorp, no libertarian himself, concurred, although with less generosity of spirit. "It is extraordinarily difficult," he noted,

> to convince the heathen Negroes that the rights which their masters exercise over them are well-founded. They follow only their own irrepressible natural drives and consider any and all means of gaining their freedom to be just. To this end, they run away from their masters and flee into the mountains and forests, and they even raise planned revolts which threaten the lives of their masters, in order to escape servitude through the use of force.[82]

By running away as they had always done, and in the numbers they did to Tortola, slaves reinforced the truth of Hesselberg's observation. In the 1840s they began to press the issue of their freedom by bringing the metropolitan authorities urgently to consider concrete measures for emancipation. Their initiatives helped embolden liberal opinion in Denmark, already critical of absolute monarchy and colonial policy and favorably disposed to emancipation on economic as well as humanitarian grounds.[83] *Fædrelandet*, organ of the opposition, declared it "impossible for all practical purposes to place limits on the longing for freedom."[84]

Indeed, when a deserted slave spoke into the record, he gave poignant endorsement to *Fædrelandet's* sentiments. Such a man was William F. A. Gilbert, the only escaped slave from the Danish West Indies from whom we have a personal written testament. We do not know when or how he reached Boston, Massachusetts, but it was from that city on 12 August 1847, a year before emancipation, that he addressed to Christian VIII an impassioned plea not only on his own behalf but for every member of his race who had ever been or was still oppressed by slavery:

> To His Supreme Magistrate, King Christian VIII, Copenhagen, Denmark. Sir: I taken my pen in hand a runaway slave, to inform your excelcy of the evil of slavery. Sir Slavery is a bad thing and if any man will make a slave of a man after he is born free, i should think it an outrage becose i was born free of my Mother wom and after i was born the Monster, in the shape of a man, made a slave of me in your dominion now Sir i ask your excelcy in the name of God & his

kingdom is it wright for God created man Kind equal and free so i
have a writ to my freedom I have my freedom now but that is not all
Sir, i want to see my Sisters & my Brothers and i now ask your excelcy
if your excelcy will grant me a free pass to go and come when ever i
fail dispose to go and come to Ile of St. Croix or Santacruce the west
indies Sir i ask in arnist for that pass for the tears is now gushing from
mine eyes as if someone had poar water on my head and it running
down my Cheak. Sir i ask becose i have some hopes of getting it for i
see there your Nation has a stablished Chirches and Schools for
inlightning the Slave, that something the American has not done all
though she is a republican my nam is Frederick August Gilbert now
i has another name thus

Wm F. A. Gilbert

Sir, when i see such good sines i cannot but ask for such a thing as
liberty and freedom for it is Glorius. Sir i make very bold to write to
a King but i cannot help it for it have been a runaway slave i hope
your excelcy will for give me if i is out in order Please to sind you
answer to the Deinish Council in Boston

His withered hands he holds to view
with nerves once firmly strung,
And scarcely can believe it true
That ever he was yong,
And he thinks o'er all his ills,
Disease, neglect, and scorn,
Strange pity of himself he feels
That slave is forlane

William F. A. Gilbert.[85]

8

"An Intermediate Sort of Class:" The Emergence and Growth of the Freedman Population

IN ALL OF THE SLAVE SOCIETIES OF PLANTATION AMERICA there emerged an intermediate group of non-European free persons, separating the superordinate whites from the blacks over whom they exercised hegemonic control. The very existence of such a category of "free" persons upset the neatly symmetrical schema in which white was virtually a synonym for free and black for servitude. This group existed in the midst of the slave society rather than, as in the case of maroon communities, on its fringes. It included slaves who through grand marronage had escaped their owners and established viable identities as freedmen, but its core consisted of individuals who had been manumitted by the conscious will of white persons. The social contradiction entailed in the existence of this group was compounded by the appearance of free persons of mixed racial ancestry, who owed their origins to the sexual exploitation of slave women by European men. Such "colored" persons were in themselves powerful testimony to the impossibility – indeed, the absurdity – of prescribing limits to human interaction. The dialectical tensions between racism and sexuality, even in mature slave societies where servitude came to be justified on so-called scientific grounds, continuously found their resolution in the synthesis of Europe's and Africa's races. But that synthesis was also productive of its own contradictions: a category of persons who were not slave, nor wholly free. With free blacks they formed a class whose civil liberties were severely attenuated, and whose political rights were non-existent.[1]

Manumission

Denmark followed the tradition established by other European imperial nations of manumitting individual slaves whose services to the state were considered sufficient grounds to entitle them to this ultimate privilege. Calculations of economic self-interest were central to the process of manumission, but so too was a grudging gratitude and a reluctant acknowledgement of the humanity of non-Europeans in a slave society. Thus the known instances of state-initiated manumissions indicate that access to the privilege of freedom was limited strictly to those rare individuals whose contributions to social control were thought deserving. Mingo Tameryn's release from bondage in 1733 was inspired by his services to the state during the slave uprising in St. John that year. The manumission of Quamina in 1759 was similarly related to his role as king's evidence in the aborted St. Croix conspiracy of 1759.[2] The aged and trusty Christian Sort (Christian the Black) was accorded his freedom in 1763 as the authorities hoped that "such an example would serve as an encouragement to other slaves to serve with faithfulness and honesty."[3]

Having admitted the inadmissible, however, and thereby reinforcing the contradiction, the Danish West Indian colonial authorities had no intention of opening the floodgates for an anomalous interstitial group. From the early recorded manumissions of the state, there is every indication that client status was intended for the objects of the state's generosity. When private individuals for reasons of their own did similarly, the state intervened to control by law the conditions under which manumissions could occur and to define the place of freedmen in the society. But formal legislation to this effect did not begin to emerge before the 1740s, the decade after St. Croix's acquisition, and definitively in 1776.

Private individuals who accorded freedom to their slaves in the eighteenth century generally did so through testamentary devices, deeds of gift, or the purchase of the slaves of others for the express purpose of granting them freedom. Growth of the freedman population by natural increase and immigration did not become significant until the nineteenth century; nor did self-purchase, the possibilities for which were contingent on expanded opportunities for self-hire and capital accumulation. The protocol of wills of the Danske Cancelli, the Danish Chancery, records instances of testamentary manumissions which required royal confirmation and thus provides the basis for a lower-limit estimate of the manumitted population (Table 8.1). Wills examined for the years 1760, 1770, 1780, 1790 and 1799, mentioned a total of 25 manumissions by testamentary devices, including one case in 1770 where an unspecified number of children was to be freed.[4] The sample suggests a mean of five such manumissions per annum and a total of 200 for the period 1760-1800. The data suggest that the rate increased little over the 40-year period.[5]

The motivations which directed the manumittors – planters, merchants and their wives, and occasionally civil and military officials – ranged from gratitude for faithful service or sexual favors, to death-bed repentance, a sense of the impermanence of things and the mortality of all flesh, and a paternal concern for children they had fathered who were still enslaved. For example, Marcus Skerret of St. Croix had verbally promised his slave

William in 1783 that provision would be made in his will for the slave's freedom. The will, confirmed in the Danske Cancelli on 12 November 1790, described William as having shown "Omhu og troe Hengivenhed" – care and faithful devotion.[6] Similarly, Peter Nordahl, also of St. Croix, stipulated that his slave Hanna be freed for "her constancy, faithfulness and duty towards him."[7] More often than not manumissions by testament were unconditional, but from time to time, there were requirements to be fulfilled before the promised freedom became actuality. As Table 8.1 demonstrates, those conditions included defraying the expense of necessary documentation, payment of certain sums at prescribed intervals to executors or others and continuing service to the testator's heirs for specified periods. An analysis of the color of these freed slaves does not show a conclusive preference for slaves who were "mulatto" or lighter: of the 25, ten were of unspecified color, and of the remainder five were described as black and seven as mulatto. There was on the other hand, a slight preference for female slaves. Since the status of children derived from their mothers, this preference helped to lay the foundations for incremental growth of successive generations of the freeborn. The sexual balance in favor of females which became pronounced among freedmen had at least one of its roots in the patterns of manumission established before 1800.

Accumulation of Wealth

These testamentary instruments, equally importantly, contributed to freedmen's acquisition of property real and chattel, including property in slaves. In the latter regard, it had become common practice before the 1770s to devise slaves as part of the settlement on other slaves already manumitted or to be manumitted by will. As with the grant of freedom itself, eventual enjoyment of the property in slaves was sometimes unconditional; at other times it was hedged about with conditions in the nature of restrictive convenants and, on at least one occasion, by a provision that was bizarrely punitive (Table 8.1). A few examples will suffice. Cornelius Bødger of St. Thomas, whose will was confirmed in Chancery on 29 June 1770, gave to his slave Teshtie and her mulatto child, of whom he was presumably the father, the slaves Phiba, Jamba and Printz.[8] Betsy Tibetta's three daughters, Catharina, Maria and Betsy, for the acknowledgement of whose paternity Johan Friderich Habenstreit sought royal approval, were given one slave each without condition, and their mother inherited three.[9] Lucas Benners settled a domestic slave, Dorothea, on Maria Griffin, described in the will as "mulatinde;"[10] John Aikene bequeathed to Elizabeth Aikene, who must be presumed to have been his daughter, a slave Rachel and all her offspring; Habenstreit's Hanna was made to inherit her own son Francis.[11] Cornelius Bødger's "mulatto Abraham" provides an example of a conditional inheritance. His interest in "the black boy Mathias" was restricted to his lifetime. In the same will of Bødger's the provisions relating to Teshtie's inheritance of the three slaves suggest a

Table 8.1: *Manumissions by Testament in the Danish West Indies 1760, 1770, 1780, 1790, 1799*

Year	Manumittor	Manumitted	Sex	Color	Bequest	Special Conditions
1760	Anna Bødger	Nanny	F	N/S	None	To serve master during his lifetime and youngest daughter to age 21
		Magdalena	F	N/S	None	
	J. Robinson	Marrot	F	Black	50 Rds p.a.	None
		Esau	M	N/S	30 Rds p.a.	None
	Ann Søbøtker	Eva	F	N/S	None	None
1770	James Hansen	Gotto & children	F N/S	N/S N/S	None	None
	Cornelius Bødger	Teshtie	F	N/S	3 slaves, furniture	To have no black children or forfeit freedom to her mulatto child
		Teshtie's child	M	Mulatto	None	None
		Mathias	M	Black	None	Free after Abraham to whom he was willed died
1780	Johan von Beverhoudt	Magdalena	F	Mulatto	None	None
		Johan	M	N/S	None	None
		Frederik	M	N/S	None	None
	Chr. Jansen	Hans Jacob	M	Mulatto	None	None
1790	Rebecca Goodchild	Camilla	F	N/S	None	To pay 150 Rds. in 12 months to her estate; otherwise to revert to slavery unless her heirs willing to extend the period of payment
	John Aikene	Jacob	M	Black	None	To pay 1 Patacoon monthly to Wm. Diriksen
	Peter Nordahl	Hanna	F	Black	1,000 Rds., furniture, utensils, clothing	
	Marcus Skerret	William	M	Black	50 Rds p.a.	None
	Lucas Benners	Penny	F	Mulatto	None	None
		Malika	F	N/S	50 Rds p.a.	During daughter's lifetime
		Carolina	F	N/S	50 Rds p.a.	During daughter's lifetime
		William	M	Mulatto	None	None

Table 8.1 (continued)

Year	Manumittor	Manumitted	Sex	Color	Bequest	Special Conditions
1799	Anton Gravenhurst	Wilhelmina	F	N/S	None	None
	Anna Maria Kerwink	Anna Elizabeth	F	Mulatto	None	Proceeds of her estate to meet the
		Frederik	M	N/S	None	cost of their purchase from their owner Wm. Runnels
	Wm. Ravenschou	William	M	Mulatto	None	None
	Guert de Windt	Sebastian	M	N/S	None	To serve his wife for 5 years after his death and have the expenses of his Free Brief paid

Source: R/A, Danske Cancelli, Vestindiske Sager, 1760, 1770, 1780, 1790, 1799.

form of vindictive possessiveness that was to prevail beyond the grave. The mother of a mulatto child, Teshtie would lose the entirety of her inheritance if she had any black children and forfeit all to "the said mulatto child."[12]

These examples indicate that through testamentary benefactions freedmen were invested with a stake in slave ownership well before 1800. Whether from due deliberation or otherwise, white society gave freedmen an economic interest in slaves to defend and thus ensured that they would not lightly seek alliances with those very slaves in order to destroy an institution from which they profited. In the long term, the policy paid rich dividends. By the early nineteenth century, freedmen owned some two-thirds of all slaves in the towns of the Danish West Indies.[13] In the short term, there were early signs of how successfully freedmen were socialized into this form of property relations. It was not the case, for example, that freedmen who owned slaves by the end of the century felt any sense of obligation to manumit them by a testamentary instrument. On the contrary, when Maria Catharina Skaltenbrand, a free mulatto of St. Thomas, made her will in 1799, her directions were that her two female slaves Caroline and Dominga, who formed part of her more than modest estate, were not to be sold but were to be part of the settlement on her children.[14]

Maria Skaltenbrand owned three houses and their grounds in Charlotte Amalie. As a freedwoman she was not singular in her ownership of real property. It is not clear whether these were inheritances, although many freedmen became property owners in that way. Johan Habenstreit, mentioned above, left his daughters by Betsy Tibetta a house at 4 Dronningens Gade (Queen Street), Christiansted; their mother inherited, as sole owner, another house at 16 Dronningens Gade.[15] Lucas Benners directed that from his estate, "mulatinde" Maria Griffin was to be bought a house in the Free Gut of Christiansted for the sizeable sum of 1,000 Rigsdaler.[16] Benners also settled 100 Rigsdaler annually on "freeborn mulatto Abraham" for the first five years after completion of an apprenticeship in Scotland.[17] Other testators made similar provisions for annuities on their freedmen heirs usually in the amount of 50 Rigsdaler per annum (Table 8.1). Sometimes there were considerable sums of cash in lieu of an annuity, such as the 1,000 Rigsdaler of Peter Nordahl to Hanna.[18] Many legacies consisted of personal effects: clothing, jewelry, and household furnishings. Peter Nordahl's settlement on Hanna in this regard was extensive, and covered a range of items not usually bequeathed in combination. His will serves nevertheless as a prime example of those items of personal property inherited by freedmen. In the list were: 1 large mahogany bed and accessories; 1 mahogany closet, 1 round mahogany tea table; 6 green wood chairs; 1 gilt mirror; 12 silver forks; 6 silver tea spoons; 1 silver soup spoon; 1 gold scarf pin; 1 pair of gold cuff links; 1 pair of gold knee buckles; 1 small tureen; 1 silver serving dish; 3 dozen porcelain plates; 12 pairs of red handled knives and forks; 1 porcelain tea pot and cups; 1 gold knob for a walking stick; and all the deceased's clothing and linen.[19]

In all of these ways, fortified by the practice of some testators of declaring their black and colored beneficiaries "universal heirs,"[20] freedmen in the Danish West Indies came to have an increasing share of the islands' economic patrimony. Unlike the Jamaican authorities who imposed restrictions on the quantum of freedman inheritances in the 1760s,[21] the Danish West Indies had no comparable legislation. At least one St. Croix freedman, Johasie Abrams and his wife Catherine, owned before 1800 what was described as a "plantation." Catherine's Hope, no doubt named after his wife, consisted of 10 acres and an unspecified number of slaves. Johasie's very specific instructions left the estate in entail; it was not to be sold in any circumstances, and claims against it were to be paid in cash over two years.[22]

This modest entry into rural landholding was surpassed by the extensive ownership of real property in the towns. By the time C. G. Fleischer, Charlotte Amalie's Notary Public, compiled his list of persons living in the town in 1802 several houses were owned by freedmen. Many of those houses had also become income bearing through rental. Interestingly enough, many of the houses so owned were occupied not by freedmen but by white tenants, some of whose occupations suggest that they belonged to the town's respectable elements. There were, it is true, transient seamen among those tenants, and their proclivity for hell-raising, drunk and disorderly behavior and generally running a-foul of the law in the towns, is well documented.[23] To be sure, however, there were also trading firms like Beverhoudt and Meyer that rented premises from Hester Frederiks, a free black woman who ran a grocer's shop; a white school teacher, Manderpal, occupied a house owned by a black woman inn-keeper, Marie Joseph; Ludwig Meyer, a gunsmith, had as landlord a black grocery-store keeper,

Antony Derry; and clerks such as Heiliger and Cambert were tenants respectively, of Anna Susanna and Elias.[24]

Population Size and Growth

The freedmen's economic horizons expanded as their numbers grew in the late eighteenth century. The population data on freedmen before the first comprehensive census on all three islands in 1831/1832 are scattered and fragmentary. Despite the paucity of such data, however, there is enough evidence to point to a steady and sustained growth in the decades before 1800. No data are available for St. Croix before 1775, when freedmen made up about 20 percent of the total free population (Table 8.2). By 1797 they were 35 percent of the free and 4 percent of the total population of St. Croix. In St. Thomas freedmen accounted for nearly 30 percent of the free population in 1755, the earliest year for which data are available, but their numbers diminished steadily over the following two decades so that by 1775 they were only 10 percent of the free population. This decline is very probably to be explained by intra-island migration to St. Croix, whose agricultural production and prosperity had been stimulated at the end of the Seven Years' War. Although St. Thomas had been created a free port in the decade of the 1760s, that development does not appear to have influenced an influx of immigrant freedmen before the beginning of the nineteenth century. But the freedman population of St. Thomas doubled between 1789 and 1797 when they accounted for 25 percent of the free population and 4 percent of the total, to come much closer to the St. Croix pattern. There were never more than 20 freedmen in St. John before the end of the eighteenth century – about 10 percent of the free population of the island.

In 1797 the freedman population of the Danish West Indies numbered about 1,418, more than 80 percent of them living in St. Croix. In that year the white population of the islands was 3,062, a ratio approaching one freedman for every two whites. Thus the free as a group were overwhelmed by the slaves, who numbered 32,213 in 1797 (Table 1.1), in the ratio of 7:1. But this disproportion did not lead the whites to seek allies among the freedmen. Rather, their growing numbers and wealth were seen as a threat to white hegemony and means were sought, long before the end of the eighteenth century, to restrict that growth.

Restrictive Legislation

In the preamble to the definitive ordinance of 10 October 1776, Christian VII declared his intention to protect "the negroes who either have purchased their freedom, or have obtained the same through their owners' liberality" from "fraudulent debtors [who] sometimes endeavor, by giving their negroes their freedom designedly to diminish their property"

Table 8.2: *The Freedman Population of the Danish West Indies, 1755-1797*

Year	St. Thomas	St. Croix	St. John	Total
1755	138	n.d.	n.d.	138
1760	151	n.d.	n.d.	151
1765	72	n.d.	n.d.	72
1770	67	n.d.	n.d	67
1775	50	368	n.d.	418
1780	88	374	n.d.	462
1789	160	953	16	1,129
1797	239	1,164	15	1,148

Sources: R/A, Diverse sager, Visdomsbog I, "Specification paa alle Blankes, Frinegeres og Slaves Antal paa St. Thomas fra 1755 til 1774," ff. 342-43; ibid., "Tabel over de paa Hans Majestæts Vestindiske Øers vaerende Indvaanere, Frinegere og Slaver," ff. 461, 529; West, "Beretning;" Oxholm, *De Danske Vestindiske öers Tilstand.*
n.d. no data.

attempted to defraud their creditors.[25] Under the ordinance all freedmen, local and émigré, were required to have "Free Briefs" or freedom certificates approved and signed by the governor general, to be produced on demand. All intended manumissions were to be publicized beforehand, so that creditors' interests could be protected. If unchallenged after two months, "none under what cause or pretext soever shall be permitted further to molest" the beneficiaries of freedom. A protocol of freedmen was established, to include the names of persons whose manumissions, though challenged by creditors, were of at least two years' standing. An additional register of freeborn children was made incumbent on the churches. The ordinance required every slave, prior to manumission, to state how he intended to earn his living, "and it shall be carefully observed that every negroe ... live up to his declaration." It stipulated, finally, that failure to secure a Free Brief carried the penalty either of leaving the island within a year or forfeiture of freedom. Taken in its totality, the ordinance was a mixture of disciplined regulation, whose purpose was to bring order to a situation with potential for chaos, and a degree of enlightened, if guarded, liberality.

Christian VII's approach was informed by the same spirit that had influenced his predecessor Frederik V, author of the 1755 "Reglement for Slaverne." That document, though primarily devised as a slave code, spoke to the status of freedmen, especially the manumitted, in its very last clause: "The freed are to enjoy all rights on par with the free-born and are to be esteemed and respected in all regards equally with the free-born subjects of the Crown."[26] Danish West Indian freedmen regarded the Reglement as their fundamental charter of liberties. Its grant of equal status was absolute and without condition. It represented a radical departure from the legislative developments of the two previous decades during which various administrators of the Danish West India Company had devised a series of measures severely limiting the civil liberties and social rights of freedmen.

The first definitive code of 1733 made no discernible qualitative distinction between slaves and freedmen, perhaps because the numbers of the latter were still negligible. The code's author, Governor Gardelin, did address himself specifically in paragraph 15 to the subject of free blacks: if convicted of sheltering maroons or dealing in goods stolen by slaves they would lose all their rights (which the clause did not define), have their goods confiscated and be deported. However, in the concluding clause 19, the only other clause that mentioned freedmen, Gardelin declared that the preceding eighteen were "the articles by which free negroes and slaves would be governed." There is an element of ambiguity in the provision that was probably deliberate, but in theory it could have meant that freedmen were subject to the entire punitive apparatus designed for slaves.[27] By the following decade, Governor Jens Hansen had instituted segregated residential arrangements. No freedman was allowed to construct a dwelling except in those areas of the towns specified by the chief surveyor. These areas, in which what came to be known as the Free Guts had their origin, were to be laid out in regular streets and the structures with their grounds were limited to 30 square feet. Hansen's ordinance also forbade slaves to reside in the Guts, a strict interpretation of which would have inhibited freedmen's ownership of slaves.[28] During the decade of the 1740s as well, two other ordinances of 1741 and 1746 respectively forbade freedmen purchasing rum after dark, and their ownership of rum shops or of dogs, unless the latter were lame in the legs.[29]

In 1765, Peter de Gunthelberg, the Commandant in St. Thomas, in an Ordinance designed to enforce an already existing curfew for slaves in the towns, established the first formal curfew legislation for freedmen. Although they were allowed to be on the streets two hours later than plantation slaves, and an hour later than house slaves, like slaves they were required to have legitimate permission from an authorized person if present on the streets after 10 p.m.[30] This law, like many of its predecessors, reflected an automatic presumption of criminality on the part of all non-whites, irrespective of condition. The identical presumption informed Governor General Clausen's ordinance of 1767, effectively prohibiting freedmen from engaging in cotton cultivation. Before its decline in the 1790s, cotton as a staple was as profitable as sugar and less risky.[31] Clausen's intention was to guard against the theft of the staple. Freedmen could only avoid the suspicion of theft if they possessed an official affidavit, showing how much land they owned and how many slaves to cultivate it.[32] In the circumstances, it would not be unreasonable to conclude that on the ordinance's hidden agenda was the important purpose of eliminating the possibility of serious freedman competition in the export economy.

The year following Clausen's ordinance, Jens Krag, the Commandant in St. Thomas, made a concerted effort to rid the island's town of night time disturbances caused by slaves' dances and shouting on the streets.

Freedmen were equally liable to arrest for "rowdy behavior, music, shouts and screams" that disturbed the peace after dark. Krag's ordinance of 1768 therefore specified that "to bring an end to the prevailing disorder, and to ensure that free negroes can at all times be distinguished from slaves, they are hereby required to wear a cockade of white and red linen or a ribbon on their hat." Commandant Krag also emphasized that freedmen were not permitted to wear arms of any sort unless they were undertaking some public duty under supervision.[33]

Further restrictions on freedmen's night time activity were contrived in the 1770s. Governor General Clausen, like most of his predecessors and some of his immediate successors, had an almost paranoic preoccupation with night noises, the alien registers of which particularly when accompanied by drumming, no doubt conjured up images of the bloody slave uprising on St. John in 1733. Already in 1765 de Gunthelberg had proscribed "noises, dances and drinking assemblies in the Free Negro Quarter" of St. Thomas beyond 10 p.m. and particularly "the so-called Goombay."[34] For St. Croix, Clausen retained the 10 p.m. curfew but required freedmen to have written permission from the governor general when they held dances. No slaves were allowed at those affairs; nor were whites, "irrespective of their station." If they attended, danced, drank or worst of all created a disturbance, they faced a heavy fine or two weeks imprisonment on bread and water.[35]

One conclusion prompted by most if not all of this restrictive legislation is that it represented the local authorities' persistent attempts to blur the line of distinction between freedmen and slaves. In this way they were at odds with what the crown appears to have intended in 1755 and again, if to a lesser degree, in the Ordinance of 1776. The structure of local administration, mirroring in miniature the absolute monarchy of the metropolis, permitted the decrees of governors general to have immediate effect. Using such extensive discretionary powers, an activist Governor General such as Clausen could attempt not only to close the divide separating slave and freedman, but also to further widen the gap separating freedman and white. In this latter regard his Ordinance of 1775 is instructive. Clausen claimed that it had come to his attention that former slaves of both sexes, black as well as mulatto, had taken the names of their former owners and had baptized their children using the same names. He condemned the practice as both disrespectful and lacking in gratitude, and as a source of future confusion for white families of the same name. He therefore decreed that no free black or mulatto of either sex would thenceforth be allowed such patronymics, unless they used the formula "N.N. manumitted by N.N." Failure to do so was to result in corporal punishment.[36]

Restricted use of "white" family names was not the only mechanism to which the local authorities resorted in an attempt to define rigidly the freedman's place. The most arresting device by far was the sumptuary Ordinance of Governor General Schimmelmann in 1786. In a long preamble

Schimmelmann observed that he could no longer remain indifferent to the increasing tendency, common to both slaves and freedmen, particularly women, to bedeck themselves in finery. The costliness of such dress, he maintained, was "inappropriate to their rank and condition." He hinted darkly at prostitution and its immoral earnings and fulminated against the infidelity, deception and theft that this love of splendor brought in its wake. Since "banquets and festivities given by people of color" provided the occasions for the display of luxury, Schimmelmann proposed to regulate these more closely and to institute "more modest and proper forms of dress." Accordingly all people of color, slave as well as free, were expressly forbidden to wear jewelry of precious stones, gold or silver, material of silk, brocade, chintz, lawn, linen, lace, or velvet; gold or silver braid; silk stockings; elaborate up-raised hair styles, with or without decoration; or any form of expensive clothing whatsoever. Under the Ordinance freedmen were permitted to wear the "more modest and proper" dress prescribed for domestic and field slaves. Also permitted were wool, cotton, coarser varieties of lace, silk ribbon of Danish manufacture, a simple gold cross or silver ornament worn on the head, chest, or around the neck. The ornament was not to exceed 10 Rigsdaler in value. Pinafores of simple cambric were acceptable, as were head- or neck-scarves of the same material, and silver jewelry and silver pocket watches. Freedmen could also wear whites' cast-off clothing, provided they could prove which whites had either sold or given such clothing away. Exceptions would only apply to "officers and men of the Free Negro Company who while on duty would use their regulation uniforms." For the first offenses the punishment was public humiliation: the person concerned would have to parade the streets in a "Spansk Kappe," a sort of dunce's cap used for minor offenders in Denmark and abolished in 1792. Subsequent violations entailed corporal punishment. So far as the "banquets and festivities" went, the original cause of Schimmelmann's concern, he was not minded "to deprive the people of color of the freedom to enjoy their dancing pleasures or tea assemblies." However, as those occasions had encouraged disorderly conduct, all future parties could have no more than six invitees from elsewhere, unless the host had received police permission. Final authorization for the party rested with the Chief of Police; it could only take place under police supervision. The constables present were to ensure decorum in the observance of the sumptuary regulations, moderate consumption of food and drink, and an end to the festivities by 11 p.m. Violators would receive 50 lashes, and whereas the regulations governing dress would be implemented in six months, those governing entertainment would have immediate effect.[37]

Gender and Demographic Concerns

Schimmelmann was not alone in his negative reaction to the developing culture of the freedmen. The St. Croix Burgher Council, in a lengthy

Table 8.3: *The Adult Freedman Population of St. Thomas, 1755-1770*

Year	Women	Men	Total	Women as % of Total
1755	69	23	92	75.0
1760	73	32	105	69.5
1765	37	35	72	51.4
1770	27	17	42	64.3

Source: R/A, Diverse sager, Visdomsbog I, "Specification paa alle Blankes, Frinegeres og Slaves Antal paa St. Thomas fra 1755 til 1774," ff. 342-43.

memorandum of 1778, had suggested that social assemblies involving food and drink, "should in certain respects be controlled and in others forbidden altogether."[38] The Burgher Council's advisory and Schimmelmann's executive act both represented a view of freedmen, whose numbers were markedly increasing in the 1770s and 1780s, as pathogens in the body politic. It was not a view shared by the crown; nor for that matter by the colonial "laity," whose manumissions by deed, bequests of property real and personal, and sexual interaction with freedwomen represented a countervailing tendency. In its most unambiguous terms, the views of officialdom were stated by von Roepstorff in a memorandum in 1783. It was no good thing, he remarked, "to tolerate an all too large number of free negroes." His solution envisaged regulations governing manumissions, the repatriation of foreign freedmen and, above all, of freedwomen. He observed:

> One recalls that it is only a free mother who provides the country with free children. Every negro man's freedom dies with him; in other words, there is nothing of importance to fear from that quarter. On the other hand the problem is of far greater significance when it comes to the young females ... My proposal would be that everyone, as the extant ordinances permit, can free a slave woman in her own right; but if this is to extend to her children, the manumitted shall be required to pay five hundred Rigsdaler to the Treasury, and if this is approved the sum would certainly not be too large.[39]

The central focus of von Roepstorff's disquiet was the freedwoman and the free offspring she would bear. While Schimmelmann's sumptuary ordinance looked to the present, Roepstorff's memorandum looked to the future. Together they shared an unease about women as central to the development of the social culture of freedmen and their prospects for numerical increase. There were always more freedwomen than men in St. Thomas between 1755 and 1770 (Table 8.3), and Hans West maintained in 1792 that more than half of the 797 free non-whites in Christiansted were women.[40]

The concerns did not end with the preoccupation over numbers and the demographic implications they carried. They went beyond to an unarticulated ambivalence about the freedwoman as a person, a concrete reality for which nothing in their experience would have prepared Schimmelmann,

Roepstorff or their colleagues. Unlike contemporary white women in the West Indies, freedwomen from force of circumstances were obliged to exercise a considerable degree of independence in child-rearing, in relationships with men and in ordering their material affairs. The paradox of their oppression was that in all the above regards they had risen above the conventional constraints of gender that still affected their white counterparts. The reaction of white males wavered between contempt and a presumption of loose sexual morality on the one hand, and admiration on the other. At one extreme was an anonymous memorialist at the turn of the century, who condemned all young freedwomen as innately salacious and seekers of sexual adventures with white men by the age of thirteen.[41] Somewhere between the two extremes was Hans West, who admired freedwomen for their physical grace, but nevertheless found it possible to traduce them as incarnations of everything that was evil:

> With measured tread these proud queens sail, erect, through the streets, adorned with straw or hats of best English felt, long gold earrings, gold necklaces, several rings on their golden fingers and bracelets; dressed in fine clothes of the costliest English or East Indian chintz, the best muslin or transparent lawn ... which proclaims their importance as they susurrate through the streets ... But more despicable persons with the airs and good manners that they truly possess could scarcely be imagined ... The Free Gut where they live is a den of venereal disease and ill-gotten goods of every imaginable description, but these honest folk do not steal themselves. They hire house slaves exclusively to do it![42]

Such views held by the official classes in the Danish West Indies reek suspiciously of over-compensation: vigorously condemning what was desirable but not decently attainable. By the nineteenth century, these same classes were to become a byword for their relationships with freedwomen "housekeepers." Time, in short, helped them to resolve the contradictions of their double standards. The unofficial classes were never seriously faced with that difficulty. Unrestrained by any need to set society's moral tone, some of them were capable of relating to freedwomen as women and not exclusively as former slaves or descendants of slaves. This is not to say that these relationships were founded in equality. They could never be, given the social context of slavery and the status of women generally. Nor is it to say that there was an absence of exploitation of a racial or sexual character. Indeed there were instances of heartless abandonment when a favored mistress was past her prime.[43] Marriages were out of the question.[44] Within those limitations, however, there had evolved a sexual modus vivendi between the races. It did not match in scale or intensity the experience of a Brazil where, notwithstanding Gilberto Freyre's overdrawn picture, there was a joyful celebration of inter-ethnic sexual relationships.[45] In the Danish West Indies, such relationships during the eighteenth century became the "custom of the country," although the arbiters of the convention were exclusively the islands' white males.

Table 8.4: *Adult Whites in the Danish West Indies, 1755/6-1774**

Year	St. Thomas Women	Men	St. Croix Women	Men	St. John Women	Men	Total	Women as % of Total
1755/6**	99	110	247	301	65	76	898	45.8
1760	111	124	384	472	63	68	1,222	45.7
1765/6***	72	111	385	519	35	37	1,159	42.5
1770	106	146	362	478	30	62	1,184	42.1
1773/4+	89	146	445	556	37	51	1,324	43.1

Source: R/A, Diverse sager, Visdomsbog I, "Specification paa alle Blankes, Frinegeres og
    Slaves Antal paa St. Thomas fra 1755 til 1774," ff. 339-43.
* Exclusive of servants of unspecified sex in the case of St. Croix.
** There are no St. Croix data for 1755.
*** There are no St. Croix data for 1765.
+ There are no St. Croix data for 1774.

In this connection the remarks of Edvard Colbiørnsen in 1788 are instructive: "To prevent unmarried white men from involving themselves with freedwomen, having regard to local circumstances, would be a pious hope and perhaps impossible to prevent even with the severest legislation."[46] Some of these relationships were clearly situational, inspired by the perennial shortage of white women (Table 8.4). At the same time Colbiørnsen himself provided evidence of what it would not be exaggeration to call color-blind passion. He observed further: "When the abuse reaches the point that young men sacrifice their time, health and welfare and ... the married forsake their duty as husbands and fathers, and are not ashamed to let a concubine occupy the bed of a wife they have driven away, then it is time for the legislator to take note."[47]

Freedwomen, then, intensified the complexity of an already complex situation for the authorities. The dynamics of miscegenation, its effect on the white gene pool, the social and somatic consequences, did not make this problem easier of resolution. Already in the 1750s, Richard Haagensen writing from St. Croix had remarked on the evolving mosaic of colors. Addressing an uninitiated metropolitan readership, he simplified the calculus by explaining that an admixture of mulatto and white resulted in a "mucediser;" the latter with a white produced an almost white person, known variously in the early nineteenth century as "casticer," "pusticer" or "griffe."[48] One does not find in the Danish West Indies the same obsession with a fractional formulation of the "degree of distance from the white ancestor" found in the Anglo-Saxon colonies of the Americas. Nevertheless, before the end of the eighteenth century the authorities were obliged to confront the problem of who was to be defined as white and how. The Danish West Indian government, for its part, never adopted a definitive legislative position. It came closest in the draft slave code of A. G. van der Østen in 1785 in which it was proposed that the descent rule should not be operative.[49] But this code was never legislated.

Some colonial legislators agonized over the social implications. Colbiørnsen, for example, responding to van der Østen's draft, commented that many reputable white families in the Danish West Indies and elsewhere could trace their ancestry to blacks. Accordingly, he thought it would be "useful to prescribe certain generations after which, descendants of negroes, who have white ancestry in an unbroken line could be declared white."[50] Having made the suggestion, however, he had reservations. Any such decision, he thought, would be impolitic and morally inadvisable for it could be construed as "authorisation for such inter-mixtures ... even though in view of the local situation they have to be considered almost as a necessary evil."[51]

The miscegenation that the authorities viewed as a problem and made various efforts to resolve did not occur in reverse. The white male dominance and irreducible racism, fundamental to this and all other New World slave societies, made unthinkable the possibility of mating between white women and freedmen. In van der Østen's words, it would constitute "a shameful occurrence" and was "contrary to all expectation."[52] The threat to white dominance, noted by Roepstorff in 1784, did not come from male freedmen. Indeed in a number of ways they were potential contributors to its reinforcement: as part of the oppressed labor force or by co-option into the local security and para-military organizations. The employment prospects of male freedmen in the later eighteenth century were far from promising. In the first place plantations tended to create their own pool of skilled labor for obvious reasons of economy. In the second place, a large part of the unskilled labor pool in the towns was provided by slaves. West described such urban slave artisans, especially those who were creole, in terms approaching hyperbole. Their accomplishments as shoemakers and barbers, he thought, would put some of Copenhagen's best artisans to shame.[53] In St. Croix, he pointed out, there were several good freedmen shoemakers, tailors, carpenters and cabinet-makers in the decade of the 1790s, when there were some 300-400 male freedmen in Christiansted alone. But a decent living from these and other trades was unlikely and not for reasons of laziness which West maliciously imputed.[54] Far more germane was the economics of slave labor in the urban setting. Competition from that quarter not only narrowed the openings to artisanal employment, but also closed those to domestic service for freedmen and freedwomen. West calculated that it cost 300-400 Rigsdaler to purchase a slave, on which interest at 6 percent amounted maximally to 24 Rigsdaler per annum or 2 Rigsdaler per month. A freedman servant on the other hand cost 6-10 Rigsdaler per month, exclusive of food.[55]

The army of domestic slaves that most urban households characteristically maintained by the 1790s suggests that others like West had made the same calculation and arrived at the same conclusion.[56] Since there was no manufacturing in the plantation economy apart from the production of rum and sugar, West considered their prospects bleak.[57] These daunting prospects, a function of numbers, competition and the nature of the economy, were not always thus. Some 40 years earlier, for example, Haagensen painted a far more sanguine picture of freedmen in the urban economy.[58] By and large, their female counterparts fared somewhat better. The areas of economic activity into which they settled such as island-wide huckstering, using their slaves, or providing board and lodging, were not as fiercely competitive as the male artisanal trades.[59] Moreover, some women with bequests from white men had been able to establish the foundations for capital accumulation. As the century approached its end, most male freedmen did little more than merely survive. There were indications in the 1790s that alternative sources of employment as ship masters were beginning to materialize. But that particular development on the employment front did not achieve significance until the first two decades of the nineteenth century.[60] Without access to employment that could generate surpluses for themselves, or even for whites to appropriate, male freedmen far moreso than women constituted an economically vulnerable underclass.

Social Control

In a more direct physical way, male freedmen contributed as well to white political dominance by their incorporation into the security apparatus of the colonial state. Given the overwhelmingly superior numbers of the slave population, the plurality of slaves in the towns, and the feebleness of colonial military resources, the formation of freedman paramilitary organizations became part of the solution to the problems of internal and external security.[61] In this Denmark merely followed the example of the rest of the hemisphere in entrusting to freedmen those security functions in a slave society that slaves could not be trusted to perform and white men were not sufficiently numerous to execute.[62] By 1765, freedmen provided the "town watch" in St. Thomas with a patrol from 8 p.m. to 4 a.m.; by the 1780s, and probably before, they were also established in St. Croix and by that date such patrols were armed and uniformed. Their duties included patrolling the coasts in the vicinity of the towns for contraband activity; hunting and apprehending runaway slaves; monitoring the curfew; maintaining order at freedmen's dances and giving character references for their promoters; administering corporal punishment to other freedmen of both sexes; and taking censuses of freedmen from time to time.[63]

This para-military organization was led by a Captain of the Freedmen, one of whose qualifications for the position was his trustworthiness. It is not without significance that the first such "reliable" freedman was Mingo Tameryn, whose appointment reflected the authorities' gratitude for his part in suppressing the 1733 uprising in St. John. His son Pieter Tameryn held similar office in St. Croix in the 1770s.[64] By the turn of the century, the organization formed a critically important part of the law-enforcement apparatus in the towns and their environs, as the police diaries of the period eloquently attest.[65] These police powers helped to separate freedmen from slaves. Their exercise also bred hostility from some whites. According to de Gunthelberg in 1765, the latter "from whom one would have expected assistance and support in the maintenance of public order have instead debased themselves to make common cause with the common people and have been so bold as to attack the patrol and release vagabond negroes whom the patrol had orders to arrest."[66] Another observer noted with some asperity in 1788 that freedmen para-military "officer" personnel were invited to government house on some official occasions.[67]

These reactions on the part of lay white colonists were part of the price the authorities were prepared to pay for promoting internal security. They did make concessions to contemporary conventions and racist sensibilities by physically segregating the freedmen in an adjoining room at Government house functions, with an open communicating door, where they ate and drank separately. This apartheid won the approval of the observer quoted above, who saw it as one means of making freedmen "sensible of the Europeans' superiority."[68] But when all was said and done, the Danish West Indian authorities had established the islands' police force at little cost to themselves. Government house invitations were a mark of social status in that and many other colonial polities and they helped to buy the freedmen into collaborating with the extant social order.

At the end of the eighteenth century, the place of freedmen in that social order had more or less taken shape. Their numbers had grown in all three islands. The male freedman leadership had been co-opted, and whilst some degree of status might have attached to ranks such as Freedman Captain, the avenues to status and economic mobility were firmly barricaded. Their women folk with marginally more access to the avenues of economic mobility, were no more mobile in status terms, notwithstanding the physical attractions they held for some white men. The intention of the law, and the conventions as they evolved, was to ensure that the boundaries of ethnicity and ascriptive class remained inviolate. The law emphasized the lowliness of all freedmen as a status group by insisting on the "Free Brief" or certificate of freedom, but denying the burgher's certificate held as a matter of course by the most inconsequential white resident or itinerant. No freedman held any position of trust under the crown except as security personnel and then largely for reasons of expediency; no freedman's evidence was admissible against a white person in the local courts.[69]

There were freedmen, however, who did not share the superordinate whites' circumscribed view of their place in society, their status possibilities or appropriate desserts by way of economic opportunity. As early as the 1750s at least two freedmen in St. Croix, registered their dissatisfaction with the status quo. This was the significance in part of the leadership given by the freeborn William Davis and his collaborator French or Frank to the 1759 slave conspiracy. The depositions taken after the conspiracy was exposed, indicated that Davis was to have become Governor General in a new dispensation without whites.[70] No evidence has yet come to light that others subsequently sought such a radical denouement. Nevertheless, there had emerged before the end of the eighteenth century a certain sense of individual, if not communal, self-esteem. West noted the phenomenon but with scarcely concealed ridicule:

> There is another sort of negro here who in all respects ranks above [house slaves] and who have conferred on themselves the most extensive claims to every imaginable preferential treatment. These are the free negroes and mulattoes, or more properly mulatto women. Through their masters' generosity or their own efforts they have achieved freedom and prosperity. They consider themselves GENTLEMEN and LADIES and greet each other in the following style: HOW DO YOU DO *SIR*. I HOPE YOU WELL *MAM*.[71]

From West's point of view such forms of greeting were pretentious in the extreme. From another perspective, it was an early index of self-conscious behavior that would grow incrementally as the nineteenth century unfolded and force a re-examination of the status quo by local authorities and the crown.

9

"The Rights and Privileges of Rational Creatures:" The Freedman Petition of 1816

AS THE NINETEENTH CENTURY BEGAN, THE EMBRYONIC self-identity of Danish West Indian freedmen struggled for survival in the essentially hostile atmosphere of white society's irreducible racism. While they needed to defend themselves on that front, too close an identification with the slaves would compromise their aspirations, so that they were faced with the task of carving out for themselves a discrete yet viable middle ground between whites and slaves, within the structure of the slave society. Caught between the abrasions of these challenges, the freedmen's sense of self became increasingly refined and defined. The process of definition was greatly aided by the numerical growth of the freed population, the effects of the British occupation from 1807 to 1815, and by the presence of a substantial cohort of immigrants, whose expanding numbers had a leavening ideological influence.

Between 1797 and 1815 the freedman population of the islands more than trebled, increasing from 1,418 to 5,035 (Table 1.1). This rapid growth in the freedman population was the combined result of immigration, natural increase and manumission. To arrange these factors in any order of magnitude poses difficulties, since the necessary data are virtually non-existent. Nevertheless, some data for 1815 pertaining to St. Thomas are indicative. Of the 464 freedmen in Charlotte Amalie that year, 47 percent were immigrants. The free-born were the next largest group at 29 percent, whilst those manumitted were third with 24 percent.[1]

St. Thomas and St. John experienced the most spectacular growth, the number of freedmen increasing more than ten-fold in the period 1797-1815 (Table 1.1). In St. Croix the population merely doubled and by 1815 there were almost as many freedmen living in St. Thomas as in that island. In the same period the white population of the Danish West Indies increased by only 35 percent, while the slaves decreased. Freedmen outnumbered whites in each of the islands by 1815, accounting for 55 percent of the total free population.

White Attitudes

The deep-seated racist antipathy towards freedmen found an appropriate occasion for its expression in the debates that immediately preceded the abolition of the slave trade in 1802. Many of the white participants in the discussion, especially those opposed to abolition, envisaged freedmen exclusively in terms of their potential contribution to the islands' labor resources. They argued not merely that there was a labor shortage, but justified the maintenance of the trade and the inclusion of freedmen in the labor force expressly on racial grounds. In this regard an anonymous memorandum, attributable to the Chief of Police of St. John, is instructive. It rehearsed the well-known argument of the incapacity of whites to withstand the tropical sun, and argued that even if there were examples of a few whites whose labors indicated the contrary, they were invariably creoles inured to the climate from childhood and in any event an etiolated species constantly given to illness. "Thus," the author proposed, "negroes are essential for cultivation in the colonies. The question which therefore arises is whether this could be accomplished with the paid labor of free negroes." The question implied an affirmative answer, but the author ruled out the possibility on the grounds of the freedmen's perception of themselves and their aversion to manual labor: "when free negroes consider themselves as good as, if not better than whites, they regard it as a shame to serve the whites and prefer to support themselves either by stealing or receiving goods stolen from whites by their slaves, than to earn a livelihood by regular work."[2]

This anonymous author also quoted with approval a report on Antigua's freedmen that came to the conclusion that "they may in general be regarded as a useless, dissipated race of people," adding that in the case of the Danish West Indies they were a public burden as well. Not surprisingly, he was bitterly opposed to manumission by testament and hinted darkly at his own final solution by which this "pernicieuse race de vipères pourrait au moins être diminuée sinon extirpée." The argument was reinforced by an appeal to eugenics and an early appeal to "scientific" racism. Pointing to St. Domingue and Martinique, he dismissed as unachievable the racial equality that the National Assembly had imposed in both islands:

> Beside the natural distinctions separating black and white, there is this essential difference: the negro has no cartilage in the tip of his nose; a mulatto has little, a mustee more, a castee somewhat more again, and a pustee just as much as a white. These latter represent the first generation that might be manumitted with royal approval, if their owners are in a position to do so.[3]

From racial views of this extreme character, it was not difficult for the author to fashion a description of freedmen as "the plague of the colonies," capable of the worst and most dangerous forms of social deviance. Apart from their alleged propensity for theft and laziness, freedmen were also condemned for learning neither to read nor write – though the memorialist did not trouble, like West earlier, to relate lack of initiative to economic opportunity, nor their illiteracy to an educational system that was deficient even for whites. As for the young women among the freed:

> they already begin at that age [12-13] to support themselves by salacious living. The comely ones become the declared mattress of somebody or another; the less attractive openly become whores, having three or more children, as often as not for different fathers who can provide a little support for their offspring. As quickly as they flower, as quickly they fade in this climate. By age 25 to 30 when they have lost all their attractions, they are left for the most part to their own devices and their resources of support for themselves and their children consisting of no more than a little clap-board house and a couple of slaves. This is all their compensation for this sacrifice of their morals.[4]

Without morals, a sense of duty or desire to engage in regular employment for a living, driven moreover by "an exaggerated sense of the advantages of their freedom," freedmen were "both the most useless and most dangerous persons."[5]

This perception of freedmen as a danger to the state was heightened by the circumstances of an era and a region wracked by political upheaval and revolution. At one level this preoccupation with freedmen as potential disturbers of the public peace had been a constant of the eighteenth century. It found expression in curfew legislation, restricting ownership of taverns and issue of rum shop licences to whites, and prohibiting the retail rum trade in the Free Guts. It was not without significance that the original liquor licensing ordinance of 1746 was reissued in 1803 and went so far as to spell out that only a white person could be appointed locum tenens if the substantive tavern owner was absent for a protracted period.[6]

At yet another level, freedmen were presumed to be bent on breaking a fragile public order in the most destructive manner conceivable, by the promotion of revolutionary ideas and the violent overthrow of the colonial state. Not surprisingly therefore, when in 1807 Baron Friderich de Bretton Jr. was accused of plotting to overthrow the government of St. Croix evidence led at the investigation pointed accusingly at freedmen, and it was noted both that he lived with a "mulatto wench" and that on the eve of the English invasion those freedmen who had been inducted into an artillery corps and under arms were far from being reliable.[7]

The same rankling suspicion of subversion suffused the views of the anonymous memorialist of 1802. The problem, as he saw it, was at its most severe in St. Thomas where the population of émigré freedmen was growing very rapidly. He recommended that the émigrés, whose points of origin he identified as the French West Indies, Curaçao and Grenada, be permitted to land for a maximum of four days. If they remained any longer they should be either deported immediately or detained in chains until deportation. They possessed what he described as "an erroneous understanding of freedom," with those from Curaçao being the worst offenders. If the island's commerce prospered, he felt, their views did not represent a threat to peace, public order or political orthodoxy. Once trade declined, however, he was less sanguine about the prospects "for their violence and depravity will increase in inverse proportion to their loss of livelihood."[8]

White officialdom, unwaveringly racist, was equally unwavering in its determination to narrow the avenues of economic opportunity open to freedmen, and to define their social space. This is well exemplified in observations by Adrian Bentzon expressed in 1802. Bentzon, ironically, achieved a certain notoriety for abandoning his wife, a New York Astor, in favor of his freedwoman mistress Francisca Henrietta Coppy, popularly known as Miss Chigger and mother of two sons from this liaison.[9] Like his anonymous contemporary, Bentzon saw the proper role of freedmen in the society as contributors to the labor supply once the transatlantic slave trade had been abolished. In advocating a ban on the purchase of slaves for use as household servants except in special circumstances, he proposed also "that none of that class called free coloreds should by gift, inheritance or any other means be allowed to possess any slaves unless they are planters." Such a provision had a triple objective: restriction of slave labor exclusively to agriculture; widening the distance between slave owner and slave; and reinforcing "the restrictive boundaries fashioned by in-built prejudice." Whites would no longer enjoy the comparative advantage of using domestic slave labor, as West had foreseen. Indeed, in the scenario envisaged by Bentzon freedman ownership of slaves would be a virtual impossibility. The contemplated dispensation would oblige freedmen to offer their services on the labor market to replace unavailable slaves and, by increasing the supply, force wages down. The competition, moreover, would lead to an abandonment of freedmen's habitual "idleness ... folly and debauchery." Bentzon remarked further that if such legislation were found inappropriate, specific guidance in the descent rule would be required. "It is obvious," he concluded, "that it would need to be determined after what degree a person with white ancestry should be deemed white."[10]

Before Bentzon, both van der Østen and Colbiørnsen had addressed their attention to this issue. Neither they, he nor any subsequent administrator definitely disposed of it, although their prejudice in favor of a European somatic norm was clearly evident. It is also clear that at the beginning of the nineteenth century the attitudes of officials such as Bentzon towards freedmen as a group were colored by the freedmen's closeness in ethnicity and social organization to the slaves, even though the latter were below them in legal status. These were readily observable phenomena and obscured, for even the most observant white, the reality of incipient class formation among the freedmen, based on economic achievement, education, life-style and some degree of internalization of the very somatic criteria to which whites subscribed.

Interaction with Slaves

The records of the police jurisdictions of Christiansted and Frederiksted at the beginning of the nineteenth century shed important light on the symbiotic social contact slaves and freedmen shared. Freedmen had wives or women who were still slaves. John Messer, a Captain in the Frederiksted town watch, had a slave wife, Sarra, with whom he organized cock fights. These sometimes included a supper to mark the occasion, and participants as well as guests were free as well as slave. The catering was the responsibility of Sarra and another slave, Cudjoe. It is significant that Messer, by his own admission, could not read. It is aso instructive that when he was arrested he remarked that "he didn't think he had done anything wrong as it was common practice all over the countryside for slaves and free negroes to have cockfights."[11]

These intimate forms of social interaction are also well illustrated by the freedmen's continued abetting of petit marronage by providing shelter for slaves. For example, Aletta, a free black woman, was sentenced to four days detention on bread and water in Christiansted's fort for having housed a runaway in March 1805.[12] A year later, almost to the day, the police of Christiansted conducted what would now be vulgarly described as a "sweep" in the Free Gut. Several constables and twenty freedmen took part, and they no doubt regarded their efforts as richly rewarded. They apprehended Caritta from Beeston Hill estate who was being sheltered by a free black woman; Molly, from Frederiksted, absent from her owner since the previous Christmas; Elisabeth from Castle Coakley estate, housed by Peter a free black man and Hanna absent from her owner for two days without permission.[13]

Evidence of freedman cooperation in grand marronage, on the other hand, is not overwhelming.[14] One reported case in 1805 suggests that pliant freedmen whether with connections in Puerto Rico, the collaboration of willing Puerto Rican colonists resident in the Danish West Indies or the cooperation of a discreet ship master, could engineer a slave's escape. In the case in question, William Rogiers, owner of Fountain estate, sought police assistance in finding Augustus who had been absent for two months. The subsequent investigation revealed that Augustus' sister, Johanna Marie, a free "mulatinde," had lived in Christiansted for two years previously with a Puerto Rican colonist, Castillo, a cigar finisher by trade; that the mother of Johanna Marie and Augustus was also a slave on Fountain; that Fountain's slaves often came on errands to Johanna Marie from her mother; and that an aunt of Johanna Marie and the missing Augustus had been banished to Puerto Rico two years earlier for allegedly attempting to poison a family. It also transpired that a second slave from Fountain, Mathilda, who had twice run away for short periods, had been engaged as cook in the Castillo house. Rogiers' affidavit to the police concluded, not unreasonably, that there was enough evidence for the "strong supposition" that Castillo and Johanna Marie had concealed Augustus and had shipped or intended to ship him out to Puerto Rico.[15]

Both in the case of Messer's cock fights and Johanna Marie's apparent complicity in grand marronage the close fraternization of freedmen and slaves was buttressed by ties of kinship. There were other forms of social intercourse, however, based entirely on shared interests and common behavioral patterns. On Christmas Day 1806 Elisa Messer and Fillis, two free black women, were arrested in the streets of Christiansted along with a slave woman, Hanna, for singing bawdy satirical songs. A few months earlier, Juliana, a slave woman owned by free "mulatinde" Susanna Campbell got 30 lashes for the same offense. On New Year's Day 1807, Marie, a free black woman, was taken up on the same charge.[16] The performance of outrageous lyrics on the streets singly or in company bridged the legal divide separating slaves and freedmen, especially where the latter were black.

If such common activity had its season, other forms of socializing took place throughout the year. The police arrested a slave Thomas in January 1805 for playing cards with freedmen; two freedmen in December that year for playing cards at night with slaves, and a freedwoman for taking part in a game of chance, Baksen Deus, with two slaves in July 1807.[17] The incidence of arrests over these two years was not great and suggests both inefficiency on the part of the police as well as the adroitness of the participants in escaping arrest. In any event, the incidents themselves tell their own story of close contact. Overwhelmingly, however, it was at the dance that the social exchanges were at their most complete. The law did not permit freedmen and slaves to attend each other's dances. The prohibition notwithstanding, free people of both sexes often attended these affairs, and where their color was given they were almost invariably black. Of five arrests in Christiansted between September 1805 and New Year's Day 1807, only one was of a freedman described as "mustice."[18] Mostly black freedmen then appeared to have attended and actively participated in slave dances. But it is also worth recording that they were known to have played intermediary roles in securing necessary authorization. Josephus, a free black man in Christiansted, sought and obtained such permission for a slave dance in April 1807.[19]

While the evidence points to mutually reinforcing cordiality between slaves and some freedmen, it is equally certain that a process of internal differentiation was in train, producing a stratum of freedmen with habits and views that separated them from the mass of their legal peers. This elite sought actively to distance themselves from slaves and to disassociate themselves from those of their class whose patterns of social activity were often indistinguishable from those of slaves. By keeping their distance, they reduced the possibility of becoming involved in unseemly street brawls such as that involving a free black woman Genet Francis and a slave woman, also called Genet.[20] They were also unlikely to befall the fate of a Frederiksted free black man who was set upon by three male slaves early in 1797, or to face the prospect of verbal abuse.[21]

If anything, freedmen with aspirations to higher social status were wont to overcompensate, and treat slaves as harshly or more harshly than did whites. Since there was substantial ownership of slaves in the towns by freedmen, in the case of St. Thomas as high as 28 percent by 1802, there was ample opportunity to indulge the tendency to harshness where it existed.[22] It was not unusual for freedmen, irrespective of sex, to have their slaves detained in the town forts which did additional duty as prison and workhouse. Used extensively by whites both in town and on the plantations to deal with refractory slaves, the town forts had become well established by 1800 as disciplinary centers. Slave-owning freedmen frequently emulated this white practice,[23] though less, one suspects, out of a desire to avoid private punishment and a reputation for cruelty, than to demonstrate their authority over the slaves they owned.[24]

Certainly, many contemporary white observers claimed that in the private domain freedmen slave owners were notoriously given to ill-treatment. Theirs is largely hostile testimony, however, and incapable of the same evidential verification as the police files. Bentzon, in 1802, supported his general opposition to freedman ownership of slaves by arguing that it "would put an end to one of the worst forms of slavery, for it is quite readily comprehensible that of all masters, the colored are the least compassionate and the most demanding."[25] His anonymous contemporary's assessment was that "the most tyrannical towards negroes are the emancipated, Jews and creole women." According to this account, their preference in punishment was to avoid the police and exercise their own arbitrary discretion at home where it was not subject to any limits: punishments of more than 100 lashes administered by a hired chastiser using a plaited cow-skin whip were not uncommon. He alleged further that there were many occasions on which the police had declined to punish the pregnant or the weak, and their owners, made indignant by the refusal, proceeded to take matters into their own hands, beating their defenseless slaves in the most brutal manner. Many of these owners, he added, put their slaves in heavy chains, partly as punishment, partly as deterrent. Frightened at the prospect of worse treatment, the slaves would not complain and would only run away when they were able.[26] This tale of unrelieved tyranny, at least in so far as it applied to freedmen, was perhaps overdrawn. Nevertheless, there would have been psychological motivation for such behavior, and it makes the phenomenon, if not the alleged degree and frequency, eminently plausible.

Internal Differentiation

The process of internal differentiation, of which the over-compensatory behavior towards slaves formed part, generated tensions of its own kind among freedmen themselves. The evidence, though not conclusive, would also seem to suggest that such conflicts might have had their roots in, or were partly inspired by, considerations of color. When Christian Muller, a free "mustice" and member of the Frederiksted town watch, arrested Roderick Conner, a mulatto, for disturbing the peace in 1804, the act was accompanied by the significant admonition: "You shall have respect for me just as though I were the governor general himself."[27] If not his office, then his color was intended to have a certain cachet. Those instances of physical confrontation between freedmen recorded in the police files for the early years of the nineteenth century, almost invariably involved persons of different gradations of color. For example, Nanny Heyliger, a free black woman and free "mulatinde" Maria Messer were both arrested for fighting on the streets of Christiansted in January 1805; Thomas Barry, a mulatto, had Rimont Lamberg, a free black from Curaçao, arrested for "impertinence and threatening behavior" in June 1806; later that year, Pedro Peterson, a free black, wounded Hanna Ravene, a free mulatto, in her head with a stone; the following year Robert, a free black, was arrested on a complaint from Daly, a free mulatto, for creating a disturbance outside his house and threatening him.[28]

The patterns of litigation and complaint in the police courts tell virtually the same story as the examples above. The very day after Robert's arrest, two mulatto freedwomen Rachel Beverhoudt and Sara Heiliger were in court to air a complaint against a free black woman, Nancy Blizard. The same pattern of litigation is evident in another case. Three Heiligers, Maria, William and a third whose initial only is given, and all described as "mustice," appeared in court on 19 September 1805, along with a slave owned by Maria, presumably as an unsworn witness. None of the opposing party was as light complexioned as the Heiligers: there was "mulatinde" Elizabeth Stallard; a free black woman, Elizabeth Pedrino; William Purcell, described as mulatto; two witnesses in free blacks Sally Daly and Janton Towers, and a third in Walker, a carpenter, whose color was not recorded.[29]

Unfortunately, the police diaries do not indicate the outcome of the hearing nor, more importantly, the nature of the complaint. It may well be that the constricted spatial ambience of the small towns of the Danish West Indies, in the physical as well as social senses, was a fertile breeding ground for fiercely competitive battles of recognition in the war of status. Ultimately, the important engagement would be on the white front. In the meantime, the skirmishes among the freedmen themselves seemed to be in the nature of a contest to establish claims to leadership for the assault on the other front. Undeniably, color was one component of the contest but in the highly textured complexity of freedman society in the process of formation there were other layered subtleties. For example, where there were instances of confrontation between freedmen in the town patrols and their peers who lived in the so-called Free Guts, these were to an important degree nourished by the desire of the black and colored para-military, as Christian Muller so cogently expressed it, to command "respect."[30]

It is also interesting to note in this regard that while there were no public assembly rooms for freedmen, such as The Lonely Hearts Club for whites in Frederiksted,[31] some aspiring freedmen attempted private equivalents. Access was by invitation only. In a house in Christiansted's Free Gut occupied by T. Smith, "billiards [were] often played behind closed doors." On a Sunday morning in April 1806 when the police arrived there, card games were in progress. William Heiliger, mentioned above, was one of the guests present. He and all the others were fined.[32] This was a far cry from street corner card games with slaves. Yet Smith's was not the only house in the Free Gut where billiards were available. On the same Sunday morning, William Purcell and his two guests were charged and fined for playing billiards in Purcell's house while church services were in progress.[33]

Challenging Inequality

The Purcells and Heiligers, even though in apparently competing coteries, were instrumental in giving momentum to the drive for status reinforcement, though not quite yet for equality, vis-à-vis whites. They rankled at the notion of wearing the cockade, required by law of all freedmen and designed to identify doubtful claimants to free status.[34] It is not surprising, therefore, to learn that in December 1805 the combative William Heiliger was fined 6 pistoles for not wearing his cockade. Similarly, in September 1806 John Abraham, a free mulatto, arrested for being drunk and disorderly at the Christiansted Sunday market, insisted to the police that he was free but wore no cockade; and freedman Johannes Jacob when arrested as a curfew violator by the Christiansted patrol in January 1807 wore no cockade.[35] There are also examples from Charlotte Amalie in St. Thomas, and St. Croix's other town, Frederiksted, of antipathy to a badge considered demeaning.[36] There were also at least two occasions in 1806 when the law was turned on its head, perhaps deliberately to demonstrate its perceived absurdity. John Fransisko, whose name suggests he might have been a mestizo from Puerto Rico, was apprehended in September 1806 for wearing a cockade but he had no Danish papers of any sort. Late that year freedman John Franklin was properly displaying his cockade but had nothing else to authenticate his free status.[37]

Objection to the cockade was a form of passive resistance. So too was the attempt by a "mulatinde" whom the police dignified with the title of Miss before her family name, Benders, to travel from St. Croix to St. Thomas without a pass.[38] But there were other more active methods by which freedmen sought to challenge the status quo, or express their irritation at it. This could involve recourse to the courts; a route chosen by freedwoman Genet Dyer to get satisfaction from a white man, Bellony, who, fired up by drink, took away her slave-higgler's tray of cakes and made them unsaleable. Bellony was made to pay for the cakes and fined 6 Rigsdaler.[39] It could also involve sublimating their pent up aggression by stoning the property, but not the persons, of whites. This kind of vicarious assault, mostly at night, had a long history,[40] and as a gesture of defiance it continued to have currency in the early nineteenth century.[41] Slaves, however, had no monopoly on this kind of violence. In 1805 Diderich Raahauge, a white shopkeeper in Frederiksted, had all the windows of his house and those at street level in his shop destroyed. His fellow white tormentors had made use not only of stones but also of stale bread.[42] When therefore freedman Jems Nicolas stoned the house of a Mrs. Watlington, a white woman, in Christiansted, he was making use of a well established convention for expressing displeasure.[43]

Challenges to the established order also involved a range of verbal responses in altercations with whites that ran along a continuum from lack of deference to positive abuse.[44] Early in 1797 when Hans Simon, a Frederiksted free black man, was set upon by three slaves, the freedman patrol was quickly on the scene. Two of the slaves taken into custody were the property of Ludwig Heitman who arrived shortly afterwards in the company of the town's Chief of Police Frederich Eylitz. In making the arrest the patrol's swords had come into play and both of the apprehended slaves had received flesh wounds. From the welter of allegation and counterallegation at the inquiry there does not appear to have been a shortage of abuse. What is also clear is that the freedmen gave as good as they got. Christian Muller, a free mustice patrolman, told Eylitz that he would not have troubled himself to come to the scene of the assault if it had not involved a rich man's slaves. Indeed, with a proper sense of his position and protocol, Muller further informed Eylitz that he was doing the King's duty and that "if there were no justice in the West End [Frederiksted] there was a General [Governor General] in the Basin [Christiansted]." Isaac Barnes, a mulatto, who was visiting nearby with a free mustee, Jenny Almeyda, rushed to help even though he was not on duty. Being without uniform, he was told by Eylitz that he had no business there. Barnes' rejoinder was that he had as much right there as anyone. Another patrolman, Samuel van Brackle, did not take kindly to Eylitz's apparent objection to use of their side arms and observed, "Why should we carry side arms and not use them on occasions such as this?"[45]

Freedmen, then, were not given to meek retreat into silence when the occasion in their view required a vigorous verbal defence. The very Isaac Barnes who took Eylitz to task in 1797 demonstrated five years later that he had lost none of his ability to defend himself with the spoken word, even to the point of abusiveness. Early in 1802 Barnes was a member of a patrol party in search of a deserted Danish soldier. In the course of the search, the patrol crossed the estate of John Willet Morrel, where they apparently helped themselves to pawpaws and bananas. Barnes' version of the story, told in his affidavit to the police court in Frederiksted was that "he began to abuse me repeatedly call'd me a dam rascal dam Negroe that I might kiss his backside several times drew his sword & told me to look sharp or he would cut off my dam head that he would look out & call'd God to witness."

The deposition of another freedman, Ben Challender, showed that Barnes was not to be outdone when it came to abuse. Challender's account of Barnes's reply was more than likely an edited version, since his rendering of Morrel's vituperative attack only made mention of "rascal and other abusive words." Notwithstanding, Barnes' language as he related it to the court was opprobrious enough. He had told Morrel that "he was no more of a rascal than the rascal that called him that; that he was green just come from his country, done digging potatoes."[46]

However indignant Barnes was and however rich his vocabulary of abuse, there was no altering the objective fact of freedman inequality. There was nothing that whites had actually proposed or undertaken in these early years of the nineteenth century to alter in any fundamental way the terms of their relationship with freedmen. They had toyed with the idea of accepting as equals those made in their somatic image and relaxed for some freedmen the otherwise rigidly restrictive residential apartheid. There were other minimal concessions such as the 1806 grant of a three year liquor licence to the free black Benjamin Jeppe in St. Thomas and the permission granted in January 1807 to William Cosvelt, a free mulatto, "to hold cockfights for the free colored once per month for the next five months" in Christiansted.[47] But whites remained, as they had always been, hostile, suspicious and unyielding in their belief in the freedmen's innate inferiority. They were even ready to dismiss with scarce-concealed contempt the freedmen's attempts to advance their claims on status. The patrol was tolerated as a useful security adjunct, but hardly respected by some of the official classes like Eylitz, nor indeed by the lay colonist. In the latter regard nothing had changed since 1765 when Commandant de Gunthelberg in St. Thomas upbraided white colonists for ridiculing the patrol and obstructing it in the performance of its duty.[48] If anything they had gone a step further in inventing derisory names. On New Year's Eve 1803 a party, mostly of Anglo-Irish, foregathered at Samuel Gumbs' house in Frederiksted to celebrate. The party got somewhat out of hand with even the young women taking part in the illegal throwing of squibs. When the patrol came by they were stoned so violently that a passerby was hit in the back by a brick that felled him. The patrol were also jeered and called "Black Coat."[49]

The first significant shift in attitude towards freedmen appears to have been the result of the changes accompanying the major British occupation from 1807 to 1815. Already under the first brief occupation of 1801-1802 the British had shown a predisposition to rule by division, going so far as to encourage slaves to bring complaints against their masters to the occupying authorities.[50] So far as freedmen were concerned, the terms of the capitulation in 1801 stipulated that "the free coloured people ... shall be regarded as protected as heretofore under the Danish Government and they shall not be forced to do any military duty" provided they took an oath of allegiance to the British crown.[51] Altogether the military governors of the occupation showed a far more accommodating attitude towards freedmen than their Danish predecessors. Throughout the occupation, for example, proclamations were issued from time to time requiring freedmen who were without the obligatory Free Brief, prescribed by the seminal ordinance of 10 October 1776, to collect them at the government secretary's office. The last such proclamation was made in August 1813.[52]

Towards the end of the occupation, however, when apparently many freedmen had not complied, the last British military Governor General George Ramsey issued a proclamation that was virtually an amnesty:

> taking into consideration the general good conduct of coloured inhabitants ... and the various circumstances that may have prevented the individuals from making the proper application, I do hereby recall and annul the said Proclamation and authorize the Government Secretary to deliver up the ... emancipations, which are by virtue hereof fully confirmed, and shall be held valu'd and effective to all intents and purposes.[53]

After the restoration, Danish colonial officials regarded the interregnum of the occupation as a bad influence on the freedmen, in as much as they deemed the British to have paid insufficient attention to the laws and conventions defining their status.[54] The relaxation of residential segregation and freedman ownership to real property in "white" areas of the towns were developments that antedated the substantive British occupation of 1807-1815 and the Danish authorities were so aware. But there was the clear implication that these were undesirable trends the British had done nothing to arrest and may even have encouraged.[55]

Certainly by the third year of the second occupation, the freedmen of St. Croix were submitting for the first recorded occasion, "petitions, representations and requests" to the British authorities, and apparently in such numbers that the latter felt obliged to invoke extant regulations governing such submissions.[56] There is nothing in the evidence to indicate active encouragement on the part of the British. At the same time, however, an atmosphere more conducive to petitioning may have inspired this burst of activity on the freedmen's part. Though it has not been possible to determine the content of these petitions, their presentation suggests a gathering momentum in the quest for status and social mobility.

It is significant that this activity coincided with the first recorded attempt to provide schooling on an organized basis for the freedman community. In the absence of any public provision for their instruction, the initiative was seized by an immigrant freedman, Samuel Hackett who, in February 1811, "respectfully inform[ed] his friends and the public, that he will receive coloured children as boarders, and likewise schooling on moderate terms ... with the accustomed assiduity, and strictest attention, good discipline and exemplary conduct."[57] Hackett's endeavors represent an important input by émigré freedmen in leavening the consciousness of their Danish West Indian counterparts. This émigré presence provided the major conduit through which the main currents of bourgeois revolutionary ideology reached the shores of the Danish West Indies, and brought information about contemporary freedman initiatives in Barbados, Jamaica and

Trinidad.[58] Restiveness among freedmen in these British outposts of Caribbean empire were unlikely to have gone unnoticed in the Danish islands, themselves a part, however recently and temporarily, of the same empire. There is strong presumptive evidence for the existence of a Caribbean brotherhood of freedmen. It shared information transmitted, if in no other way, by the number of schooners and other craft operating out of St. Thomas and St. Croix that had freedmen masters.[59] It was in a position to determine goals and identify appropriate strategies for their achievement.

The cumulative effect of these internal and external influences led to the freedmen's most daring and direct confrontation with authority; their refusal in St. Croix to perform para-military duties, from which the British had exempted them, shortly after the restoration in 1815. Thirteen years earlier, in May 1802, following the end of the first British occupation, the Danish crown had decreed that freedmen in future would form an auxilliary corps of artillery. Now, however, in a written remonstrance followed by oral representations, several freedmen unequivocally declared their unwillingness to serve except under certain conditions. This behavior, characterized by Governor General Oxholm as "presumptuous and punishable disobedience," derived its inspiration in his view from "an erroneous interpretation of their rights and privileges" prompted by "foreign mischief-makers who from time to time have illegally settled among the locals."[60]

All the participants in what was technically mutiny were sentenced to terms of imprisonment with one exception in John Hennesy, who was deported. The sentences appeared to have had a sobering effect on some and they were all subsequently pardoned.[61] The pardons apart, the Danish colonial authorities were not in a conciliatory frame of mind. If anything they were driven to even greater inflexibility. One immediate effect of the freedmen's presumed presumptuousness of May 1815 was that the Danish West Indian government tightened the regulations for the authentication of the freedom certificate, particularly for those persons who had arrived after, or had been granted freedom certificates since the occupation of 1807.[62]

The Petition of 1816

Given the context, it was predictable that the freedmen's extreme step to advance their cause in May 1815 would have ended in failure. It also prompted a change of strategy on their part. The solution as they saw it lay not in securing piecemeal reform in the colonies but in the more fundamental departure of seeking full equality from the metropolis. In this sense the "mutiny" of 1815 has a direct causal relationship with the Petition of 1 April 1816 addressed to the King by the freedmen of the Danish West Indies. Signed by 331 freedmen, the Petition was both a plea for privileges and complaint against long standing grievances deeply felt.[63] Not surprisingly, in view of the main provisions of Oxholm's recent proclamation regarding freedom certificates, the petitioners requested "that distinguished badge of fealty, conferred on your Majesty's other subjects, called Burgher Briefs," in place of the obviously hated freedom certificate that only conferred an inferior kind of citizenship. In less enlightened times, they argued, "there might have been wise and politic grounds for such a denial, but such a prohibition is now inappropriate." Ultimately therefore the Petition was about full citizenship and its corollary, equality of treatment with whites.

Organizationally the Petition consisted of a preamble followed by an enumeration of the privileges asked for and a statement of extant grievances. The petitioners indicated to the crown that the two freedmen entrusted with the document's presentation, William de Windt and William Purcell, were persons of weight and respectability in their community. They were charged to seek "an extension of certain privileges, favors and immunities; and ... relief from sundry grievances, which for some years we have labored under, contrary we are persuaded, to the knowledge of your Majesty, and in direct opposition to the well known clemency of your Majesty's character ... and also in direct opposition and contempt of various Rescripts and Ordinances, which from time to time, have been promulgated by your Majesty's predecessors, and yourself, in favor of us the free people of color."

The freedmen were thus tactfully, respectfully but firmly, drawing attention to the dichotomy between the crown's policy intention and its colonial execution at least the Reglement of 1755. In the meantime, their numbers had grown by their accurate estimate to more than 5,000 and their quantitative increase, they argued, had been matched by their qualitative enrichment of society. By indirection, Windt and Purcell were exemplars of a class whose members had established themselves "in various useful and honest callings, occupations and employments;" who had acquired lands, tenements and slaves to the value of 6 million Rigsdaler; who constituted, in addition, a militia of 1,000 effectives. They drew these points to the crown's attention, they said, not out of ostentation but in the hope that this would make them worthy of royal approbation.

The Petitioner's preamble is stamped throughout by positive self-perceptions and an awareness of important contributions to Danish West Indian society. Citizenship, that "distinguished badge of fealty," was therefore a privilege they thought they had more than justly earned. Once it had been confirmed and recorded in the islands' courts, it should replace all physical badges except those used in their para-military capacity. Secondly, the freedmen asked to be under the same militia law that applied to others, for whereas there were standing orders for the white militia there was nothing comparable for freedmen. In the absence of such standing orders they often found themselves charged and fined without knowing the nature of their offense.

An application for permission to operate inns for freedmen in the towns of St. Croix and St. Thomas on the same basis as obtained for "other inhabitants," sought a third privilege that would expand their horizons of economic opportunity. It would also facilitate social intercourse especially with "our brethren from neighboring islands [who] have occasion to visit the respective towns in these islands, either upon business or duty; and it being denied us to open such houses as they might repair to for their accommodation or their entertainment, they have been and are put to great inconvenience."

The fourth privilege sought was not rationalized in the terms employed for the third but the two were clearly related. Their exclusion from the retail rum trade had been stringently observed since the eighteenth century. Exceptions such as Benjamin Jeppe, mentioned earlier, did not alter the rule but simply reinforced it. At the time of the Petition there were only three freedmen, all resident in St. Thomas, who had permission to operate rum shops.

The first in a long catalog of grievances that followed the request for privileges, was the absence of due process. In this connection, the infliction of corporal punishment, irrespective of sex, as has been seen, and administered with the same casual violence with which slaves were treated, was particularly objectionable. Slaves received such punishment for neglect of their masters' service. Freedmen who were not legally in servitude could not be said to be free of that particular yoke when all that was required for them to be beaten was a directive from the governor general to the Chief of Police, his assistant or one of the freedmen "Captains." The freedmen complained that they were on the receiving end of "the severest and most ignominious punishments ... for the slightest offenses, and sometimes indeed without the form of a trial," whilst whites when they were the offending party in an altercation were merely fined for offenses for which freedmen were whipped, regardless of age or sex.

The ill will generated by corporal punishment made it in the petitioners' view a fit subject for abolition in much the same way that the crown had seen fit to terminate the slave trade. That compelling argument from recent history was reinforced by another drawn from less recent events and specifically related to freedmen. Explicitly invoking the Reglement of 3 February 1755, they pointed out that it had entitled them to the same privilege of trial and the same adminstration of justice. Indeed, the violence of this ordinance, their "Magna Carta," was a source of particular grievance, inspiring an appeal to the crown for the strictest observance of *all* the ordinances in force.

The arbitrary and discriminatory nature of corporal punishment was associated in freedmen's minds with the general problem of denial of due process. In another form it manifested itself in the refusal of bail even for the most trivial offenses. The result was often imprisonment without trial, prejudicial not alone to health and property but also to the interests of families. Such treatment, the aggrieved freedmen submitted, cast them "into a state of degradation which neither Nature nor the God of Nature intended us to descend to." Nor did they consider their treatment consonant with the crown's ordinances "which by extending to us the rights and privileges of rational creatures, encourage us to the performance of those duties, by which societies are upheld and life rendered desirable."

The conditions obtaining during imprisonment for debt constituted a related grievance. Their rates of daily subsistence in debtors' jail were lower than those for white debtors who received twice as much. Their conclusion, for which there was ample justification, was that "prejudice against us runs so deep that we are allowed to eat neither as much as nor as well as whites."

Of all the vexatious impositions few were more insupportable than the obligation to provide the entire manpower "to *hunt* for negroes that have absconded from their masters." Refusal to join in the search for runaway slaves involved mandatory corporal punishment and solitary confinement on bread and water. The "maronjagt" was an outstanding illustration of the degradation to which as a group they were continuously subjected. It involved long absences from home, frequently in the remotest parts of the islands and during inclement weather. They suffered loss of income during these searches but could claim no compensation. Yet they often faced substantial medical bills for illnesses contracted during the course of this obligatory tour of duty. The work involved had never been remunerated. Indeed, it was only as recently as the occupation that the more compliant British introduced a per diem of 4 Reales under General Harcourt. In 1816, however, that per diem was claimed to be insufficient to feed a man's family or compensate for loss of income. Any planter or other white person whose slave had run away, merely had to request the governor general for a freedman search party, took no part themselves and showed little concern for the dangers or discomforts involved. Equally if some white person committed a capital crime and escaped custody, it was the duty of a freedman search party to find him. The petitioners submitted that all free persons, irrespective of color, should be required to pursue criminals and runaway slaves.

Naturally enough the physical badge of inferiority symbolized by the cockade figured prominently among the petitioners' grievances. A badge bearing no relationship to service performed on behalf of the state was considered by freedmen as a gross insult to their dignity. They submitted that two circumstances argued for its discontinuance. Firstly, a lost or forgotten cockade exposed them to the arbitrary discretion of the chief of police, and could attract either corporal punishment or incarceration on bread and water for 48 hours. Secondly, it was demeaning to wear the insignia when any slave inventive enough could acquire it, run away for months and, protected by the cockade, commit the gravest crime while at large. The petitioners also pointed out that this formed the basis of stories frequently in circulation among planters and others that such and such a freedman had been apprehended, but either resisted arrest or made good his escape leaving his freedom badge in the hands of his pursuers.

No freedman, the petitioners complained, was eligible for a public loan. The single exception, so far as they were aware, was Samuel de Windt, a captain in St. Croix's freedman corps of artillery established in 1802. One consequence of this discriminatory practice was that many pieces of real property owned by freedmen had been sold for sums considerably below their market value. Had they been eligible for loans, the petitioners claimed, such properties could have been saved.

On the social plane, the "innocent pleasures of dancing and many others equally innocent" which whites indulged without restriction, still required the written permission of the chief of police. The petitioners alleged, however, that he was known to have played favorites. If they received official permission they were required to pay a fee, and remain under police supervision for the duration of the dance. The constables on duty were empowered to break up the festivities if they went beyond the permitted hour, but for a further fee would exercise their discretion to extend the time limit.

The petitioners also raised the delicate and deeply felt issue of the sexual exploitation of their women, particularly their young women. Contrary to the views of the anonymous memorialist of 1802 who condemned all freedwomen as innately salacious, the freedmen vigorously defended their virtue. Certainly, at least one white official would have agreed with the freedmen's position. Edvard Colbiørnsen had observed as long ago as 1788 that the blame could be laid squarely at the door of the unmarried white men, whose unbridled priapic tendencies were beyond the effective control of legislation.[64] The petitioners asserted that it was unfortunately all too common a practice among white men to seduce and corrupt the morals of young freedwomen, habituating them to prostitution and loose living. The authorities had turned a blind eye to violations of the law against prostitution and the issue of these immoral liaisons, if girls, they were condemned like their mothers to prostitution. The crown was called upon to put an end to sexual abuse and to protect the virtue of freedwomen by insisting on an observance of the relevant ordinances.

The Petition was personally taken to Copenhagen by Windt and Purcell. It achieved little on the short term. Indeed there was royal reproof for the two emissaries for having left the West Indies without the permission of the Danish West Indian government.[65] There was, however, one marginal short-term gain; the creation by 1817 of a Fire Service in which, apart from a white commanding officer, the other officers and rank and file consisted of freedmen. In effect, this was another interstitial group-service of the kind Marvin Harris identifies. It was a critically necessary service, given the frequency of destructive fires in the islands' towns.[66] For the freedmen, however, it could be seen as a positive development. If only in the sense that it lacked the degrading associations of maroon hunts.

In the long term, the crown's decision to review the situation of the freedmen was part of an overall re-examination of the laws with the intention of drafting a definitive Consolidated Slave Code.[67] But that process had been in train since the 1780s and had made notoriously little progress, caught up as it was in the cumbrous machinery of the collegiate structures of Denmark's absolute monarchy.[68] Against this background, the crown's decision was a prescription to do exactly nothing. As late as 1833, almost two decades later, nothing had materialized by way of a Consolidated Slave Code.[69] If the monarch proposed, however slowly at home, it was the local authorities who disposed in the corners of the colonial empire. Events up to 1816 had demonstrated only too clearly that if freedmen were to expect relief, it would have to await colonial administrators sympathetically disposed to their cause.

After 1816

The period after 1816, although meager in institutional gains, was an era of consolidation, growth and material advance by the freedman community of the Danish West Indies. The political leadership represented by de Windt and Purcell had its parallels on the social, professional and economic fronts. Jean Reneau, for instance, anonymously put up 7,500 kroner to finish the rebuilding of the Lutheran Church in St. Thomas destroyed by the hurricane of 1788. When Reneau died in 1819 he had recovered neither principal nor interest.[70] By the beginning of the 1830s, there was at least one non-white attorney-at-law in St. Croix, and in St. Thomas a freedman, Johannes Friborg, practiced as an estate executor. By that date freedmen, having long breached the provisions for residential segregation, had broken into the forbidden sanctum of sugar estate ownership. In St. Croix, John Daly owned one such estate, and in St. John the Hillsne family, brought up in England, and probably anciens libres, owned two of the largest sugar plantations on that island.[71]

The period after 1816 also produced one of the most fascinating freedmen of the early nineteenth century in the person of Apollo Miller of St. Croix. He began promoting cock-fights in Frederiksted in 1814, profiting from its endemic popularity among the English and Spanish speaking elements of the community. By 1815 he was promoting inter-island contests, and in the following year was a steward of the Cock Fighters' Club. His promotions became more selective over time, so that for the bouts on Shrove Tuesday 1820, he produced printed cards to prevent "the intrusion of unwelcome guests." This activity in all probability provided the seed capital with which Miller was able to diversify and expand into the ownership of a tavern cum restaurant, reading room and lodging house, that provided a horse and gig service as well as stables. With an eye for the "main chance" he was one of the first persons in St. Croix to have ice cream on sale commercially, as well as a catering service for parties. Later in the 1820s he moved to St. Thomas, perhaps in search of wider opportunities. A house he occupied in Charlotte Amalie was taken over by N. Caydle and run as the Commercial Hotel in 1824 to "accommodate gentlemen with board and lodging in the best style." In the 1830s he bought the City Hotel, beside the King's Wharf, that had been gutted in the 1832 fire. The Hotel was made "fire-proof," an important consideration in fire-prone Charlotte

Amalie, and re-opened. When Miller died, in about 1836, it continued to be operated by his wife Frances.[72]

Persons like Apollo Miller, John Daly, the Hillsnes, Johannes Friborg, and others like the brothers Dennery, Jacob and August, who owned and operated a sloop trading in the northern Leewards,[73] demonstrated by their achievements the injustice of their relegation to second class citizenship. They and many others like them were prosperous and prospering, in arrears just like whites for their horse and carriage taxes.[74] Yet when a Mr. Weiss came to Christiansted's Crown Hotel in October 1828 with his magician's bag of tricks, he advertised that he would "fit up a separate place for free coloureds, and admit them by a separate entrance on the south side of the room."[75]

In the period after 1816 also, freedwomen as unofficial hostesses for public officials, up to and including the governor general, achieved a degree of notoriety.[76] Governor General Bentzon in the years just before 1820 had a more than casual affair with Francisca Henrietta Coppy who bore him two children whose paternity he acknowledged in his will of 1823.[77] Anna Heegaard, the best known of these hostesses, had a long attachment with the Colonial Adjutant, Captain Knudsen, after which she became Governor General von Scholten's unofficial consort. Knudsen was profoundly affected by the experience and twelve years later was still lovelorn.[78] When she took up residence with Governor General von Scholten in 1829, she was already a woman of substantial means, purchasing a house in Christiansted for the substantial sum of 6,250 Rigsdaler, owning numerous slaves as well as costly household and personal effects.[79]

Material success was unequally yoked, however, with the de jure disabilities complained of in the 1816 Petition and with the social ostracism from which only a favored few were exempt. But working on this situation were three catalytic agencies of change: Anna Heegaard herself,[80] von Scholten, with whom she cohabited for another two decades, and the external conditions elsewhere in the West Indies. By the time Anna Heegaard had taken up residence in the governor general's manorial establishment at Bülowsminde, the British had issued the Order in Council of 1829 which lifted the civil and legal disabilities under which freedmen in the British West Indies labored.[81] Influenced by this example, the imperatives of his own domestic situation, and a degree of personal idealism, von Scholten drew up a Report in 1830 which began the process by which freedmen of the Danish West Indies achieved full legal equality.

This 1830 Report proposed inter alia to abolish the freedom certificates; to grant unconditional equality of "first class" status to the senior officers of the militia who had served for at least fifteen years; to grant "second class" status and patents of freedom to junior officers, and "third class" status to other ranks. Lawfully married women would be placed in the same "class" as their husbands. Other freedwomen were to be classified "conformably to the education, conduct, and the other good qualities of the individual, as also to their pecuniary circumstances."[82]

For all its apparent idealism, however, the Report was marred by touches of ethnocentrism. It clearly intended to distinguish first generation manumitted, the militia's other ranks and those long separated in time from slavery, in an ascending order of preference. In this regard the Report contained an instructive provision: "Only the second generation of a person, emancipated by gift or by purchase, can ascend to the first division, unless the first generation proceeds from parents lawfully married, and of good conduct, or unless the Governor General deems an individual of this description particularly deserving of such an advancement." Further, the Report was unambiguously biased in favor of freedmen most closely approximating the European phenotype: "Where free persons of color of both sexes assimilate in color to the whites, and they otherwise by a cultivated mind and good conduct render themselves deserving to stand, according to their rank and station in life, on an equal footing with white inhabitants, all the difference which the color now causes ought to cease." For all its shortcomings, the Report represented a forward step. It was approved in substantive form by the crown in April 1830 and was jubilantly greeted by the freedmen of St. Thomas, 282 of whom signed a petition requesting the crown to strike five gold medals, for members of the royal family and von Scholten, to commemorate the occasion.[83]

The Report and the Plan of 14 March 1831 which elaborated its details,[84] justified the newspaper *Fædrelandet's* comment that von Scholten had a passion for "projectmageri" or scheme-making of the most involved sort. The attempt to divide the freedmen into classes, it said, was risible and had to be abandoned before it started.[85] That might very well have been wisdom after the event from a notoriously hostile anti-von Scholten quarter. The fact, however, was that the crown did order a re-drafting in 1832.[86] The new draft emerged in 1833, shorn of the complexities of the 1830 Report but with a major recommendation for a ten year "apprenticeship" period for all those manumitted after 10 April 1830, the date on which the Report had been approved.[87] For their part, the freedman communities of Christiansted, Frederiksted and Charlotte Amalie had lost some of the initial enthusiasm of 1831. After mature reflection, they were unanimous in their reservations about the "apprenticeship" proposal in the new draft.[88] Von Scholten claimed that his advice, from the more "cultivated" freedmen, was against a sudden transition to unconditional freedom. He was nevertheless prepared to compromise with a five year probationary period instead of the previously proposed ten years.[89] The Danish Chancellery which was asked to comment, supported von Scholten on the length of the probationary period and recommended to the crown accordingly.[90]

Four years of drafts, reports and plans were ended by the royal ordinance of 18 April 1834. It gave unconditional equality without distinction to all those who were in legal possession of their freedom at the date of the ordinance. However, those to be manumitted in future, were to serve a three-year probation before their final incorporation into the free citizenry.

Children over fifteen were made subject to the three-year probation and so too were recently arrived foreign freedmen.[91]

Legislation, however, did not bring social acceptance immediately. White society was still scandalized at appointments of free non-whites to positions of trust and their invitation to the governor general's dinner parties.[92] But by the early 1840s one observer noted free non-whites in public office and other non-white "gentlemen" – he even used the English word – were no longer being served in adjoining rooms at government house receptions.[93]

Free non-white women had a more difficult passage. The prejudice towards them by white women was described in 1833 by Magens, the landfoged in St. John, as an insoluble problem which coercion could only compound.[94] They were openly snubbed at government house balls when they ventured to go.[95] The weak link in this chain of snobbery and prejudice, however, was the social cachet attaching to government house functions. Von Scholten and Anna Heegaard kept glittering court at Bülowsminde; gala evenings, soirées dansantes, festive occasions and elaborate dinners at which the best crystal, silver service and fine china complemented the menu.[96] But there was an anomaly and an arresting incongruity in accepting such hospitality from a non-white hostess, the first lady of the Danish West Indies, whilst turning up one's nose at other non-white women, especially those of "education, conduct ... other good qualities and pecuniary circumstance." Bit by bit, the bastions of prejudice appear to have crumbled during the 1840s, so that when van Dockum, von Scholten's adjutant ended his tour of duty in 1846, he noted that white women and free non-white women could meet each other without the former turning their heads away. As he appropriately concluded, "Dette var en begyndene social omvæltning" – That was the beginning of a social revolution.[97]

10

Strangers Within the Gate: Émigré Freedmen in the Nineteenth Century

AN IMPORTANT ASPECT OF THE EXPERIENCE OF THE FREEDMAN community in the slave society of the Danish West Indies, noticed in passing in previous chapters, was its location within a wider Caribbean brotherhood. By the beginning of the nineteenth century a developing regional perspective had begun to express itself in a little documented intra-Caribbean migration, reinforced by ties of ethnicity, family and commerce, and by the vicissitudes of politics. The significance of this migratory movement was most apparent in the case of St. Thomas. The island's neutral status in the political upheavals of the early nineteenth century and Charlotte Amalie's growing importance as a commerical entrepot offered refuge and employment to freedmen from around the region. The immigrants brought not only their skills but also a degree of political awareness that radicalized the creole freedmen into a self-aware community and united them in their efforts to achieve equality. There is no evidence of tensions between creole and foreign freedmen or between freedmen of different nationalities. Nor is there any evidence that local adult freedmen, themselves a minority, complained of unfair economic competition from or sharp practice by a foreign minority within their minority. Rather, the evidence points in the direction of communal solidarity and cooperation that found eventual expression in the Petition of 1816.

Origins

The notarized enumeration of Charlotte Amalie's able-bodied male adult freedman population on 28 May 1802 indicated that of those 221, one originated from St. John, ten from St. Croix and 122 from St. Thomas. The remaining 89, 40 percent of the total, were of foreign origin. Among these émigré males a majority numbering 39, or 44 percent, derived from

Curaçao, but there was also a significant number from neighboring St. Eustatius: 30 or 34 percent. The remainder came variously from contiguous islands of the northern Leewards, Guadeloupe, Martinique, Barbados and Jamaica.[1] Conspicuous by their absence from the enumeration are free persons of color originating in St. Dominigue/Haiti. Their absence should come as no surprise, however, considering that the Danish West Indian like most colonial governments in the region, had placed that country in quarantine and interdicted the movement of persons and vessels from it to the Danish islands.[2] Equally conspicuous by their absence are freedmen from other French West Indian colonies, apart from three from Guadeloupe and Martinique identified in the enumeration. Their absence is readily explained by the fact of their expulsion.

The expulsion of the French freedmen from the Danish West Indies occurred immediately after the restoration of the islands following the British occupation of 1801-1802. Casimir von Scholten, Commandant of St. Thomas, lamenting his incapacity to defend the islands, complained particularly of their dependence on a militia composed almost entirely of Britons and British sympathisers and "a Freedman Company whose loyalty was doubtful."[3] Although there is nothing to indicate a lack of loyalty on the part of the freedmen or an unwillingness to perform militia duties, von Scholten vented his xenophobic wrath against a perceived fifth column, the status- and state-less freedmen of French extraction connected however tangentially with a country with whom Denmark shared a common enemy in England. In a frank but unintended confession of his prejudices, the Commandant remarked that he had always been of the view, as most people in Denmark were, that there was a mass of French émigrés of all colors in Charlotte Amalie. The town's narrow streets, always bustling with people augmented by crews of ships in harbor, contributed to that impression. He was surprised, therefore, to discover in a submission officially requested from the French Consul Citoyen Michel, that there were only 29 white Frenchmen and 116 adult freedmen of French extraction in the island.[4] Some of these, unlike the equally foreign Anglophone burghers, were professional soldiers of some experience; Jean Castaign, aged 31, was or had been a Lieutenant in the 12th Regiment. J. M. Florentin, 25, and Le Févre fils, had both seen service in the different French colonies; L. Pernon, aged 38, held or had held the rank of Lieutenant in the Garde Nationale. Others among the 116 were rank and file infantrymen. The entire complement of Francophone émigré freedmen, soldiers as well as artisans, formed a special detachment of the St. Thomas Freedman Militia, under the subordinate command of their "Chef de Batallion" Frédéric Laure.[5] However, this entire corps in Commandant von Scholten's judgment was full of "purely revolutionary colored persons," unruly and insubordinate advocates of freedom, and extremely dangerous. They were therefore expelled.[6]

Of the 221 able-bodied freedmen, foreign and indigenous, in 1802, 109 possessed artisanal skills related to seafaring, whether as carpenters, ships' carpenters, joiners or sailmakers. There was a single goldsmith, Domingo

Table 10.1: *Whites and Freedmen in the Danish West Indies, 1797, 1815, 1835*

	1797			1815			1835		
Island	Whites	Freed-men	Freed-men as % of Free	Whites	Freed-men	Freed-men as % of Free	Whites	Freed-men	Freed-men as % of Free
St. Thomas	726	239	24.8	2,122	2,284	51.8	1,977	5,204	72.5
St. Croix	2,223	1,164	34.4	1,840	2,480	57.4	1,892	4,913	72.2
St. John	113	15	11.7	157	271	63.3	208	202	49.3
Total	3,062	1,418	31.7	4,119	5,035	55.0	4,077	10,319	71.7

Sources: R/A, Diverse sager, Forskellige Oplysninger, VI; R/A, AVS/FC, II, von Scholten's Comments on G. W. Alexander's "Anmærkning to Kongen af Danmark m.h.t. de danske Øer;" P. L. Oxholm, *De Danske Vestindisk öers Tilstand* (1797), "Statistisk Tabelle."

Morases, aged 24, from Curaçao.[7] His other 38 compatriots would have come to St. Thomas in search of work and opportunity directly arising from its maritime activity and free port status. Such inflows from Curaçao and elsewhere at the turn of the century explain in large measure the rapid expansion in the number of freedmen which increased almost seven-fold from a total of 239 in 1797 to 1,521 in 1803. Of that number, 665 or 43 percent were of foreign origin (Tables 10.1-10.2).

The rapid increment in the size of the freedman population, its high émigré component and the suspicions entertained about the latter in 1801 and 1802, influenced Governor General von Walterstorff to establish the first "St. Thomas Commission for the Registering of the Free Colored" in February 1803.[8] In its report, one of the Commission's first submissions drew attention to what it described as the "unwontedly large" number of foreign freedmen. It forced the question whether their presence was necessary or advantageous, or in the alternative harmful and a burden on the island's resources. The Commission's immediate concern was the excessive disproportion in living standards between creole freedmen and their foreign counterparts. So far as the former were concerned the Commission's view was that "their circumstances have not all improved. Rather, the foreigners have in large measure deprived them of the traditional sources of livelihood handed down by their ancestors as their most precious inheritance."[9]

The Commission declared that it had no wish to reflect on the Government's generosity in providing a haven for foreign freedmen in those troubled times. It observed, however, that among those foreigners there was a large number of women from Curaçao and elsewhere who, describing themselves as seamstresses and cooks, were really petty traders whose knowledge of Spanish and Spanish customs, placed creole freedmen at a disadvantage. They acquired and sold locally the "most worthless"

Table 10.2: *Creole and Émigré Freedmen, by Sex and Skill, St. Thomas, 1803*

Origin	Women	Men	Children	Total	Skilled	Unskilled
St. Thomas	316	115	425	856	73	358
French						
Islands	154	107	49	310	–	–
English						
Islands	51	33	16	100	–	–
Curaçao	146	63	45	254	–	–
Spanish						
Territories	1	–	–	1	–	–
Émigré						
Sub-Total	352	203	110	665	132	423
All Freedmen	668	318	535	1,521	205	781

Source: N/A, RG 55, Box 583: St. Thomas Commission for the Registering of the Free
    Coloured, 1803.

merchandise from Puerto Rico at more than 100 percent profit. Further, the
Commission observed, they and their innumerable offspring were a charge
on the public purse.[10] As Table 10.2 indicates, however, the 110 children of
foreign freedmen numbered nowhere near the 425 of the creoles. Nor
indeed were the 146 freedwomen from Curaçao as numerous as their 154
French-speaking counterparts. Nor is there evidence to suggest conflict
between the creole and foreign freedmen of Charlotte Amalie.

White Fears

Objections to the foreign presence came not from those members of the
host community most immediately affected, the creole freedmen, but rather
from the whites. The Commissioners in choosing to complain of the situation highlighted the women from Curaçao, who constituted a smaller
group than the French-speaking freedwomen, because their economic
activity was the most visible and demonstrated a degree of enterprise that
was objectionable, presumably, because it was so highly profitable. The
Commissioners' recommendations were consistent with their prejudices.
Foreign freedmen were superfluous and their presence undesirable; the
island should either rid itself of them at the earliest opportunity or impose
additional taxes on them as a group. Deportation would not be an inconvenience as Curaçao had been returned to the Dutch with freedmen's
privileges intact. The Commissioners were also minded to deport all freedmen originating from Grenada as undeserving of succor, since Fédon's
uprising in that island had been the work of freedmen. Finally the Commissioners commented that émigré artisans should not be considered a
burden as long as they were industrious and could contribute manpower
for the island's defense. It was the Commission's hope, however, that they
would re-migrate voluntarily rather than being forcibly evicted, and find

encouragement to go to Puerto Rico and other Spanish-speaking places where they were in great demand.[11]

The Commissioners made no pretense that there were inadequate employment opportunities for artisanal skills or that émigrés were in competition with creoles. They nevertheless considered their ultimate departure politic. As Table 10.2 demonstrates, the ratio of skilled to un-skilled was somewhat higher among foreign freedmen at 24 percent than among creoles at 17 percent, and the foreign cohort also represented 64 percent of all skilled freedmen in St. Thomas in 1803. Attention has already been drawn to the Commissioners' spurious submission on the Curaçao freedwomen and their children. What they may also have allowed to escape their notice is that although there were proportionately more women among the foreign-born than among locals, there was a higher proportion of women among the adult creole freed population (73 percent) than among the émigré adults, where women comprised 63 percent.

Although the deportation proposed by the Commissioners in 1803 seems not to have materialized, the suspicion, ambivalence and presump-tion of potential disloyalty characterizing white attitudes to free people of color generally, applied in additional measure to those originating outside St. Thomas. The continuous political upheaval in the Caribbean and Latin America for the first two decades of the nineteenth century, associated with the struggles in Haiti and the movement for independence in Latin America, were fertile grounds in which the prevailing antipathies could flourish. Those external developments coincided with and were partly responsible for what one Danish official called an "unbelievable increase" of the freedman population. The attractiveness of St. Thomas for the Caribbean "boat people" of the early nineteenth century increased rather than diminished with time. Christian von Holten, Commandant of St. Thomas in 1815, reported that of the 464 able-bodied male freedmen then in the island, 215 were of foreign origin.[12] This represented 46 percent and compares with the situation 13 years earlier when they represented 40 percent. If the origins of the free women of color, numbering some 1,365 in 1815, and of children of both sexes, are taken into account it is probable that the cohort of émigré freedmen exceeded 50 percent.[13]

It was the view of some colonial officials that the second British occupa-tion of the islands 1807-1815 had worked to increase the disaffection of the freedmen towards Denmark. Only the creoles and a few Curaçaoans were well disposed, wrote one official, while "among the others defiance and insolence have taken over."[14] For his part, Commandant von Holten claimed that the British had paid scant attention during the occupation to the colonial ordinances from the previous century delimiting the rights of freedmen.[15] He claimed that the British had been pliant in their issue of "Free Briefs." The proclamation issued by Ramsey shortly before the islands' return to Denmark in April 1815 seems to support this view. An earlier proclamation of August 1813 had informed the freedman com-munity that some 50 certificates uncollected at the Governor's office would be declared null and void.[16] That of 1815 advised the certificates would remain valid and ready for collection.[17]

The metropolitan government expressed considerable unease at the time of the restoration over the presence of foreigners generally and colored foreigners particularly in the Danish islands. Royal directives on 28 July 1815 and 9 April 1816 advised the Danish West Indian government to be on its guard against foreign refugees and foreign persons of color especially who, they warned, should not be allowed to remain without freedom certificates issued by the Governor.[18] P. L. Oxholm, the Governor General, thought these instructions timely. Vagabonds and vagrants of all colors, as he described them, had flocked to St. Thomas after the restoration, attracted by the apparent ease with which they could establish themselves there.[19] The authorities at St. Thomas had distributed freedom certificates with a certain largesse; over the first two months after the British left certificates were issued at an average of more than one per day.[20] This appears, however, to have been less out of concern for the incoming stream of refugees than for considerations of personal gain. As Oxholm explained, foreign freedmen could enter St. Thomas, stay as long as they wished, and give no account of the nature of their business to the authorities provided the fees for a certificate were paid. For each white foreigner issued with a residence certificate, or freedman receiving a certificate or Free Brief, the Chief of Police collected 2 Patacoons ($2) as an entry tax in the first instance; for longer periods, up to three months, the fee was $4, and for periods up to six months, $8. These "sportler" as the Danes described such perquisites of office went only in part to the Chief of Police. The major share, some two-thirds, went to Commandant von Holten. As Oxholm concluded, the Commandant's authority over his Chief of Police would be hopelessly compromised in the event of disorder, since he too had reaped material benefits in legitimising the foreigners' presence.[21]

The collusion and venality of St. Thomas officialdom was compounded by insubordination or at least an unwillingness to cooperate. The island's physical separation from the central jurisdiction of St. Croix was an additional factor tending to inaction. In the past, Oxholm observed, there had been a "curious principle" in the administration of St. Thomas and St. John by which regulations issued in St. Croix were either ignored or suppressed.[22] For example, the seminal ordinance of 10 October 1776 regulating the procedures by which freedmen were issued certificates of freedom, required foreign freedmen to present their original certificates and passport before being issued with a local certificate authenticated by the Governor General.[23] A protracted correspondence between Governor General and Commandant brought neither acknowledgement of error on the part of the latter, nor a resolution of the issue. It eventually required the intervention of the Generaltoldkammer, reaffirming in unequivocal terms the validity of the 1776 Ordinance and the subordination, in all matters civil, of the Commandant to the Governor General.[24]

In the meantime, threats to law and order from émigré refugees including freedmen, were a source of constant worry to Governor General Oxholm. He alleged that refugees from Spanish America, arriving in boats he insisted were stolen, had made common cause with freedmen to engage in acts of piracy with Charlotte Amalie as their base. He claimed further that they had managed to get hold of boats with the Danish royal coat of arms and had plundered cargo vessels on the high seas, including vessels that had cleared from St. Thomas.[25] His proposed solution to these difficulties envisaged a policy that would differentiate various categories of freedmen. Those born free, and who could claim several generations of free ancestry, should be distinguished from those only recently emancipated from slavery.[26] Equally, persons manumitted in the Danish West Indies were to be treated differently from those who had migrated from overseas. In practical terms this would involve two different kinds of legitimation. Creole freedmen who could authenticate their status would receive "Free Briefs," or freedmen's certificates; émigrés who could authenticate their bona fides would be issued with resident certificates. The former would confer civil rights of the kind that only due process could nullify; the latter left its recipient liable to continuous police surveillance and deportation for undesirable conduct.[27] Implementing such a policy, however, entailed major jurisdictional problems.

Émigrés and the Freedman Community

The metropolitan government's settlement of the jurisdictional dispute with St. Thomas, mentioned earlier, also ruled on the proposed resident certificates by insisting on the continuance of the traditional Free Briefs of 1776.[28] The decision was colored by the home government's concern that modifications of established practice would heighten the possibility of Spanish American insurgents' creation of a staging post in the island to further rebellion against a legitimate government that Denmark recognized.[29] On receipt of the government's definitive ruling, Oxholm drew attention to a development that is of interest not only as an argument in support of the policy he had proposed, but also because it serves as an index of the growing group dynamics among the freedman community. Most of the freedman residents of St. Thomas, he reckoned, were illegal entrants. There were, however, signs of strong family nucleation: they had contracted legal marriages and were parents of children from whom they could not be arbitrarily separated by deportation for failure to have a Free Brief. Even though there were no fees required to obtain freedom certificates, freedmen as a group had failed to come forward to claim them.[30] The potential consequence was mass deportation. But as Oxholm recognized, deporting the numbers involved entailed considerable difficulty, and no such deportations took place.[31] By combined communal inaction the entire freedman community had called the home government's bluff. Indeed, one of Oxholm's senior advisors, Major Stabell, was of the view that their solidarity on this issue merely reflected a unanimity that had prevailed in their opposition to the introduction of the resident certificates.[32] Though their opposition was not a factor in the defeat of the Governor General's proposal, there is no denying the fact that by 1815-1816, the freedmen of St. Thomas had begun to forge a sense of group identity.

To an important degree that phenomenon is attributed to the presence of the émigrés. As "strangers within the gate" they had a far greater psychological need than creole freedmen for a sense of community and coherence as a group. Their horizons extended beyond the parochial frontiers of Charlotte Amalie. They kept their lines of communication open to family or trading associates overseas, many of whom came to St. Thomas to visit from time to time.[33] It was precisely to further these regional liaisons that the Freedmen's Petition to the Crown in 1816 decried the lack of accommodation for "our brethren of the neighboring islands" on visits to the Danish West Indies.[34] The 1816 Petition, arguably, arose from a growing self-awareness and a capacity for united action not previously in evidence. Although authored in St. Croix, it addressed itself to the problems of all freedmen in the Danish West Indies. Such developments also help to explain the collective refusal of St. Croix's freedmen to do militia duty in May 1815. It was an extraordinary act, enjoying the unanimous support of the entire freedman community.[35] Oxholm himself attributed the refusal in large measure to the influence of "foreign troublemakers," promoting, "an erroneous interpretation of rights and privileges."[36]

The presence of the émigré freedmen did indeed have a leavening effect on the freedman community of St. Thomas in terms of ideology, perceptions, roles and expectations. They came from many areas of the Caribbean where the certitudes of the ancien régime had already been successfully challenged, or were in the process of being challenged, by bourgeois-democratic revolutionary ideology. It was not to be expected that the presence of mestizo refugees intent on Venezuela's independence, nor the "free colored generals and formerly outstanding personalities from the French West Indies and St. Domingue" would leave the creole community unaffected.[37] The connections with the outside world, sustained by seafaring activity and the visits of relatives and business associates, also maintained important and continuous contact with the freedman communities of the British West Indies. News of campaigns for civil rights in those islands provided models for the radical agenda of 1815-1816. Adrian Bentzon, reflecting on these developments, observed that "This idea of civil liberty was a poorly developed fragment of British philosophical traditions, based on which some foreign free colored or other had got the notion of putting the Memorial together."[38] Commandant von Holten, in the aftermath of the Petition, drew attention to freedman "unrest" in Barbados, to rumors that St. Vincent and St. Lucia would shortly "explode," and hinted strongly at a causal relationship between developments in the British West Indies and those in the Danish islands.[39]

Von Holten raised a point of further interest in relation to the ideology of freedmen in St. Thomas. He attributed the spirit which had lately prevailed among them, by which he meant their demand for equality of treatment, to the "dangerous teaching propagated by Methodists ... seeking to impose notions of freedom and equality as substitutes for submission and obedience."[40] From their arrival in the West Indies in the 1780s, the Methodists had never secured royal approval for any establishments in the Danish West Indies. They remained in bad odor. "To be a Methodist," Gurney remarked in 1840, "seems to be tantamount to being excluded from the Danish colonies." Governor General Peter von Scholten found them not only contemptible but dangerous, sharing the antipathies demonstrated earlier in the century that had resulted in the destruction of Methodist chapels in Jamaica and Barbados, and harassment of their missionaries.[41] There were no Methodist chapels in St. Thomas. This did not prevent, however, the dissemination of an ideology that while it emphasized brotherhood and equality in the sight of God also helped to fulfill some of the freedmen's social aspirations and legitimized their desire for political rights. Lacking established meeting places the Methodists met in private homes.[42] In the absence of a clergy, leadership of congregations fell to lay persons, whose participation Methodism tended generally to emphasize. As Mary Turner has pointed out, Methodists and other sectarians in the West Indies during slavery, did not, as a matter of policy, accept freedmen into the formal ministry before they had been granted full civil rights.[43] That event did not occur in the Danish West Indies before 1834. It is therefore tempting to speculate that in all of these circumstances, the revolutionary gospel of Methodism accompanied its migrating freedman adherents to St. Thomas. Antigua suggests itself as the most plausible source, not only because of its geographical proximity but because it was the Methodist stronghold of the Eastern Caribbean. Whatever their provenance émigré freedmen have a paramount claim to be considered as the unidentified originators of the "dangerous teaching" that so alarmed von Holten in 1816.

By the time of the islands' restoration to Danish sovereignty in 1815, the freedman population of St. Thomas outnumbered the white and contained a plurality of immigrants. Demographic weight was not in itself sufficient to forge the collective perception of unity which emerged. Freedmen emerged as an identifiable group, in the sense that they were treated as such by the superordinate whites, in the early stages of colonization. In the course of the eighteenth century, their somatic traits had become socially relevant, forcing them into perceptual and cognitive categories. Theoretically, this formed the basis on which certain behavioral norms were expected of, and certain opportunities were denied or made available to, them. Freedmen in this sense had been externally designated as a group. This does not, however, exhaust the theoretical possibilities for group dynamics or group formation. Groups also cohere deliberately for specific objectives that involve influencing the course of events in particular directions. Such deliberate formation of social or political action groups arises

Table 10.3: *Émigré and Creole Adult Male Freedmen, St. Thomas, 1831*

Category	Émigré	Creole	Unspecified	Total	Émigré as % of Total
Free Corps	85	179	4	268	31.7
Unorganized	43	88	–	131	32.8
Fire Corps	169	166	5	340	49.7
Fire Corps Supernumeraries	303	117	8	428	70.8
Total	600	550	17	1,167	51.4

Source: Calculated from N/A, RG 55, Box 585: St. Thomas Commission for Registering of the Free Coloured, 1831.

out of a realization that individuals acting qua individuals are rarely in a position to exert the influence of a collectivity.[44] The historical conjuncture at which the freedmen of the Danish West Indies in general, and of St. Thomas in particular, made the transition from external designation to deliberate formation, coincided with the considerable influx of freedmen in the period immediately prior to 1815. Affected by the ferment of ideas which formed part of the émigrés' ideological baggage, they began for the first time systematically to pursue interdependent goals.

The Census of 1831

The enumeration of the freedman population undertaken in 1831 in connection with Governor General von Scholten's proposed reforms showed St. Thomas to be the home of a persistently plural community. As Johannes Mouritzen, one of von Scholten's senior advisers remarked, the island was "an assembly point for free coloureds of all the surrounding islands."[45] Creole freedmen were a minority among the adult males eligible for compulsory duty in the security services (Table 10.3). Of the 1,167 enumerated, émigrés numbered 600 or 51 per cent of the total. They were particularly numerous in the Fire Corps' Supernumeraries, where they constituted almost 71 percent of its membership. Historically there had been a significant Dutch cultural and economic influence at work in St. Thomas since the end of the seventeenth century but that influence had virtually disappeared by the beginning of the 1830s.[46] The cultural continuities were such, however, that Curaçaoan freedmen found the ambience of Charlotte Amalie particularly agreeable. Overall, as Table 10.4 indicates, they comprised 36 percent of the 600 foreign adult freedmen in the internal security services.

The largest cohort of foreigners, 323 or 54 percent, came from other West Indian islands. The Francophone territories, Martinique, Guadeloupe and Haiti contributed more than a third of that number, but there was representation from practically every island in the archipelago of the Greater and

Table 10.4: *Foreign Adult Male Freedmen by Origin, St. Thomas, 1831*

Category	Curaçao	All Other West Indies	North & South America	Europe	China	Africa	Total	Curaçao as % of Total
Free Corps	38	43	1	2	–	1	85	44.7
Unorganized	9	32	–	–	–	2	43	20.9
Fire Corps	51	100	9	1	–	8	169	30.2
Fire Corps Super-numeraries	118	148	24	2	1	10	303	38.9
Total	216	323	34	5	1	21	600	36.0

Source: As for Table 10.3.

Lesser Antilles, from Jamaica to Trinidad. The composition of the foreign community was not exclusively Caribbean, however. There were freedmen from North and South America, Europe, China and 21 from Africa. Of the latter five were bosales with a median age of 42, who had purchased their own freedom. Two had been manumitted and the remaining fourteen ranging in age from 25 to 80 were enumerated as "freeborn in Africa." The most likely explanation for this conundrum is that they had seen service with black West India Regiments that were already in existence, but as recaptives from the illegal slave trade, and had been pressed into service by British government policy after 1808. That policy also provided that such troops disbanded because of old age or injury, could settle on islands of their choice.[47]

By and large, Charlotte Amalie's economic opportunities for freedmen lay firstly in the building trades in a town notorious for its fires: between 1804 and 1832 damages resulting from fires were estimated at some $US30 million.[48] The creation of the freedman Fire Corps had a strictly utilitarian purpose, and while membership in it conferred some degree of status on its members, they could find, more importantly, ready employment in rebuilding activity as carpenters, plumbers, masons, painters and joiners. The enumeration of 1831 showed émigré freedmen well represented in these crafts (Table 10.5).

The seafaring trades constituted the second major area of employment. Those trades appear to have been particularly attractive to Curaçaoans. More than half of the 188 enlisted in the Supernumeraries of the Fire Corps were seamen and, of the total of 129 local and foreign seamen in the Supernumeraries, Curaçaoans accounted for 48 percent. Among the artisanal aristocracy, the practicing goldsmiths, the foreigners, particularly those from Curaçao, made a strong showing. Only six of the 22 goldsmiths in Charlotte Amalie were identifiably creole.

Table 10.5: *Adult Male Freedmen by Skill, St. Thomas, 1831*

Skill	Free Corps	Un- organized	Fire Corps	Super- numeraries	Total	% of Skilled
Carpenters*	62	28	101	24	215	18.4
Masons	17	10	18	26	71	6.1
Painters	2	2	5	4	13	1.1
Plumbers	2	–	1	1	4	0.3
Stone-breakers	1	1	–	1	3	0.3
Joiners	28	8	18	18	72	6.2
Sub-Total in Building Trades	112	49	143	74	368	31.5
Sailmakers	3	–	5	8	16	1.4
Seamen	1	10	26	129	166	14.2
Shoemakers	35	5	34	45	119	10.2
Tailors	45	14	22	45	126	10.8
Goldsmiths	6	1	7	8	22	1.9
Other**	55	31	67	95	248	21.2
Unspecified	11	21	36	24	92	7.9
Total Skilled	268	131	340	428	1,167	100.0

Source: As for Table 10.3.

* These figures include a handful of ship-carpenters whose numbers would not be sufficiently significant to increase the percentages of those involved in seafaring trades.

** The alphabetical breakdown of this category shows the following: Barbers, 10; Bakers, 2; Butchers, 9; Cigar-makers, 21; Cooks, 10; Coopers, 36; Fishermen, 24; Gardeners, 4; Grocers, 4; Hatmakers, 1; Mattress-makers, 5; Planters, 6; Printers, 1; Restaurateurs, 1; Saddlers, 2; School Teachers, 3; Service Assistants, 59; Smithies, 1. In addition there were 25 odd-job men.

The census of 1831 demonstrated the substantial growth of the freedman population of St. Thomas in the early nineteenth century. At 3,408 it had more than doubled since 1803 and had increased by almost 50 percent from 2,284 in 1815. Freedmen in Charlotte Amalie and its environs were almost three times as numerous as whites (Table 5.3). An analysis of the census also indicates that from being liabilities as some public officials had been wont to believe, the significant foreign elements were community assets. They provided the greater part of the internal security forces, and supported themselves and the economy of St. Thomas in a wide range of services and occupations, some of which required considerable levels of skill. Such indices helped to dampen any tendency there might have been to treat émigrés differently for purposes of granting full civil equality.

In the discussion which preceded that decision in 1834, the possibility of differential treatment had been raised. One suggestion in 1833 had been that the legal status of émigré freedmen in St. Thomas should correspond with the status they enjoyed in their country of origin.[49] However, it was anticipated that with emancipation imminent in the British West Indies large numbers of ex-slaves from those islands would shortly find their way to St. Thomas. Since by virtue of their emancipation they would enjoy full equality and unrestricted civil liberties, their presence would have been potentially productive of a problematic asymmetry. As it transpired, the problem never arose, as the grant of full civil rights to freedmen in the Danish West Indies in April 1834 antedated British West Indian emancipation by some months. The policy dispositions in respect of foreign freedmen eventually adopted were suggested by Michael Lange, a member of the Danske Cancelli, the metropolitan government's legal advisory body. In a circular memorandum of 21 January 1834, Lange expressed the view that foreign freedmen already resident should be treated no differently from creoles, and that they too should receive unconditional equality.[50] This was the position taken in the seminal ordinance of 18 April 1834. The paragraphs in it relating to foreign freedmen addressed themselves only to those who might take up residence in St. Thomas at some future date. Such persons, it stipulated, would be governed by the regulations previously in force and required to apply for "Free Briefs." Thereafter, they would be subject to a probationary residence period of three years, at the end of which they would qualify for citizenship provided they had led exemplary lives.[51]

The émigré freedman community of St. Thomas not only benefited by the reform of 1834 but played an important role in its coming to pass. Wittingly or unwittingly, they were bearers of the ideological perceptions of the Age of Revolution. By their presence they posed a challenging antithesis to the traditional thesis of race and ethnicity. Out of that confrontation emerged the synthesis of 1834. In the process, they helped the entire freedman community of the Danish West Indies to define itself as a group with greater acuity and to establish its goals. Their struggle for civil liberties was, however, a limited battle. The very structure of the slave society in which they moved and had their being created the categories within which they conceived their fate. Certainly freedmen of the Danish West Indies interacted with slaves in a supportive fashion and often they belonged to the same kinship networks, but they saw their own achievement of civil liberties as separate and apart from the struggle of the slaves for freedom. The movement towards the abolition of slavery and the removal of the entire structure of slave society, with its special place for freedmen, occurred in parallel with the freedmen's struggle and was influenced by it, but it remained a separate story.

11

"Religion and Enlightenment:" Education, Amelioration and the Road to Abolition

ON 16 MAY 1841, SEVEN YEARS AFTER THE GRANTING OF CIVIL rights to the freedman population and seven years before the abolition of slavery in the Danish West Indies, the first school for slave children was officially opened on the St. Croix plantation of La Grande Princesse. The occasion was marked with flourishes of congratulatory oratory from the Anglican Bishop of Barbados and the Roman Catholic Bishop of Trinidad. The director of the school system, the Moravian missionary Römer, who gave the main address, dwelt on the occasion's symbolic and historical significance: on that very estate, in almost the exact spot, the first Moravian missionary had been buried almost a hundred years before. St. Croix was then still largely covered with virgin forest, and the slaves whose labor would tame that forest were "without morals or religion." From primal chaos had been brought agricultural order, a material development which had a spiritual correspondence, said Römer, in the spread of "religion and enlightenment" among the slaves, and to which the schools' erection bore witness.[1]

As in most slave societies of the West Indies, public schooling was granted a low priority, for whites, freedmen and most particularly for slaves. The compelling imperatives of production and profit left little time for contemplation of such a non-material objective. Planters with means who desired an education for their children would send them to the ancient foundations in Denmark – Sorø Akademi or Herlufsholm – if they were Danish; or if they were Anglophone, to establishments in Boston, Philadelphia or New York, or to English boarding schools. Those without means or motivation contented themselves with the local offering from itinerant pedagogues.[2] It was not until 1788 that a public school for whites was established in Christiansted with Hans West as headmaster.[3] Comparable facilities for slave children were difficult to rationalize. A pervasive

Eurocentrism deemed Africans ineducable and, worse, questioned their membership in the human family. Custom and the law "even if not faithfully observed, had always been that education was forbidden to blacks."[4] Indeed, the crown itself left the issue in no doubt when it informed the colonial administration in St. Croix in 1768 that a public school system for slaves would serve "no useful purpose."[5] The extent to which received practice and theory in this regard began to be breached is attributable to a series of developments which began in the 1730s; the beginnings of proselytizing activities among slaves by Moravian and Lutheran missionaries, the effect of German Pietism on the conduct of Danish West Indian policy after the 1750s, and the humanitarianism of the closing decades of the eighteenth century.

Early Attempts at Slave Education

The Moravian endeavor which began in St. Thomas in 1732, was distinguished by its zeal, self-sacrifice and devotion. If the planters at an early date perceived them as revolutionaries, bent on the total overthrow of the prevailing social order, they were wrong only to the degree that they attributed a conscious revolutionary purpose to the Moravians. It was clear from the outset that the missionaries from Herrnhut did not feel themselves bound by the conventions of slave society; one of their number, Freundlich, took as his wife a free woman of color in 1739 in a wedding ceremony conducted by the missionaries' leader, Friedrich Martin.[6]

The Moravians were nothing if not resourceful. Johann Dober and David Nitschman, potter and carpenter respectively, the first two missionaries, took the trouble to learn the slaves' lingua franca, the Dutch based "creolsk." This simplified the task of instruction from the pulpit and at class meetings. It also re-inforced the use of creole and laid the essential foundations on which a creole grammar was eventually produced, along with creole translations of the New Testament and other religious works, a hymnal and a catechism.[7] From the very start the Moravians' concern for the slaves' afterlife created the possibility for slaves to become literate in this life, in creole if nothing else.

By 1800 that possibility had been achieved in some measure.[8] It was due largely to a sustained and informed interest in the slaves which the Moravians were the first and for some time the only ones to show. That interest consisted not only in an insistence on the necessity of the slaves learning to read, but also in raising earlier than anyone else the question of a school system. The organization since 1749 of missionary work into "classes" of communicants, baptized members not yet communicants, and candidates for baptism, was in practice nothing more or less than emphasizing for slaves that dimension of education which contemporary pedagogy had appointed for the poor. The work of Moravians as teachers among slaves was so successful before 1800, that Finance Minister Count Ernst Schimmelmann, (one of the more enlightened Danes of his time and a concerned if absentee proprietor in the Danish West Indies) approached them in 1799 to send teachers to his estate, La Grange and to his sister's, La Grande Princesse, in St. Croix. In the previous year, Thomas de Malleville, a West Indian creole who was not only governor but also a convert of the Moravians, took up with them the question of establishing in St. Croix a school system for slaves.[9] But in that very year de Malleville died; the Moravians lost an influential adherent, and with him for the time being, the prospect of bringing his embryonic plan to maturity.

Denmark's state Lutheran church began missionary and educational work among the slaves in the West Indies a good 25 years later than the Moravians. The creation of the Lutheran Mission to the West Indies, aimed at slaves and free people of color, was in part the belated outcome of the Pietist movement in its Danish phase. The movement placed considerable emphasis on the welfare and religious education of the underprivileged. Pietism was institutionally expressed in the foundation of country schools and of the Missionary College. In 1755, following the crown's acquisition of the islands from the company, Frederick V endorsed a proposal for starting a mission among West Indian slaves, and by 1756 ten missionaries had arrived in the islands, among them Johannes Kingo who produced the first creole ABC book in 1770.[10]

The purpose of this mission was set out in the Reglement for slaves issued in 1755: the preaching of God's word among slaves and a Christian education for them.[11] The mission, however, was ill-fated from the outset. Its goals were over-ambitious and the instructions betrayed a singular ignorance of the logistic context of the work missionaries were being called on to perform. They were expected to preach and teach adult slaves between 6 p.m. and 5 a.m.; devote an hour per week to children of working age, teaching them Danish, reading and religion, and preparing them for confirmation; and spend a minimum of six hours per week on each plantation. This latter provision as it applied to St. Thomas could involve a missionary in a 22 hour work day that required 16 hours of travel on foot. But there were also instructions from scientific societies to collect botanic specimens and the like. As Lose, the church historian, drily remarked, the missionary had a longer working day than the slave.[12]

The consequence of overwork and exposure to a new disease environment was high mortality. By 1773 Lutheran missionary activity was effectively confined to Charlotte Amalie, Frederiksted and Christiansted, and it is hardly surprising that Governor General Walterstorff, reporting on the mission in 1796, characterized it as a failure. He suggested that the missionary endeavor be brought under the control of the Generaltoldkammer, with a phased withdrawal of the personnel then in the islands.[13]

It was this failure of the Danish mission that strengthened the claims of the Moravians, who the Danish government itself identified in 1793 as best suited for the task of educating slaves. Its only reservation was that it would not support an itinerant system, since plantation owners might construe this as violation of their rights of property, and slaves might see in their instructors an alternative source of authority, partisan to their interests. The logical extension of this position was that the secular and religious instruction of slaves should take place in established locations. Indeed Miecke, the leader of the Moravians, said as much in a submission to the colonial administration in St. Croix.[14] The administration itself led by the sympathetic de Malleville reported to the government in Copenhagen that a large number of school houses should be erected all over the islands to facilitate the education of the young. Adult slaves, they reckoned, could only with difficulty benefit from instruction. At the very least the West Indian government envisaged one school in each of the nine quarters into which St. Croix was divided, at least two each for the less populous St. Thomas and St. John, and the immediate erection of two buildings in Christiansted and Frederiksted.[15] De Malleville's administration wanted the Moravians to work out their own methods but saw the necessity of obliging masters to allow slave children to go to school on certain specified days. Adult slaves would continue as in the past to receive instruction in the evenings and on Sundays and, if any of their number could be identified as of sufficiently good character, they could with their masters' permission assist with discipline in the children's schools.

So far as the costs of erecting the schools were concerned, the government proposed that in the long term, the charges could be borne by public funds or by the Moravians. For the time being the Lutheran Mission Fund could sustain the costs. There remained the question of the schools' location and the acquisition of the land on which to erect an initial two in St. Croix. In an obvious attempt to avoid planter hostility, it was suggested that a member of the colonial bureaucracy, Chamberlain Heyliger, could be persuaded to grant some lands on his Mt. Bijou estate for one location. For the other, the name of another colonial official, customs officer Miller, whose estate in the East End was mortgaged to the crown, was canvassed.[16] The East End, however, was agriculturally the least significant area in St. Croix with a relatively small slave population.[17] The Danish West Indian government, while endorsing the principle of established locations, specific times and public funding for an educational system for slaves, was treading exceedingly warily. It feared giving offense to the planter community but appreciated that the success of any scheme required, if not the active cooperation, at least the tolerance of the planter community.[18]

The Moravians, however, were beginning to have reservations. This was partly an effect of de Malleville's passing but it was also a realistic appraisal of the task at hand. Regardless of the projected increase in the physical facilities for slave education, the Moravians were not at all sure that they could take on a general educational system such as was contemplated. In the first place, there was an element of coercion on both planter and slave which could conceivably produce a negative reaction from both. The Moravians claimed that they could only consider the religious instruction of slave children and would not be undertaking secular instruction in reading and writing. The most they were prepared to do was to take some slave children of outstanding ability and teach them to read creole. The missionaries' objectives, in short, were more modest than the colonial government's. They found it desirable, for example, to give secular education momentum by encouraging slaves to re-read at home what they had heard in church and in this way develop literacy in creole.[19] A further source of misgiving for the Moravians was the proposed location of one of the schools on Heyliger's estate, for they found its situation insufficiently central. In 1803 it was said that "In the absence of a convenient location for a teaching establishment, the whole question was dropped." Two years later the Moravians were reportedly breaking stones and assembling material, presumably waiting on the government to provide a site, the public school system for slaves had effectively been laid to rest for the time being.[20]

The Danish Lutheran church continued to provide a combination of secular and religious education, supervised by its ordained clergy and with the assistance of four teachers in St. Croix, and one each in St. Thomas and St. John, but this was hardly more than a token. In 1832 Governor General von Scholten proposed that the Lutheran mission service be abandoned altogether, "since its primary object was to Christianize newly arrived Africans and that object was past."[21] The Moravians for their part continued unobtrusively with their work, operating from their mission stations: New Herrnhut and Niesky in St. Thomas; Bethany and Emaus in St. John, Fridensthal and Friedensfeld in St. Croix. Their methods were simple and direct: classes of enquirers and communicants were kept in the meeting houses and prayers were said every evening for any slaves wishing to attend. Unlike the Lutherans, they were not culture bound and felt no sense of compulsion to teach slaves Danish.[22] Yet literacy was high on their agenda and the success of their efforts in this connection was evidenced by the increasing number of slaves who could read in the first three decades of the nineteenth century.[23]

Effects of Metropolitan Humanitarianism

If sustained interest in providing education for society's oppressed persisted in the colonies only among the Moravians, in Denmark itself developments were taking place which would be of long term consequence for the colonies. Within Denmark there had been an ongoing concern since the late 1780s for an educational system appropriate to the country.[24] The law provided for compulsory elementary education, the erection of school buildings, remuneration of teachers and fines for withholding children from school. But the performance hardly matched the profession and the situation was ripe for the attention of Denmark's enlightened social reformers, whose agenda by the 1780s included reforms in land tenure and agriculture, the abolition of serfdom (1792) and the curtailment of the slave trade (1802). These reformers gave low priority to classical learning and memorizing; they emphasized in their stead useful knowledge, education for citizenship and "mens sana in corpore sano." For reformers like Bernstorff, Ludvig and Christian Reventlow and Ernst Schimmelmann, reforms as they related to serfdom and the rural poor, made little sense unless they were wedded to a thoroughgoing educational reform embracing serfs and the peasantry. Largely due to their efforts, the Great School Commission was brought into being in 1789, and for the next 25 years profoundly affected the course of educational developments, not only in Denmark but in her West Indian colonies as well. By the time the Commission had sat for the last time in 1814, the law enforcing compulsory education and creating state supported schools for the poor had been passed.

Frederick VI, first as crown prince and subsequently as king, helped to initiate these reforms and was active in their promotion. Von Scholten's close relationship with him particularly in the period 1808-1814, placed him in intimate contact with the reformist ideas with which the king was associated. It is difficult to imagine entry into that circle without sharing its ideals; it is equally difficult to imagine anyone not being profoundly affected by its central concerns once within it. It is also of some importance to notice the fact that von Scholten's career as a colonial official, properly speaking, began immediately after his long association at close quarters with a reform-minded king, and close on the heels of the law establishing a publicly funded educational system for Denmark's poor in 1814. His appointment in that very year to his first post, that of Weighmaster in St. Thomas, was the start of a period of colonial service for the next 34 years, the last 20 of which he spent as Governor General of the Danish West Indies.

Von Scholten personified the important bridge that linked humanitarian activity in Denmark to its colonial manifestation. The slave in the colonial context was a factor in a mode of agricultural production different in degree but not significantly in kind from the Danish manorial system of the eighteenth century. The oppression and subordination which characterized slavery and serfdom were essential to both as closed systems of unequal social relationships. The social reformers of late eighteenth century Denmark sought to rectify the imbalances, if not equalize the relationships, by the moral upliftment of and increased social opportunities for that class which serfs comprised. The slaves in the colonies, from the reforming humanitarians' point of view, comprised an equally imperative category for amelioration. The movement for the abolition of the slave trade was the first major point of contact between metropolitan reform and the colonial situation, where the ameliorative intent towards slaves was consistently articulated.[25] Von Scholten represented this tradition; his appointment as Governor General in 1828 provided the opportunity to promote amelioration with vigor.

Von Scholten's Initiatives

As early as 1829 von Scholten expressed satisfaction at and encouragement for the work of the Moravians among blacks, and promised material
support.[26] He came early to hold the Moravians in high regard because he
perceived that their methods and their successes in evangelizing and
teaching among the slaves made them crucial to his future plans. As an
earnest of this regard, 3 August 1832 was declared a public holiday to
permit the celebration of the Moravian centenary jubilee. Ten thousand
slaves attended the Friedensfeld mission house; von Scholten himself was
present with an official party and military escort, and authorized a 19 gun
salute before and after the service.[27]

On von Scholten's own admission he had committed his energies from
the very outset of his administration to promote the slaves' welfare and the
amelioration of their situation. Both, he emphasized in 1834, were inextricably yoked with the immediate and future fortunes of the colonies. The
Emancipation Act in the British West Indies gave a compelling urgency to
von Scholten's plans, for he recognized that with the termination of Apprenticeship scheduled for 1840, all other colonial possessions in which
slavery persisted could not escape the seismic shock-waves of emancipation.[28] What von Scholten therefore began with in 1828 as a program of
ameliorative reforms came to be conceptualized as an Emancipation Plan.
In it, education for slaves on a publicly funded basis formed an important
part.

Initial response to the plan was at best unenthusiastic and at worst
hostile. In many respects the planters' reaction was characterized by the
same kind of hysteria evident at the time of the abolition of serfdom in
Denmark. Even among the Moravians there were important reservations
on the question of emancipation. Brother Bonhoff thought slaves far too
unenlightened to make proper use of their freedom and shared in no way
the Governor General's view that there was a compelling necessity for
change in the threatening circumstances of the time. Bonhoff did concede,
however, a need for a properly organized school system, and supported
von Scholten in a proposal for allowing slaves Saturday free for market so
that Sunday could be devoted to schooling and religious instruction.[29]
Moravian support for that part of von Scholten's plans relating to slave
education was crucial in the face of generalized hostility among the islands'
white communities.

The metropolitan government, or more particularly Frederick VI whose
confidence von Scholten enjoyed, responded by establishing a commission
of senior officials to "enquire into the circumstances of the several Danish
West Indian Islands."[30] Its report, submitted in November 1834, endorsed
the establishment of a school system and suggested that its details be
worked out by a local commission in the islands.[31] The local committee,
composed of planters, clergy and members of the Burgher Council of St.
Croix, decided that eight schools should be erected on appropriate sites,

and that materials and labor which the plantations could not provide would be paid for from public funds.[32] Important gains were made among the planter community between 1834 and 1838 in securing their support. Von Scholten reported early in 1839 that the "school project had little by little won public attention and support."[33] In 1841 H. B. Dahlerup observed that the more aware planters appreciated the significance of British West Indian emancipation for the Danish islands, and had come to understand that the most efficacious means of preventing a violent upheaval when the inevitable emancipation came was to prepare the slaves to make good use of their freedom by education and "moral upliftment." This conviction led some planters to build small schools on their plantations, imitating the example of those who at an earlier time had done so out of motivations of "philanthropy and religious sentiment."[34]

If this latter motivation had masked a consideration of self-interest insofar as such schooling facilitated greater social control in conditions of slavery, it now apparently gave way to another form of self-interest, although of a more enlightened kind, relating to the future. Von Scholten for his part was evidently committed after 1834 to the inevitability of emancipation. But he envisaged a measured progress and an orderly denouement in which his school plans were an important input. "Concern for the lower classes including the unfree," he remarked to the Burgher Council of St. Croix in 1839, "was a matter of simple wisdom." The Burgher Council was entirely in agreement; education for the lower classes (freed-men included), their moral upliftment and character-betterment would be amply repaid by greater public peace and security.[35]

Considerations of public order had been a major stumbling block to the introduction of any system of instruction, as indeed they had been during the heyday of the St. Domingue and later the Cuban slave regimes.[36] The Danish West Indian plantocracy looked with as much displeasure at non-conformist, especially Methodist, missionary activity as they regarded republican black Haiti, a land they deemed "without resources, industry, religion and morality" after 40 years of independence.[37] Von Scholten himself reacted very negatively to the presence of "the host of American Methodists who came to winter in St. Croix for their health" and were steadily gaining influence among slaves, freedmen and the women of St. Croix. He was well aware of the disruptive effect which Methodists were deemed to have on the even tenor of slave plantation societies and had no difficulty declaring them prohibited immigrants. Similar proscriptions existed under von Scholten against Quakers and Baptists.[38]

Once enough planters were convinced that the proposed school system was unlikely to be prejudicial to public order, the major obstacle to its acceptance by any but the most determined defender of the status quo was assured of removal. The County School Ordinance of 1839 formally established the system although construction of the first school actually began in 1838.[39] The Ordinance authorized the erection of eight schools in St. Croix, five in St. Thomas and four in St. John, the capital costs of which would be met from the colonial treasury in those instances where they were not met by gifts and voluntary contributions. The recurrent annual expenditure, estimated at 10,000 Rigsdaler, would be met from a capitation tax on slaves.[40] To placate planter opposition, the arrangements called for children over nine to be taught on Saturday mornings; children below that age would have three hours of instruction daily in the mornings, Saturdays apart.

Instruction was to be in English, for, as the Danish West Indian government argued in 1838, Danish was a minority language and creole, the slaves' lingua franca, was inappropriate as a medium of instruction. Moreover, the slaves' English was sufficiently passable to permit the use of that language in schools and churches.[41] There was the additional advantage in using English: it would help to win the support of the adult slaves for the system. Official instruction in English, the language of the majority of the planter community, was an earnest of the recognition of the slaves' humanity. The adult slave population was sufficiently perceptive to grasp this implication, and to distinguish between a state supported generalized system and the earlier private individual efforts, which some slaves had tended to view with suspicious caution. By contrast they greeted the new dispensation with considerable enthusiasm.[42]

Von Scholten had in the meantime insisted that the Moravians were crucial to his purpose, and having obtained the crown's permission to seek eight missionaries to get the project underway, traveled to the Moravian headquarters at Herrnhut.[43] The allowing of exclusive rights to the Moravians in education was by no means an unreasonable concession, given both the size of their following (Table 11.1), and their past record; in any event it would not have been possible to denominationalize the system, given the existing financial constraints. The Moravians for their part regarded this as an opportunity for additional missionary endeavor. One of their number was sent to England to learn English. Bishop Breutel reported to his principals from St. Croix in 1841 that their mission was fulfilling a long and deeply felt need and that the schools would facilitate greater reading of the Bible and a sharpened moral sense among the coming generation.[44]

The decision not to denominationalize the educational system for slaves brought difficulties in its train, although not immediately. Confessional conceits and liturgical subtleties could only with difficulty or not at all be reconciled in this omnibus arrangement, where secular instruction for the most part was rooted not merely in the basics of common morality but also in the tenets of religion as well. The Danish Lutheran pastor in Christiansted was charged with the task of producing a generally acceptable manual, and his 61-page *Schoolbook for the Religious Instruction of the Unfree in the Danish West India Islands* proved sufficiently neutral to serve as a text with which to begin.[45]

In metropolitan Denmark an important manifestation of that enthusiasm was represented by the crown princess Caroline Amalie. The

Table 11.1: *Church Affiliation of the Free and Unfree Population in the Danish West Indies, 1835*

Island	Lutheran		Moravian		Church of England and Presbyterian		Methodist	
	Free	Slave	Free	Slave	Free	Slave	Free	Slave
St. Croix	2,120	1,904	276	6,244	3,363	5,111	–	–
St. Thomas	1,748	461	447	1,895	1,534	398	51	28
St. John	80	86	237	1,369	146	118	1	3
Sub-total	3,948	2,451	960	9,508	5,043	5,627	52	31
Total	6,399		10,468		10,670		83	

Island	Quaker		Roman Catholic		Jews		Unbaptised	
	Free	Slave	Free	Slave	Free	Slave	Free	Slave
St. Croix	1	–	916	6,433	42	–	87	184
St. Thomas	7	–	4,056	2,265	425	–	66	251
St. John	–	–	19	46	–	–	6	307
Sub-total	8	–	4,991	8,744	467	–	159	742
Total	8		13,735		467		901	

Source: R/A, CANS, 5, von Scholten's Report, 2 January 1839, Encl. 16B.

princess was a woman of deep religious feeling and remarkable piety, profoundly affected, it would appear, by the movement for educational reform and spiritual regeneration set in train by Denmark's great reformer of the nineteenth century, N. F. S. Grundtvig. She congratulated von Scholten on the introduction of the school system, particularly its religious component and asked to be kept informed of the progress of the experiment.[46]

Metropolitan and Local Opposition

The princess' enthusiasm was hardly a national phenomenon, however. Denmark's Liberals, distrustful of the court, of absolute monarchy and von Scholten as its colonial expression, damned the experiment with faint praise. Their objections were not to the schools in principle but to von Scholten. His very presence, they claimed, was an obstacle to progress in the colonies. They went so far as to suggest that the schools were hardly more than a symbol of von Scholten's capacity for vain gloriousness. The schools were sited along the main road, the Centreline, from Christiansted to Frederiksted and it was impossible not to see them; so far as the Liberals could discern, the determining criterion in their location had been optimal visual effect.[47] Although von Scholten had a justifiable reputation for love of magnificence and show, the Liberals' ad hominem criticism was unworthy.

They were on firmer ground in calling into question the use of the Moravian missionary instructors. They made the crudely chauvinist but eminently understandable point that the Moravians were being favored at the expense of Danish Lutheran missionaries. It was of little significance that the Lutheran mission had been a declared failure since the beginning of the nineteenth century. The Liberals were embittered at the declining importance of the Danish language and Danish culture in the West Indian Islands, and in large measure blamed it on von Scholten. The appointment of unlettered Moravians as instructors, it was said, would conduce to the continued use of creole among the slaves and defeat one of the stated objectives of the school system. Learning creole from the slaves, the Liberals argued, missionaries seldom learnt English themselves, and rarely came into contact with the "educated classes."[48]

The Liberals proposed that the teacher corps be indigenized by the use of freedmen. Although von Scholten had spent a great deal of energy fighting for civil equality for freedmen and had been equally energetic in promoting their social acceptance, he had failed to connect this enthusiasm with zeal for slave education.[49] Certainly, encouragement for the use of freedmen as teachers had not been lacking. As early as 1829, on the occasion of a public celebration in St. Croix marking the wedding of Prince Frederick Carl Christian to Princess Wilhelmina, there had been a proposal that a fund be started to educate "two young natives, one white and one of color, to become teachers of the schools of these islands." Von Scholten is reported to have warmly approved but that is as far as the proposal appears to have got.[50] The Liberals pointed out that while von Scholten merely talked about schools, the British West Indies provided many examples of the identification and training of local freedman teachers, with excellent results. Further they argued that if one wanted to improve the situation of blacks and coloreds vis-á-vis whites and bring them into contact with the latter, then logic required that one look among them for teachers to train. If, moreover, English was to be the medium of instruction, the choice of free black and free colored teachers would reinforce its more widespread use among the slaves, thereby replacing creole as the lingua franca.[51] Whatever the reason, their German provenance or their lowliness in the contemporary class scale, the Moravians' lack of competence in English was a decided disadvantage given the promotion of competence in English as one of the stated objectives of the school system.

The Liberal misgivings about the school system have to be understood not only as suspicion of von Scholten but also as distrust of his mentor Frederick VI. Van Dockum, who was von Scholten's adjutant at the beginning of the 1840s, observed in his memoirs that "when, following Frederick VI's death, Liberal voices in Denmark rose in concert against everything his regime had stood for, planters found a ready support in the Danish press which saw von Scholten only as a servant of absolutism." The Liberal press, according to van Dockum, not only articulated the planters' point of view, but also identified von Scholten as the major obstacle to progress in the colonies. In van Dockum's view, it was the planter community which obstructed every attempt at progressive change. Indeed the Liberal press had gone to such lengths to incite opinion against von Scholten that street riots took place in front of his house in Copenhagen.[52] Although van Dockum was likely to be partisan, there is ample evidence to support his charge of the hostility of the press and *Fædrelandet*, in particular, which published a series of articles in 1841 under the title "The West Indies from a Planter Perspective." There is also considerable justice in his stricture on the planters, a significant number of whom put up a determined resistance to the school experiment between 1840 and 1846.

The planters found little difficulty with the education of slave children below the age of eight or nine. The education of older slaves, however, raised knotty issues. In the age group nine to twelve, in St. Croix alone, there were some 930 children whose labor planters calculated they would lose for whatever period of schooling was prescribed. In St. Thomas there were some 122 and in St. John 94 (Table 11.2). Although these figures for 1841 represented no more than 4.6 percent of the 24,738 slaves counted in the October 1841 census, they had a qualitative significance far outweighing their quantitative import.[53] For von Scholten, the anticipated difficulties would be happily resolved if slaves were allowed a free day other than Sunday. The crown, broadly supportive of von Scholten's ameliorative intent, was guarded in its support of the free day proposal. It took a compromise position in an ordinance of 1 May 1841, calling on planters to grant their slaves one free week day during the "dead season" from July to November and a weekly payment of 2 Danish crowns to all slaves over eight years old during crop time.[54] Von Scholten, however, exercised his discretion to propose to the planters a free day weekly for the entire year. In a circular letter to the planter community he argued that in this way the planters would be saved the additional cash outgoings and slaves would achieve an opportunity to use the arrangements being made for their children. No slave child of eight years and over, in the counterdispensation proposed by von Scholten, would be allowed to go to school during the working week, now deemed by him to mean Monday to Friday.[55]

The proposal had a mixed reception. In St. Croix, of the 170 sugar plantations and cattle farms listed in 1840, the owners or agents of some 83 describing themselves as a "considerable majority" accepted the greater part of the circular's contents, adding however that although children aged four to eight would be permitted to attend school on days other than the free day, this would be "without prejudice to their early training in field work."[56] Further, regarding the education of older children and adult slaves, they stated firmly that they would not consent to the appropriation of any part of the working week to the instruction of adults or those above age eight.[57]

Table 11.2:   *Estimated School Age Population of Slaves in the Danish West Indies, 1841*

Age Groups	St. Croix			St. Thomas			St. John		
	Catholic	Non-Catholic	Total	Catholic	Non-Catholic	Total	Catholic	Non-Catholic	Total
Weekday School for Children Ages 5-9	501	960	1,461	15	215	230	5	187	192
Saturday School for Children 9-12	320	610	930	8	114	122	3	90	94
Total	821	1,570	2,391	23	329	252	8	278	286

Source: R/A, Indiske Forestillinger og Resolutioner, 1845-1846, 53b, Appraximativo Oversigt over de ufrie Born paa plantagerne paa St. Croix, St. Thomas og St. Jan, som efter Folketællingen af 1ste October 1841 Kunne ansees Skolepligtige.

Opponents of von Scholten among the plantocracy saw the school system and the free day which would help to make it viable as no more than a means of hastening emancipation, their ultimate ruin. Nor did some of the dissenting planters see virtue in attempting to educate slaves in a secular or religious mode: the slave was ineducable, "work [was] exacted of the Black, in strict conformity with the doom of the Almighty" and there was "no proof that his race is peculiarly fitted for any much more noble or useful career."[58] From St. Thomas, the public prosecutor Sarauw, an implacable enemy of von Scholten's, made a detailed submission to the king on 31 December 1840, casting doubt on the authenticity of von Scholten's "considerable majority." According to Sarauw many planters had signed, not because they thought the weekly free day right or good, but to avoid the greater evil of allowing free time during the normal work week for adults and adolescents to go to school. Sarauw submitted that the entire planter community was particularly fearful of adult slaves being sent to school, and suggested that this was the reason why even those who had consented to a free Saturday weekly laid down the express condition that no slave over eight years should be sent to school during the work week.[59]

Some planters however felt that there was no reason to despair of change for the better in the slaves' morality if they were allowed the benefit of instruction. They took special objection to the racial pessimism of von Scholten's opponents and the notion of the slaves' ineducability. Such a position they claimed was "infected with ... Colorphobia," since its proponents had no proof that the slave was not peculiarly fitted for a nobler career than unremitting labor. A reasoned counter-argument by one of von

Scholten's partisans advocated with remarkable vigor that slaves' entitlement to membership of the human family was no less than the white man's:

> we in fact *have* proof abundant that he is fitted with every sense and facility, which have raised the white man to the elevated stand, which he now holds in the scale of creation; that the same thirst after knowledge, the same inventive genius is his, and that in no case, we assert, has it been observed, that placed in parallel circumstances of advantage for education the black man has ever failed to keep pace with the white man; but on the contrary we can say, that well known instances have occurred, in which he has surpassed *him,* who had been early taught to look on himself as superior to the *Negro Race.*[60]

Whatever the weight of opinion, it is clear that von Scholten had determined that the school system, (and the weekly free day which would facilitate its expansion to older slaves) was an object of the first importance; partly in its acculturative aspect as a method of promoting social control and public order; partly also in its ameliorative aspect, as a mechanism of social engineering, and expression of optimism for the future of the islands' blacks. While few planters would have quarreled with the first, the second objective was a source of hysterical misgiving. It smacked suspiciously of "democracy," which Sarauw pointedly reminded the king was a phenomenon unknown in Denmark; worse, it conjured up visions of Haiti.[61] The grudging response and outright opposition were to be explained only in terms of a mortal fear of social leveling. The point was not lost on the king's advisers in the Generaltoldkammer who subsequently remarked: "There are grounds for believing that several planters treat with suspicion any arrangements for the education of the youth, for they fully appreciate that the establishment of a properly organized educational system would entail the destruction of the most important obstacle to the freer development of social relationships in the colony."[62] Christian VIII for his part, once he became king in 1839, was anxious to proceed with caution, working towards a gradual emancipation by free birth, with compensation paid to the owners of the mothers in question. Education, he felt, would help to prepare the slaves for their freedom. But at the same time he was at pains to point out that, with this and other ameliorative measures, it was just as much a point of concern "to make emancipation unnecessary for as long as possible, for when the unfree are treated in a lawful and considerate manner, the necessity for such a costly step would cease to be so compelling."[63]

This was a very conservative approach to the question of emancipation. Yet Christian VIII, like his wife, supported the experiment in slave education; in his case if for no other reason than to buy time and postpone the day of reckoning. Accordingly, he issued a Royal Rescript on 18 February 1843 which by transferring market day from Sunday to Saturday made the latter the slaves' free day. The Rescript instructed the Governor General to draw up a regulatory ordinance for the school system in collaboration with the colonies' law officers, the Lutheran priest and some planters.[64] It gave

royal approval to the instruction of all slave children over the age of nine
on the free day. But conflict over timetabling and the upper age limit
for instruction continued down to 1846 when a compromise was finally
hammered out.

The 1846 Ordinance

The ordinance known as the "Reglement for Landskolerne paa de
danske vestindiske Øer" was the detailed instrument for institutionalizing
a publicly supported school system for slaves in Denmark's three West
Indian Islands. It reiterated the Generaltoldkammer's final position on the
upper age limit (12 years), prescribed the days and times at which school
would be held, the times of admission, and the periods of vacation.[65] It
established a school board consisting of the Lutheran priest as secretary
and chairman with a casting vote; the chief of police; a member nominated
by the Burgher Council but approved by the governor general, and a fourth
member appointed at the governor general's discretion.[66]

The regulations recognized the critical importance of slave parents and
estate management, more particularly overseers, to the success of the
experiment. Priests were to impress upon older slaves and slave parents
the advantage of schooling, and if they proved refractory, they were to be
punished suitably. Overseers were charged with the responsibility of ensuring children's regular attendance; keeping an up-to-date list of
school-age children; providing a trustworthy adult to accompany children
to school; and explaining absence, illness and late-coming. Dereliction in
the execution of these duties on the part of the overseers could lead to
investigation by the police and heavy fines, especially if it was established
that children were being made to work during school hours.[67]

The Generaltoldkammer dwelt heavily upon this point of attendance in
the Ordinance, for it had earlier observed that the record of attendance had
been less than satisfactory. It attributed this to a lack of interest on the part
of many planters, of whom the signatories to the memorial of August 1845
were particularly representative. None of them, the Generaltoldkammer
submitted, had the least interest in ensuring that slave children on their
estates derived any advantage from the schools. Only total lack of interest
on the planters' part, it concluded, could explain absences to such a degree
that from many plantations not a single child attended school in 1844.[68]

The missionaries from Herrnhut were retained in their teaching posts
and charged with keeping up-to-date lists of attendance and a school
journal. They were immediately responsible to the Moravian authorities
locally, by whom they were hired and could be fired for neglect of duty and
bad conduct. The school inspector was similarly Moravian, immediately
responsible to the School Board and ultimately to the governor general. He
was required to pay unscheduled visits, inspect the journal for the incidence of absence, keep an inventory of the physical facilities and make an
annual report to the board. Above all the inspector was charged with the

preparation of written instructions for teachers, to which they were scrupulously to adhere so as not to offend religious sensibilities. Such methods of instruction as the teachers used were also to be prepared by the inspector.[69]

The syllabus as laid down in the Ordinance was not overly ambitious: reading, the basics of arithmetic, memorizing and singing hymns, and studying Bagger's catechism. A public examination once per year in June was to test the accomplishments of school leavers or those about to enter Saturday school, and the results along with a character testimonial recorded on a certificate. Outstanding pupils were eligible for a cash prize on the inspector's recommendation.[70]

In scope, the school system which this Ordinance regularized was not dissimilar to schools for the rural poor established in Denmark in 1814. The latter had been called into being hard on the heels of the abolition of serfdom, their creation motivated by the same kind of humanitarian idealism, the same desire to create a useful citizenry from a formerly oppressed class. Von Scholten was not only deeply influenced by this metropolitan tradition but was also one of the major conduits through which it reached the colonies. His stated purpose was the achievement of the slaves' eventual emancipation in which their education, publicly supported, would play an important preparatory part. But whilst one recognizes humanitarian purpose, there was also utilitarian intent: a concern born of what von Scholten had described as "simple wisdom;" an insurance policy purchased by more enlightened planters against the possibility of violent upheaval. A concern for social control was therefore an important component in the experiment with the slave school system. Good citizenry, or an "orderly *denouement*" to slavery, involved an acceptance by the unfree community of the implicit premises of the superordinate class. Indeed the particular importance of religious education in this regard was expressly articulated as early as 1796.[71]

The paradox was that among the more conservative elements of the plantocracy, from whom one would have expected greatest support for heightened social control, there was the greatest resistance. The paradox is explainable by reference to the fact that they were more interested in the long term than in the short term considerations: in protecting their ascribed status against potential social leveling which education could eventually bring, than in forestalling the more immediate potential threat of violent upheaval.[72] The ultimate paradox was that those who opted for social control were rudely awakened, and in only two short years after 1846.

In the final analysis, the school system contributed significantly to the achievement of what it was supposed to help prevent; the slaves' seizure of their freedom by their own revolutionary initiative. To the same degree and for the same reason that some planters were suspicious of education, slaves responded positively to it. Above all, the availability of education heightened their perceptions of their own worth as a race and raised their expectations for freedom. Those expectations were legitimized in the royal proclamation of 28 July 1847 which conferred freedom on all slaves born after that date and set a date for emancipation in twelve years.[73] Von Scholten had been uncompromisingly opposed to a law of free birth, anticipating that "it would create discontent and have the most regrettable consequences while adult slaves remained in servitude."[74] His calculations could not have been more correct.

The Free Birth Proclamation of 1847 gave an urgency, born of impatience, to the expectations for freedom raised by the school system. The adult slave population would not postpone their inheritance of a freedom to which they felt their children were no more legitimate heirs than themselves. The uprising of 2-3 July 1848 by which the slaves forced the issue of their emancipation has been associated in conventional historiography with the law of Free Birth as its important proximate cause.[75] While this is the case, the chain of causation has other significant backward linkages. The introduction of the school system has serious claims to be considered in the re-appraisal of explanations for 2-3 July 1848.

12

The Victor Vanquished:
Emancipation and Its Aftermath

THE ST. CROIX SLAVE UPRISING OF 2-3 JULY 1848 BELONGS TO
that splendidly isolated category of Caribbean slave revolts which succeeded if, that is, one defines success in the narrow sense of the legal
termination of servitude. The sequence of events can be briefly rehearsed.
On the night of Sunday 2 July, signal fires were lit on the estates of western
St. Croix, estate bells began to ring and conch shells were blown, and by
Monday morning, 3 July, some 8,000 slaves had converged in front of
Frederiksted fort demanding their freedom. In the early hours of Monday
morning, Governor General von Scholten, who had only hours before
returned from a visit to neighboring St. Thomas, summoned a meeting of
his senior advisers in Christiansted (Bass End), the island's capital. Among
them was Lt. Capt. Irminger, commander of the Danish West Indian naval
station, who urged the use of force, including bombardment from the sea
to disperse the insurgents, and the deployment of a detachment of soldiers
and marines from his frigate Ørnen. Von Scholten kept his own counsels.
No troops were despatched along the arterial Centreline road and, although he gave Irminger permission to sail around the coast to beleagured
Frederiksted (West End), he went overland himself and arrived in town
sometime around 4 p.m. before Irminger did. No sooner had he alighted
from his coach than he addressed the swarming multitude of slaves insisting on their freedom: "Now you are free, you are hereby emancipated."[1]

Emancipation by gubernatorial fiat abruptly terminated sixteen hours
of riotous but surprisingly bloodless activity. The absence of bloodshed and
the denouement of freedom distinguishes this uprising from other "late"
slave rebellions in the Caribbean. Bussa's 1816 rebellion in Barbados, the
Demerara uprising in 1823 and the Jamaica Christmas rebellion of 1831
were all characterized by spectacular blood-letting and no immediate
consequential change in the slaves' legal status.[2] None of those uprisings
in the British West Indies had been predicated on the declared, as distinct
from the rumored, intent of the metropolitan government to emancipate

the slave population. The slaves in the Danish West Indies, on the other hand, had had the crown's assurance in the previous year that general emancipation would take place in 1859, with an interim dispensation of Free Birth to take effect from 28 July 1847.[3] Nevertheless, the St. Croix rebellion shares common ground with those of the British and French West Indies in that it derived as much from aroused expectations as it did from a perception of oppression.

The uprising followed more than a decade and a half of ameliorative changes introduced under the liberalizing stewardship of von Scholten. During the 1830s, the work day's length was strictly regulated, slave owners' discretionary powers of punishment drastically reduced, public auctions banned and the keeping of plantation journals for regular inspection made mandatory.[4] In the 1840s, Saturday was conceded as a free day, to facilitate its use as a market day in place of Sunday, which was now consecrated to religious observance and secular instruction. Wage payments at the rate of 4 Rigsdaler per day were introduced for plantation work undertaken on the prescribed free day. Significant improvements were also registered in the quality of slave housing which was approvingly viewed by an eye as critical as Victor Schoelcher's. The first publicly supported elementary schools for slave children were opened in 1841, and by 1846 their existence had been formalized by an ordinance authorizing the establishment of seventeen schools.[5] Von Scholten's strategy was based on a calculation of the inevitability of emancipation in the Danish, once emancipation had taken place in the British, West Indies. Since he deemed it no longer a question of whether but when, he sought by this reforming dispensation to smooth the transition to full freedom when it should arrive. His metropolitan principals and the increasingly vocal Liberal politicians in Denmark's provincial assemblies gradually came to share the governor general's emancipationist perspective and by 1847 the issue had been sealed by royal proclamation.[6]

For all the world, therefore, the Danish West Indies appeared set on a course for an untraumatic termination of chattel slavery. Amelioration and the royal proclamation apart, there were other favorable auguries which suggested a smooth passage. There was no well developed tradition of slave revolts. The Danish West Indies had passed but once through the fiery crucible of actual revolt, and that 1733 uprising in St. John had been conclusively put down with assistance from the French. Ethnic rebellions typical of other Caribbean plantation colonies while their slave populations were predominantly African, were never a feature of the Danish West Indian experience. As for conspiracies, only that in St. Croix in 1759 created a briefly sustained ripple of anxiety.[7] Nor were there to be further conspiracies, actual or attempted revolts, as the slave populations of the Danish West Indies became increasingly creolized after the late eighteenth century. In St. Croix itself, a useful index of the creolization process was the astonishingly high incidence of church affiliation, which by 1835 was 99 percent of the island's total slave population (Table 6.2). Yet those confessional affinities appear, if anything, to have reinforced the quest for "respectability" at the expense of "reputation."[8] That emphasis, and its concomitant, an accommodating rather than an adversary mind-set, is perhaps best explained not so much by religion's opiate effect, as by the structures within those denominations permitted to practice in the Danish West Indies: the state Lutheran Church, the Roman Catholics, the Moravians, and to a lesser extent the Dutch Reformed Church. None of these offered the same possibilities as the non-conformist Baptists and Methodists for slave leadership within the congregation; nor, by the same token, the possibilities for the emergence of movements such as the "native Baptists" with their potential for political radicalization.[9]

Notwithstanding the apparent order and calm of mature creolized slave society in the Danish West Indies, there were persons, as late as 1847 who recognized that the will to resist was as constant as servitude itself; that the grace period – virtually apprenticeship before emancipation – could conceivably be interrupted by what was euphemistically called "unforeseen circumstances."[10] The slaves for their part had responded to the Law of Free Birth not with unalloyed enthusiasm as might have been anticipated, but rather with impatience born of dissatisfaction that their children were beneficiaries of an imperial largesse which they would have to wait more than a decade to enjoy. Free Birth as policy had respectable international pedigree: the Venezuelans had implemented it in 1821; Buxton had canvassed it in the British Parliament in 1823.[11] But in the Danish West Indies, the asymmetry which it established was productive of the very tensions the metropolitan government sought to avoid.

There is evidence, moreover, which indicates that since at least 1800, the slaves particularly in St. Croix, were less and less in thrall to whiteness as a megalithic instrument of social control. Its erosion as a formidable deterrent had been promoted by intimate contact with a growing cadre of Anglo-Irish plantation supervisory personnel which did not exactly command respect. Nor were there grounds to be in awe of a colonial polity whose power traditionally had been less than hegemonic. Most particularly, its exiguous resources of force, which had virtually invited the 1733 uprising, encouraged the conspiracy of 1759 and proved risibly inadequate to respond to the British invasions of 1801 and 1807, were no more prepossessing in 1848 than they had ever been. Whatever other calculations the slaves might have made in 1848, there is very little doubt that they considered the odds favorable because of the feebleness of the colonial military posture.

Emancipation by gubernatorial fiat foreclosed the possibility of the Akan-style alternative polity envisaged by some earlier Caribbean slave rebellions, and of which the regime of Dessalines, as Michael Craton has perceptively noted, was the ultimate expression.[12] The St. Croix insurgents had no such political order in contemplation. Their aspirations, like those of their Jamaican counterparts in 1831 or Barbadian equivalents in 1816 did not transcend the regularization of a proto-peasant status well established by 1848. Victory achieved through the mediation of state approval also left intact, with the exception of legal slavery, the institutional structures of the colonial polity, including the mechanism for the administration of law and order. Many of the predominantly non-Danish planter class and some sectors of officialdom, moreover, shared little of von Scholten's reforming enthusiasm or racial optimism, however guarded. Soured by an emancipation which they thought premature, angered by a rebellion which they deemed impertinent, they sought an early opportunity to restore the social order which had prevailed up to Monday 3 July 1848.

The Court Martial

In the early hours of Tuesday morning, 4 July, a group of the recently emancipated was shot down just outside Christiansted. There was retaliatory looting and destruction for the next three days on estates in the center, south, west and north of the island. On Thursday, 6 July, von Scholten suffered what would now be diagnosed as a nervous collapse and the lieutenant governor of St. Thomas, Frederik Oxholm assumed command of the civil government.[13] Oxholm arrived on Saturday, 8 July, and the 530 troops which he requested of the governor of Puerto Rico arrived the same day.[14] But long before then, Irminger had moved decisively to assert the power of constituted authority, to demonstrate to the newly emancipated that freedom was not licence. On Tuesday, Frederiksted was put under a state of emergency by a commission consisting of Irminger, Capt. Frederik von Scholten, the governor general's brother, Capt. Castonier, the fort commandant, and the Chief of Police Øgaard: if the freedmen came back to town and assembled in groups of more than ten, they would be fired on by the fort cannon and the frigate, still at anchor in the harbor.[15]

Irminger's role as primus inter pares in this commission can be assumed from the superiority of his rank and the fact that he commanded resources far superior to anything Castonier had at his disposal. By Wednesday he had manifestly taken charge, relieving Castonier, albiet temporarily, of the command of the fort, and using his marines to demolish a block of buildings obscuring the fort's line of fire towards the landward approaches from the north and east. By Thursday 6 July, the commission had been enlarged to include the commanding officer of Frederiksted's Fire Corps, Major Gyllich, and Crown Prosecutor Sarauw. This enlarged commission issued a second proclamation on Thursday which had the effect of extending the emergency beyond Frederiksted: "any person or persons opposing the authorities or in any other manner combining for illegal or violent purposes will be dealt with as rioters and instantly shot."[16] The mass arrests began the same day and the court martial proceedings in Frederiksted on Friday, 7 July.

The court sat uninterruptedly for the next five weeks. It examined more than 100 prisoners, heard evidence from other recently emancipated slaves, from freedmen before emancipation, from estate owners, agents, overseers, bookkeepers and from government officials. Those apprehended were far more than could be accommodated in the very fort to which most of the terrified whites of western St. Croix had fled only a few days before. The others were confined on the Ørnen and on cargo boats in harbor.[17] The court consisted essentially of the members of the commission mentioned above, with High Court Assessor Louis Rothe as chairman. Irminger did not participate, but the draconian spirit of the trials breathed his love of discipline and strong measures as the only effective method to deal with the perpetrators of the uprising and participants in its destructive aftermath. Within a week, eight persons had been executed on charges ranging from felonious wounding and arson to riotous assembly.

In resorting to the Court Martial, Irminger and the commission drew upon an instrument with the best antecedents. In the previous century a parallel had been drawn with frequency and facility between the slave society of the Danish West Indies and one in which Martial Law or the Articles of War were in force. The population disparity between slaves and whites fostered a desire for absolute obedience and a state-of-siege mentality which manifested themselves in actual or proposed provisions of the Slave Codes and the manner of their administration. Summary justice of the drumhead variety followed in the wake of the 1759 conspiracy and there were resonances of approval from eighteenth century commentators such as Hans West and a governor general in the 1780s, Major General Schimmelmann.[18]

Above all, however, the elaboration and justification of the military parallel was the work of State Counsellor Lindemann, who produced in 1783 one of the better known draft slave codes.[19] With Danish War Articles 600 and 601 to guide him, Lindemann proposed that punishment should be terrifying and as summarily swift as a military court. Experience had shown, he said, that slave cases were not only costly but time consuming, and as a result the significance of the punishment was lost by the time it came to be administered. To obviate protracted hearings, Lindemann called for the use of military process, specifically the "Stand Ret" or Court Martial.

Riotous assembly on the part of slaves aimed at rebellion, had thus been deemed mutiny as far back as 1783. Little did Lindemann realize that his prescriptions would come to apply where the "mutiny" had "succeeded." Those were the paradoxical foundations on which free society was established in St. Croix. The victors were made to suffer the fate of the vanquished. This was the heavy price required of those who dared to turn the wheel but not full circle. That price was inherent in a strategy of revolution which eschewed violence and had objectives of too limited a character to disturb the balance of power relations. Free society's parturition in such inauspicious circumstances boded ill for its healthy growth. The cataclysmic eruption of the "Great Fire Burn" in St. Croix 30 years later can only be fully understood in the light of the unresolved tensions of 1848.[20]

At another level of significance, the Court Martial through its depositions,[21] provides the only source from which the revolted slaves of 1848
speak. For comparable trials conducted during the slave period the
reliability of the evidence, invariably given under duress, must always be
treated with a certain caution. But in the instant case the fact that those on
trial were ex-slaves, of however recent vintage, is an important distinction
lending weight to a presumption of greater reliability. Moreover, in its
totality, the evidence from ex-slave as well as other deponents, has a degree
of internal consistency which puts its plausibility beyond reasonable doubt.
The trial transcript is thus an important source of information. Inter alia, it
sheds light on the modalities of planning and mobilization; the leadership
role of individuals; the objectives of the planned revolt; collective expectations and attitudes; the particular role of women, now, no less than before,
more than silent bystanders in Afro-Caribbean resistance to oppression.[22]
It demonstrates the rage and passion with which the ex-slaves settled old
scores and, inadvertently, provides from the inventory of destruction a
view of the life-style of plantation whites and the internal appointments of
their houses.

The officers of the Court, for their part, were motivated by a range of
concerns narrower than those which might preoccupy subsequent historians. Apart from the dispensation of exemplary punishments, the
purpose of the Court Martial from their perspective was twofold: to enquire
into the origins of the emancipation movement and to determine the extent
of, participation in, and culpability for the disturbances between Tuesday
and Thursday, 4-6 July. Naturally, they led evidence to establish
foreknowledge, preparation, motive, timing and leadership; and, attempting to anticipate the thrust of the eventual metropolitan enquiry to probe
the connection, if any, between the governor general and those who
planned it.[23] Reading through the transcript, the distinct impression
prevails that the members of the Court merely went through the motions
in the interrogations relating to the post-emancipation disorders. One
senses them springing to life, alert and more attentive in the heat and
tedium of those long tropical summer days, when there was evidence
bearing on the emancipation movement, even though involvement in it
could not be deemed an offense after 3 July.

The Trial Evidence: Prolegomenon to Revolt

As was the case with so many previous slave uprisings in the Caribbean,
that in St. Croix derived some of its inspiration from rumor, garbled
intelligence and misplaced belief in the imminence of emancipation. A
great many of the ex-slaves examined confessed to having heard months
before that emancipation was impending. Such talk of emancipation, it
appears, gathered momentum after the provisional government of the
Second Republic had decreed general emancipation in the French islands
in April 1848. This was the tenor of the depositions respectively of Cuby

from Envy and Jack from Prosperity.[24] Johannes from Bog of Allen said that at least since June he had heard slaves out in the country say "it was their understanding that the King had already for some time past granted freedom to people here, but that this emancipation had not been publicized because the planters opposed it."[25] This view, that emancipation had already been granted, recurs in the examination of Frederik from Mt. Pleasant. Chamberlain Ferral's recollection was that when the emancipation proclamation was read on that estate on Tuesday 4 July, Frederik had remarked that if the proclamation had not been printed that day, "it had stuck in their throats for a very long time." Frederik denied the remark, but conceded having said that the proclamation was printed neither on Monday nor on Tuesday. This was a view shared by many slaves in Frederiksted on Monday. According to Frederik they claimed that they had been free for a long time but that the proclamation had been withheld.[26] If Moses from Butler's Bay is to be believed, at least one white person felt similarly, namely a Mrs. Beech whom he alleged to have heard berating her husband on Tuesday for being a party to withholding the proclamation.[27] None of these deponents, however, admitted to knowing anything about the planned march on Frederiksted before Sunday night.

There were others who had heard from a week before that Monday was the target day on which they would withdraw their labor and demand their freedom.[28] A slave, George Francis, was alleged to have told the Rosehill workforce on Saturday to turn out with sugar bills and sticks on Monday, but nothing was said about going to Frederiksted. Similar advice had also been given at Rosehill by Richard from neighboring Mt. Stewart and Patrick from Punch, another northside estate. Adam from Rosehill admitted, before being sentenced for setting fire to a canefield, that a week in advance Gotlieb Bordeaux, also known as General Buddoe, an artisan from La Grange, had told him that they should all "look to their time" and to inform others.[29] But Buddoe himself denied knowing anything about the planned events of Monday before Sunday afternoon. Indeed Buddoe claimed that his source of information was Charles of Butler's Bay. But the latter denied that allegation, insisting he knew nothing prior to Sunday evening.[30] Martin King, whom the Court said was commonly believed to be a leader of the emancipation movement, also denied any foreknowledge of a plan before Sunday evening. If he is to be believed, he did not fancy its chances of success even as late as Monday morning.[31]

As it transpired none of the persons examined admitted knowledge of a plan earlier than the preceding Friday. On that day, Moses of Butler's Bay said he heard slaves on the way to and from the West End saying there would be no work on Monday. Even so, he knew nothing of a concrete development before he heard the conch shells, known in local creole as tuttue,[32] being blown on Sunday night. There was even one witness who claimed to have heard nothing before Monday at lunch time.[33] It is also interesting to notice that not even those freedmen from Martin King's Bog of Allen or Buddoe's La Grange seemed to have, or admitted to having, any previous information as to what was to transpire. One witness from Bog of Allen told the Court that when the bells started to ring and the shells were blown on Sunday evening, neither he nor anyone else on the estate, so far as he knew, had any idea of what was afoot. Joseph from Prosperity, who lived on neighboring La Grange, said he knew nothing before Sunday evening.[34]

Counsels of discretion aside, this suggests that the plan had been conceived and passed on to a few chosen persons whose task was to organize their individual estates, and to sound the signals on Sunday night. Limiting knowledge of the plot to a few trusted lieutenants explains the success with which disciplined secrecy was maintained to such a remarkable degree in the planning of the uprising. Further, it enabled its implementation to enjoy all of the optimal advantages of surprise. There were no betrayers in a slave population of nearly 20,000. The compact size, favorable terrain and intense development of St. Croix, where no estate was ever much more than a kilometer from its neighbor, facilitated ease of communication between the leadership without the need to rely on intermediaries of questionable trustworthiness.

Leadership

Whilst the evidence led at the trial is not especially forthcoming with details of prior planning, it positively identifies leadership roles and suggests the identity of ultimate leadership. Specific individuals either unilaterally assumed, or, more plausibly were delegated specific tasks for the occupation of Frederiksted. On Monday evening when the crowd there was in front of the office of the Chief of Police, a building which was subsequently destroyed, Augustus from Concordia was self-confessedly "in command to get the crowd in line." His leadership role was emphasized by the sword he had in hand, and by way of further emphasis, the blood of a duck, killed by the same sword, smeared on the front of his shirt.[35] On Monday evening, still in his bloodstained shirt, he was at Høgensborg estate shouting that he had orders "to decapitate anyone who didn't declare himself free since all were now free." One man for whom the notion of general emancipation was too much to accept, told Augustus he was not free since he had not been manumitted by his master. Augustus promised to decapitate him too. His role as leader is also confirmed by his participation on Monday in a symbolic act of climactic catharsis: the rooting up of the beating post, the Justitsstøtte, in Frederiksted's market square and its dumping into the sea.[36]

The first shred of evidence relating to ultimate leadership came from Will of Annally estate. Questioned about his activities in Frederiksted on Monday, he admitted being there and having in his possession a demi-john of rum stolen from the premises of the grocer Moore. But the demi-john was "taken from him or rather smashed." He did not say by whom.[37] However, Frederik von Scholten in his eyewitness account published subsequently, pointed out that the crowd in front of the fort and adjacent to

Moore's grocery, was being commanded by Buddoe. He forcibly prevented the looting of goods and spirits and "smashed the containers with his sword."[38] Will either suffered a genuine bout of amnesia, or like so many other witnesses would give nothing away regarding preparation or leadership. One other shred of evidence on leadership came from Edward of Rosehill estate. He told the Court that when George Francis enjoined the workforce on Saturday to turn out on Monday, he made it sound as though Moses of Butler's Bay was the "chief organizer."[39]

Despite intensive interrogation, neither Buddoe nor Martin King admitted to organizing the uprising. Such an admission in any case, with emancipation accomplished, would have been a work of supererogation. However, there was a direct attribution of leadership to Buddoe and Martin King from the four men condemned to death on 11 July: Decatur from Bethlehem for rioting and theft; Friday from Castle for a similar offense; Augustus from Concordia for felonious wounding and Adam from Rosehill for arson. In his original examination on 9 July, Friday deposed that Martin King was to be blamed for everything. On the day he was sentenced, Friday first admitted to using the general's name, Buddoe, not the governor general, to stir up the crowd, but later came back at his own request to inform the Court that "Bordeaux was at the head of everything."[40]

Decatur, who admitted breaking open Moore's iron safe from which a lot of money had been removed, also asked to make a statement to the Court after his death sentence had been pronounced. As far as the Court could make out, he explained that it was Buddoe who made the slaves on northside estates rise for freedom and come into town.[41] Adam too, asking the Court to make a statement after his condemnation, reaffirmed his earlier testimony that Buddoe had instructed slaves that they should take their freedom by fair means or foul. Augustus for his part reinforced these statements by adding that on Sunday Buddoe had told slaves that come Monday they should "tell the white man they would no longer be slaves."[42]

What is of further interest about this group of testimonies, is that with the exception of Friday, they all stated in the most emphatic terms that Buddoe gave no orders for looting or destruction. Friday claimed that Buddoe gave instructions on Tuesday to destroy the Carlton estate.[43] But there was an abundance of countervailing evidence from other ex-slaves, from white plantation help and government officials that Buddoe strove to maintain order on Monday and on the days following.[44] Friday's statement about Tuesday, even if true, does not alter the weight of the evidence from the other three in relation to Monday. One would have good grounds to believe that Decatur, Augustus and Adam, their minds wonderfully concentrated by the prospect of impending execution, were unlikely to have given collectively misleading testimony. There was nothing to be gained by exonerating Buddoe from instigating violence on Monday. If that part of their testimony stands the test of reliability, so should the other portion relating to Buddoe's ultimate leadership.

Strategy and Objectives

If the proceedings help to clarify the locus of leadership, they also shed some light on organizational strategies. None of the testimony is explicit on this point, but there were enough statements at the trial to indicate that the slaves intended to use the strike weapon as a lever to force the issue of their freedom. Industrial action as a form of ultimate protest was no novelty among Caribbean slave populations. It had been advocated, though unsuccessfully, by Nanny Grigg in Barbados in 1816, Deacon Quamina in Demerara in 1823 and more recently by Sam Sharpe in the Jamaica Christmas uprising of 1831.[45] The predetermined signal for Monday's strike was the blowing of tuttues and the ringing of plantation bells. Both signaled emergencies such as fire, or work-start and stoppage. But when the signals were given, Frederik von Scholten, whose house lay high enough for a good view of the countryside, could see no fire.[46] At that time of night, work could not, obviously, be beginning. This was indeed an emergency signal, but for a final work-stoppage.

The most concrete testimony of the connection between withdrawal of labor and its use as a bargaining counter for freedom, came from the condemned Augustus. Buddoe, according to him, had told slaves on Sunday that they were not to go to work on Monday *and* to tell the whites they would no longer be slaves. The connection was also made explicit by Edward of Rosehill. Where connection was not explicit, others nevertheless showed awareness of an impending strike. Moses from Butler's Bay, as mentioned earlier, had heard about this on Friday, and Robert Lucas, the carpenter at Betty's Hope, said that when he went to town on Saturday to buy turpentine, "several persons" had informed him that there was to be no work on Monday.[47]

The seriousness with which the work-stoppage was enforced is well illustrated by Martin King's experience on Monday. By his own account, the workforce at Bog of Allen had gone to work on Monday, a circumstance which raises questions about his leadership influence up to this point. On instructions from the overseer, Williams Næst, King took the plantation wain to drive to the West End. Having descended the escarpment to the Centreline as far as St. George's, where his wife Severine lived,[48] Martin King stopped to get a cart whip. He was met by an angry crowd, led by Decatur among others, who unhitched the mule and drove the cart into the cane piece, telling Martin he was not to drive to the West End. It may well be that Martin wanted to use the opportunity of his instructions to be present in Frederiksted for reasons connected with the events of later that day. But so far as Decatur and the others were concerned, the mere appearance of collaboration on Monday morning, which driving the cart symbolized, was a betrayal. Phillipus of Mt. Pleasant was sufficiently enraged to hit Martin over the arm with a cutlass and force him to join in the march to the West End.[49]

The difficulty of implementing a work-stoppage aimed at emancipation is illustrated not only by what Martin King reported as happening at Bog of Allen on Monday morning. Habits of a lifetime were not easily dispelled. Even at Mt. Pleasant to which the enraged Phillipus was attached, some work had begun on Monday morning. The driver there, Jørgen, told the Court however that he was threatened with decapitation for his lapse by John Simmons, one of the men eventually condemned, and two others.[50] Whatever the difficulty of its implementation, the strategy obviously struck a responsive chord. Forced labor was the essential badge of a servitude they were being asked to endure patiently for another eleven years until general emancipation in 1859. But in the meantime freedom had already come since 1847 for their newborn children; since 1838 for the British West Indies, including Tortola scarcely a cannon shot from St. John; and more recently since April for the French West Indies.

The deeply felt resentment is expressed in the language and behavior of Decatur, Phillipus and John Simmons. Comparable freedom, to work not at all, or on their own terms, was the substance of that independence they hoped to achieve that Monday and to maintain thereafter. This was the spirit which informed the behavior of Edward of Rosehill on the morrow of emancipation. In an encounter with his erstwhile owner van Brackle from neighboring Spring Garden on the northside, Edward announced: "Mr. van Brackle here is your hoe and your cutlass. I will no longer work for you and if I work I will buy them myself." Where upon, he threw the tools at van Brackle's feet.[51] The principle of voluntary work on freely negotiated terms was, before Monday and after, the only acceptable and dignified basis on which to establish the status of a free peasantry to which they aspired. It would take another generation to achieve. But for the present the objective was a powerful motivating force, and the strategy had a certain attractiveness, particularly when it promised the circumscription at worst and the avoidance at best of bloodshed.

Violence Manqué: 2-3 July 1848

St. Croix's birthday of freedom was not, however, entirely bloodless nor characterized by an absolute absence of violence. Only incredible levels of discipline, universally applied, could have restrained physical assault on persons and property on that day. Yet the evidence indicates that those levels of discipline were in large measure realized. Two incidents involving attacks on white persons were proof of the rule by the proverbial exception. The first is contained not in the trial transcript but in Frederik von Scholten's account. It involved Major Gyllich, commander of the Fire Corps. Riding into town on Monday, he was chopped at by someone as he passed through a crowd, managed to parry the blow and after shouting, "I am a friend not an enemy," and throwing his sword to the ground, was allowed to pass.[52] Gyllich subsequently proved his bona fides by riding around on Tuesday, accompanied by Buddoe, and attempting to restore calm without force on several mid-island estates.[53] The conviction that he was sympathetic may have saved Gyllich when discipline briefly disintegrated on Monday morning.

The second incident involved Augustus from Concordia and John Lang, owner of Paradise, on the road between that estate and Good Hope on Monday afternoon. Each gave a slightly different version of how the incident began, but they agreed on how it developed, namely, that Lang who was unarmed took a stick from a man and fetched Augustus two smart blows. In retaliation Augustus slashed with his sword at Lang inflicting a serious wound to the arm and a lesser wound to the hand. By Augustus' own admission, and that of William McFarlane who saw him shortly after the event, he was pretty far gone in drink.[54] There were thus important extenuating circumstances attending Augustus' loss of self control.

The other exceptional incidents of violence immediately preceding emancipation involved the destruction and plunder of three houses in Frederiksted in the course of Monday: the Police Station and residence of Frederiksted's Chief of Police Andresen; Police Adjutant Didrichsen's house and Moore the grocer's shop cum house. The evidence led at the trial is not especially helpful as to motive in the case of the first two. It is possible to infer, however, that Peter von Scholten's absence in St. Thomas was widely known among the slave community and that in his absence the revolting slaves directed their protest at those whom they perceived as representing authority. This would help in accounting for the assault on Major Gyllich. Such an interpretation also lessens, if not discredits, the conspiratorial theory which suggests links between the governor general and the plot to revolt.[55] Frederik von Scholten records it as his understanding that the slaves had come into town on Monday morning to "negotiate" with Frederiksted's Chief of Police for their freedom.[56] The destruction of the Police Station and the Police Adjutant's house must therefore be construed as a consequence of the slaves' frustration at not being able to extract freedom from this quarter, as an expression of the seriousness of their intent and a symbolic gesture of defiant uncompromising militancy.[57] No examinee confessed to being in either police building and the trial record thus contains nothing to convey the electric atmosphere of that highly charged morning. The closest it comes is in the deposition of Malvina of Big Fountain who, standing outside Didrichsen's house, was unable to get in "as it was filled with people."[58]

A similar crushing throng was present at grocer Moore's. The sack of his building on Strandgade (Waterfront Street), in close proximity to and in full view of the fort, was inspired by the slaves' belief that Moore had advised the Fort Commander to "shoot them down like dogs." Moore's cook, Edward, who was present heard the crowd shouting the accusation. There was such an enormous crowd that he was unable to identify anyone as particularly responsible or who led the charge. They burst through the street door which gave access via a staircase to the rooms above which were locked. The doors to them were broken down by crow bars and axes obtained from the cellar.[59]

It was impossible for the Court to apportion individual responsibility for the destruction and sack of any of the three houses, although Decatur's condemnation was specifically related to the rifling of Moore's iron safe.[60] But on the day in question, the destruction of Moore's house gave the slaves an important psychological boost by emphasizing their considerable advantage in tactical and strategic terms. It would have been easy to follow Moore's alleged advice, strafe Strandgade and mow down the insurgents either from the water battery or the gun emplacements at the fort's entrance. But this was not an option the whites would exercise. The slaves, in effective control of the town, had accomplished this without bloodshed. A burst of grape shot would have indiscriminately killed those in the streets while the looters in Moore's shop needed only to go through the back entrance into the street behind. This was the reason that Irminger demolished all the buildings obstructing the cannons' line of sight towards the north and east on Wednesday. Had the Fort Commander opened fire on Monday, the likelihood was that the slaves would not only have killed whites in retaliation but also put fire to Frederiksted.[61]

The vulnerability of the towns to fire was notorious. The slaves knew this and it led them to deploy a strategy in which the threat of Frederiksted's total destruction was their ultimate bargaining counter. When Frederik von Scholten ventured out of the fort with the Roman Catholic priest and some of the more courageous whites to calm the slaves in the streets, one of the leaders told him: "We can't fight the soldiers since we have no weapons, but we can burn and destroy if we don't get our freedom – and we will do it." This was no idle boast; it was clearly part of a well laid plan: "close to the fort, behind a corner house and out of the cannons' reach was a large group of slave women with trash and dry cane leaves which, at the first volley from the fort, they would have lit and thrown through windows and doors. Since most householders had by then left their houses there would thus have been nothing to prevent such a fire spreading rapidly through the town."[62]

Attitudes to the Future: Race and Class

The proceedings of the Court Martial also help to answer the question whether the slaves had developed ideas relating to a future less immediate than the acquisition of freedom. Accompanying the desire for freedom was an aspiration to property in land. There even seemed to be a sense in which that aspiration was born of a conception of land as patria to which they and not the whites had an exclusive claim. A similar view prevailed among the equally creolized slave population of Barbados in 1816.[63] Nelson, interestingly enough a bosal, who had worked at Mt. Pleasant, declared on Tuesday that if anyone attempted to arrest him he would cut them down "since the island belonged to them." A virtually identical expression came from Andreas of Envy, who told John Randall Findlay, a freedman before emancipation, that "the land would now belong to them, namely the blacks."[64] Land as property was the indispensable basis of their independence as peasants. Beyond that, however, there were visions that transcended mere peasant subsistence and looked to the continuance of the mono-crop export economy run by freedmen. John Simmons told Richard Doute the bookkeeper at Big Fountain that there was enough land to plant cane and that they could build their own ships to bring provisions in. James Heyliger, one of those executed, made an important distinction between the destruction of plantation buildings and the destruction of cane in the field, since the latter "would be the country's loss."[65] This desire to own land and to maintain on it the production of cane as an export staple, probably explains why Adam's arson attempt at Rosehill was the only one such.

The corollary of those ambitions was that the whites would have to leave the estates or remain on them on a footing of equality at best or subordination at worst. The collective attitude of the slaves, where it did not celebrate their own race, condemned whites qua whites, denigrated them as figures of authority and judged them unflatteringly in terms of class. By the 1840s a great many of the overseers and bookkeepers on estates in the Danish West Indies were Irish or Anglo-Irish, usually humble crofters in search of their fortune. More often than not, they were less familiar with plantation routine and management techniques than the slaves they were supposed to supervise. Their penchant for liaisons with slave women had a long history and this, with a predilection for drink and general hell-raising, made them a disruptive force on most plantations.[66] Such white estate help did not invite the respect of the slave gangs. Karen Fog Olwig has graphically illustrated this in the case of St. John, instancing an 1847 case in which a slave Johannes abused the overseer Glasco in the most derogatory and scatological terms: "You are a come-and-go, my master is head-judge. You, pskaw! You a shitting ass (sic) Blanco."[67] The heat and excitement of the emancipation uprising and its aftermath was an opportunity for the expression of race consciousness; for the villification of whites generally and plantation help in particular; for expressions of challenge to and rejection of their authority.

Racial consciousness inspired the threat on Tuesday by Martin William of Hamsbay to Emilia of the same estate that "he would take off her head if she was on the white people's side."[68] Charles of Butler's Bay on the previous Sunday evening had threatened anyone taking the whites' side with similar punishment. John Simmons, for his part, had a utilitarian concept of racial solidarity: he told the bookkeeper at Montpelier that it was a good thing to proceed against whites as they had, or it would be the worse for blacks.[69] From racial consciousness and solidarity it was an easy transition to racial animosity. According to Eveline, a domestic in Frederiksted, Christian, a former house servant to the regimental surgeon, took very unkindly to a remark from a white school teacher to behave himself on Tuesday. Christian's reply was that he would not permit any white man to speak to him like that, and he would consider it a small matter to sever his head from his body. Christian denied the remark, but conceded that he was unable to recall everything he had done, drunk as he was at the time.[70]

Indeed, even before the disturbance began on Sunday evening, racial animosity was in evidence. At Montpelier, Henry, incensed at the overseer's rebuke for impertinence on Sunday afternoon, declared that "his spirit was such that white people should be very careful with him.[71]

The decision to revolt was an effect of the renting of that veil of respect which clothed whites in slave society. But it was also cause. Several incidents involving manhandling, attempted manhandling and abusive remarks on and after Monday 3 July, demonstrate the extent to which the blacks of St. Croix were no longer contained by the established devices of social control. At Envy on Tuesday, several blacks from Negro Bay armed with machetes charged the bookkeeper, who was only rescued by the timely intervention of some of Envy's workforce. Charles Conally, overseer at Hope, had a similar experience on Tuesday when he lost a silver watch and a watch chain.[72] Comparable examples can be cited from Camporico, Carlton, Sprathall, Mt. Pleasant and Spring Garden estates in the period between Monday and Tuesday.[73]

What this as product suggests, is a process of "demystification" of whites, and it was exemplified preeminently in the behavior of Isaac of Prosperity, from Tuesday a close associate of Buddoe. On Thursday at Hamsbay, Buddoe arrived with Isaac and others to remind the owner, John Elliot, that slavery was abolished and along with it, the whip from the field. Elliot was told that if he did not agree to working conditions which the ex-slaves found acceptable, the plantation would be taken from him and any other likeminded white. To emphasize the point, Isaac struck the floor with his sword, declaring, "No nonsense Elliot." On Wednesday at Prosperity, again accompanying Buddoe, Isaac let his old bookkeeper know that he had "an account to settle with him" and that it was a good thing he had not met him. The rapid evaporation of deference which this signifies is well illustrated by the third incident involving Isaac. With Buddoe at the estate The William on Tuesday, they both wanted to know who had given orders for work to resume there. Thomas Murphy, the overseer, assured them that he had given the orders and that the workforce would be paid. Whereupon, Isaac grabbed Murphy by the scruff of the neck, told him to behave himself and be quiet or he would rough him up.[74]

Hated and disrespected, overseers and bookkeepers were also objects of distrust. An important aspect of the immediate management of freedom, therefore, appears to have been to get white plantation help to leave the estates and to disarm them. The first objective was consonant with an aspiration to property; the second with a desire to minimize their vulnerability and to protect themselves, if the need arose, with weapons other than sugar-bills and cudgels. The depositions at the trial do not suggest by their number that the desire to drive the whites from the estates was a widespread phenomenon. But its existence on widely separated estates points not so much to spontaneous indignation on the part of individuals, as to a pre-arranged plan. At Adventure on Wednesday, Peter from Kingshill, a central estate along the Centreline, exclaimed: "Why is this white man still on the plantation?"[75] At Sprathall on the northside, "a large part of the workforce" demanded on Tuesday that the overseer, book-keeper and owner should never set foot on the property again.[76] At Montpelier, another northside estate on Wednesday, Henry, cutlass in hand, told Hewson the overseer in threatening tones that he wanted whites "cleared away from the estates" and that it was best if they hid themselves.[77] Moorehead, the lessee of Camporico in the south was similarly threatened on Wednesday.[78] The geographical spread of these estates – Kingshill from which Peter derived, in the island's center; Sprathall in the northwest; Montpelier in the north; Adventure in the south and Camporico in the southwest – is sufficiently wide to discount pure spontaneity as an explanation.

The plan to disarm whites on Tuesday and subsequently, was said to have originated with Buddoe. Samuel and John from Camporico, both of whom engaged in a spectacular if unsuccessful horseback chase to seize the bookkeeper's gun, claimed to have received such orders.[79] Buddoe disclaimed responsibility, although he admitted to riding around to several estates on the northside on Tuesday, requiring the usual distribution of food allowances and enjoining the workforce to look after animals.[80] There is no doubt, however, that he used the occasion to get overseers and others to hand over their firearms. Such was the case, for example, at The William on Tuesday, when in the company of Isaac from Prosperity, he demanded and got overseer Murphy's gun.[81]

Buddoe's denial has the ring of veracity. If he intended to collect the guns himself, he might well have given no order. The fact is that the discipline which had prevailed up to Monday, had begun to wear thin by Tuesday and individuals like Samuel and John simply took matters into their own hands. The breakdown was facilitated, in the absence of regular rations in those confused days, by hunger and by drink. The continuance of the allowance arose as a specific issue on Tuesday at several estates.[82] A cow was slaughtered at Montpelier, sheep there and at Concordia; pigs at Sprathall and at Mt. Stewart where ducks were also slaughtered.[83] Numerous witnesses confessed to being heavily under the influence of drink after emancipation was declared.[84] There is some evidence too that some of the rum consumed so extensively might have been ritually drunk to symbolize binding engagement. Cuby testified that on Wednesday morning he was offered a mixture of rum and gunpowder by some of the workforce from Negro Bay.[85] In such circumstances the revolting freedmen were less susceptible to the restraints of leadership. It is interesting to observe that after Buddoe had collected arms at The William, the workforce from Sprathall arrived some hours later to make the same demand on overseer Murphy.[86] At Carlton on the southside on the same day, there was also an attempt to seize the bookkeeper's gun.[87] At Montpelier on Tuesday a freedman, Frederik, had already come into possession of a firearm. Asked to give it up by the Roman Catholic priest accompanying the party to read the emancipation proclamation, Frederik is alleged to have claimed that they had taken all the overseers' guns in the country. Making allowances for hyperbole, the remark reinforces the view that the disarming of white plantation help by Buddoe alone or by increasingly indisciplined subordinates, was a cardinal feature of the planning post-Monday. More importantly, Frederik is again alleged to have said that the guns would only be returned when they could have greater trust in overseers, or when they behaved better.[88]

Here, distilled, was the very essence of the matter. Overseers and bookkeepers, standard bearers of the "mission civilisatrice" had been weighed in the scales and found severely wanting. They generated hatred, animosity, contempt, distrust and bitterness. Augustus at Concordia smashed up the sick house precisely "because he had been locked up in it many times." Others too like Catherine from Carlton or Isaac from Prosperity, mentioned earlier, equally victims of arbitrary detention and the whip, had searing recollections as the basis for settling old scores.[89] Persistent bitterness inspired Joseph from Anguilla to shout threateningly at Envy estate: "Where is that fellow Lorentz? It's him I want."[90] It would equally explain the insistence independently by Neddy from Grove Place and Present from Jealousy that Lucas' house at Mt. Pleasant should be destroyed, as it was a prison.[91] The fact that Thomas Clarke was overseer at both Jealousy and Mt. Pleasant which were contiguous was, in all probability, not an unrelated circumstance.[92]

Property Destruction: 4-5 July 1848

Against this background, it is no matter of surprise that the extensive looting and destruction which characterized Tuesday and Wednesday, 4-5 July, were directed almost exclusively at the houses and personal effects of white plantation personnel.[93] The trial transcript is replete with instances, not of mere destruction of such property on several estates, but symbolic acts of violation and humiliation fuelled by extremities of rage. The many occasions on which ex-slaves bedecked themselves with three-cornered hats, swords, military jackets and belts of whites who had fled in terror, were not so much gasconade as calculated demonstrations of the fact that the mighty have fallen.[94] The looting of food supplies: salted fish and beef, flour, cornmeal, sugar, rum, beer and wine from the provision cellars of several estates answered similarly not merely to the needs of hunger.[95] Such looting represented as well the symbolic rejection of that authority in which control of plantation rations was vested. Chopping off the locks of provision cellars or breaking down the doors to them was arguably a form of cathartic release no less satisfying than the uprooting of the Justitsstøtte on Monday.

The almost endless catalog of destroyed houses and personal property belonging to overseers and bookkeepers invites a similar interpretation. Mannings Bay, Envy, Lower Love, Castle, Concordia, Adventure, Golden

Grove, Jealousy, Sprathall, Hamsbay, Diamond, Ruby, St. George, Wheel of Fortune, Mt. Pleasant, Mt. Stewart, Good Hope among others, suffered in varying degrees. Apart from houses partially or wholly destroyed, the inventory of items most frequently mentioned as destroyed or stolen included clothing, bed linen, beds, bedsteads, wardrobes, cupboards, washstands, dining tables, porcelain, glassware, silverware, goldplate, objets d'art.[96]

Another common leitmotiv of all the accounts of destruction is the extraordinary violence. The explanation inheres only in part in the freedom with which rum was available from plantation stores. It inheres even less in Adam's religious assignment of cause to "the devil in his head" for setting fire to the fields at Rosehill. One has to look elsewhere for the springs of that volcanic passion which led individuals systematically to demolish a dining room at Concordia; reduce a divan, clock and clock-stand there to splinters; or impale Lucas' globe at Mt. Pleasant on an improvised bayonet.[97] The effects in question could simply have been taken away as booty. Rum and "the devil" merely quickened an impluse to destroy whose roots lay deep in the long suffered indignities and abuses of servitude.

Women

One interesting aspect of the rampage between Tuesday and Thursday was the important contribution of women. It was pointed out earlier that they had assembled the trash with which to set fire to Frederiksted, should that prove necessary. At Negro Bay on Wednesday they again compromised another trash detail when Big Robert threatened to burn the owner's house down.[98] Frederik von Scholten in this connection made the very interesting observation that:

> Among the black population, women play a role of great importance. They do the same work that the men do and their physical build and size render them formidable adversaries in the rough and tumble of a fight. Throughout the disturbances they were more aggressive, vengeful and altogether more violent in their passion than the men.[99]

The trial transcript bears this out substantially. Rosaline, described by her former owner Jane Jackson as giddy-headed and childish, underwent no instant metamorphosis when she made the soberingly pointed remark: "Is there a war on? That can't be for in that case they would have burnt the town just as in St. Dominigue."[100]

Women displayed a rage no less primordial than the men's. Slavery had after all made no distinction as to gender, and their sex laid them open to the additional disadvantage of harassment, not to mention the perversion of normal maternal relations. It is no wonder therefore that Mathilda from Frederiksted was an active instigator outside Moore's grocery; that a woman was co-leader with Big Robert in the sack of Negro Bay; that Sey, a woman from neighboring Manning's Bay was also identified as a moving spirit at Negro Bay.[101] Another Manning's Bay woman, Sara, chopped off the legs of Knight's piano at Negro Bay, and was only prevented from chopping up the rest when Martha, who belonged to the estate workforce, lay on top of it to protect it.[102] At Lucas' Mt. Pleasant, Penny from adjoining River took the first blow at the door with a cudgel, and when it did not give, proceeded to attack another door. The overseer Thomas Clarke commented that Penny distinguished herself with "threats of murder and cutting people's head off." At the same estate, Present from Jealousy who had described Lucas' house as a prison to be destroyed, chopped up a cupboard.[103] It was Rachel wielding an axe who reduced the divan at Concordia to splinters.[104] Violent in destruction, the women were remarkably resourceful in plunder. Unable to remove a whole mattress at Sprathall, Else removed the ticking and took the cover.[105] Women were the main removers of plunder at Concordia and a large number of other estates.[106]

Differential Responses

It should be emphasized that not all the ex-slaves succumbed to such transports of fury. Notwithstanding the fact that Buddoe's writ had ceased to run island-wide since the morning of Tuesday 4 July, and such influence as Martin King possessed had begun to wane, their stand against destruction and plunder, of which the Court took note, apparently had some effect.[107] For some freedmen the psychological bond with familiar things and places, masters' as well as their own, or a Weltanschauung defined by the plantation as world, was not readily rupturable by the transition to freedom. Many drivers were as resistant to plundering as others were active in instigating it. Some like Jacob Washington, former crookgang driver at Spring Garden and son of the bookkeeper Jasper Washington, perhaps had special reason to resist the rioters.[108] The same would be true of William Borch, former driver of the same estate, who had a reputation for excessive use of the whip in the field, and from whom a number of ex-slaves sought "satisfaction."[109] But there are no special circumstances to explain why John Peru, former driver at Upper Love, or Isaac at Paradise both attempted to prevent destruction and pillaging on Wednesday.[110] Drivers apart, there were many former slaves, male as well as female, who protected property on many estates in the immediate aftermath of emancipation. They hid household effects in the quarters, in canefields and in trash, or bravely barred entrance to provision cellars at Enfield Green, Camporico, Bog of Allen, Rosehill, Carlton, Mt. Pleasant, Negro Bay, Adventure, Envy and elsewhere.[111]

Among those free before emancipation, the events on and immediately after Monday 3 July, also produced no unilinear response. In Frederiksted there was a strong suspicion of this group as originators of the plot and potential allies of the insurgents. Nevertheless, it was their restraining influence, according to Frederik von Scholten, which accounted for the destruction in town being limited to three houses.[112] That restraining influence was also in evidence in the rural milieu, where by a growing convention in violation of a 1747 law, some freedmen were allowed to live before emancipation. Thus Edward Hein who lived on Negro Bay did his best to prevent destruction at neighboring Golden Grove, Richard Gumbs disarmed the leader of the invading band at Hamsbay, and Samuel William openly deplored the use of violence at Bog of Allen.[113] The latter's wife and five children were slaves up to emancipation. But his response is in radical contrast with that of Mathaeus, another freedman, whose wife Sally had been a slave. Mathaeus was the driver of one of the carts in which effects were removed from Negro Bay. At Negro Bay too, it was another ancien libre, Christopher from Manning's Bay, who allegedly helped in the removal of a hogshead of rum.[114] No common pattern of behavior emerges. But this is hardly a matter for surprise in view of the disparities of economic achievement, aspiration and status among pre-emancipation freedmen.[115]

Epilogue

The evidence from the trial establishes that the slaves of St. Croix pursued their purpose of achieving emancipation with unwavering single-mindedness. However, on the very morrow of emancipation there were signs of atomization. In the trial itself ex-slaves freely accused other ex-slaves for their part in the events after Monday. Those who had achieved freedom earlier were themselves no more united programmatically. Such internal divisions weighted the scales in favor of constituted authority which remained intact despite the upheavals. The executions, and Buddoe's deportation at his own request,[116] robbed the ex-slaves of their best potential leadership. Vanquished victors, the ex-slaves of St. Croix were poorly placed to confront the challenges of the first generation of freedom.

Notes

CHAPTER 1

1. Useful introductory material on the Danish West Indies published in English can be found in Isaac Dookhan, *A History of the Virgin Islands of the United States* (1974); Jens Larsen, *Virgin Islands Story* (1950); Florence Lewisohn, *St. Croix under Seven Flags* (1970); Waldemar Westergaard, *The Danish West Indies under Company Rule (1671-1754)* (1917); and Gordon K. Lewis, *The Virgin Islands: A Caribbean Lilliput* (1972).
2. See John Macpherson, *Caribbean Lands: A Geography of the West Indies* 3rd ed., (1973), pp. 3, 123; P. P. Sveistrup, "Bidrag til de tidligere dansk-vestindiske Øers Økonomiske Historie, med særligt Henblik paa Sukkerproduction og Sukkerhandel," *Nationaløkonomisk Tidsskrift for Samfundsspørgsmaal Økonomi og Handel* 80 (1942):65, 87.
3. J. L. Carstens, "En Almindelig Beskrivelse om Alle de Danske Americanske eller West-Jndiske Ey-Lande," *Danske Magazin* 8 (3) (1970): 260-61.
4. Svend E. Green-Pedersen, "The Economic Considerations behind the Danish Abolition of the Negro Slave Trade," in *The Uncommon Market: Essays in the Economic History of the Atlantic Slave Trade*, edited Henry A. Gemery and Jan S. Hogendorn (1979), pp. 407-408; idem., "Slave Demography in the Danish West Indies and the Abolition of the Danish Slave Trade," in *The Abolition of the Atlantic Slave Trade: Origins and Effects in Europe, Africa, and the Americas*, edited David Eltis and James Walvin (1981), pp. 234, 245.

5. Franklin W. Knight, *The Caribbean: The Genesis of a Fragmented Nationalism* (1978), p. x, and idem., *Slave Society in Cuba During the Nineteenth Century* (1970), p. 194.
6. Christian Degn, *Die Schimmelmanns in atlantischen Dreickshandel: Gewinn and Gewissen* (1974), p. 122, quoted in Jørgen Bach Christensen, *Kolonisamfundet på St. Croix i sidste halvdel af det 18 århundrede, med særligt henblik på aristokratiet blandt plantageejerne*, Cand. mag. dissertation, Aarhus University, 1978, p. 7.
7. R. I. Moore ed., *The Hamlyn Historical Atlas* (1981), p. 94, Plate 4. See also Gunnar Olsen, *Den unge enevælde 1660-1721*, vol. 8, *Danmarks Historie* edited John Danstrup and Hal Koch (1964), p. 106.
8. Kay Larsen, *Guvernører, Residenter, Kommandanter og Chefer. Samt enkelte andre fremtrædende Personer i de idligere danske Tropekolonier* (1940), p. 30.
9. Ibid.; Waldemar Westergaard, *The Danish West Indies Under Company Rule* (1917), p. xxi.
10. Carstens, "En Almindelig Beskrivelse," pp. 260-61.
11. J. O. Bro-Jørgensen, *Dansk Vestindien indtil 1755*, vol. 1 *Vore Gamle Tropekolonier* edited Johannes Brøndsted (1966) vol. 1, pp. 176-78.
12. Kay Larsen, *Guvenører, Residenter*, p. 30.
13. Christensen, *Kolonisamfundet på St. Croix*, p. 7.
14. Bro-Jørgensen, *Dansk Vestindien*, p. 172.
15. Enid M. Baa, "The Brandenburgers at St. Thomas," a paper presented at the 10th Annual Conference of the Association of Caribbean Historians, St. Thomas, 1978, pp. 19 et seq.

16. Bro-Jørgensen, *Dansk Vestindien,* pp. 149-50.
17. Ibid., pp. 160-63.
18. Jean-Baptiste Labat, *Nouveaux Voyages Faits aux Isles de l'Amérique* (1972 edition, first published 1742) vol. 4, p. 147.
19. Bro-Jørgensen, *Dansk Vestindien,* p. 171. Cf. Westergaard, *Danish West Indies,* p. 30.
20. See, for example, Bancroft Papers (University of California, Berkeley), Z A 1: 3, Orders of Governors 1672-1727.
21. Bro-Jørgensen, *Dansk Vestindien,* p. 171.
22. Labat, *Nouveaux Voyages,* vol. 4, p. 148.
23. Bro-Jørgensen, *Dansk Vestindien,* pp. 171-72.
24. Cornelius Ch. Goslinga, "The Fall of the Dutch West India Company," a paper presented at the 11th Annual Conference of the Association of Caribbean Historians, Curacao, 1979, p. 2.
25. Westergaard, *Danish West Indies,* p. 151.
26. Bro-Jørgensen, *Dansk Vestindien,* pp. 220, 222.
27. Westergaard, *Danish West Indies,* p. 247.
28. Christensen, *Kolonisamfundet på St. Croix,* p. 9.
29. Bro-Jørgensen, *Dansk Vestindien,* pp. 242, 248, 250-54; Christensen, *Kolonisamfundet på St. Croix,* pp. 9, 72.
30. Bro-Jørgensen, *Dansk Vestindien,* pp. 248-49, 255; Lewisohn, *St. Croix,* pp. 90-91.
31. Sveistrup, "Bidrag," pp. 76-77.
32. Bro-Jørgensen, *Dansk Vestindien,* p. 255; Lewisohn, *St. Croix,* pp. 191-92.
33. Lewisohn, *St. Croix,* p. 92.
34. Christensen, *Kolonisamfundet på St. Croix,* pp. 102-103.
35. Lewisohn, *St. Croix,* pp. 121 et seq.
36. Christensen, *Kolonisamfundet på St. Croix,* pp. 86-87, 98, 100-104.
37. See, for example, R/A, NEER, Louis Rothe to Generaltoldkammer og Commerce Collegiet, 10 September 1847. Ibid., Louis Rothe, "Beskrivelse over Antigua."
38. Richard B. Sheridan, "The Rise of a Colonial Gentry: A Case Study of

Antigua," *Economic History Review* 13 (1960-61): 355-57.
39. RDAG, 1770-1802, passim.
40. Hans West, "Beretning om det danske Eilande St. Croix i Vestindien," *Iris* 3 (1791):71, 82.
41. RDAG, July-December 1770, passim.
42. Ibid., 29 June 1776.
43. SCG, 23 July 1814.
44. Vagn Dybdahl, *De nye Klasser 1870-1913,* vol. 12, *Danmarks Historie* edited John Danstrup and Hal Koch (1965), p. 422. See Richardson Wright, *Revels in Jamaica 1682-1838* (1937) for a history of the theater in that island.
45. Jens Vibæk, *Dansk Vestindien 1755-1848,* vol. 2 *Vore Gamle Tropekolonier* edited Johannes Brøndsted (1966) vol. 2, pp. 44-45.
46. Dybdahl, *Danmarks Historie,* p. 422.
47. Hans West, *Bidrag til Beskrivelse over Ste. Croix* (1793), p. 325.
48. R/A, Gtk, Vestindisk Kopibog, 1838, no. 91, Dansk Vestindisk Regering to Danske Cancelli, 24 February 1838, f. 57.
49. See chapter 11.
50. *Fædrelandet,* 19 March 1841.
51. Herman Lawaetz, *Peter von Scholten, Vestindiske Tidsbilleder fra den sidste General-guvernørs Dage* (1940), pp. 159-60; R/A, NEER, passim; Grethe Bentzen, *Debatten om det Dansk-vestindiske Negerslaveri 1833-1848 med særligt henblik på de igennem tidsskriftpressen og stænderdebatter udtrykte holdninger,* Cand. mag. dissertation, Aarhus University, 1976, pp. 65 et seq.
52. Hans Jensen, *De danske Stænderforsamlingers Historie 1830-1848* (1931-34) vol. 2, p. 609.
53. Victor Prosch, "Om Slaveemancipationen paa de dansk-vestindiske Øer," *Dansk Tidsskrift* 2 (1848):419.
54. "Irske og Skotske Colonier paa St. Croix," *Fædrelandet,* 17 October 1840.
55. Ibid., 1 April 1841.
56. Bro-Jørgensen, *Dansk Vestindien,* pp. 261-75, 278; Lewisohn, *St. Croix,* p. 102.
57. Bro-Jørgensen, *Dansk Vestindien,* p. 280; Christensen, *Kolonisamfundet på St. Croix,* p. 10.
58. Sveistrup, "Bidrag," p. 63.

59. Christensen, *Kolonisamfundet på St. Croix*, p. 11
60. J. P. van de Voort, *De Westindische Plantages van 1720 tot 1795: Financien en Handel*(1973), pp. 220, 274-76; Christensen, *Kolonisamfundet på St. Croix*, p. 11.
61. Christensen, *Kolonisamfundet på St. Croix*, p. 11.
62. *Fædrelandet*, 9 September 1840.
63. Ibid., 17 October 1840.
64. R/A, FAN, 2 Bd, 1787, de Malleville's Betænkning, 19 October 1787.
65. Christensen, *Kolonisamfundet på St. Croix*, p. 11.
66. *Fædrelandet*, 2 April 1841.
67. Ibid., 17 October 1840.
68. Frances Armytage, *The Free Port System in the British West Indies: A Study in Commercial Policy 1766-1822* (1953), especially pp. 2, 42, 72, 84.
69. R/A, Gtk, Diverse sager, Forskellige Oplysninger, VII, "Angaaende Øen St. Thomas som Frihavn og Toldvæsnet," f. 183.
70. Ibid., f. 184.
71. R/A, Forskellige Oplysninger, VII, ff. 184-85.
72. Armytage, *Free Port System*, p. 129, quoting Young to Bathurst, 28 September 1822.
73. Vibæk, *Dansk Vestindien 1755-1848*, p. 322.
74. P. P. Sveistrup, "Det Kongelige Danske octroyerede Vestindiske Handelsselskab," *Historisk Tidsskrift*, 10 (6) (1943): 386, 389, 391, 406-407.
75. Ibid., pp. 412-13; W. A. Cole and Phyllis Deane, "The Growth of National Incomes," in vol. 6 *Cambridge Economic History of Europe* edited H. J. Habakkuk and M. Postan (1966), p. 28.
76. Svend Green-Pedersen, "Danmarks ophævelse af negerslavehandelen, Omkring tilblivelsen af forordningen af 16, Marts 1792," *Arkiv. Tidsskrift for Arkivforskning* 3 (1) (1969): 19-37; Green-Pedersen, "The Scope and Structure of the Danish Negro Slave Trade," *Scandinavian Economic History Review* 19 (1971): 170.
77. Green-Pedersen, "Scope and Structure," p. 171.
78. Ibid., pp. 154-55, 181. See also Svend Green-Pedersen, "The History of the Danish Negro Slave Trade, 1733-1807. An Interim Survey Relating in Particular to its Volume, Structure, Profitability and Abolition," *Revue Française d'histoire d'outre mer* 62 (226-27) (1975): 196-220.
79. Green-Pedersen, "Scope and Structure," p. 149.
80. Green-Pedersen, "Danmarks Ophævelse," p. 22.
81. Green-Pedersen, "Scope and Structure," pp. 176-77.
82. Cf. *Fædrelandet*, 17 October 1840.
83. R/A, Forskellige Oplysninger, I, Christian VII to Clausen, 4 November 1782.
84. R/A, Forskellige Oplysninger, V, 1803, f. 119.
85. R/A, Diverse sager, Visdomsbog I, n/p.
86. R/A, Forskellige Oplysninger, V, 1803, f. 120, "... et ordnet Politi til at vedligeholde indvortes Roelighed, end en virklig Kongsmagt."
87. R/A, Den engelske Okkupation 1801, 1807, Udkast til Forsvars Plan, 17 September 1798.
88. Ibid., Generaltoldkammer Forestilling, 14 June 1801.
89. Ibid., Generaltoldkammer Forestilling, Casimir von Scholten, Report, 11 January 1801.
90. The data are derived from R/A, Forskellige Oplysninger, VII, ff. 81-82, 95.
91. R/A, Den engelske Okkupation 1801, 1807, Casimir von Scholten, Report, 11 January 1801.
92. R/A, Forskellige Oplysninger, VII, Generaltoldkammer Betænkning og Forestilling, 18 April 1837.
93. R/A, Forskellige Oplysninger, V, 1803, f. 120.
94. Roger N. Buckley, *Slaves in Red Coats: The British West India Regiments 1795-1815* (1979), pp. 100-103, 181 n. 72.
95. R/A, Den engelske Okkupation 1801, 1807, Casimir von Scholten, Report, 11 January 1801.
96. Ibid., Defense Commission Report, 1798.

97. R/A, AVS/FC, Generaltoldkammer to Walterstorff, 15 December 1791.
98. Ibid., Generaltoldkammer to Dansks Vestindisk Regering, 23 November 1793; cf. R/A, Forskellige Oplysninger, VII, 1837, f. 86.
99. R/A, Den engelske Okkupation 1801, 1807, Casimir von Scholten to Military Investigation Commission, 20 May 1802.
100. Ibid., Casimir von Scholten to Citoyen Michel, 27 October 1800 and enclosure.
101. Ibid., Casimir von Scholten to Military Investigation Commission, 20 May 1802.
102. Ibid., West to Lindemann, 30 March 1801.
103. Ibid., Casimir von Scholten, Report, 11 January 1801.
104. Ibid., St. Thomas Burgher Council Proceedings, 13 March 1801.
105. Ibid., Military Investigation Commission Proceedings, 3 May 1802; St. Thomas Burgher Council to Military Investigation Commission, 3 May 1802.
106. Ibid., Generaltoldkammer Forestilling, 14 June 1801.
107. Ibid., Capt. Roeder, 5th Line Battalion, to Generaltoldkammer, 8 November 1844.
108. Ibid., Enclosure, Copie af et den 15de December 1807 i undersøgelses Commission i Sagen mod Baron Friderich de Bretton Junior fremlagt preliminanter Forhør optaget af Hr. Regeringsraad Bentzon og Kammerraad Smidt: St. Croix, Christiansted den 15de December 1807.
109. R/A, Forskellige Oplysninger, V, 1803, Walterstorff Memorandum 27 March 1802.
110. R/A, Den engelske Okkupation 1801, 1807, Capt. Roeder, 5th Line Battalion, to Generaltoldkammer, 8 November 1844, Enclosure, Copie.
111. Ibid., Proceedings of the Danish West Indian Government, 17 December 1807.
112. Ibid., Capt. Roeder, 5th Line Battalion, to Generaltoldkammer, 8 November 1844, Enclosure, Copie.
113. As late as 1826 an observer in Copenhagen noted: "The soldiers who are now sent to the colonies can in no way be trusted and in case of a possible uprising might be very well more dangerous than the free coloureds themselves." N. A. T. Hall, *Forslag til Ordning af Vestindisk Forfatningsforhold angaaende Negerne med mere* (1979), p. 11. On de Bretton, see R/A, Den engelske Okkupation 1801, 1807, Capt. Roeder, 5th Line Battalion, to Generaltoldkammer, 8 November 1844, Enclosure, Copie; and chapter 9.
114. Michael Craton, *Testing the Chains: Resistance to Slavery in the British West Indies* (1982).
115. R/A, Den engelske Okkupation 1801, 1807, Udskrift af Frederiksteds Jurisdiction Politi Protocol, 30 March 1801; ibid., Lindemann Memorandum, 29 March 1801.
116. R/A, AVS/FC, Walterstorff to Generaltoldkammer, 20 July 1802.
117. Ibid.
118. R/A, DVK, Adrian Bentzon, "Om Negerne paa de danske Øer," St. Croix, 24 July 1802.
119. George M. Fredrickson, *White Supremacy. A Comparative Study in American and South African History* (1981), pp. 91-92.
120. For these developments see Palle Lauring, *A History of the Kingdom of Denmark* 4th ed. (1973), pp. 189-206.
121. Hall, *Forslag*, pp. 10-11.
122. R/A, Forskellige Oplysninger, VII, 1837, Generaltoldkammer Betænkning, April 1837, f. 85.
123. R/A, AVS/FC, Generaltoldkammer to Dansks Vestindisk Regering, 23 November 1793; cf. R/A, Forskellige Oplysninger, VII, 1837, f. 86.
124. R/A, CANS, Commission Forestilling, 8 April 1843; Bentzen, *Debatten*, p. 89.
125. Bentzen, *Debatten*, p. 89.
126. Lauring, *History*, pp. 213-214.
127. R/A, CANS, von Scholten, Afskrift af det at Generalgouverneuren forfattede Udkast til en Emancipationsplan for Slaverne paa de danske vestindiske Øer, 13 October 1834, f. 12. See also R/A, Møstingske Papirer (b), Forestilling

om Forandring i Slavernes Kaar, 18 November 1834.

128. The same was also true to a lesser degree for St. Thomas. On the incidence of grand marronage from both islands after 1840, see R/A, NEER, Louis Rothe, "Om Populationsforholdene i de Danske Vestindiske Colonier og Fornemlig paa St. Croix, " 1847.

129. "Om Vestindien: betragtet fra Planteurernes Standpunckt, IV," *Fædrelandet*, 5 January 1842. A Lt. Hedemann was formally charged with the murder of one of the escaping slaves. The investigation ended in his court-martial and two months' imprisonment. According to Hans Birch Dahlerup, who conducted the investigation in the West Indies, the sentence was "mere for at tilfredsstille England og det dengang saa indflydelsesrige Abolisationspartie i dette Land, end for den Brøde, man kunde tillægge ham:" more to satisfy England and its then so powerful abolitionist lobby than for the offense itself. H. B. Dahlerup, *Mit Livs Beginveheder* (1909), vol. 2, pp. 189, 270.

130. N/A, RG 55, Box 9, Søbøtker to Christian VIII, nos. 3 and 4, 11 and 28 November 1845. See also R/A, NEER, Louis Rothe, "Om Populationsforholdene."

131. R/A, NEER, Garliebs Betænkning, 20 February 1847.

132. Ibid., Rothe to Generaltoldkammer, 10 September 1847.

133. See chapter 12; and Bentzen, Debatten, passim.

134. R/A, NEER, Peter von Scholten, Forslag to Generaltoldkammer, 9 November 1846.

135. Ibid., Direction for den Statsgeld og den Synkende Fond to Generaltoldkammer, 29 July 1847: "Der ligger allerede i sig selv noget compromitterende i, at Regjeringen offentlig udtaler sin Beslutning, men tillige giver tilkjende, at den mulige vil savne Kraft til atsætte den igiennem. En saadan Tilkiendgivelse vilde desuden let kunde fremkalde urolige Ideer hos den ufrie Befolkning, som ellers ikke vare opstaaede, ja næsten vare en Opfordring til ved slige Demonstrationer at tiltvinge sig hvad Regjeringen selv syntes kun at vente disse for at tilstaae især da Udsigten til Emancipation først efter 15 Aars Forløb egentiig ikke ere synderlig tillokkende for de Ufrie."

136. Ibid., Royal Reskript of 28 July 1847. The Chancellery's final submission on 24 July 1847 was heavily influenced by one of its members and a leading jurist of his time, A. S. Ørsted. His own views, on the compensation question, inter alia, were expressed in a submission to the Generaltoldkammer, to be found in the same bundle, on 25 May 1847.

137. See chapter 12.

138. Prosch, "Om Slaveemancipationen," p. 419.

CHAPTER 2

1. R/A, UBAN, no. 24, Forslag til en Negerlov for de Kongelig Danske Vestindiske Eylande med tilfiede Anmærkninger.

2. U. N. Fugl, "Om Negerslaveriet i Vestindien," *Juridisk Tidsskrift* 24 B, 1 H (1834):10.

3. A. S. Orsted, "Beholdes Herredømmet over en vestindisk Slave, naar han betræder dansk-europæisk Grund," *Arkiv for Retsvidenskaben og dens Anvendelse* 1 (1824):462-63. On the medieval Danish law codes, see Ruth Mazo Karras, *Slavery and Society in Medieval Scandinavia* (1988), pp. 173-76.

4. Ørsted, "Beholdes Herredømmet," pp. 462-63. Cf. David Brion Davis, *The Problem of Slavery in Western Culture* (1966); idem., *The Problem of Slavery in the Age of Revolution, 1770-1823* (1975); Orlando Patterson, "Slavery: The Underside of Freedom," *Slavery & Abolition* 5 (1984):87-104.

5. "Dom i sagen General-Majorinde Henriette de Schimmelmann contra Mulat Hans Jonathan Afsagt den 31 te Mai 1802," *Arkiv for Retsvidenskaben og dens Anvendelse* 1 (1824):36.

6. Ibid., p. 37. Cf. W. W. Buckland, *The Roman Law of Slavery* (1908).

7. "Dom i sagen General-Majorinde Henriette de Schimmelmann," p. 38. On the Somerset case, see James Walvin, *Black and White: The Negro and English Society 1555-1945* (1973), pp. 117-29.

8. Ørsted, "Beholdes Herredømmet," p. 460.

9. Ibid., p. 461.

10. Ibid., p. 464.

11. Ibid., pp. 465, 469.

12. R/A, FAN, 1785, Schimmelmanns Anmærkninger, 20 April 1784, f. 38.

13. Hans West, *Bidrag til Beskrivelse over Ste. Croix* (1793), p. 134.

14. R/A, UBAN, No. 24, Part 1, Remarks on Article 1.

15. Ibid., Remarks on Article 2.

16. Ibid., Remarks on Article 3.

17. Ibid., Article 4.

18. Ibid., Article 5.

19. Ibid., Remarks on Article 5. "Men i denne Anledning maa her anmærkes, at Slaverne i Nord America langt fra ei holdes saa strænge som paa Eilandene hvor en haardere Disciplin bliver en Fornødenhed i Betragtning af de Blankes ringe Antal imod Slave Mængden."

20. Ibid., See Remarks on Article 8, 16, 18, 20, 21, 32, 36.

21. R/A, FAN, 1785, Schimmelmanns Anmærkninger, 20 April 1784, f. 38. His view was that recovered maroons got off too lightly with 50 strokes, when deserting soldiers were obliged to run the gauntlet six times between 300 men.

22. Ørsted, "Beholdes Herredømmet," p. 468.

23. Fugl, "Om Negerslaveriet," p. 15.

24. Ibid., p. 8.

25. R/A, UBAN, no. 24, Part 3 (1783), Remarks on Articles 1 and 22.

26. R/A, Om Negerhandelens Afskaffelse 1788-1847, Letter to the Commission considering a Slave Law for the Danish West Indies.

27. Ibid.

28. West, *Bidrag*, p. 24.

29. Hans West, "Beretning om det danske Eilande St. Croix i Vestindien," *Iris* 3 (1791):53-55.

30. R/A, DVK, Mühlenfels Bemærkning, 8 July 1805. "Det er uimodsigelig Sandhed, at kun Negere, fødte i samme Clima eller i eet endnu varmere end det Vestindiske, ere de eneste skikkede til Sukker Cultivationen, uden at deres Sundhed derved lider."

31. R/A, NEER.

32. R/A, UBAN, no. 4, 5 September 1733.

33. R/A, UBAN, 2 (1755), para. 38. "I øvrigt skall Slaverne ansees som en Part og Deel af Eyendom og altsaa skal det være deres Husbonder tilladt efter Lovens Tilhold at disponere over dem, ligesom deres øvrige Midler og Eyendom."

34. K. L. Rahbek, "Om Negerhandelens Ophævelse i Hensyn til de danske vestindiske Øer," *Minerva* 1 (1805):199-201.

35. Ibid., pp. 201-203. For sugar prices, see Jens Vibæk, *Dansk Vestindien 1755-1848*, vol. 2 *Vore Gamle Tropekolonier*, edited Johannes Brøndsted (1966), p. 73, Table 6 "Auktionspriser på brunt råsukker, skilling pr pd."

36. Rahbek, "Om Negerhandelens," p. 204.

37. Ibid., p. 239. "...synderlig er dog den Formodning, at fordi Planterne ville drage mere Omhu for deres Negere, at fordi de vilde forbedre kisses Kaar, at fordi de ville give dem Leilighed til at føle Fordelen af huuslig Vel, saa skulde dette anledige Urolighed. Just det Modsatte kunne vi antage, og man feiler neppe, naar man troer, at om endog andensteds fra skulde skee Forsøg derpaa, da vil dette blive af saameget mindre Virkning, som Herrerne ere mere opmærksomme, og Negrene fatte mere Kiærlighed og Tillid til dem."

38. Svend E. Green-Pedersen, "Negro Slavery and Christianity: On Erik Pontoppidan's Preface to L. F. Roemer, *Tilforladelig Efterretning om Kysten Guinea," Transactions of the Historical Society of Ghana* 15 (1974):85-102.

39. C. G. A. Oldendorp, *History of the Mission of the Evangelical Brethren on*

the Caribbean Islands of St. Thomas, St. Croix, and St. John (1974), pp. 243-49. English edition and translation by Arnold R. Highfield and Vladimir Barac. German edition first published 1777.

40. R/A, UBAN, no. 4, 5 September 1739, Preamble.

41. R/A, UBAN, 26, Placater, Anordninger og Publicationer betræffende Negervæsnet, 1726-1780, no. 15, Governor Hansen's Placat, 16 August 1748: "hvortil de dog af Gud Naturen ere forbunden."

42. Richard Haagensen, *Beskrivelse over Eylandet St. Croix i America i Vestindien* (1758), p. 51. "...jeg...sige min Mening om dem i Almindelighed ... at de ere alle onde af Natur, og at lidet godt boer hos dem, ja om jeg tør sige det, troer jeg virkeligen at deres sorte Hud vidner om deres Onskab og at de ere destinerede Trældom saaledes de ingen Frihed bør have."

43. Ibid., p. 58.

44. There is little doubt from the internal evidence that "RH" is none other than Haaagensen. See *Thotts Samling*, no. 816, f. 19, 20 March 1755, Kongelig Bibliotek, Copenhagen. I am very grateful to Bibliotekar Stuhlmann for bringing the above to my attention. "...ja disse slavers Ondskab er saa stor at om de ikke blive holt Ligeelse Viis som Hunden i Lænker, turde eller kunde ingen Leve med dem."

45. West, *Bidrag*, p. 128-29.

46. West, "Beretning," p. 39.

47. West, *Bidrag*, p. 129.

48. West, "Beretning," pp. 53-55.

49. West, *Bidrag*, p. 25. "Negernes Uddunstning er saa væsentligen forskiellig fra Europærnes og ofte saa vederstygelig stinkede, at den længe kan efterlade Ulugt i et Værelse, og man undertiden er nød til at træde ud af Negers Spor, for at undgaae denne qvalende Ubehagelighed skiønt man tillige maae gør dem den Ret at de som oftest holde sig renlige, og dagligen vaske Legemet."

50. West, "Beretning," pp. 63-64. See also West, *Bidrag*, p. 5 and Haagensen, *Beskrivelse*, pp. 14-15.

51. West, "Beretning," pp. 48-49.

52. Oldendorp, *History*, pp. 243-45.

53. R/A, FAN, 1785, Skrivelse fra Hr. Oberst Malleville til Hr. Gouvernør Clausen, 20 February 1784, f. 21. Compare also Malleville's Anmærkning, ibid., 7 April 1784, f. 33.

54. Ibid., ff. 22-23.

55. R/A, UBAN, Miscellaneous Papers, Avokat Balling's written submission 5 November 1784, in Udskrift af Christiansteds Dom Protocol Anno 1784 den 13 d. December. "...det alleene er Frygt for Straf og ikke Religion eller Opdragelse, der kan afholde den vilde og uoplyste Neger fra, at begaae Forbrydelser."

56. Green-Pedersen, "Negro Slavery and Christianity."

57. West, *Bidrag*, pp. 88-89. "Jeg maae ... igientage, at ikke alene de fleste Negere, som have vant sig til Landet, ingenlunde ønske at gaae tilbage til Kysten ... Efter at have levet nogle Aar i Vestindien, ansee de endog Kysten og nyskomne enfoldige Kystnegere med saadan Ringeagt, at det er blevet et Skieldsord mellem Landets Negere at kalde hverandre Busal eller Guinea-Neger."

58. Bruno Bettleheim, "Individual and Mass Behaviour in Extreme Situations," *Journal of Abnormal Psychology* 38 (1943):439, 448-50 quoted in Stanley Elkins, *Slavery: A Problem in American Institutional and Intellectual Life* (1963), pp. 108, 112-13.

59. West, *Bidrag*, p. 90.

60. R/A, DVK, Leinrich's Remarks, 11 March 1801.

61. Ibid., Mühlenfels Bemærkning, 8 July 1805.

62. R/A, Akter vedkommende Slaveemancipationen 1834-1847, 111, Etatsraad Berg to Governor General von Scholten, 12 May 1841. The Biblical reference is to Genesis 3:19, "Det kommer af at Negeren ei vil Arbeide, at han ei vil følge Guds lov: 'I dit Ansigts Sved skal de [sic] æde dit Brød.' Ikke beskylde

man den europæiske Slavehandel for denne gyselige Tilstand, der har existeret inden Europærne kjendte Africa."

63. Davis, *Problem of Slavery in Western Culture*, pp. 78-108, 187-89.

64. Herman Lawaetz, *Brødremenighedens Mission i Dansk-Vestindien 1769-1848* (1902).

65. Oldendorp, *History*, pp. 425-27, 446-47, 457-61.

66. Davis, *Problem of Slavery in Western Culture*, pp. 237-47. See chapter 6, this volume. Cf. Mary Turner, *Slaves and Missionaries: The Disintegration of Jamaican Slave Society 1787-1834* (1982), pp. 65-83.

67. Davis, *Problem of Slavery in Western Culture*, p. 227.

68. Cf. Michael Craton, *Testing the Chains: Resistance to Slavery in the British West Indies* (1982); Turner, *Slaves and Missionaries*.

69. See Table 6.2.

70. Davis, *Problem of Slavery in Western Culture*, p. 233.

71. R/A, UBAN, 2, Reglement for Slaverne, 3 February 1755: "Slaverne skulde altsaa, naar de blive Christne, derved ikke blive frie, men ikke destomindre derfor være og blive Slaver, og ikke mindre være skyldige til at beviise deres Husbonder og Eyere, efter den Tid som forhen, Lydighed, Flittighed, Troeskab og andre Pligter."

72. Davis, *Problem of Slavery in Western Culture*, pp. 124-28.

73. Green-Pedersen, "Negro Slavery and Christianity."

74. Oldendorp, *History*, p. 247.

75. Davis, *Problem of Slavery in the Age of Revolution*; Ronald Kent Richardson, *Moral Imperium: Afro-Caribbeans and the Transformation of British Rule, 1776-1838* (1987); Christine Bolt, *Victorian Attitudes to Race* (1971).

76. R/A, Om Negerhandelens Afskaffelse 1788-1847, Byfoged, St. Jan to Slave Trade Commissioners, undated.

77. R/A, DVK, Vanderbourg, Rapport sur l'etat present des Negres et sur les Moyens de l'ameliorer, 22 October 1798.

78. Ibid.

79. Ibid.

80. R/A, DVK, Adrian Bentzon, "Om Negerne paa de danske Øer i Vestindien," 24 July 1802.

81. R/A, Akter vedkommende Slaveemancipationen 1834-1847, 111, Etatsraad Berg to Governor General von Scholten, 12 May 1841.

82. R/A, CANS, von Scholten to Christian VIII, 15 January 1841, Enclosure 6, undated, f. 6. The internal evidence suggests the authorship of B. Burt. See ibid., Enclosure 10.

83. R/A, CANS, Prokurator Sarauw, Udkast til en Skadeløs Emancipation, undated.

84. *Fædrelandet*, 15 January 1841.

85. *Kjøbenhavnsposten*, 14 August 1838.

86. Victor Prosch, "Om Slaveemancipation paa de dansk-vestindiske Øer," *Dansk Tidsskrift* 2 (1848):390-93. "...der vel ofte antager Præg af nysgjering Efteraben."

87. Ibid., pp. 394-95.

88. R/A, UBAN, no. 2, 3 February 1755, Preamble.

89. R/A, UBAN, no. 3 (1759), n/p.

90. R/A, UBAN, Roepstorff's Nota, no. 17, 7 February 1784, ff. 3-4. "Og paa grund af alt foranmeldte, troer jeg det gjørligt, at betragte de ufrie Negere, som Trælbønder, deres Afkom at tilhøre Proprietaire some deres Vornede, og deres Arbeide for Føde og Klæde som et billigt Hoverie."

91. *Kiøbenhavnske Lærde Efterretninger*, no. 42, July 1791, pp. 657-58.

92. Haagensen, *Beskrivelse.*, pp. 55-56.

93. *Kiøbenhavnske Lærde Efterretninger*, no. 42, July 1791, p. 658.

94. Ibid., pp. 659-61.

95. Ibid., pp. 662.

96. West, "Beretning," pp. 61-62.

97. *Kiøbenhavnske Lærd Efterretninger*, no. 42, July 1791, pp. 662-63. "... at stadfæste nemlig, den ædle Tanke, at disse forvorpne sorte Mennesker, denne Chams Afkom, bør forblive i Trældom til evig Tid."

98. R/A, CANS, Peter von Scholten, Afskrift af det af Generalgouverneuren forfattede Udkast til en Emancipation for Slaverne paa de danske vestindiske Øer, 13 October 1834, f. 12.

99. Ibid., f. 9.
100. James Smith, *The Winter of 1840 in St. Croix* (1840), pp. 22-24, 97-105; G. W. Alexander, "Om den moralske Forpligtelse til og det Hensigtmæssige af strax og fuldstændigt at ophæve Slaveriet i de danske-vestindiske Kolonier," *Dansk Ugeskrift* 2 (76) (1843): 374-96.
101. Victor Schoelcher, *Colonies étrangères et Haïti* (1843), vol. 2, pp. 4, 6.
102. H. B. Dahlerup, "Skizzer fra et kort Besøg paa vore vestindiske Øer i Sommeren 1841," *Nyt Archiv for Søvæsenet* 1 (1842):34-35.
103. Ibid, pp. 42-43.
104. *Fædrelandet,* 14 October 1840. "Parlamentsacten af 28 de August 1833 har afgjort Spørgsmaalet om Negerslavernes Emancipation for hele Vestindien, idet den ikke blot har givet det fulde Bevis for, at denne store Forholdsregel lader sig udføre, og det endog uden væsentlig Ulempe, men tillige har givet Slavebefolkningen paa de Øer, hvor deres Lænker endnu ikke ere brudte, en saa energisk Længsel efter Frihed, at den ikke laengere lader sig tilbageholde, end sige undertrykke. Det Spørgsmaal, der altsaa navnligen foreligge ogsaa den danske Regering med Hensyn til dens vestindiske Smaaøer er ikke *om,* men naar og *hvorledes* den vil forskaffe de derværene Slaver Friheden."
105. Hans Jensen, *De danske Stænderforsamlingers Historie 1830-1848* (1931-1934), vol. 2, pp. 609-10.

CHAPTER 3

1. Useful discussions of these definitions can be found, for example, in Richard Quinney, Critique of the Legal Order (1973), p. 16, and J. L. Gillin, *Criminology and Penology* (1943), p. 9.
2. Douglas Hay, "Property, Authority and the Criminal Law" in Douglas Hay et. al., *Albion's Fatal Tree* (1975), p. 25.
3. R/A, UBAN, no. 38, Peter Clausen's Placat, 5 October 1774, para. 3; N. A.

T. Hall, "Slaves and the Law in the Town of St. Croix 1802-1807," *Slavery and Abolition* 8 (1987):162. On the slave laws generally see Elsa V. Goveia, *The West Indian Slave Laws of the 18th Century* (1970).
4. R/A, UBAN, no. 4, September 1733, Gardelin's code, paras. 1-2
5. Ibid., paras. 3-5.
6. Ibid., para. 9.
7. Ibid., para. 11.
8. Ibid., para. 12.
9. Ibid., para. 6.
10. Ibid., para. 7.
11. Ibid., para. 18.
12. Ibid., para. 16.
13. Ibid., paras. 13-14.
14. Ibid., para. 17.
15. Preben Ramløv, *Brødrene og Slaverne* (1968), pp. 53-54; Waldemar Westergaard, *The Danish West Indies under Company Rule* (1917), p. 167.
16. R/A, UBAN, no. 1, Extract af de for de Kongelige Danske Vestindiske Eilande Udkomne Reglementer og Placater, Negerne Betræffende, Moth's Articler for Negerne, 11 December 1741, Articles 1-2, 6-7.
17. Ibid., Lindemark's Placat, 31 January 1746, para. 2.
18. Ibid., Lindemark's Placat, 23 December 1746, para. 1.
19. Richard Haagensen, *Beskrivelse over Eylandet St. Croix i America i Vestindien* (1758), p. 24.
20. R/A, UBAN, no. 1, Extract af de for de Kongelige Danske Vestindiske Eilande Udkomne Reglementer og Placater, Negerne Betræffende, Moth's Placat, 3 February 1742, para. 6.
21. R/A, UBAN, no. 2, Reglement for Slaverne, 3 February 1755, paras. 17, 19, 22.
22. Ibid., paras. 21-22.
23. Ibid., paras. 1, 6.
24. Ibid., para. 3.
25. Ibid., para. 5.
26. Ibid., para. 6.
27. Ibid., para. 39.
28. Ibid., paras. 7, 38.
29. Ibid., paras. 42-43.
30. Ibid., para. 23.
31. Ibid., paras. 10-11.
32. Ibid., paras. 15-16.
33. Ibid., paras. 15-16
34. Ibid., paras. 25-27.

35. Ibid., paras. 28-30.
36. Ibid., para. 32.
37. Jens Vibæk, *Dansk Vestindien 1755-1848*, vol. 2 *Vore Gamle Tropekolonier* edited Johannes Brøndsted (1966), p. 49.
38. Haagensen, *Beskrivelse*, p. 49.
39. R/A, Haandsriftsamlingen, Species facti over den paa Eilandet Ste. Croix intenderede Neger Rebellion, forfattet efter Ordre af Byfoget Engelbreth Hesselberg.
40. R/A, UBAN, no. 27, Placater, Anordninger og Publicationer betræffende Negervæsnet 1726-1780, no. 22, von Pröck's Placat, 23 December 1759, para 1.
41. Ibid., paras. 2, 6, 13, 14, 16.
42. Ibid., paras. 3-4, 7-9, 12.
43. R/A, UBAN, no. 27, Placater, Anordninger og Publicationer betræffende Negervæsnet 1726-1780, no. 29, Peter de Gunthelberg's Placat, 9 February 1765, para. 4.
44. Ibid., para. 9.
45. Ibid., para. 12.
46. R/A, UBAN, no. 27, Placater, Anordninger og Publicationer betræffende Negervæsnet 1726-1780, no. 38, Peter Clausen's Placat, 5 October 1774, para. 3.
47. Ibid., para. 5.
48. R/A, UBAN, no. 27, Placater, Anordninger og Publicationer betræffende Negervæsnet 1726-1780, no. 43, Borgerraadet Forestilling, St. Croix, 2 December 1778.
49. Ibid., para. 3.
50. Ibid., para. 4.
51. Ibid., para. 5.
52. R/A, UBAN, no. 8, Exemplar paa Negerne som er dømte efter Placater af 5 September 1733 og 16 Augusti 1748.
53. R/A, UBAN, Bilag 5a, 3 September 1785. See also ibid., Udskrift af Christianstæds Dom Protocol, 13 December 1784. For the case of Jochum and Sam, see chapter 2.
54. R/A, FAN, 1785, Bind 1, Skrivelse til den Vestindisk Regiering fra det Kongelig Vestindisk Rente og Generaltoldkammer, 23 December 1782, ff. 83-87.

55. R/A, AVS/FC, Dansk Vestindisk Regiering to VGRG, 30 September 1783.
56. R/A, UBAN, no. 24, Forslag til en Negerlov for de Kongelig Danske Vestindiske Eylande med tilføiede Anmærkninger, Pt. 3, Article 13.
57. Ibid., Part 1, Articles 1-6, 8, 11-15, 19, 67.
58. Ibid., Articles 32-40.
59. Ibid., Articles 77-93, 96.
60. Ibid., Articles 94-95, 98.
61. Ibid., Articles 100-103, and Remarks on Article 103.
62. Ibid., Part 3, Articles 2-4, 6, 41.
63. Ibid., Articles, 1, 36, 14-16.
64. Ibid., Part 4, Article 3.
65. Ibid., Article 2.
66. Ibid., Article 11.
67. Ibid., Part 3, Articles 21, 10-12.
68. Ibid., Article 46.
69. Ibid., Articles 6-7.
70. Ibid., Part 4 Tillæg, Article 6.
71. Ibid., Article 8.
72. R/A, FAN, 1785, Bind 1, ff. 295-349.
73. Ibid., Bind 2, ff. 93 et seq.
74. E. Kirstein, "Udtog af Forestilling en til Kongen angaaende Negerhandelens Afskaffelse," *Minerva* (1792):71-73, 78. See also C. A. Trier, "Det danske-vestindiske negerindførelsforbud af 1792," *Historisk Tidsskrift* 5 (1904-1905):437.
75. Trier, "Det danske-vestindiske negerindførelsforbud," p. 437.
76. R/A, DVK, Kirstein to Bentzon, 28 October 1805.
77. Ibid., Oxholm to Dansk Vestindisk Regiering, 21 December 1792. See also ibid., Adrian Bentzon, "Om Negerne paa de Danske Øer i Vestindien," 24 July 1802; ibid., St. Croix Burgher Council to Dansk Vestindisk Regiering, 5 September 1792; ibid., VGRG to St. Croix Burgher Council, 2 June 1804; and P. L. Oxholm, "Nogle Anmærkninger over en Afhandling om Negerhandelens Ophævelse udi Maanedskrift Minerva af Februarii 1805," *Minerva* 2 (1806):160.
78. R/A, VJ, 1796, nos. 458, 609.
79. R/A, DVK, Bentzon, "Om Negerne."
80. R/A, UBAN, no. 24, Forslag til en Negerlov for de Kongelig Danske Vestindiske Eylande med tilføiede

Anmærkninger, Part 1, Remarks on Article 93. See also R/A, DVK, Gen. Walterstorff, Forløbige Anmærkninger ved det Regierringen tilsendte Udkast fra Commissionen betræffende de Laan ... til fleere Negeres Afskaffelse, 21 September 1792; and Trier, "Det danske-vestindiske negerindførelsforbud," p. 460.

81. R/A, VJ, 1796, no. 609.

82. R/A, Vestindiske og Guineiske Kongelig Resolutioner 1771-1816, Resolution of February 1800.

CHAPTER 4

1. The estimate of 75,000 for net imports of slaves is that of Noel Deerr, in his The History of Sugar (1949-50) Vol. 2, p. 283. Philip D. Curtin, The Atlantic Slave Trade (1969), p. 86, reduced the estimate to 28,000, based on the assumption that the total slave population of the Danish West Indies was 20,000 at the end of the eighteenth century rather than the actual 33,000 (see Table 1.1) and that the economies of the islands were all mercantile rather than agricultural. Svend E. Green-Pedersen, "The Scope and Structure of the Danish Negro Slave Trade," Scandinavian Economic History Review 19 (1971): 178-79, shows that Christiansted retained 19,057 slaves in 27 years between 1766 and 1802, an annual average of 706; and Frederiksted retained 3,517 in sixteen years between 1767 and 1802, an annual average of 219. Assuming a similar rate for the whole period 1733-1802 produces an estimate of 64,000 for St. Croix alone. It seems probable that imports were higher rather than lower than average in the years before 1766, so this may be regarded as a lower limit estimate. Paul E. Lovejoy, "The Volume of the Atlantic Slave Trade: A Synthesis," Journal of African History 23 (1982): 483-84, produces an estimate of 73,900, based on data presented in Svend E. Green-Pedersen, "The History of the Danish Negro Slave Trade: An Interim Survey Relating in Particular to its Volume,

Structure, Profitability and Abolition," Revue française d'histoire d'outre mer 62 (1975):201.

2. Curtin, Atlantic Slave Trade, p. 216.

3. Thorkild Hansen, Slavernes Kyst (1967).

4. Green-Pederson, "Scope and Structure," pp. 149-77. Cf. J. O. Bro-Jørgensen, Dansk Vestindien indtil 1755, vol. 1, Vore Gamle Tropekolonier, edited Johannes Brøndsted (1966), pp. 269-71.

5. Sidney W. Mintz and Richard Price, An Anthropological Approach to the Afro-American Past: A Caribbean Perspective (1976), p. 8.

6. C. G. A. Oldendorp, History of the Mission of the Evangelical Brethren on the Caribbean Islands of St. Thomas, St. Croix and St. John (1987), pp. 159-70. On the ethnic identification of the "Amina" see Curtin, Atlantic Slave Trade, pp. 185-86.

7. Pauline Holman Pope, Cruzan Slavery: An Ethnohistorical Study of Differential Responses to Slavery in the Danish West Indies (Ph.D. dissertation, University of California at Davis, 1969), pp. 87-88, 131. See also Pierre J. Pannet, Report on the Execrable Conspiracy Carried Out by the Amina Negroes on the Danish Island of St. Jan in America 1733, edited by Aimery P. Caron and Arnold R. Highfield (1984); Oldendorp, History, p. 678, n. 7; Monica Schuler, "Akan Slave Rebellions in the British Caribbean," Savacou 1 (1970):8-31.

8. Schuler, "Akan Slave Rebellions," p. 23.

9. Ibid., p. 10.

10. Green-Pedersen, "Scope and Structure;" Schuler, "Akan Slave Rebellions," p. 10; Curtin, Atlantic Slave Trade, pp. 223-27.

11. Curtin, Atlantic Slave Trade, p. 221; Pope, Cruzan Slavery, pp. 101-102.

12. See RDAG, passim.

13. Green-Pedersen, "Scope and Structure," pp. 150-65, 177.

14. Melville J. Herskovits, The Myth of the Negro Past (1962), pp. 83-112; George P. Murdock, Africa: Its Peoples and Their Culture History (1959), pp. 257-84; Mintz and Price, Anthropological Approach, p. 1; Mervyn Alleyne, Roots of Jamaican

Culture (1988), p. 8. Cf. Oldendorp, *History*, pp. 159-70.

15. Jerome S. Handler and Frederick W. Lange, *Plantation Slavery in Barbados* (1978), p. 289, n. 1.

16. Richard Haagensen, *Beskrivelse over Eylandet St. Croix i America i Vestindien* (1758), pp. 65, 138; Oldendorp, *History*, p. 214.

17. P. L. Oxholm, *De Danske Vestindiske öers Tilstand* (1797), p. 42.

18. Ibid., pp. 42-43, 57.

19. Ibid., Statistisk Tabelle.

20. Ibid., Statistisk Tabelle.

21. Ibid., Statistisk Tabelle.

22. I. C. Schmidt, "Blandede Anmærkninger, samlede paa og over Eylandet St. Croix i America 1788," *Samleren* 2 (1788): 203-204.

23. Ibid., pp. 204-205, 215.

24. Hans West, *Bidrag til Beskrivelse over St. Croix* (1793), p. 71.

25. Schmidt, "Blandede Anmærkninger," p. 204.

26. Ibid., p. 217; Oxholm, *De danske vestindiske*, Statistisk Tabelle.

27. *Oeconomisk Journal* (April 1757): 287.

28. Handler and Lange, *Plantation Slavery*, p. 72.

29. Ibid., p. 203.

30. R/A, VLA, Frederiksfort Standret, 7 July - 12 August 1848.

31. Schmidt, "Blandede Anmærkninger;" Peter von Scholten, *Orders for the Regulation of Labor Conditions 7 May 1838* (1838).

32. Jens Vibæk, *Dansk Vestindien 1755-1848*, vol. 2, *Vore Gamle Tropekolonier*, edited Johannes Brøndsted (1966), p. 131. Cf. R/A, Rentekammeret, Vestindiske Kommissionsforretninger vedrørende salg af plantager og ulovlig handel paa St. Croix, 1759.

33. R/A, DVK, Oxholm's General Report St. Croix, 1792.

34. R/A, DVK, Oxholm's Plantation Returns St. Croix, West End Quarter, 1792.

35. E. Kirstein, "Udtog af Forestilling til Kongen angaaende Negerhandelens Afskaffelse," *Minerva* (1792):68.

36. R/A, DVK, Returns for Company Quarter, 1792.

37. R/A, DVK, Oxholm's Anmærkninger ved den Kongelige Commissions til Negerhandelens bedre Indretning paa de Vestindiske Eylande og Kysten Guinea, dens Promemoria af 7 April 1792 - elter Ordre, 1 August 1792.

38. Oldendorp, *History*, p. 222.

39. Oxholm, *De Danske Vestindiske*, Plan I.

40. R/A, DVK, Returns for Queen's Quarter, 31 December 1792.

41. Vibæk, *Dansk Vestindien*, p. 136.

42. Per Eilstrup and Niels Eric Boesgaard, *Fjernt fra Danmark* (1794), p. 97.

43. R/A, DVK, Returns for King's Quarter, 31 December 1792.

44. Oldendorp, *History*, p. 571. Cf. Gabriel Debien, *Les Esclaves aux Antilles Francaises* (1974), pp. 219-34; Handler and Lange, *Plantation Slavery*, pp. 46-54.

45. Haagensen, *Beskrivelse*, p. 58.

46. Oldendorp, *History*, p. 221. Cf. Edward Brathwaite, *The Development of Creole Society in Jamaica, 1770-1820* (1971), pp. 234-36.

47. West, *Bidrag*, p. 84.

48. Schmidt, "Blandede Anmærkninger," p. 215.

49. West, *Bidrag*, p. 71.

50. Oldendorp, *History*, pp. 221-22.

51. R/A, FAN, Bind 2, Part 2, p. 28.

52. Victor Schoelcher, *Colonies étrangères et Haïti* (1843), vol. 2, p. 24. Cf. Debien, *Les Esclaves*, pp. 219-34.

53. Schoelcher, *Colonies étrangères*, vol. 2, p. 21.

54. R/A, Walterstorff, Forestilling Anmærkninger, 21 July 1792.

55. Schoelcher, *Colonies étrangères*, pp. 20-21; H. B. Dahlerup, "Skizzer fra et kort Besøg paa vore vestindiske Øer i Sommeren 1841," *Nyt Archiv for Søvæsenet* 1 (1842): 32. Cf. G. W. Alexander, "Om den moralske Forpligtelse til og det hensigtmæssige af strax og fuldstændigt at ophæve Slaveriet i de dansk-vestindiske Kolonier,"*Dansk Ugeskrift* 2 (1843): 7; Thorkild Hansen, *Slavernes Øer* (1970), p. 323.

56. R/A, CANS, 3. Generalguvernør Scholtens Indberetning, 2 January 1839, Bilag 8, Circular 14 May 1838.

57. West, *Bidrag,* p. 81; Schmidt, "Blandede Anmærkninger," p. 243.
58. Schmidt, "Blandede Anmærkninger," p. 243.
59. West, *Bidrag,* p. 81.
60. Haagensen, *Beskrivelse,* pp. 55-56.
61. Oldendorp, *History,* p. 222.
62. West, *Bidrag,* pp. 330, 339-40.
63. R/A, DVK, Adrian Bentzon, "Om Negerne paa de danske Øer i Vestindien," St. Croix, 24 July 1802.
64. Haagensen, *Beskrivelse,* pp. 54-58.
65. Oldendorp, *History,* p. 223.
66. Brathwaite, *Development of Creole Society,* p. 219.
67. Schmidt, "Blandede Anmærkninger," pp. 246-50.
68. Ibid., pp. 249-250.
69. West, "Beretning," p. 43.
70. Cf. chapter 3, on the slave codes of Gardelin and Lindemann.
71. Bentzon, "Om Negerne;" R/A, FAN, Bind 2, Part 3, p. 17. Cf. Neville A. T. Hall, "Slave Laws of the Danish Virgin Islands in the Later Eighteenth Century," *Annals of the New York Academy of Sciences* 292 (1977):174-86.
72. See for example R/A, FAN, Bind 2, Part 3, p. 27.
73. West, *Bidrag,* pp. 109-110. Cf. R/A, DVK, Oxholm's Anmærkning 1 August 1792, p. 8.
74. Schmidt, "Blandede Anmærkninger," pp. 260-261. See also Oldendorp, *History,* p. 262; Brathwaite, *Development of Creole Society,* p. 214.
75. R/A, Rentekammeret, Vestindiske Kommissionsforretninger vedrørende salg af Plantager og ulovlig handel paa St. Croix, 1759.
76. Haagensen, *Beskrivelse,* p. 60.
77. Von Scholten, *Orders for the Regulation of Labor,* p. 3.
78. Haagensen, *Beskrivelse,* p. 60.
79. R/A, FAN, Bind 2, 1785, Oxholm's Anmærkninger, 24 September 1788.
80. Schmidt, "Blandede Anmærkninger," p. 261.
81. Haagensen, *Beskrivelse,* pp. 65-66.
82. Schmidt, "Blandede Anmærkninger," p. 261.
83. Reglement 1755, p. 9. See chapter 3.
84. Cf. Lindemann in R/A, UBAN, Part 1, p. 85.

85. Ibid, p. 83; Vibæk, *Dansk Vestindien,* p. 143.
86. Reglement 1755, pp. 6, 39.
87. West, *Bidrag,* p. 137.
88. R/A, DVK, Oxholm, 31 December 1792.
89. R/A, DVK, 1805. Analysis of the available data on family and kinship is problematic. Cf. Karen Fog Olwig, *Cultural Adaptation and Resistance on St. John: Three Centuries of Afro-Caribbean Life* (1985), pp. 56-60; Michael Craton, "Changing Patterns of Slave Families in the British West Indies," *Journal of Interdisciplinary History* 10 (1979):1-35; B. W. Higman, *Slave Populations of the British Caribbean, 1807-1834* (1984), pp. 364-73; Ira Berlin, "Time, Space, and the Evolution of Afro-American Society on British Mainland North America," *American Historical Review* 85 (1980):44-78.
90. Oldendorp, *History,* pp. 488-90.
91. Mintz and Price, *Anthropological Approach,* p. 37. Cf. Karen Fog Olwig, "Finding a Place for the Slave Family: Historical Anthropological Perspectives," *Folk* 23 (1981):345-58; idem., *Cultural Adaptation and Resistance,* pp. 56-68; Marietta Morrissey, *Slave Women in the New World: Gender Stratification in the Caribbean* (1989), p. 95.
92. Oldendorp, *History,* p. 263.
93. Kirstein, "Udtog af Forestilling," p. 61.
94. Bentzon, "Om Negerne," p. 6.
95. DVRA, 7 September 1818. Cf. Richard B. Sheridan, *Doctors and Slaves: A Medical and Demographic History of Slavery in the British West Indies, 1680-1834* (1985), pp. 249-67.
96. Bentzon, "Om Negerne;" Kirstein, "Udtog af Forestilling."

CHAPTER 5

1. *RDAG,* 30 June and 15 September 1792.
2. C. H. Holten, "Af en gammel Hofmands Mindeblade (Konferensraad Carl Henrik Holtens Optegnelser)," *Memoirer og Breve* 11 (1909):51. In contrast Holten observed that in Europe he had two chambermaids and a man

servant. Cf. R/A, VJ, 1793, #911, where it was claimed that in the West Indies a married man needed a household staff of five, an additional servant for each member of the family, one for each child, plus a coachman.

3. Hans West, *Bidrag til Beskrivelse over Ste. Croix* (1793), p. 61.

4. Hans West, "Beretning om det danske Eilande St. Croix i Vestindien," *Iris* 3 (1791):64.

5. R/A, AVS/FC, Betænkning no. 3, 10 February 1818. Cf. R/A, VJ, 1793 #911.

6. R/A, DVK, Gen. Walterstorff's "Foreløbige Anmærkninger," 21 September 1792.

7. West, "Beretning," p. 42. Cf. B. W. Higman, *Slave Populations of the British Caribbean, 1807-1834* (1984), pp. 237-42.

8. R/A, UBAN, no. 27, Placat #43, 2 December 1778. See also Frederiksted Police Chief Behagen's call for an inventory of trays' contents as a means of preventing the sale of stolen goods: *SCG*, 13 February 1812.

9. R/A, Diverse Dokumenter, Om Negerhandelens Afskaffelse (korrespondence m. kommissionen) 1788-1847, Anonymous Pro Memoria c. 1802, f. 11.

10. West, "Beretning," p. 47.

11. R/A, DVK, Burgher Council of St. Croix to Danish West Indian Government, 5 September 1792.

12. R/A, VJ, 1793 #911: "den tilsyneladende Overflødighed af Huusnegre i Mange Tilfælde kan fortjene Forsvar, naar man lægge Mærke til, at ofte ere de deres Ejers eneste Opholds-Middel, der enten gjør sig Fordeel ved dennes Haandarbejde eller ved at udleje den."

13. R/A, Om Negerhandelen Afskaffelse, Anonymous Pro Memoria c. 1802

14. R/A, VJ, 1793 #911

15. *SCG*, 25 July 1808.

16. See respectively *RDAG*, 1 February 1770; *RDAG*, 25 June 1777; *RDAG*, 17 October 1770; *SCG*, 14 January 1815; *RDAG*, 4 August 1770; *SCG*, 24 March 1817; *RDAG*, 30 October

1776; *RDAG*, 25 August 1770. These bits of bio-data all derive from advertisements for runaways.

17. West, "Beretning," p. 42: "Nogle lære haandværke, og bringe det saavidt i deres kunst, at jeg nedlægge min Aere paa, at ingen fuld udlært Messerssvend imellem Kiøbenhavns høiberømte Laug, der indskrænke al muelig Industrie, skal kunne sye et Par Sko eller en Klædning, end ikke et Knaphul saa net og skønt, som en creolsk Neger."

18. R/A, UBAN, no. 17, von Roepstorff's Nota, 7 February 1784.

19. Victor Schoelcher, *Colonies étrangères et Haïti: Resultats de l'Emancipation Anglaise* (1843) vol. 2. pp. 20-21.

20. West, "Beretning," p. 47.

21. R/A, FAN, Bind 1, no. 63, Schimmelmann's Placat, 26 May 1786, para. 2 (b), ff. 72-73.

22. Holten, "Af en Gammel Hofmands Mindeblade," pp. 51-52. West makes a comparable observation in *Bidrag*, p. 60.

23. *RDAG*, 14 August 1817.

24. *STT*, 24 May 1821.

25. R/A, DVK, Oxholm's Anmærkninger ved Kongelige Commissions til Negerhandelens bedre Indretning paa de Vestindiske Eylande og Kysten Guinea, dens Promemoria af 7 April 1792 - elter Ordre, 1 August 1792, para. 8 (b).

26. Jens Vibæk, *Dansk Vestindien 1755-1848*, vol. 2 *Vore Gamle Tropekolonier* edited Johannes Brøndsted (1966), p. 13.

27. R/A, Rentekammeret, Vestindiske Kommissionsforretninger vedrørende salg af plantager og ulovlig handel paa St. Croix, 1759.

28. See chapter 6.

29. R/A, UBAN, no. 17, von Roepstorff's Nota, 7 February 1784.

30. West, *Bidrag*, p. 75.

31. Ibid., p. 76.

32. N. A. T. Hall, *Forslag til Ordning af Vestindiske Forfatningsforhold Angaaende Negerne med Mere* (1979), p. 18.

33. Holten, "Af en Gammel Hofmands Mindeblade," p. 52.

34. R/A, UBAN, 27 #22, von Prock's Placat, 23 December 1759, para. 7. See also R/A, UBAN, no. 1, Moth's

"Articler for Negerne" 11 December 1741, para. 2. Cf. R/A, UBAN, no. 27, #35, Schimmelmann's Placat, 20 August 1773, para. 4; #38, Clausen's Placat, 5 October 1774, para. 2. For the situation regarding St. Thomas see #27, 12 November 1762.

35. Ibid., #30, 18 October 1766.

36. Ibid. #39, 27 September 1775.

37. SCG, 29 February 1808; DVRA, 21 March 1808 and 26 February 1816; West "Beretning," pp. 48-49; R/A, UBAN, no. 27, #34, Clausen's Placat, 27 September 1775; R/A, FAN, 1785, Bind 2, Borger Raads Betænkning, 1 August 1787, f. 76.

38. R/A, FAN, 1785, Bind 2, Borger Raads, Betænkning, 1 August 1787, f. 76: "Sælge Negre infinde sig især i Crop Tiden paa Plantagerne, op muntre Slaverne til Tyverie, selv tilbytte for Skamkjøb hvad Rum, Sukker eller Bomuld de kunde have i Besiddelse, og endeligen anvise dem nederdrægtige Blanke og Frie Negere i Byerne, hos hvem de frit og i Sikkerhed kan afsætte større QVANTITETER."

39. Ibid.

40. Ibid., Colbiørnsen's Anmærkninger, 20 September 1788, f. 114.

41. R/A, UBAN, no. 27 #38, 5 October 1774.

42. Ibid., no. 1, Moth's "Articler," 11 December 1741.

43. R/A, UBAN, no. 27 #38, 5 October 1774.

44. R/A, UBAN, no. 27 #38, Clausen's Placat 5 October 1774 para. 6. Cf. Ibid., no. 1 #24, Forslag til en Neger Lov for de Kongelige Danske Vestindiske Eylande, Part 1 para. 83, 1773; and R/A, FAN, Bind 2, Neger Lov for de Danske Vestindiske Eylande, Part 2 para. 38. See also chapter 6.

45. West, "Beretning," p. 49.

46. R/A, UBAN, no. 27 #43, 2 December 1773.

47. R/A, FAN, Bind 2, de Malleville's Betænkninger 19 October 1787, f. 94; ibid., de Malleville's Anmærkninger, 7 April 1784, f. 33.

48. Ibid., de Malleville's Betænkninger, 19 October 1787, f. 84.

49. For examples see RDAG, 14 June 1775; DVRA, 23 April 1807; ibid., 25 May 1807.

50. Bryan Edwards, The History, Civil and Commercial, of the British Colonies in the West Indies (1793) vol. 3, p. 25. Jerome S. Handler, The Unappropriated People: Freedmen in the Slave Society of Barbados (1974), pp. 56, 152; Gad J. Heuman, Between Black and White: Race, Politics and the Free Coloreds in Jamaica, 1792-1865 (1981), p. 14.

51. R/A, Diverse Dokumenter, Om Negerhandelens Afskaffelse 1738-1847, Anonymous Pro Memoria c. 1802, f. 8.

52. STT, 29 January 1822.

53. N. A. T. Hall, "The 1816 Freedman Petition in the Danish West Indies: Its Background and Consequences," Boletin de Estudios Latinamericanos y del Caribe, 29 (1980): 55-73.

54. R/A, AVS/FC, Bentzon's Betænkning no. 3, 10 February 1818.

55. Ibid.

56. West, "Beretning," p. 42. For coincident freedmen's skills see West, Bidrag, pp. 57-58.

57. See for examples RDAG, 19 September 1772, reporting the case of the runaway tailor Wanico who "tis well known … would not absent himself so often from his master, if there was [sic] not bad people to employ him in hopes of getting their work cheaper done than by a white person."

58. Claudia Dale Goldin, Urban Slavery in the American South (1976), pp. 47 et seq. Cf. Mary C. Karasch, Slave Life in Rio de Janeiro 1808-1850 (1987), pp. 55-91.

59. R/A, DVK, St. Thomas Raad to Danish West Indian Government, 9 November 1792.

60. Ibid.

61. Ibid., Walterstorff's "Foreløbige Anmærkninger," 21 September 1792.

62. Ibid., St. Croix Burgher Council to Danish West Indian Government, 5 September 1792.

63. For the case of Jochum and Sam, see chapter 2.

64. R/A, FAN, Bind 1, "Geinpart af Adskillige Placater Negerne Betræffende 1672-1787," no. 60,

Schimmelmann's Placat, 14 October 1785, para. 1.

65. Ibid., de Malleville's "Uforgribelige Tænker over Herr General Gouverneurens Placat," 10 December 1787.

66. R/A, UBAN, no. 4, 5 September 1733, paras. 12, 17, 18.

67. Ibid., no. 1, Moth's "Articler for Negerne," 11 December 1741 para. 1; ibid., no. 27 #29, de Gunthelberg's St. Thomas Placat, 9 February 1765, paras. 2 and 3; ibid., no. 27 #38, para. 6.

68. Ibid., no. 27 #18, 17 May 1756, para. 8; #22, 23 December 1759, para. 12; #22, 23 December 1757, para. 9 (cf. #38 Clausen's Placat, 5 October 1774, para. 3); no. 1 30 December 1758, para. 2 (Cf. no. 27 #33, Clausen's Placat, 21 October 1770, and #41 Clausen's Placat 21 October 1771.

69. Ibid., no. 27 #29, 9 February 1765, paras. 6, 8, 10, 14. Cf. #38, 5 October 1774, para. 4.

70. Ibid., no. 27 #43, St. Croix Burgher Council's Forestilling, 2 December 1778, paras. 4 and 5.

71. See Neville A. T. Hall, "Slavery in Three West Indian Towns: Christiansted, Fredericksted and Charlotte Amalie in the Late Eighteenth and Early Nineteenth Century," in *Trade, Government and Society in Caribbean History 1700-1920* edited B. W. Higman (1983); idem., "Slaves and the Law in the Towns of St Croix 1802-1807," *Slavery & Abolition 8* (1987):147-65.

72. Assaults were rare. The journals contain one incident of an assault on a white with a weapon: Bladwell's Hendrik hitting a white man on his back with a sword in Christiansted. He received 50 lashes as punishment: N/A, RG 55, Box 485, Udskrift af Christiansteds Jurisdictions Politi Journaler, 3 March 1806. Also in Christiansted a slave, Faucett's Joseph, tore a police constable's clothing while resisting arrest for fighting: ibid., 12 April 1807.

73. Ibid., 13 October 1806; 1 May 1807.

74. Ibid., 9 October 1806.

75. David Findlay, an executor and litigant in a case of a disputed will in 1793 informed Notary Public, Otto Müller, that one of his opponents in the litigation lusted after proceeds of the estate "like Jews in Copenhagen whose beards are set in motion at the sight of gold." N/A, RG 55, Box 793, Proceedings of the Common Probate Court of St. Croix, Findlay to Müller, 23 October 1793.

76. N/A, RG 55, Box 485, Udskrift af Christiansteds Jurisdictions Politi Journaler, 25 August 1806.

77. Ibid., 25 December 1806.

78. See chapter 7. Cf. *Out of the House of Bondage: Runaways, Resistance and Marronage in Africa and the New World* (1986) edited Gad Heuman.

79. N/A, RG 55, Box 485, Udskrift af Christiansteds Jurisdictions Politi Journaler, 2 February 1807.

80. Ibid., 19 February 1807.

81. Ibid., 15 August 1807.

82. Ibid., 26 December 1805, 19 November 1806, 4 December 1806, 25 January 1807, 22 and 29 April 1807; *DVRA*, 23 April 1807.

83. Wade, *Slavery in the Cities*, p. 186.

84. See for example N/A, RG 55, Box 485, Udskrift af Christiansteds Jurisdictions Politi Journaler, 9 January 1805.

85. Ibid., 4 and 9 January 1805.

86. Ibid., 4 February 1806; 19 November 1806.

87. Ibid., 3 April 1807; cf. 3 March 1806.

88. R/A, UBAN, Miscellaneous Papers, Judge Edvard Colbiørnsen's Judgment in the case of John Hart vs. Jochum and Sam, 3 September 1785. On the 1759 conspiracy, see Monica Schuler, "Akan Slave Rebellions in the British Caribbean," *Savacou* 1 (1970): 23, and Waldemar Westergaard, "Account of the Negro Rebellion on St. Croix, Danish West Indies, 1759," *Journal of Negro History* 11 (1926):50-61.

89. N/A, RG 55, Box 487, Udskrift af Christiansteds Jurisdictions Politi Journaler, Governor General Walterstorff to Chief of Police Smith, 31 January 1803, in docket Governor General vs Bogholder Beverhoudt in the matter of Mulatto Marie, January 1803. The birch

whip was also in use and appeared to be less lethal. The evidence is not, however, conclusive as to choice of whip for particular offenses, degree of punishment and location i.e. within the prison or at the public whipping post. On the birch or "Riis" see R/A, FAN, Bind 2, Walterstorff's Bemærkninger, 8 October 1788, ff. 126-27.

90. See for example R/A, FAN, Bind 1, Van der Østen's Neger Lov for de danske vestindiske Eylande, 1785, f. 304.

91. N/A, RG 55, Box 496, Udskrift af Frederiksteds Jurisdictions Politi Journaler, 8 September 1806.

92. Ibid., Box 485, Udskrift af Christiansteds Jurisdictions Politi Journaler, 9 October 1805; Box 487, Udskrift af Christiansteds Jurisdictions Politi Journaler, docket Governor General vs Bogholder Beverhoudt in the matter of Mulatto Marie, January 1803.

93. DVRA, 13 July 1815.

94. R/A, RG 55, Box 485, Udskrift af Christiansteds Jurisdictions Politi Journaler, 8 and 9 December 1806.

95. Fædrelandet, 22 December 1840.

96. See for example N/A, RG 55, Box 485, Udskrift af Christiansteds Jurisdictions Politi Journaler, 14 September 1806.

97. Ibid., 24 January 1805; 9 February 1805; 26 June 1805; 21 December 1805; 21 January 1806; 15 February 1806; 1 April 1806; 28 April 1806; 18 June 1806.

98. Wade, Slavery in the Cities, pp. 94-95.

99. N/A, RG 55, Box 485, Udskrift af Christiansteds Jurisdictions Politi Journaler, Walterstorff to Chief of Police Smith, 31 January 1803, in docket Governor General vs Bogholder Beverhoudt in the matter of Mulatto Marie, January 1803.

100. Ibid., 19 and 25 February 1807.

101. For example, ibid., 1 February 1805; 1 July 1805; 6 July 1805; 12 January 1807.

102. R/A, UBAN, #27, de Gunthelberg's Placat no. 29, 9 February 1765, Preamble.

103. N/A, RG 55, Box 485, Udskrift af Christiansteds Jurisdictions Politi Journaler, 16 March 1802. By way of

comparison, Louisville, Kentucky, with a population of 1,000 slaves in 1820 had three constables, a ratio of 1 for approximately 330 slaves. Wade, Slavery in the Cities, pp. 99, 326.

104. For example, N/A, RG 55, Box 485, Udskrift af Christiansteds Jurisdictions Politi Journaler, 14 February 1806; 17 December 1806; 15 February 1807.

105. R/A, Gtk, Kongelige Resolutioner, 1800, no. 87, 19 February 1800, enclosing Dansk Vestindisk Regerings Pro Memoria, 27 September 1799.

106. N/A, RG 55, Box 485, Udskrift af Christiansteds Jurisdictions Politi Journaler, 6 April 1807.

107. Ibid., 30 July and 1 August 1807.

108. Ibid., 26 July 1805; 29 July 1805 in docket Johannes vs. Hennings; 9 and 10 August 1805.

109. Ibid., 3 September 1805.

CHAPTER 6

1. R/A, CANS, von Scholten to Christian VIII, 15 January 1841, Enclosure 3, 29 October 1840; Enclosure 5, 26 May 1840. For an earlier instance see I. C. Schmidt, "Blandede Anmærkninger, samlede paa og over Ejlandet St. Croix i Amerika 1788," Samleren 2 (1788):244.

2. Bronislaw Malinowski, "Introduction," in Methods of Study of Culture Contact in Africa (1938), p. xvii.

3. Edward Brathwaite, The Development of Creole Society in Jamaica 1770-1820 (1971), p. 296.

4. Serghei Arutuniev, "Cultural Paradigms: The Process of Change Through Cultural Borrowings," Cultures 5 (1978):95.

5. Jerome S. Handler and Frederick W. Lange, Plantation Slavery in Barbados: An Archaeological and Historical Investigation (1978), p. 289 n. 1.

6. Schmidt, "Blandede Anmærkninger," p. 239. See also R/A, FAN, 1785, Bind 2. Commandant de Mallevilles Betænkninger, 19 October 1787, f. 92.

7. Schmidt, "Blandede Anmærkninger," p. 245.

8. See Brathwaite, *Development of Creole Society*, pp. 253-60; Mary Turner, *Slaves and Missionaries: The Disintegration of Jamaican Slave Society 1787-1834* (1982), p. 11.

9. R/A, UBAN, no. 4, Philip Gardelin's Placat, 5 September 1733, para. 13. Cf. ibid., no. 24, Forslag til en Neger Lov for de Kongelige Danske Vestindiske Eylande, 1783, Pt. 1. para. 10. Cf. also R/A, FAN, 1785, Bind 1, Negerlov for de Danske Vestindiske Eylande, Pt. 3, para. 18.

10. Monica Schuler, "Akan Slave Rebellions in the British Caribbean," *Savacou* 1 (1970):21-23.

11. See chapter 1 and 11.

12. H. B. Dahlerup, *Mit Livs Begivenheder* (1909), vol. 2, p. 277.

13. Malinowski, "Introduction," p. xvii.

14. See chapter 11.

15. Dahlerup, *Mit Livs,* vol. 2, pp. 296-97. See also H. B. Dahlerup, "Skizzer fra et kort Besøg paa vore Vestindiske Øer i Sommeren 1841," *Nyt Archiv for Søvæsenet* 1 (1842):28.

16. See chapters 11 and 12.

17. Sidney W. Mintz and Douglas Hall, *The Origins of the Jamaican Internal Marketing System* (1960).

18. On the markets see Hans West, *Bidrag til Beskrivelse over Ste. Croix* (1793), pp. 75-76; idem., "Beretning om det danske Eilande St. Croix i Vestindien," *Iris* 3 (1791):72-74; Schmidt, "Blandede Anmærkninger," pp. 242-44; J.P. Nissen, *Reminiscences of a 46 years' residence in the Island of St. Thomas in the West Indies* (1838), p. 34; Thurlow Weed, *Letters from Europe and the West Indies, 1843-52* (1866), pp. 353-55.

19. R/A, UBAN, no. 2, paras. 14 and 15.

20. Ibid., no. 27, Governor Clausen's Placat, 11 August 1767, paras. 1-5.

21. West, "Beretning," p. 72. Cf. Schmidt, "Blandede Anmærkninger," pp. 241-43.

22. West, *Bidrag,* pp. 75-76.

23. Weed, *Letters,* p. 354.

24. Ibid., p. 353.

25. R/A, UBAN, no. 4, Philip Gardelin's Placat, 5 September 1733, para. 16.

26. Ibid., no. 1, 11 December 1741, para. 6. Cf. ibid., no. 27, #18, Governor von Pröck's Placat, 17 May 1756, para. 7.

27. Ibid., no. 27, #29, 9 February 1765, para. 9.

28. Ibid., no. 27, #38, 5 October 1774, para. 6.

29. R/A, UBAN, no. 24, Forslag til en Neger for de Kongelige Danske Vestindiske Eylande, 1783, Part 3, paras. 33-36.

30. West, "Beretning," p. 77. Although he does not specifically say so, it is likely that his remarks were based on his own observations of, or reports on, the situation in Christiansted, not on the plantations.

31. C. H. Holten, "Af en gammel Hofmands Mindeblade (Konferensraad Carl Henrik Holtens Optegnelser)," *Memoirer og Breve,* 11 (1909):53: "Jeg mindes iblandt andet en Haarskjærer, som anskaffede sig et Par Briller til at valtse med, fordi han havde seet Waltersdorffs Secretair, Captain Manthey, at gjøre dette, og at han, da de andre Couleurte dog fandte dette vel latterligt, svarede den ganske mug-gent: 'I ere nogle Tosser, some ikke vide at dette er Mode ved Hoffet'."

32. R/A, UBAN, no. 27, #43, 2 December 1778, para. 5.

33. R/A, FAN, 1785, Bind 1, Schimmelmann's Placat, 26 May 1786, paras. 1 and 2.

34. *SCG,* 27 July 1814.

35. Weed, *Letters,* p. 346.

36. Ibid. See also R/A, UBAN, no. 33, Clausen's Placat, 21 October 1770.

37. For representative samples of proclamations see R/A, UBAN, no. 1, 30 December 1758; ibid., no. 27, 12 December 1761; ibid, no. 33, 21 October 1770; ibid, no. 41, 21 October 1777.

38. R/A, UBAN, No. 24, Forslag til en Neger for de Kongelige Danske Vestindiske Eylande, 1783, Part 1, para. 93. Author's emphasis.

39. See for example *SCG,* 25 December 1813.

40. R/A, UBAN, no. 27, #22, 23 December 1758, para. 3.

41. R/A, UBAN, no. 24, Forslag til en Negerlov for de Kongelige Danske Vestindiske Eylande, 1783, Part 1, para. 98; R/A, FAN, 1785, Bind 1,

Negerlov for de Danske Vestindiske
Eylande, Part 3, para. 104.
42. Nissen, *Reminiscences*, p. 164.
43. R/A, UBAN, no. 27, #22,
23 December 1759, para. 3.
44. Nissen, *Reminiscences*, p. 164.
45. Ibid., pp. 164-65. Author's emphasis.
46. Weed, *Letters*, pp. 346-47.
47. Ibid., p. 347.
48. Ibid., p. 347.
49. Ibid., p. 348.
50. Schmidt, "Blandede
Anmærkninger," pp. 232-33.
51. Brathwaite, *Development of Creole
Society*, p. 230. See also Robert Dirks,
*The Black Saturnalia: Conflict and Its
Ritual Expression on British West
Indian Slave Plantations* (1987).
52. Weed, *Letters*, pp. 349-50. On "Set
Girls" see Brathwaite, *Development of
Creole Society*, p. 231.
53. R/A, UBAN, no. 27, #38, Governor
General Clausen's Proclamation,
5 October 1774, paras. 1 and 5.
Cf. R/A, UBAN, no. 24, Forslag til
en Negerlov for de Kongelige
Danske Vestindiske Eylande, 1783,
Part 1, para. 87; R/A, FAN, 1785,
Bind 1, Negerlov for de Danske
Vestindiske Eylande, Part 3,
para. 74.
54. R/A, UBAN, no. 27, #38, 5 October
1774, para. 5.
55. Dahlerup, *Mit Livs*, p. 48. See also
DVRA, 25 August 1836.
56. R/A, UBAN, no. 24, Forslag til en
Negerlov for de Kongelige Danske
Vestindiske Eylande, 1783, Part 1,
para. 94: "Sielden seer man en
Neger paa Gaden uden en Steen i
Haanden; men det ses med
Ligegyldighed, saalænge Steenen
ey trætter nogen Blank. Det gaar
endog saavidt, at man ei kan være
sikker i Huusene og paa Gallerierne
for saadan letsindig Steenkasten
hen i Veiret. Man hitter allerede
paa at bruge Slynger. En saadan
Øvelse, naar den blev almindelig,
vist blive en farlig Tidsfordriv og
Fornøielse."
57. R/A, FAN, 1785, Bind 2,
Commandant de Malleville's
Betænkninger, 19 October 1787.
58. See for example R/A, UBAN, no. 27,
#29, Commandant de Gunthelberg's
Proclamation, 9 February 1765.

59. R/A, UBAN, no. 24, Forslag til en
Nergerlov for de Kongelige Danske
Vestindiske Eylande, 1783, Part 1,
para. 76.
60. Dahlerup, *Mit Livs*, pp. 47-48, 274.
61. R/A, UBAN, no. 27, #38, 5 October
1774, para. 3.
62. R/A, UBAN, no. 24, Forslag til en
Neger for de Kongelige Danske
Vestindiske Eylande, 1783, Part 1,
para. 77.
63. R/A, FAN, 1785, Bind 1, Negerlov
for de Danske Vetindiske Eylande,
Pt. 3, para. 73.
64. R/A, FAN, 1785, Bind 2, 1 August
1787, f. 68.
65. Ibid., de Malleville's Betænkninger,
19 October 1787, f. 91.
66. R/A, UBAN, no. 24, Forslag til en
Negerlov for de Kongelige Danske
Vestindiske Eylande, 1783, Part 1,
para. 84.
67. R/A, FAN, 1785, Bind 1, Negerlov
for de Danske Vestindiske Eylande,
Part 3, para. 98. Cf. ibid., Bind 2,
1 August 1787, f. 76, and ibid., Etatz
Raad Colbiørnsen's Anmærkninger,
24 September 1788.
68. R/A, UBAN, no. 24, Forslag til en
Negerlov for de Kongelige Danske
Vestindiske Eylande, 1783, Part 1,
para. 2.
69. R/A, UBAN, no. 4, Philip Gardelin's
Placat, 5 September 1733, para. 11.
70. R/A, FAN, 1785, Bind 1, Negerlov
for de Danske Vestindiske Eylande,
Part 3, para. 59.
71. R/A, UBAN, no. 27, #18, 17 May
1756, paras. 8, 22. Cf. ibid., #22, 23
December 1759, para. 12, and *SCG*,
7 July 1812, Police Chief Gjellerup's
Ordinance.
72. R/A, UBAN, no. 24, Forslag til en
Negerlov for de Kongelige Danske
Vestindiske Eylande, 1783, Part 1,
para. 97.
73. *DVRA*, 13 May 1815.
74. See for example, *SCG*, 9 February
1807; 5 October 1814.
75. Sidney W. Mintz and Richard Price,
*An Anthropological Approach to the
Afro-American Past: A Caribbean
Perspective* (1976), p. 10.
76. Ibid., p. 16.

CHAPTER 7

1. Richard Price, ed., *Maroon Societies: Rebel Slave Communities in the Americas* (1973), p. 3.

2. See chapter 5, and N. A. T. Hall, "Slavery in Three West Indian Towns: Christiansted, Fredericksted and Charlotte Amalie in the Late Eighteenth and Early Nineteenth Century," in *Trade, Government and Society in Caribbean History, 1700-1920* edited by B. W. Higman (1983), p. 23.

3. Price, *Maroon Societies*, p. 9.

4. That number is not to be taken at face value since West made no distinction between *petit* and *grand* marronage. Hans West, "Beretning om det danske Eilande St. Croix i Vestindien," *Iris* 3 (1791):43-72, ("Mandtal Optaget for 1789").

5. R/A, DVK, Oxholm's Generaltabel, St. Croix, 1792.

6. R/A, Den engelske Okkupation 1801, 1807, Recapitulation of the State of the Different Quarters of the Island of St. Thomas, 13 May 1802. For comparative statistics, see for example B. W. Higman, *Slave Populations of the British Caribbean, 1807-1834* (1984), pp. 387-88.

7. Waldemar Westergaard, *The Danish West Indies under Company Rule (1671-1754)* (1917), p. 121.

8. University of California, Berkeley, Bancroft Papers, Z-A 1, 3, Copies of Orders Issued during Governorships, 1672-1727.

9. Ibid., Z-A 1, 48, Kongelig Secretaire Schwartkopf's Report, 13 October 1786.

10. In the case of St. Croix, contemplated legislation in 1783 against illegal felling of trees was justified on the basis that "since almost all the forests have been cut down, illegal felling of trees is of greater importance than previously." R/A, UBAN, no. 24, Part 1, Article 48. See also David Watts, *The West Indies: Patterns of Development, Culture and Evironmental Change since 1492* (1987), pp. 393-95.

11. J. L. Carstens, "En Almindelig Beskrivelse om Alle de Danske Americanske eller West-Jndiske Ey-Lande," *Danske Magazin* 8 (3) (1970):225-59.

12. See chapter 1.

13. Bro-Jørgensen, *Dansk Vestindien indtil 1755*, vol. 1 *Vore Gamle Tropekolonier*, edited Johannes Brøndsted (1966), p. 225.

14. Westergaard, *Danish West Indies*, p. 160.

15. Ibid., p. 161.

16. Arturo Morales-Carrión, *Albores Históricos del Capitalismo en Puerto Rico* (1974), p. 83.

17. Luis M. Diaz Soler, *Historia de la Esclavitud Negra en Puerto Rico* (1965), pp. 233, 236.

18. Cayetano Coll y Toste, ed., *Boletin Histórico de Puerto Rico* (1914), vol. 1, pp. 16, 20.

19. Fernández Méndez, *Historia Cultural de Puerto Rico, 1493-1968* (1971), p. 165

20. Peter H. Wood, *Black Majority: Negroes in Colonial South Carolina from 1670 through the Stono Rebellion* (1974), pp. 305-307.

21. Westergaard, *Danish West Indies*, p. 162. See also C. G. A. Oldendorp, *History of the Mission of the Evangelical Brethren on the Caribbean Islands of St. Thomas, St. Croix, and St. John* (1987), pp. 233-34, 609; and chapter 3 above.

22. Bancroft Papers, Z-A 1, 52, Governor General Walterstorff's Placat of 21 November 1791, quoting earlier proclamations of 1742, 1744, 1750 and 1756.

23. Oldendorp mentioned amputations for which the definitive slave code of 1733 made provision (*History*, pp. 233, 609). But by the 1780s there were already voices critical of the code's provision as barbaric. See, for example, R/A, UBAN, Miscellaneous Papers, Judge Colbiørnsen's Opinion, 3 September 1785; R/A, FAN, Bind 1, 1785, Generaltoldkammerets skrivelse to Danish West Indian Government, 23 December 1782.

24. Richard Haagensen, *Beskrivelse over Eylandet St. Croix i America i Vestindien* (1758), p. 42.

25. Ibid., p. 43.

26. Oldendorp, *History*, pp. 233-34. Oldendorp did not say whether he knew of any slaves who managed to reach Puerto Rico or adjacent islands by swimming.

27. Bancroft Papers, Z-A 1, 52, Governor General Walterstorff's Placat, 21 November 1791.

28. *SCG*, 12 March 1811.

29. R/A, AVS/FC, Dansk Vestindisk Regerings Deliberations Protocoller, 30 April 1816.

30. N/A, RG 55, Box 9, Søbøtker to Christian VIII, 13 December 1845.

31. Haagensen, *Beskrivelse*, p. 43.

32. Oldendorp, *History*, pp. 233-34; E. V. Lose, "Kort Udsigt over den danske-lutherske Missions Historie paa St. Croix, St. Thomas og St. Jan," *Nordisk Missions-Tidsskrift* 1 (1890):22-23; Diaz Soler, *Historia de la Esclavitud*, pp. 234-36; Morales Carrión, *Albores Históricos*, p. 67; R/A, FAN, 1785, Bind 2, ff. 74, 89.

33. Westergaard, *Danish West Indies*, p. 161. Diaz Soler is of the view that the settlement of the claim under the 1767 convention was facilitated by the demise of the Danish West Indian Company, whose illicit trading with Puerto Rico had always been an obstacle to negotiations (*Historia de la Esclavitud*, p. 234).

34. Bancroft Papers, Z-A 1, 43, Clausen to de Muesos, 4 July 1775.

35. *SCG*, 8 February 1811.

36. Ibid., 9 April 1811.

37. R/A, CANS, von Scholten to Christian VIII, 13 January 1841, in which reference is made to an unfiled letter of 18 November 1840. See also R/A, Privat Arkiv 6795, Christian VIII to von Scholten, 7 October and 4 December 1840, 1 August 1841.

38. C. Van Dockum, *Livserindringer* (1893), pp. 74-77. See also Isaac Dookhan, "Vieques or Crab Island: Source of Anglo-Spanish Conflict," *Journal of Caribbean History* 7 (1973): 1-22.

39. Andrés Ramos Mattei, *La Hacienda Azucarera: Su Crecimiento y Crisis en Puerto Rico (Siglo XIX)* (1981), pp. 23-24. Demand for labor inspired the decree of 1849 establishing an obligatory work regimen for free labor in Puerto Rico. See ibid., p. 24, and Labor Gomez Acevedo, *Organización y Reglamentación del Trabajo en el Puerto Rico del Siglo XIX* (1970), pp. 449-53; Francisco A. Scarano, *Sugar and Slavery in Puerto Rico* (1984), pp. 25-34.

40. R/A, FAN, 1785, Bind 2, Etats Raad Laurbergs Erindringer, 12 January 1784, ff. 10-11. Cf. ibid., Bind 1, f. 326.

41. It is possible that cane field deserters were simply engaging in short-term absenteeism. The length of absence and the construction of shelter that made absence of that duration possible would suggest, more plausibly, an intention to remain at large and ultimately leave the island.

42. *STT*, 16 September 1815.

43. Ibid., 5 March 1822.

44. R/A, UBAN, no. 27, Clausen's Placat, 39, 29 July 1775; R/A, FAN, 1785, Bind 2, de Malleville's Anmærkning, 7 April 1784, and de Malleville's Betænkning, 19 October 1787, ff. 33, 84. See also chapters 3 and 5.

45. R/A, Diverse sager, Forskellige Oplysninger V, Bentzon's Ordinance of 11 September 1817, f. 315.

46. Ibid., VI, Søbøtker's Proclamation of 22 July 1831, f. 216.

47. A. S. Ørsted, "Beholdes Herredømmet over en vestindisk Slave, naar han betræder dansk-europæisk Grund," *Arkiv for Retsvidenskaben og dens Anvendelse* 1 (1824):459-85.

48. *STT*, 9 February 1827.

49. Ibid., 9 March 1819.

50. *DVRA*, 15 May 1806.

51. *STT*, 9 March 1833.

52. Svend E. Green-Pedersen, "Slave Demography in the Danish West Indies and the Abolition of the Danish Slave Trade," in *The Abolition of the Atlantic Slave Trade* (1981), p. 245. See also G. W. Alexander, "Om den moralske Forpligtelse til og det hensigtmæssige af strax og fuldstændigt at ophæve Slaveriet i

de dansk-vestindiske Kolonier,"
Dansk Ugeskrift 2 (76) (1843):5-7.

53. Jamaica Government Archives,
Spanish Town, Calendar of
Records, High Court of Vice
Admiralty, Jamaica, 1796, f. 17.
Freedmen sometimes also owned
their own vessels. The brothers
Jacob and August Dennerey
jointly owned a boat in St. Thomas
in 1820.

54. R/A, AVS/FC, Generaltoldkammer
skrivelse to Dansk Vestindisk
Regering, 23 November 1793, and
Dansk Cancelli to
Generaltoldkammer, 8 August 1807,
enclosure 4, 29 October 1805. For
further examples of boat legislation
directed at St. Domingue/Haiti see
N. A. T. Hall, *Forslag til Ordning af
Vestindisk Forfatningsforhold
angaaende Negerne med Mere* (1979),
pp. 3, 7, n. 16.

55. R/A, Akter Vedkommende
Slaveemancipation 1834-1847, von
Scholten's comments on G. W.
Alexander's "Anmærkninger til
Kongen af Danmark m.h.t. de
danske Øer" [n.d.].

56. The scarcity of white labor was a
continuous problem, especially for
plantations, forcing von Scholten to
pass deficiency legislation in the
1830s. See chapter 1.

57. *Royal Gazette* (Kingston),
Supplement, 8-15 August 1788.

58. *Jamaica Courant* (Kingston), 17 May
1806.

59. *Royal Gazette*, 2-9 December 1797.

60. Ibid., 7 November 1793.

61. The total tonnage of shipping into
St. Thomas 1821-1830 doubled that
of the previous decade. There was
an annual average of 2,890 vessels
with a total tonnage of 177,441. See
Westergaard, *Danish West Indies*,
p. 252.

62. Hall, "Slavery in Three West Indian
Towns," p. 30.

63. *STT,* 10 April 1819.

64. The newspapers of the Leewards,
Windwards, Barbados, and
elsewhere in the eastern and
southern Caribbean can be expected
to be good sources for marronage
from the Danish West Indies.

65. R/A, NEER, Louis Rothe, "Om
Populations Forhold i de danske
vestindiske Colonier og fornemlig
paa St. Croix" [n.p.].

66. Van Dockum, *Livserindringer,*
pp. 74-77.

67. Rothe, "Om Populations Forhold."

68. Ibid.

69. The figures for 1840 are derived
from Alexander, "Om den moralske
Forpligtelse," p. 7. Those for 1846
are from P. P. Sveistrup, "Bidrag til
de tidligere dansk-vestindiske Øers
Økonomiske Historie,"
*Nationaløkonomisk Tidsskrift for
Samfundsspørgsmaal, Økonomi og
Handel* 80 (1942):78-79.

70. Rothe did not make any attempt to
quantify the effects of *grand
marronage* from St. John, but did
state marronage to Tortola would
have a "conclusive influence upon
the structure of [St. John's] slave
population" ("Om Populations
Forhold").

71. R/A, CANS, von Scholten to
Christian VIII, 15 January 1841.

72. Alexander, "Om den moralske
Forpligtelse," p. 15.

73. *Fædrelandet,* 15 and 22 December
1840.

74. H. B. Dahlerup, *Mit Livs
Begivenheder* (1909), vol. 2, pp. 270,
289; idem., "Skizzer fra et kort Besøg
paa vore vestindiske Øer i
Sommeren 1841," *Nyt Archiv for
Søvæsenet* 1 (1842):1.

75. Statistics on the sex distribution
of deserters or groups of deserters
are not abundant, but the available
data do point to a heavy
preponderance of males. For
example, of the 86 deserters in
St. Thomas in 1802 (see above, n. 6),
73 were male and 13 female. The 7
men and 1 woman in the incident
in 1819 (see above n.63) represent a
not dissimilar proportion. The party
of 5 in 1840 (see above n. 72),
assuming the two escapees were
men, appears to be almost evenly
balanced. But that distribution, on
the basis of other evidence, can be
considered unusual.

76. N/A, RG 55, Box 9, Søbøtker to
Christian VIII, 11 November 1845,

no. 3, Copies of Letters Sent to the King, ff. 2-3.

77. For letters reporting the incident, see ibid., 28 November and 13 December 1845, 27 and 28 January 1846, nos. 4-7.

78. For examples see R/A, UBAN, no. 4, Gardelin's Placat, 5 September 1733; R/A, AVS/FC, Walterstorff to Generaltoldkammer, 20 July 1802; R/A, FAN, 1785, Bind 2, Laurbergs Erindringer, 12 January 1784; N/A, RG 55, Box 9, Søbøtker to Christian VIII, 28 January, 12 June 1846, nos. 7, 19; Haagensen, Beskrivelse, p. 35.

79. R/A, CANS, von Scholten to Christian VIII, 14 May 1842.

80. N/A, RG 55, Box 9, Søbøtker to Christian VIII, 28 January 1846, no. 7.

81. R/A, Haandskriftsamlingen, Species facti over den paa Eilandet Sainte Croix Aaret 1759 intenderede Neger Rebellion, forfattet efter Ordre af Byfoget Engelbreth Hesselbjerg, No. 3.

82. Oldendorp, History, p. 233.

83. For a detailed discussion of opposition liberal and other positions on the emancipation debate in Denmark see Grethe Bentzen, Debatten om det dansk-vestindisk Negerslaveri 1833-1848 med særligt Henblik på de igennem Tidsskriftpressen og stænderdebatter udtrykte holdninger, Cand. mag. dissertation, Aarhus University, 1976.

84. Fædrelandet, 5 January 1841.

85. R/A, VJ, 1848, no. 141.

CHAPTER 8

1. On the "in-betweenity" of freedmen in the hemisphere, see for example David W. Cohen and Jack P. Greene, eds., Neither Slave Nor Free: The Freedmen of African Descent in the Slave Societies of the New World (1972); Jerome S. Handler, The Unappropriated People: Freedmen in the Slave Society of Barbados (1974); Ira Berlin, Slaves Without Masters: The Free Negro in the Antebellum South (1975); Edward Cox, Free Coloreds in the Slave Societies of St. Kitts and Grenada, 1763-1833 (1984).

2. R/A, Haandskriftsamlingen, Species facti over den paa Eilandet Sainte Croix Aaret 1759 intenderede Neger Rebellion, forfattet efter Ordre af Byfoget Engelbreth Hesselbjerg; Jens Larsen, Virgin Islands Story (1950), pp. 57-58.

3. R/A, Rentekammeret, Relationer og Resolutioner angaaende Vestindien og Guinea, 1760-65, no. 62, 11 November 1763.

4. R/A, Danske Cancelli, Vestindiske Sager, 1746-71, 1773-86, 1787-99.

5. In comparative terms, this was a low rate of manumission at about 0.02 percent of the slave population per annum, but it must be emphasized that comparison is hazardous because the sample is partial and includes only those wills which for some reason were submitted to royal confirmation. Cf. B. W. Higman, Slave Populations of the British Caribbean, 1807-1834 (1984), p. 381; John D. Garrigus, A Struggle for Respect: The Free Coloreds of Pre-Revolutionary Saint Domingue, 1760-69, Ph.D. dissertation, Johns Hopkins University, 1988; David W. Cohen and Jack P. Greene, eds., Neither Slave Nor Free.

6. R/A, Danske Cancelli, Vestindiske Sager, 1787-99, f. 167.

7. Ibid., f. 145.

8. Ibid., 1746-71, f. 570.

9. Ibid., 1773-86, f. 340.

10. Ibid., 1787-99, f. 171.

11. Ibid., ff. 143, 145.

12. Ibid., 1746-71, f. 570.

13. Cf. Svend E. Green-Pedersen, "Slave Demography in the Danish West Indies and the Abolition of the Danish Slave Trade," in The Abolition of the Atlantic Slave Trade edited David Eltis and James Walvin (1981), pp. 234-37.

14. R/A, Danske Cancelli, Vestindiske Sager, 1787-99, f. 668.

15. Ibid., 1773-86, f. 341.

16. Ibid., 1787-99, f. 171.

17. Ibid., f. 171.

18. Ibid., f. 143.

19. Ibid., f. 143.

20. See for example ibid., 1773-86, f. 340; ibid., 1787-99, ff. 143, 687.

21. Gad J. Heuman, Between Black and White: Race, Politics, and the Free Coloreds in Jamaica, 1792-1865 (1981), pp. 5-6.

22. R/A, Dansk Cancelli, Vestindiske Sager, 1787-99, f. 525. The will was confirmed on 2 June 1797.

23. N/A, RG 55, Boxes 485-87, Udskrift af Christiansteds Jurisdictions Politi Journaler; Boxes 496-97, Udskrift af Frederiksteds Jurisdictions Politi Journaler.

24. R/A, Den engelske Okkupation 1801-1807, "Liste over Byens Indvaanere, 28 de Mai 1802," ff. 10-12, 14-16, 18-20.

25. J. H. Schou (ed.), *Chronologisk Register over de Kongelige Forordninger og Aabne Breve* (1848).

26. R/A, UBAN, no. 2, "Reglement for Slaverne," 3 February 1755, para. 45: "I ligemaade skulde de Friegivne nyde alle Rettigheder som Friebaarne, og med de Friebaarne Kronens Undersaatter i alle Maader lige agtes og ansees."

27. Ibid., no. 4, Gardelin's Placat, 5 September 1733, clauses 15, 19, 3, 6, 9, 12-13, respectively.

28. Ibid., no. 1, "Extract af de for de Kongl. Danske Vestindiske Eilande udkomne Reglementer, Ordonnancer, og Placater Negerne betræffende," Governor Hansen's Placat, 27 November 1747, clause 4.

29. Ibid., Governor Moth's "Articler for Negerne," 11 December 1741, clause 2; ibid., Governor Lindemark's Placat, 31 January 1746, clause 2.

30. R/A, UBAN, no. 27, Placater Anordninger og Publicationer Negerne Betræffende 1726-80, no. 29, de Gunthelberg's Placat, 9 February 1765, clauses 2-3, 5.

31. P. L. Oxholm, *De Danske Vestindiske öers Tilstand* (1797), p. 39. Cf. Richard Haagensen, *Beskrivelse over Eylandet St. Croix i America i Vestindien* (1758), pp. 46-47.

32. R/A, UBAN, no. 27, Placater Anordninger og Publicationer, no. 31, Clausen's Placat, 11 August 1767, clauses 1-4. Cf. R/A, FAN, 1785, Bind 1, Governor General Schimmelmann's Placat, 13 June 1787, clause 5.

33. R/A, UBAN, no. 27, Placater Anordninger og Publicationer, no. 32, Commandant Krag's Placat, 21 May 1768, clauses 1-4.

34. Ibid., no. 27, Placater Anordninge og Publicationer, no. 29, 9 February 1765, clause 9.

35. Ibid., no. 27, Placater Anordninger og Publicationer, no. 38, 5 October 1774, clause 6.

36. Ibid., no. 27, Placater Anordninger og Publicationer, no. 40, 12 October 1775.

37. R/A, FAN, 1785, Bind 1, Schimmelmann's Placat, 26 May 1786. On the "Spansk Kappe" there is a discussion as well as an illustration in Jens Vibæk, *Reform og Fallit 1784-1830*, vol. 10 *Danmarks Historie* edited John Danstrup and Hal Koch (1971), p. 115.

38. R/A, UBAN, no. 27, Placater Anordninger og Publicationer, no. 43, St. Croix Borger Raads Forestilling, 2 December 1778.

39. R/A, UBAN, no. 17, Roepstorff's Nota, 7 February 1784.

40. Hans West, *Bidrag til Beskrivelse over Ste. Croix* (1793), p. 58.

41. R/A, Om Negerhandelens Afskaffelse 1788-1847, Anonymous Pro Memoria [1802?], f. 14.

42. Hans West, "Beretning om det danske Eilande St. Croix i Vestindien," *Iris* 3 (1791):50.

43. See for example R/A, FAN, 1785, Bind 2, Clausen's Anmærkninger, 4 May 1784, f. 143.

44. Ibid., Bind 1, "Neger Lov for de danske vestindiske Eylande af A. G. van der Oesten," cap. 1, clause 29, f. 301.

45. See Gilberto Freyre, *The Masters and the Slaves: A Study in the Development of Brazilian Civilization* (1964); Carl N. Degler, *Neither Black Nor White: Slavery and Race Relations in Brazil and the United States* (1971); Katia M. de Quierós Mattoso, *To Be a Slave in Brazil 1550-1880* (1986); Mary C. Karasch, *Slave Life in Rio de Janeiro 1808-1850* (1987), pp. 205-207, 291-95.

46. Ibid., Colbiørnsen's Anmærkninger, 24 September 1788, f. 121. Cf. ibid., Ernst Walterstorff's Betænkninger, 8 October 1788, f. 137.

47. Ibid., Colbiørnsen's Anmærkninger, 24 September 1788, f. 121.

48. Haagensen, *Beskrivelse*, p. 63; N/A, RG 55, Boxes 583-86, Commission for the Enumeration of the Free

49. R/A, FAN, 1785, Bind 1, "Neger Lov," cap. 3, clause 115, f. 334. Cf. Higman, *Slave Populations*, pp. 147-57.

50. R/A, FAN, 1785, Bind 2, Colbiørnsen's Anmærkninger, 24 September 1788, ff. 103-104.

51. Ibid., f. 104.

52. Ibid., Bind 1, "Neger Lov," cap. 1, clause 30, f. 301.

53. West, "Beretning," p. 42.

54. West, *Bidrag*, pp. 57-58, Cf. Karasch, *Slave Life*, pp. 199-203; Claudia Dale Goldin, *Urban Slavery in the American South, 1820-1860* (1976), p. 18.

55. West, *Bidrag*, pp. 58-59.

56. See chapter 5.

57. West, *Bidrag*, p. 59.

58. Haagensen, *Beskrivelse*, p. 66.

59. Huckstering was the more highly favored occupation since it did not require a fixed asset in the form of owner-occupied housing or accommodation of the sort needed to board lodgers. References to both forms of endeavor can be found for example in R/A, UBAN, no. 27, Placater Anordninger og Publicationer, no. 43, Borger Raads Forestilling, 2 December 1778; and R/A, Den engelske Okkupation, ff. 10-12, 14-16, 18-20.

60. N/A, RG 55, Box 558, Regulatory Functions: Sea Pass Protocols for Vessels, 1782-1806, 1806-7, 1815-68. Whereas there was a solitary St. Croix freedman, William Cruse, as ship master in the late 1790s, there were ten by 1805: ibid., 1782-1806, ff. 41-51, 92-104.

61. Oxholm, *De Danske Vestindiske*, "Statistisk Tabelle." See also chapters 1 and 5.

62. Marvin Harris, *Patterns of Race in the Americas* (1964), pp. 86-89. Cf.Roger Norman Buckley, *Slaves in Red Coats: The British West India Regiments, 1795-1815* (1979).

63. R/A, UBAN, no. 27, Placater Anordninger og Publicationer, no. 29, de Gunthelberg's Placat, 9 May 1765; ibid., no. 37, Clausen's Placat, 20 January 1774; R/A, FAN, 1785, Bind 1, Schimmelmann's

64. See Larsen, *Virgin Islands Story*, pp. 57-58; R/A, UBAN, no. 27, Placater Anordninger og Publicationer, no. 37, Clausen's Placat, 20 January 1774, clause 4.

65. N/A, RG 55, Boxes 485-87, Udskrift af Christiansteds Jurisdictions; ibid., Boxes 496-97, Udskrift af Frederiksteds Jurisdictions.

66. R/A, UBAN, no. 27, Placater Anordninger og Publicationer, no. 29, de Gunthelberg's Placat, 9 May 1765.

67. I. C. Schmidt, "Blandede Anmærkninger, samlede paa og over Ejlandet St. Croix i Amerika 1788," *Samleren* 2 (1788):231.

68. Ibid.

69. Frederik V's "Reglement for Slaverne" had only made such evidence admissible by indirection: R/A, UBAN, no. 2, 3 February 1755, para. 45. However, the ordinance was never promulgated.

70. R/A, Haandskriftsamlingen, Species facti over den paa Eilandet Sainte Croix Aaret 1759 intenderede Neger Rebellion.

71. West, "Beretning," p. 49. Emphases in the original.

CHAPTER 9

1. R/A, AVS/FC. See also N. A. T. Hall, "The 1816 Freedman Petition in the Danish West Indies: Its Background and Consequences," *Boletin de Estudios Latinoamericanos y del Caribe* 29 (1980):64.

2. R/A, Diverse Dokumenter, Om Negerhandelens Afskaffelse 1788-1847, Letter to Commission for Danish West Indian Slave Law, Anonymous Pro Memoria [1802?], f. 2.

3. Ibid., f. 3.

4. Ibid., ff. 14-15.

5. Ibid., f. 15.

6. *DVRA*, 8 February 1803.

7. R/A, Den engelske Okkupation 1801-1807, Capt. Roeder, 5th Line Battalion, to Generaltoldkammer/CC, 8 November 1844; ibid., Danish West Indian Government, Deliberations

Protocoller, 17 December 1807; ibid., Encl., Copie af et den 15de December 1807 i undersøgelses Commission i Sagen mod Baron Friderich de Bretton Junior fremlagt preliminanter Forhør optaget af Hr. Regeringsraad Bentzon og Kammerraad Smidt: St. Croix, Christiansted den 15de December 1807.

8. R/A, Om Negerhandelens Afskaffelse 1788-1847, Anonymous Pro Memoria [1802?], ff. 3, 16.

9. H. F. Garde, "Anna Heegaard og Peter von Scholten," *Personalhistorisk Tidsskrift*, 13 Række, Bind 6 (1958):28; R/A, DVK, Adrian Bentzon, "Om Negerne paa de Danske Øer i Vestindien," 24 July 1802.

10. R/A, DVK, Bentzon "Om Negerne," 24 July 1802.

11. N/A, RG 55, Box 496, Udskrift af Frederiksted Jurisdictions Politi Journaler, 22 and 23 June 1802.

12. N/A, RG 55, Box 485, Udskrift af Christiansteds Jurisdictions Politi Journaler, 9 and 12 March 1805.

13. Ibid., 3 March 1806. Cf. ibid., 18 March 1807.

14. See chapter 7.

15. N/A, RG 55, Box 485, Udskrift af Christiansteds Jurisdictions Politi Journaler, 14 September 1805, enclosing Rogiers' affidavit 30 September 1805.

16. Ibid., 25 August 1806, 25 December 1806, 1 January 1807.

17. Ibid., 12 January 1805, 24 and 30 December 1805, 30 July 1807.

18. Ibid., 24 September 1805, 4 June 1806, 14 Septembr 1806, 1 January 1807.

19. Ibid., 11 April 1807.

20. N/A, RG 55, Box 487, Udskrift af Christiansteds Jurisdictions Politi Journaler, 8 March 1802.

21. N/A, RG 55, Box 496, Udskrift af Frederiksteds Jurisdictions Politi Journaler, 13 January 1797; N/A, RG 55, Box 487, Udskrift af Christiansteds Jurisdictions Politi Journaler, 1 August 1802; N/A, RG 55, Box 485, Udskrift af Christiansteds Jurisdictions Politi Journaler, 17 October 1805.

22. R/A, Om Negerhandelens Afskaffelse 1788-1847, Anonymous

Pro Memoria [1802?], f. 11. See also Svend E. Green-Pedersen, "Slave Demography in the Danish West Indies and the Abolition of the Danish Slave Trade," in *The Abolition of the Atlantic Slave Trade* edited David Eltis and James Walvin (1981), p. 234-37.

23. For Christiansted examples see N/A, RG 55, Box 485, Udskrift af Christiansteds Jurisdictions Politi Journaler, 8 May 1805, 25 July 1805, 21 August 1805, 8 September 1805, 29 October 1805, 6 and 11 April 1807.

24. Cf. Richard C. Wade, *Slavery in the Cities: The South 1820-1860* (1964), pp. 94-96.

25. R/A, DVK, Bentzon, "Om Negerne," 24 July 1802.

26. R/A, Om Negerhandelens Afskaffelse 1788-1847, Anonymous Pro Memoria [1802?], ff. 8-9, 15.

27. N/A, RG 55, Box 496, Udskrift af Frederiksteds Jurisdictions Politi Journaler, 20 June 1804.

28. N/A, RG 55, Box 485, Udskrift af Christiansteds Jurisdictions Politi Journaler, 3 January 1805, 2 June 1806, 17 December 1806, 12 August 1807.

29. Ibid., 19 June 1805, 13 August 1807.

30. Ibid., 26 October 1805, 29 May 1806, 21 October 1806; N/A, RG 55, Box 496, Udskrift af Frederiksteds Jurisdictions Politi Journaler, 20 June 1804.

31. N/A, RG 55, Box 496, Udskrift af Frederiksteds Jurisdictions Politi Journaler, 24 December 1805.

32. N/A, RG 55, Box 485, Udskrift af Christiansteds Jurisdictions Politi Journaler, 21 April 1806.

33. Ibid.

34. Hall, "The 1816 Freedman Petition."

35. N/A, RG 55, Box 485, Udskrift af Christiansteds Jurisdictions Politi Journaler, 12 December 1805, 14 September 1806, 10 January 1807.

36. Ibid., 22 and 25 May 1806; N/A, RG 55, Box 496, Udskrift af Frederiksteds Jurisdictions Politi Journaler, 4 April 1807. (Filed with Christiansted.)

37. N/A, RG 55, Box 485, Udskrift af Christiansteds Jurisdictions Politi Journaler, 7 September 1806, 20 November 1806.

38. Ibid., 1 May 1807.
39. N/A, RG 55, Box 487, Udskrift af Christiansteds Jurisdictions Politi Journaler, 19 July 1802.
40. See chapter 6.
41. See for example N/A, RG 55, Box 485, Udskrift af Christiansteds Jurisdictions Politi Journaler, 9, 13, 19 and 23 October 1806.
42. Ibid., 28 October 1805; N/A, RG 55, Box 496, Udskrift af Frederiksteds Jurisdictions Politi Journaler, 8 and 11 March 1805, and enclosures.
43. N/A, RG 55, Box 485, Udskrift af Christiansteds Jurisdictions Politi Journaler, 17 December 1806.
44. Ibid., 15 May 1805.
45. N/A, RG 55, Box 496, Udskrift af Frederiksteds Jurisdictions Politi Journaler 13, 16 and 23 January 1797, and enclosures.
46. Ibid., 10 April 1802. This report is badly water damaged and cannot be read in its entirety.
47. N/A, RG 55, Box 485, Udskrift af Christiansteds Jurisdictions Politi Journaler, 19 July 1806 (filed in Christiansted), 10 January 1807.
48. R/A, UBAN, no. 27, de Gunthelberg's Placat, 9 February 1765, preamble.
49. N/A, RG 55, Box 496, Udskrift af Frederiksteds Jurisdictions Politi Journaler, 2 January 1804. It might also have been "Black Loaf," the writing is indistinct.
50. R/A, DVK, Bentzon, "Om Negerne," 24 July 1802.
51. R/A, Den engelske Okkupation, capitulations of 29 March 1801 (St. Thomas), 31 March 1801 (St. Croix).
52. SCG, 22 June 1813, 3 August 1813.
53. Ibid., 8 March 1815.
54. R/A, AVS/FC, Ch. Holten to P. L. Oxholm, 18 July 1815, enclosure 12 in Oxholm to Danish West Indian Government, 13 September 1815; ibid., J. W. Mouritzen to Oxholm, 2 September 1815, enclosure D in Oxholm to Danish West Indian Government, 3 January 1816.
55. Ibid., Mouritzen to Oxholm, 27 September 1815, enclosure D in Oxholm to Danish West Indian Government, 3 January 1816.

56. SCG, 8 June 1810. Cf. ibid., 6 July 1813.
57. Ibid., 8 February 1811.
58. Jerome S. Handler, The Unappropriated People: Freedmen in the Slave Society of Barbados (1974); Sheila Duncker, The Free Coloured and Their Struggle for Civil Rights in Jamaica (M.A. dissertation, University of London, 1960); James Millette, The Genesis of Crown Colony Government: Trinidad 1783-1810 (1970).
59. Johan Peter Nissen, Reminiscences of a 46 years' residence in the island of St. Thomas in the West Indies (1838), p. 46; Jamaica Government Archives, Spanish Town, Calendar of Records, High Court of Vice Admiralty, Jamaica 1796; N/A, RG 55, Box 558, Regulatory Functions: Sea Pass Protocols for Vessels, 1782-1868.
60. DVRA, 15 January 1816, Oxholm's proclamation of 15 January 1816.
61. R/A, AVS/FC, Oxholm to Dansk Vestindisk Regering, 3 January 1816, encls. H and K, Petitions of seven jailed freedmen; ibid., Extract af Gen. Gouvernementets Referat Protocol, 1815, No. 650, 12 December 1815.
62. DVRA, 15 January 1816, Oxholm's proclamation.
63. R/A, AVS/FC. The petition and its appendices are unpaginated. Further references to them are therefore not footnoted.
64. R/A, FAN, Bind 1, Colbiørnsen's Anmærkninger, 24 September 1788.
65. R/A, AVS/FC, Oxholm to Danish West Indian Government, 3 January 1816, encl. C, Draft proclamation, para. 5; DVRA, 28 August 1817.
66. DVRA, 6 October 1817; 14 February 1825; 13 July 1826; 2 January 1832. Nissen, Reminiscences, pp. 63-65, 165, pointed out that between 1804 and 1832 more than $30 million in property were destroyed in the Danish West Indies by fire.
67. DVRA, 28 August 1817.
68. Neville A. T. Hall, Forslag til Ordning af Vestindiske Forfatnings forhold Angaaende Negerne med Mere (1979).

69. R/A, VLA, Dansk Vestindisk Regerings Protocoller, 3 June 1833, ff. 127, 129.

70. E. V. Lose, "Kort Udsigt over den danske-lutherske Missions Historie," *Nordisk Missions-Tidsskrift* 1 (1890):29.

71. R/A, AVS/FC, von Scholten to Frederik VI, 2 July 1833, Enclosure 20, Magens to von Scholten, 2 June 1833.

72. A fuller account is in Neville A. T. Hall, "Apollo Miller, Freedman: His Life and Times," *Journal of Caribbean History* 23 (1989):196-213.

73. *STT*, 8 June 1820.

74. *DVRA*, 9 January 1826.

75. Ibid., 20 October 1828.

76. H. B. Dahlerup, *Mit Livs Begivenheder* (1909), vol. 2, p. 47.

77. Garde, "Anna Heegaard," p. 28; Dahlerup, *Mit Livs*, vol. 2, p. 78.

78. Garde, "Anna Heegaard," p. 34.

79. Ibid., pp. 31-32.

80. N. A. T. Hall, "Anna Heegaard – Enigma," *Caribbean Quarterly*, 22 (2 and 3) (1976):66-69.

81. See Duncker, *The Free Coloured;* Gad J. Heuman, *Between Black and White: Race, Politics, and the Free Coloreds in Jamaica, 1792-1865* (1981), p. 48; Edward L. Cox, *Free Coloreds in the Slave Societies of St. Kitts and Grenada, 1763-1833* (1984), p. 105.

82. Peter von Scholten, *Most submissive Report Proposing an Improved and More distinct Organisation for Your Majesty's Free Coloured Subjects in the West India Colonies* (1830).

83. R/A, AVS/FC, Kongelige Rescript, 10 April 1830; ibid., Freedmen's address 13 May 1831. For the crown's acceptance see ibid., Frederik VI to Generaltoldkammer, 25 February 1832.

84. Peter von Scholten, *Plan for an improved and more distinct Organisation for the Free Coloured Inhabitants of the Danish West India Islands: St. Croix, St. Thomas and St. John's submitted agreeably to His Majesty, the King's most gracious command* (1831).

85. *Fædrelandet*, 21 October 1840.

86. R/A, AVS/FC, Kongelige Rescript, 7 February 1832; 12 May 1832.

87. Ibid., Peter von Scholten, "Udkast til allunderdanigst Forslag angaanede Friecouleurte," 18 March 1833, especially paras. 2, 3.

88. Ibid., von Scholten to Frederik VI, 7 July 1833, Enclosures 16, 17 and 26.

89. Ibid., von Scholten to Frederik VI, 7 July 1833. Cf. ibid., *Allerunderdanigst Forslag til endelig Bestemmelse for Deres Majestæts Friecouleutre Und ersaaters Borgerlig Stilling i Colonierne*, 7 July 1833.

90. A. S. Ørsted (ed.) *Collegial-Tidende for Danmark* (1840), 26 April 1834, p. 296.

91. J. H. Schou, ed., *Chronologisk Register over de Kongelige Forordninger og Aabne Breve* (1848), Kongelig Forordning, 18 April 1834, pp. 50-51.

92. C. van Dockum, *Livserindringer* (1893), p. 64. One such appointment was Capt. Hans Petersen, a clerk in the public service, cousin to Anna Heegaard and a member of von Scholten's "inner cabinet." See Garde, "Anna Heegaard," p. 31 and Herman Lawaetz, *Peter v. Scholten* (1940), pp. 61, 190, 222 ff.

93. H. B. Dahlerup, "Skizzer fra et kort Besøg paa vore vestindiske Øer i Sommeren 1841," *Nyt Archiv for Søvæsenet* 1 (1842):30-31.

94. R/A, AVS/FC, von Scholten to Frederik VI, 7 July 1833, enclosing Magens to von Scholten, 2 June 1833.

95. Dockum, *Livserindringer*, pp. 64-65.

96. Dahlerup, *Mit Livs*, pp. 274-75.

97. Dockum, *Livserindringer*, p. 65.

CHAPTER 10

1. R/A, Den engelske Okkupation 1801-1807, C. G. Fleischer's "Enumeration of the Able-bodied Male Freedmen of St. Thomas," 28 May 1802.

2. R/A, AVS/FC, Generaltoldkammer to Governor General Walterstorff; ibid., Christian VII to Walterstorff, 10 January 1803.

3. R/A, Den engelske Okkupation 1801, 1807, Casimir von Scholten's Memorandum, 11 January 1801; ibid., Minutes of St. Thomas Borger Raad, 13 March 1801; ibid., Generaltoldkammer to Christian VII, 14 June 1801.

4. Ibid., Casimir von Scholten's "Deduction," 20 May 1802.
5. Ibid., "État des Français de Couleur qui sont passagères où en Résidence á St. Tomas," 31 October 1800, enclosed with von Scholten to Citoyen Michel, 27 October 1800.
6. Ibid., Casimir von Scholten's "Deduction," 20 May 1802.
7. Ibid., Fleischer's "Enumeration," 28 May 1802: Occupations.
8. N/A, RG 55, Box 585, St. Thomas Commission for the Registering of the Free Coloured, 1803. Summary, 16 June 1803.
9. Ibid., f. 3.
10. Ibid.
11. N/A, RG 55, Box 585, St. Thomas Commission for the Registering of the Free Coloured, 1803, f. 4.
12. R/A, AVS/FC, Oxholm to Generaltoldkammer, 13 September 1815, enclosing Holten to Oxholm, 18 July 1815.
13. R/A, Diverse sager, Forskellige Oplysninger VI, f. 120.
14. R/A, AVS/FC, Comments of J. W. Mouritzen, 27 September 1815, Enclosure D in Oxholm's circular to the Danish West Indian Government, 3 January 1816: "Hos de Øvrige har Trodsighed og Overmod traade i stedet."
15. Ibid., Oxholm to Generaltoldkammer, 13 September 1815 enclosing Holten to Oxholm, 18 July 1815.
16. SCG, 3 August 1813.
17. DVRA, 8 March 1815.
18. Ibid., AVS/FC, Generaltoldkammer to Oxholm, 19 February 1815; ibid., "Om Frinegere eller som de kaldes frie couleurte paa de danske vestindiske Øer," [1815?].
19. Ibid., Oxholm to Generaltoldkammer, 13 September 1815.
20. Ibid.
21. Ibid.
22. Ibid.
23. Ibid., enclosing, "Anordning hvorved Frie-Negerne paa de danske Amerikanske Eilande Forsikres deres Frieheds Stand, samt adskillig ved Negernes Frigivelse sammesteds i Svang gaaende Misbrug hemmes," 10 October 1776.
24. Ibid., enclosing Oxholm to Holten, 29 July 1815; Holten to Oxholm, 30 July 1815; Oxholm to Holten, 3 August 1815; Holten to Oxholm, 7 August 1815; Oxholm to Holten, 16 August 1815; Holten to Oxholm, 25 August 1815; Generaltoldkammer to Oxholm, 19 December 1815.
25. Ibid., Oxholm to Generaltoldkammer, 15 January 1815 (reported in Generaltoldkammer to Oxholm, 19 December 1815), 13 September 1815.
26. In this Oxholm anticipated Governor General von Scholten's initial proposals in 1830 in which he advised the King that "Only the second generation of persons, emancipated by gift or purchase, can ascend to the first division, unless the first generation proceeds from parents lawfully married, and of known good conduct, or unless the Governor General deems an individual of this description deserving of such advancement." Peter von Scholten, Most Submissive Report proposing an improved and more distinct organization for Your Majesty's Free Coloured Subjects in the West Indian Colonies (1830), "Regulations for Emancipation."
27. R/A, AVS/FC, Oxholm to Generaltoldkammer, 29 March 1816.
28. Ibid., Generaltoldkammer to Oxholm, 19 December 1815, quoting para. 9 of the Ordinance of 10 October 1776.
29. Ibid., Generaltoldkammer to Oxholm, 18 May 1816.
30. Ibid., Oxholm to Generaltoldkammer, 29 March 1816, 18 April 1816.
31. Ibid.
32. Ibid., Comments of Oberst Stabell, 8 March 1816, entered in Dansk Vestindisk Regerings Deliberations Protocoller, 10 March 1816.
33. Ibid.
34. Ibid., Petition of the Free People of Colour of the Danish West Indies, 1 April 1816.
35. Ibid., Oxholm's Proclamation, 15 January 1816; ibid., Comments of Oberst Stabell, 8 March 1816, entered in Dansk Vestindisk

Regerings Deliberations Protocoller, 10 March 1816. See also chapter 9.

36. *DVRA*, 15 January 1816, Oxholm's Proclamation of 15 January 1816.

37. R/A, AVS/FC, von Holten to Oxholm, 18 July 1815, enclosed in Oxholm to Generaltoldkammer, 13 September 1815.

38. Ibid., Bentzon's "Betænkning," no. 3, 18 February 1818.

39. Ibid., von Holten to Generaltoldkammer, 2 May 1816.

40. Ibid.

41. J. J. Gurney, *A Winter in the West Indies* (1840), p. 28; James Smith, *The Winter of 1840 in St. Croix* (1840), p. 16; R/A, Akter Vedkommende Slaveemancipationen 1834-1847, II, von Scholten to Commissionen Angaaende Negernes Stilling, 30 November 1839, 9 March 1840. Cf. J. H. Parry and P. M. Sherlock, *A Short History of the West Indies* (1956), pp. 184, 186.

42. R/A, Akter Vedkommende Slaveemancipationen, 1834-1847, von Scholten to Commission, 9 March 1840.

43. Mary Turner, *Slaves and Missionaries: The Disintegration of Jamaican Slave Society 1787-1834* (1982), p. 27.

44. See for example D. Cartwright and A. Zander, *Group Dynamics* (1968), pp. 48 et seq., et passim.

45. R/A, VLA, Dansk Vestindisk Regerings Protocoller, 3 June 1833, f. 131.

46. John Peter Nissen, *Reminiscences of a 46 years' residence in the island of St. Thomas, in the West Indies* (1838), p. 207. The women, to have been analyzed in a separate study in progress, constituted 34.8 percent (500 of 1,438), and their children less than 5 percent (36 of 803). The entire foreign cohort of emigres of all ages was exactly one third of the total freedman population (1,136 of 3,408).

47. Roger Norman Buckley, *Slaves in Red Coats: The British West India Regiments, 1795-1815* (1979), pp. 131-39.

48. Nissen, *Reminiscences*, p. 165.

49. R/A, VLA, Dansk Vestindisk Regerings Protocoller, 3 June 1833,

Comments of Regeringsraad J. W. Mouritzen.

50. R/A, AVS/FC, Lange's Circular Memorandum, 21 January 1834.

51. "Forordning angaaende nærmere Bestemmelse af de Friefarvedes borgelige Stilling paa de danske vestindiske Øer," *Chronologisk Register over de Kongelige Forordninger og Aabne Breve*, edited J. H. Schou (1848):50-51.

CHAPTER 11

1. H. B. Dahlerup, *Mit Livs Begivenheder* (1909) vol. 2, pp. 297-99; *DVRA*, 1 and 3 June 1841. For a fuller version of this chapter, see N. A. T. Hall, "Establishing a Public Elementary School System for Slaves in the Danish Virgin Islands 1732-1846," *Caribbean Journal of Education* 6 (1979):1-45.

2. *RDAG*, 6 and 27 January 1773, 2 March 1776.

3. Preben Ramløv, *Brødrene og Slaverne* (1968), p. 203. See also Hans West, *Tiltrædelsestale holden da Skolen i Christianstæd paa St. Croix blev aabnet den 8de October 1789* (1789).

4. H. Lawaetz, *Brødremenighedens Mission i Dansk Vestindien* (1902), p. 165. See also chapter 2.

5. E. V. Lose, "Kort Udsigt over den danske-lutherske Missions Historie paa St. Croix, St. Thomas og St. Jan," *Nordisk Missions-Tidsskrift* 1 (1890):16.

6. Lawaetz, *Brødremenighedens Mission*, p. 22.

7. A comprehensive list of titles published in creole is to be found in Jens Vibæk, *Dansk Vestindien 1755-1848*, vol. 2 *Vore Gamle Tropekolonier*, edited Johannes Brøndsted (1966), pp. 349-51. See also Thorkild Hansen, *Slavernes Øer* (1970), p. 143; Lose, *Kort Udsigt*, pp. 20-21, 36.

8. Lawaetz, *Brødremenighedens Mission*, p. 166.

9. Ibid., p. 166; Lose, *Kort Udsigt*, p. 30; Christian Degn, *Die Schimmelmanns in Atlantischen Dreickshandel: Gewinn und Gewissen* (1974).

10. Svend Cedergreen Bech, *Oplysning og tolerance 1721-1784*, vol. 9 *Danmarks Historie*, edited John

Danstrup and Hal Koch (1965), pp. 58, 96-102, 235-44; Vibæk, *Dansk Vestindien 1755-1848*, p. 214.

11. R/A, UBAN, no. 2, Reglement for Slaverne, 3 February 1755, para. 1.

12. Lose, *Kort Udsigt*, pp. 13-16.

13. R/A, VJ, 1796, no. 184.

14. Ibid., 1793, no. 139. Jens Larsen has argued, mistakenly in this writer's view, that the royal ordinance of 21 December 1787 authorizing the selection of four acceptable freedmen as school managers was "the first attempt ... at introducing public schools for slaves:" Jens Larsen, *Virgin Islands Story* (1950), pp. 97-98. While the principle of slave education had been long conceded, it had not yet been acknowledged, even as late as the end of the 1780s, that slave education should be a charge on public funds.

15. R/A, VJ, 1798, nos. 195, 431.

16. Ibid., 1798, nos. 431, 743.

17. R/A, DVK, 14 A, P. L. Oxholm's "General Tabell, St. Croix, 31 December 1792." Oxholm's figures, however, are of questionable reliability for the reason that after the Slave Trade Abolition Ordinance of 1792, he consistently maintained that the slave labor force was inadequate for the colonies' needs.

18. R/A, VJ, 1798, no. 431.

19. Ibid., no. 743.

20. Ibid., 1803, no. 7312: "Af mangel altsaa paa et beqvemt Sted til en Lære-Anstalt blev den heele Sag da udsat." See also ibid., 1805, no. 1865.

21. R/A, Vestindisk Kopibøger 1838, no. 91, letter to the Danish Chancellery, 24 February 1838, f. 53.

22. Lose, *Kort Udsigt*, pp. 16, 17. See also *Thottske Samling*, 816 L B, 20 March 1755, f. 7.

23. Lawaetz, *Brødremenighedens Mission*, p. 166.

24. Jens Vibæk, *Reform og Fallit 1784-1839*, vol. 10 *Danmarks Historie* edited John Danstrup and Hal Koch (1971), pp. 425-34.

25. This aspect of the abolition movement has been curiously neglected in recent writing on the Danish Slave Trade and its abolition,

and even Svend Green-Pedersen, who has written most on this subject within recent times, does not in my view emphasize sufficiently this dimension of the abolition movement. See for example Green-Pedersen, "The Economic Considerations behind the Danish Abolition of the Negro Slave Trade" in *The Uncommon Market: Essays in the Economic History of the Atlantic Slave Trade*, edited Henry A. Gemery and Jan S. Hogendorn (1979).

26. Ramløv, *Brødrene*, p. 91.

27. Lawaetz, *Brødremenighedens Mission*, pp. 162-63.

28. R/A, CANS, 1, Afskrift af de af Generalgouverneuren forfattede Udkast til en Emancipations Plan for Slaverne paa de danske vestindiske Øer, 13 October 1834. Cf. R/A, Møstingske Papirer (b), Forestillinger om Forandringer i Slavernes Kaar med bilag, 18 November 1834.

29. R/A, Møstingske Papirer (b), Forestillinger om Forandringer i Slavernes Kaar med bilag, 18 November 1834; R/A, CANS, Afskrift af de af Generalgouverneuren forfattede Udkast til en Emancipations Plan for Slaverne paa de danske vestindiske Øer, 13 October 1834, enclosing Bønhoff to von Scholten, 2 May 1834. Cf. R/A, CANS, 4, Kommissionens Betænkning, 13 November 1834, f. 103.

30. R/A, CANS, 2, Kongelig Rescript, 15 October 1834.

31. Ibid., 4, Kommissionens Betænkning, 13 November 1834, ff. 111, 138.

32. Ibid., 5, von Scholten's Indberetning, 2 January 1839, Enclosure 15, 23 May 1838, ff. 206-10; ibid., Enclosure 14, Placat, 23 May 1838, ff. 202-203.

33. Ibid., Enclosure 14, Placat, 23 May 1838, f. 29.

34. *Berlingske Tidende*, 15 September 1846: article by H. B. Dahlerup.

35. R/A, CANS, von Scholten's Indberetning, 2 January 1839, Enclosure 12, 1 May 1838, f. 186; ibid., Enclosure 13, 7 May 1838, f. 199.

36. *Berlingske Tidende,* 15 September 1841: article by H. B. Dahlerup. Cf. Gwendolyn Midlo Hall, *Social Control in Slave Plantation Societies: A Comparison of St. Domingue and Cuba* (1971), p. 51.

37. U. N. Fugl, "Om Negerslaveriet i Vestindien og sammes Ophør; med specielt Hensyn til de danske Besiddelser," *Juridisk Tidsskrift* 24B, 1 H (1834):26-27. See also Mary Turner, *Slaves and Missionaries: The Disintegration of Jamaican Slave Society 1787-1834* (1982); David Nicholls, *From Dessalines to Duvalier: Race, Colour and National Independence in Haiti* (1979).

38. R/A, Akter vedkommende Slaveemancipation 1834-1847, II, von Scholten to Commissioners, Enclosure, Draft Proclamation n/d; James Smith, *The Winter of 1840 in St. Croix* (1840), p. 16.

39. *Berlingske Tidende,* 15 September 1841: article by H.B. Dahlerup.

40. R/A, CANS, von Scholten's Indberetning, 2 January 1839, Enclosure 12 to Burgher Council, 1 May 1839, f. 193.

41. R/A, Vestindisk Kopibog 1838, no. 91, letter to the Danish Chancellery, 24 February 1838, f. 57.

42. H. B. Dahlerup, "Skizzer fra et kort Besøg paa vore vestindiske Øer i Sommeren 1841," *Nyt Archiv for Søvæsenet* 1 (1842):28.

43. R/A, CANS, 10, Kongelig Rescript, 8 June 1839.

44. R/A, CANS, 5, von Scholten's Indberetning, 2 January 1839, Enclosure 12 to Burgher Council, 1 May 1838, ff. 190-91; Lawaetz, *Brødremenighedens Mission,* p. 167; Smith, *The Winter of 1840,* p. 30.

45. R/A, CANS, 5, von Scholten's Indberetning, 2 January 1839, Enclosure 17, ff. 217-76.

46. C. H. Holten, "Af en gammel Hofmands Mindeblade (Konferensraad Carl Henrik Holtens Optegnelser), vol. 11 *Memoirer og Breve,* edited J. Clausen and P. F. Rist (1909), p. 171; Smith, *The Winter of 1840,* p. 30; Roar Skovmand, *Folkestyrets Fødsel 1830-1870,* vol. 11 *Danmarks Historie,* edited John Danstrup and Hal Koch (1971); R/A, Privatarkiv 6795, Princess Caroline Amalie to von Scholten, 27 February 1839.

47. *Fædrelandet,* 15, 22 and 29 December 1840, 14 August 1841.

48. Ibid., 19 March 1841.

49. *Fædrelandet,* 14 August 1841.

50. *DVRA,* 29 January 1829.

51. *Fædrelandet,* 19 March 1841.

52. C. van Dockum, *Livserindringer* (1893), p. 66.

53. R/A, Akter Vedkommende Slaveemancipationen 1834-1847, III, Folkemængden paa de danske-vestindiske Øer efter Folketælling, 1 October 1841.

54. *Fædrelandet,* 13 October 1840, Negerslaveriet i Vestindien, I.

55. R/A, CANS, von Scholten to Christian VIII, 15 January 1841, Enclosure 1, 29 July 1840. See also *Fædrelandet,* 13 October 1840.

56. R/A, Akter Vedkommende Slaveemancipationen 1834-1847, III, Fortegnelse over Plantagerne paa St. Croix, deres Eiere og Negerantal i Aaret 1840; R/A, CANS, von Scholten to Christian VIII, 15 January 1841, Enclosure 4, 9 September 1840.

57. R/A, CANS, von Scholten to Christian VIII, 15 January 1841, Enclosure 3, 29 October 1840.

58. Ibid., Enclosure 6, n/d, ff. 5-6, 9.

59. R/A, CANS, Sarauw's Meddelelse til Kongen, 31 December 1840.

60. Ibid., von Scholten to Christian VIII, 15 January 1841, Enclosure 6, n/d; Enclosure 10, September 1840.

61. Ibid., Enclosure 11, n/d (signed B. L.); Sarauw's Meddelelse, 31 December 1840.

62. R/A, Indiske Forestillinger og Resolutioner 1845-1846, 53c, 30 December 1846: "der er Anledning til at antage, at flere Plantere betragte enhver til Ungdommens Opdragelse Foranstaltning med Mistaenklighed, fordi de fuldtvel indsaa, at naar et velordnet Underviisningsvaesen er etableret og har baaret Frugter, er en af de vigtigste Hindringer for de sociale Forholds friere Udvkling i Colonierne bortryddet."

63. R/A, Privatarkiv 6795, Christian VIII to von Scholten, no. 10, 11 May 1843.
64. A. S. Ørsted, ed., *Collegial-Tidende for Danmark*, 23 March 1844, pp. 259-60.
65. R/A, Indiske Forestillinger og Resolutioner 1845-1846, 53a, paras. 1-5. The Ordinance is undated.
66. Ibid., paras. 37-42.
67. Ibid., paras. 6-12.
68. R/A, Indiske Forestillinger og Resolutioner 1845-1846, 52c.
69. Ibid., 53a, paras. 25-36; Herman Lawaetz, *Peter von Scholten* (1940), p. 153.
70. R/A, Indiske Forestillinger og Resolutioner 1845-1846, 53a, paras. 13-19, 24.
71. R/A, VJ, 1796, no. 184.
72. Cf. Elsa V. Goveia, *Slave Society in the British Leeward Islands at the End of the Eighteenth Century* (1965), p. 329.
73. *St. Croix Avis*, 20 September 1847.
74. Dockum, *Livserindringer*, p. 67.
75. See for example Lawaetz, *Peter v. Scholten*, p. 165.

CHAPTER 12

1. Bernhard von Petersen, *En Historisk Beretning om de danske vestindiske Øer St. Croix, St. Thomas og St. Jan* (1855), pp. 94-142; Kay Larsen, *Dansk Vestindien 1666-1917* (1928), pp. 252-67; Herman Lawaetz, *Peter v. Scholten. Vestindiske Tidsbilleder fra den sidste Generalguvernørs Dage* (1940), pp. 174-91; Jens Vibæk, *Dansk Vestindien 1755-1848*, vol. 2 *Vore Gamle Tropekolonier* edited Johannes Brøndsted (1966), pp. 286-96; Thorkild Hansen, *Slavernes Øer* (1970), pp. 355-96.
2. Michael Craton, *Testing the Chains: Resistance to Slavery in the British West Indies* (1982), pp. 254-321. See also Hilary Beckles, *Black Rebellion in Barbados: The Struggle Against Slavery, 1627-1838* (1984); Neville A. T. Hall, review of David Barry Gaspar, *Bondmen and Rebels* in *Journal of Economic History* 46 (1986):1054-56.
3. R/A, NEER.
4. R/A, CANS, 1834-1843, passim.
5. A. S. Ørsted, ed., *Collegial-Tidende for Danmark* (1840), pp. 259-61; Victor

Schoelcher, *Colonies étrangères et Haïti*, vol. 2 (1843), pp. 20-21. See also chapter 11.
6. R/A, CANS, Afskrift af det af Generalgouverneuren forfattede Udkast til en Emancipations Plan for Slaverne paa de danske vestindiske Øer, 13 October 1834; Commissions Betænkning, 13 November 1834; Hans Jensen, *De danske Stænderforsamlingers Historie 1830-1848*, vol. 2 (1931-34), pp. 608-611.
7. R/A, Haandskriftsamlingen, Species facti over den paa Eilandet Sainte Croix Aaret 1760 intenderede Neger Rebellion, forfattet efter Ordre af Byfoget Engelbreth Hesselbjerg; Waldemar Westergaard, "Account of the Negro Rebellion on St. Croix Danish West Indies 1759," *Journal of Negro History* 11 (1926): 50-61.
8. Peter Wilson, *Crab Antics: The Social Anthropology of English Speaking Negro Societies of the Caribbean* (1973).
9. Mary Turner, *Slaves and Missionaries: The Disintegration of Jamaican Slave Society 1787-1834* (1982).
10. See chapter 1.
11. John V. Lombardi, *The Decline and Abolition of Negro Slavery in Venezuela 1820-1834* (1971), pp. 48-53; Frank Klingberg, *The Anti-Slavery Movement in England* (1968), p. 182.
12. Craton, *Testing the Chains*, p. 251.
13. Petersen, *En Historisk Beretning*, pp. 94-142; Larsen, *Dansk Vestindien*, pp. 252-67; Lawaetz, *Peter v. Scholten*, pp. 174-91; Vibæk, *Dansk Vestindien 1755-1848*, pp. 286-96; Hansen, *Slavernes Øer*, pp. 355-96.
14. N/A, RG 55, Box 9, Frederik Oxholm to Frederik VII, 13 and 27 July 1848; Vibæk, *Dansk Vestindien 1755-1848*, p. 296.
15. Petersen, *En Historisk Beretning*, pp. 126-27.
16. Ibid., pp. 126-29.
17. Hansen, *Slavernes Øer*, p. 394.
18. R/A, Haandskriftsamlingen, Species facti; R/A, FAN, 1785, Bind 2, Schimmelmanns Anmærkninger, 20 April 1784, f. 38; Hans West, *Bidrag til Beskrivelse over St. Croix* (1793), p. 134.
19. On the martial model, see chapter 2.

20. Fridlev Skubbeltrang, *Dansk Vestindien 1848-1880,* vol. 3 *Vore Gamle Tropekolonier,* edited Johannes Brøndsted (1967), pp. 189-218; Clifton Marsh, *A Socio-Historical Analysis of the Emancipation of 1848 and the Labor Revolts of 1878 in the Danish West Indies* (1981), pp. 78-91.

21. The transcript records are in Danish although the depositions themselves were most probably rendered in English creole, the lingua franca of St. Croix slaves long before the end of the eighteenth century (West, *Bidrag,* p. 325).

22. The Danish Slave Trade Abolition Ordinance of 1792 abolished import duties on female slaves until the trade's final cessation in 1802, and exempted such slaves from poll tax if used for field work, while doubling that tax on male slaves (Svend E. Green-Pedersen, "The Economic Considerations behind the Danish Abolition of the Negro Slave Trade," in *The Uncommon Market: Essays in the Economic History of the Atlantic Slave Trade,* edited by Henry Gemery and Jan Hogendorn [1979], p. 408). This policy reversed a well-established bias towards males in St. Croix's slave population. By 1840 of a total of 18,605, females comprised some 52.2 percent (G. W. Alexander, "Om den moralske Forpligtelse til og det hensigtmæssige af strax og fuldstændigt at ophæve Slaveriet i de danske-vestindiske Kolonier," *Dansk Ugeskrift* 2 (76) [1843]:374-96). The preponderance was even more marked in the towns of St. Croix where in 1839 they accounted for some 62.6 percent of the slave population (see chapter 5, Tables 5.4 and 5.5).

23. Lawaetz, *Peter v. Scholten,* pp. 192-216. The popular literature holds that Gotlieb Bordeaux (General Buddoe) who played a leadership role of some significance during and just after the revolt, was an intimate of the governor general's (Preben Ramløv, *Massa Peter* [1967]).

24. R/A, VLA, Dansk-vestindisk Regerings Forhandlingsprotokol St.

Croix' Militære Jurisdiktion, Frederiksfort Standret, 7 July - 12 August 1848, pp. 132, 167-68.

25. Ibid., p. 140. It certainly would not have been the first demonstration of obstructionist behavior by the plantocracy to official policy. Frederik V's 1755 *Reglement for Slaverne* was withheld for this reason (Vibæk, *Dansk Vestindien 1755-1848,* pp. 146-47), and they were not exactly models of cooperation with the governor general's reforms in the 1840s (see chapter 11).

26. R/A, VLA, Frederiksfort Standret, 7 July - 12 August 1848, pp. 176, 178-89.

27. Ibid., p. 158.

28. Ibid., p. 177.

29. Ibid., p. 39.

30. Ibid., pp. 32, 204-205.

31. Ibid., p. 111.

32. Ibid., p. 140; I. C. Schmidt, "Blandede Anmærkninger, samlede paa og over Eylandet St. Croix i America 1788," *Samleren* 2 (1788): 204.

33. R/A, VLA, Frederiksfort Standret, 7 July - 12 August 1848, p. 171.

34. Ibid., pp. 122, 132.

35. Ibid., pp. 21-22.

36. Ibid., pp. 22, 24.

37. Ibid., p. 110.

38. Petersen, *En Historisk Beretning,* p. 110.

39. R/A, VLA, Frederiksfort Standret, 7 July - 12 August 1848, p. 178.

40. Ibid., pp. 20, 28, 35, 41.

41. Ibid., pp. 38, 39.

42. Ibid., pp. 41, 42.

43. Ibid., p. 41.

44. Ibid., pp. 61, 62, 89, 120. These are the testimonies respectively of an ex-slave from Sprathall estate, a bookkeeper from the same estate, and an overseer from Adventure and Major Gyllich, Commander of Frederiksted Fire Corps.

45. Craton, *Testing the Chains,* pp. 261, 281, 300.

46. Petersen, *En Historisk Beretning,* pp. 94, 96.

47. R/A, VLA, Frederiksfort Standret, 7 July - 12 August 1848, pp. 42, 94, 140, 157, 177-78.

48. Ibid., p. 123.

49. Ibid., p. 112.

50. Ibid., p. 71.
51. Ibid., pp. 175-76.
52. Petersen, *En Historisk Beretning*, p. 102.
53. R/A, VLA, Frederiksfort Standret, 7 July - 12 August 1848, pp. 121-122.
54. Ibid., pp. 22, 29, 33-34.
55. Petersen, *En Historisk Beretning*, p. 132; Victor Prosch, "Om Slaveemancipationen paa de dansk-vestindiske Øer," *Dansk Tidsskrift* 2 (1848): 416-17.
56. Petersen, *En Historisk Beretning*, p. 101.
57. Hansen, *Slavernes Øer*, pp. 373-75.
58. R/A, VLA, Frederiksfort Standret, 7 July - 12 August 1848, p. 87.
59. Ibid., pp. 169-70.
60. Ibid., p. 36.
61. Petersen, *En Historisk Beretning*, p. 104.
62. Ibid., p. 103.
63. Craton, *Testing the Chains*, p. 258. Cf. Beckles, *Blacks Rebellion*.
64. R/A, VLA, Frederiksfort Standret, 7 July - 12 August 1848, pp. 51, 74.
65. Ibid., pp. 4, 46.
66. R/A, FAN, 1785, Bind 2, de Mallevilles Betænkninger, 29 October 1787, f. 93; *Fædrelandet*, 2 April and 17 October 1841.
67. Karen Fog Olwig, *Cultural Adaptation and Resistance on St. John* (1985), pp. 40-41.
68. R/A, VLA, Frederiksfort Standret, 7 July - 12 August 1848, p. 78.
69. Ibid., pp. 32, 46.
70. Ibid., pp. 57, 58.
71. Ibid., p. 80.
72. Ibid., pp. 10, 162-63.
73. Ibid., pp. 48, 54, 62, 71, 90.
74. Ibid., pp. 32, 38, 108, 133, 134.
75. Ibid., p. 91.
76. Ibid., p. 29.
77. Ibid., pp. 79-81.
78. Ibid., p. 16.
79. Ibid., p. 15.
80. Ibid., pp. 32, 105.
81. Ibid., p. 133.
82. Ibid., pp. 61, 101, 133, 152.
83. Ibid., pp. 79, 80, 100, 115, 134.
84. Ibid., pp. 24-26, 29, 38, 67, 81, 97, 103, 112, 126.
85. Ibid., pp. 179-80. The absence of grave dirt was significant. Its use for ritually binding engagements in the "African" period of slavery has been noted for example by Handler and Lange in the case of Barbados (Jerome S. Handler and Frederick W. Lange, *Plantation Slavery in Barbados* [1978], pp. 202, 207-208), and it figured prominently in the preparations for the 1759 St. Croix conspiracy (Monica Schuler, "Akan Slave Rebellions in the British Caribbean," *Savacou* [1970]:23). It may well be that the absence of grave dirt in 1848 constitutes a useable index of creolization at that point.
86. R/A, VLA, Frederiksfort Standret, 7 July - 12 August 1848, pp. 83, 84.
87. Ibid., pp. 59, 82.
88. Ibid., pp. 176, 179. Frederik denied the remark although Chamberlain Ferral, Van Brackle and Edward from Rosehill each independently corroborated the others' testimony.
89. Ibid., pp. 22, 82.
90. Ibid., pp. 83, 85.
91. Ibid., pp. 51, 172.
92. Ibid., p. 71.
93. Only two houses belonging to owners appear to have been destroyed: the notorious Lucas' at Mt. Pleasant and Richard Knight's at Negro Bay (Ibid., pp. 47, 121). Remarkably high levels of absenteeism seem to have prevailed in St. Croix in the 1840s, thereby reinforcing the position of overseers etc, as the predominant point of contact with white authority on the estates. Of a sample of 83 estates in St. Croix in 1840, 41 or 49.3 percent belonged to owners who were absentee. Richard Knight also appears to have been a recent purchaser of Negro Bay as in 1840 it was owned by the heirs of John Cooper and managed by Hugh Kerr, attorney for several other estates (R/A, CANS, von Scholten to Christian VIII, 15 January 1841 enclosing Proprietors and Administrators of Estates to von Scholten, 29 October 1840).
94. R/A, VLA, Frederiksfort Standret, 7 July - 12 August 1848, pp. 6, 43, 47, 48, 51, 58, 59, 69, 76, 160.
95. Ibid., pp. 10, 18, 24.
96. Ibid., pp. 8, 18, 23, 29, 72, 83, 86, 112, 115-17.

97. Ibid., 51, 115-17.
98. Ibid., p. 8.
99. Petersen, *En Historisk Beretning*, p. 117.
100. R/A, VLA, Frederiksfort Standret, 7 July - 12 August 1848, p. 135.
101. Ibid., pp. 54, 55.
102. Ibid., p. 143.
103. Ibid., pp. 71, 172-73.
104. Ibid., p. 115.
105. Ibid., p. 135.
106. Ibid., pp. 87, 116, 142-43, 174.
107. Ibid., pp. 32, 41-42, 120.

108. Ibid., p. 90.
109. Ibid., pp. 80, 96.
110. Ibid., pp. 27, 152.
111. Ibid., pp. 5, 15, 30, 38, 53, 60, 89, 179.
112. Petersen, *En Historisk Beretning*, pp. 98-99, 101, 105.
113. R/A, VLA, Frederiksfort Standret, 7 July - 12 August 1848, pp. 3, 54, 85.
114. Ibid., pp. 44, 55.
115. See chapter 9.
116. R/A, VLA, Frederiksfort Standret, 7 July - 12 August 1848, p. 105.

Bibliography

1. Manuscripts

Denmark

Rigsarkivet, Copenhagen: Danske Kancelli
D. 36. Vestindiske Sager, 1699-1771.
F. 26. Vestindiske Sager, 1773-99.

Rigsarkivet, Copenhagen: Rentekammeret. Vestindisk-guineisk Renteskriverkontor
2249.66. Vestindiske Kommissionsforretninger vedrørende salg af plantager og ulovlig handel paa St. Crox, 1759.

Rigsarkivet, Copenhagen: Generaltoldkammeret
Vestindiske Forestillinger og Resolutioner, 1760-1815.
Indiske Forestillinger og Resolutioner, 1816-48.
Vestindiske Kopibøger, 1760-1771, 1773-1848.
Vestindiske Journaler, 1760-1771, 1773-1848.
Sager til Vestindiske Journaler.
Diverse sager: Foreskellige Oplysninger I-VII, 1782-1837. Visdomsbog I.
Udkast og Betænkninger angaaende Negerloven, 1783-89.
Forslag og Anmærkninger til Negerloven med Genparter af Anordninger og Publikationer vedkommende Negervæsenet, 1785.
Dokumenter vedkommende Kommissionen vedrorende Negerhandelens bedre Indretning og Ophævelse samt Efterretninger om Negerhandelen og Slaveriet i Vestindien, 1783-1806.
Diverse Dokumenter, Negerhandelens Afskaffelse betræffende, 1788-1847.
Mostingske Papirer: (a) Forslag til Ordning af vestindiske Forfatningsforhold angaaende Negrene m.m. 2 December 1836, (b) Forestilling om Forandring i Slavernes Kaar (med Bilag) 8 November 1834, 1826-34.
Akter vedkommende Slaveemancipationen. Den ældre sag om de Frikulørte, 1826-34.

Originale Forestillinger fra Kommissionen angaaende Negrenes Stilling i Vestindien m.m., med Resolutioner, 1834-43.
Akter vedkommende Slaveemancipationen I-III, 1833-47.
Negeremancipationen efter Reskript af 28 Juli 1847, 1847-53.
Den engelske Okkupation, 1801-1807.

Rigsarkivet, Copenhagen: Vestindiske Lokalarkiver
Dansk-vestindisk Regerings Forhandlingsprotokol St. Croix' Militære Jurisdiktion: Frederiksfort Standret, 7 Juli - 12 August 1848.

Rigsarkivet, Copenhagen: Haandskriftsamlingen
VII. D. 12: Species facti over den paa Eilandet Sainte Croix Aaret 1759 intenderede Neger Rebellion, forfattet efter Ordre af Byfoget Engelbreth Hesselbjerg.

United States

National Archives, Washington D.C.
Record Group 55, Box 9: Copy books of letters sent to the King 1845-48.
Record Group 55, Boxes 485-87: Udskrift af Christiansteds Jurisdictions Politi Journaler.
Record Group 55, Box 496-97: Udskrift af Frederiksteds Jurisdictions Politi Journaler.
Record Group 55, Box 558: Regulatory Functions, Sea Pass Protocols for Vessels, 1782-1806, 1806-7, 1815-68.
Record Group 55, Box 583-86: Commission for the Enumeration of the Free Coloured in St. Croix, St. Thomas and St. Jan, 1831.
Record Group 55, Box 793: Proceedings of the Common Probate Court of St. Croix.

University of California, Berkeley
Bancroft Papers: Z A 1: 3. Orders of governors, 1672-1727.

Jamaica

Jamaica Government Archives, Spanish Town
Calendar of Records, High Court of Vice Admiralty, Jamaica 1796.

2. Books and Articles

ALEXANDER, G. W. "Om den moralske Forpligtelse til og det hensigtmæssige af strax og fuldstændigt at ophæve Slaveriet i de dansk-vestindiske Kolonier." *Dansk Ugeskrift* 2 (76) (1843): 374-96.
ALLEYNE, Mervyn. *Roots of Jamaican Culture.* London: Pluto Press, 1988.
ARMYTAGE, Frances. *The Free Port System in the British West Indies: A Study in Commerical Policy.* London: Longmans, Green and Co. Ltd., 1953.
ARUTUNIEV, Serghei. "Cultural Paradigms: The Process of Change Through Cultural Borrowings." *Cultures* 5 (1) (1978): 87-109.

BECH, Svend Cedergreen. *Oplysning og tolerance 1721-1784.* Vol. 9, *Danmarks Historie*, edited by John Danstrup and Hal Koch. Copenhagen: Politikens Forlag, 1965.

BECKLES, Hilary. *Black Rebellion in Barbados: The Struggle Against Slavery, 1627-1838.* Bridgetown: Antilles Publications, 1984.

BERLIN, Ira. *Slaves Without Masters: The Free Negro in the Antebellum South.* New York: Pantheon Books, 1975.

——— . "Time, Space, and the Evolution of Afro-American Society on British Mainland North America." *American Historical Review* 85 (1980): 44-78.

BOLT, Christine. *Victorian Attitudes to Race.* London: Routledge and Kegan Paul, 1971.

BRADLEY, K. R. *Slaves and Masters in the Roman Empire: A Study in Social Control.* Oxford: Oxford University Press, 1987.

BRATHWAITE, Edward. *The Development of Creole Society in Jamaica 1770-1820.* Oxford: Clarendon Press, 1971.

——— . *Contradictory Omens.* Mona: Savacou Publications, 1974.

BRO-JØRGENSEN, J. O. *Dansk Vestindien indtil 1755.* Vol. 1, *Vore Gamle Tropekolonier*, edited Johannes Brøndsted. Copenhagen: Fremad, 1966.

BUCKLAND, W. W. *The Roman Law of Slavery.* Cambridge: Cambridge University Press, 1908.

BUCKLEY, Roger Norman. *Slaves in Red Coats: The British West India Regiments, 1795-1815.* New Haven: Yale University Press, 1979.

CANNY, Nicholas and Anthony Pagden, editors. *Colonial Identity in the Atlantic World, 1500-1800.* Princeton: Princeton University Press, 1987.

CARSTENS, J. L. "En Almindelig Beskrivelse om Alle de Danske Americanske eller West-Jndiske Ey-Lande." Edited Herluf Nielsen. *Danske Magazin* 8 (3) (1970): 173-268.

CARTWRIGHT, D. and A. Zander. *Group Dynamics.* New York: Tavistock Books, 1968.

CHRISTENSEN, Carlo. *Peter von Scholten: A Chapter of the History of the Virgin Islands.* Lemrig: Gadgaard Nielsens Bogtrykkeri, 1955.

COHEN, David W. and Jack P. Greene (eds.). *Neither Slave Nor Free: The Freedmen of African Descent in the Slave Societies of the New World.* Baltimore: Johns Hopkins University Press, 1972.

COLE, W. A. and Phyllis Deane. "The Growth of National Incomes." In *The Cambridge Economic History of Europe, Volume 6: The Industrial Revolutions and After*, edited by H. J. Habakkuk and M. Postan. Cambridge: Cambridge University Press, 1966.

COLL y TOSTE, Cayetano (ed.). *Boletin Histórico de Puerto Rico.* San Juan, Puerto Rico: Tip. Cantero, Fernandez and Co., No. 1, 1914.

COX, Edward L. *Free Coloreds in the Slave Societies of St. Kitts and Grenada, 1763-1833.* Knoxville: University of Tennessee Press, 1984.

CRATON, Michael. "Changing Patterns of Slave Families in the British West Indies." *Journal of Interdisciplinary History* 10 (1979): 1-35.

——— . *Testing the Chains: Resistance to Slavery in the British West Indies.* Ithaca: Cornell University Press, 1982.

CURTIN, Philip D. *The Atlantic Slave Trade.* Madison: University of Wisconsin Press, 1969.

——— . "Measuring the Atlantic Slave Trade." In *Race and Slavery in the Western Hemisphere: Quantitative Studies*, edited by Stanley L. Engerman and Eugene D. Genovese. Princeton: Princeton University Press, 1975.

DAHLERUP, H. B. "Skizzer fra et kort Besøg paa vore vestindiske Øer i Sommeren 1841." *Nyt Archiv for Søvæsenet* 1 (1842): 1-62.

——. *Mit Livs Begivenheder.* Copenhagen: Gyldendal, 1908/9, 4 vols.

DAVIS, David Brion. *The Problem of Slavery in Western Culture.* Ithaca: Cornell University Press, 1966.

——. *The Problem of Slavery in the Age of Revolution, 1770-1823.* Ithaca: Cornell University Press, 1975.

——. *Slavery and Human Progress.* New York: Oxford University Press, 1984.

DEBIEN, Gabriel. *Les Esclaves aux Antilles Francaises (XVIIe - XVIIIe Siècles).* Basse-Terre: Société d'Histoire de la Guadeloupe, 1974.

DEERR, Noel. *The History of Sugar.* 2 vols. London: Chapman and Hall, 1949-50.

DEGLER, Carl N. *Neither Black Nor White: Slavery and Race Relations in Brazil and the United States.* New York: Macmillan Co., 1971.

DEGN, Christian. *Die Schimmelmanns in Atlantischen Dreickshandel: Gewinn und Gewissen.* Neumünster: Karl Wachholtz Verlag, 1974.

DÍAZ SOLER, Luis M. *Historia de la Esclavitud Negra en Puerto Rico.* Rio Piedras: Universidad de Puerto Rico, 1965.

DIRKS, Robert. *The Black Saturnalia: Conflict and Its Ritual Expression on British West Indian Slave Plantations.* Gainesville: University of Florida Press, 1987.

DOCKUM, C. Van. *Livserindringer.* Copenhagen, 1893.

"Dom i sagen General-Majorinde Henriette de Schimmelmann contra Mulat Hans Jonathan Afsagt den 31 te Mai 1802." *Arkiv for Retsvidenskab og dens Anvendelse* 1 (1824):36.

DOOKHAN, Isaac. "Vieques or Crab Island: Source of Anglo-Spanish Colonial Conflict." *Journal of Caribbean History* 7 (1973):1-22.

——. *A History of the Virgin Islands of the United States.* St. Thomas: Caribbean Universities Press for College of the Virgin Islands, 1974.

DRESCHER, Seymour. *Capitalism and Antislavery: British Mobilization in Comparative Perspective.* London: Macmillan Press, 1986.

DYBDAHL, Vagn. *De nye Klasser 1870-1913.* Vol. 12, *Danmarks Historie,* edited John Danstrup and Hal Koch. Copenhagen: Politikens Forlag, 1965.

EDWARDS, Bryan. *The History, Civil and Commerical, of the British Colonies in the West Indies.* 2 vols. London: Stockdale, 1793.

EILSTRUP, Per, and Niels Eric Boesgaard. *Fjernt fra Danmark.* Copenhagen: Lademann, 1974.

ELKINS, Stanley. *Slavery: A Problem in American Institutional and Intellectual Life.* Chicago: University of Chicago Press, 1968.

ELTIS, David. *Economic Growth and the Ending of the Transatlantic Slave Trade.* New York: Oxford University Press, 1987.

FERNÁNDEZ MENDEZ, Eugenio. *Historia Cultural de Puerto Rico, 1493-1968.* Rio Piedras, Puerto Rico: Editorial Universitaria, 1971.

FREDRICKSON, George M. *The Black Image in the White Mind: The Debate on Afro-American Character and Destiny, 1817-1914.* New York: Harper and Row, 1971.

——. *White Supremacy: A Comparative Study in American and South African History.* New York: Oxford University Press, 1981.

——. *The Arrogance of Race: Historical Perspectives on Slavery, Racism, and Social Inequality.* Middletown: Wesleyan University Press, 1988.

FREYRE, Gilberto. *The Masters and the Slaves: A Study in the Development of Brazilian Civilization.* New York: Alfred A. Knopf, 1964. First published 1936.

FRYER, Peter. *Staying Power: The History of Black People in Britain*. London: Pluto Press, 1984.

FUGL, U. N. "Om Negerslaveriet i Vestindien og sammes Ophør; med specielt Hensyn til de danske Besiddeler." *Juridisk Tidsskrift* 24 B, 1 H (1834): 86-146.

GARDE, H. F. "Anna Heegaard og Peter von Scholten." *Personalhistorisk Tidsskrift* 78 (1958): 25-37.

GASPAR, David Barry. *Bondmen and Rebels: A Study of Master-Slave Relations in Antigua*. Baltimore: Johns Hopkins University Press, 1985.

GEGGUS, David Patrick. *Slavery, War, and Revolution: The British Occupation of Saint Domingue 1793-1798*. Oxford: Clarendon Press, 1982.

GENOVESE, Eugene D. *Roll, Jordan, Roll: The World the Slaves Made*. New York: Pantheon Books, 1974.

GILLIN, J. L. *Criminology and Penology*. New York: Appleton Century Crofts, 1943.

GOLDIN, Claudia Dale. *Urban Slavery in the American South 1820-1860*. Chicago: University of Chicago Press, 1976.

GOMEZ ACEVEDO, Labor. *Organización y Reglamentación del Trabajo en el Puerto Rico del Siglo XIX*. San Juan, Puerto Rico: Instituto de Cultura Puertorriqueña, 1970.

GOVEIA, Elsa V. *Slave Society in the British Leeward Islands at the End of the Eighteenth Century*. New Haven: Yale University Press, 1965.

——. *The West Indian Slave Laws of the 18th Century*. Barbados: Caribbean Universities Press, 1970.

GREEN-PEDERSEN, Svend E. "Danmarks ophævelse af negerslavehandelen. Omkring tilblivelsen af forordningen af 16. marts 1792" *Arkiv. Tidsskrift for Arkivforskning* 3 (1) (1969): 19-37.

——. "The Scope and Structure of the Danish Negro Slave Trade." *Scandinavian Economic History Review* 19 (1971): 149-97.

——. "The History of the Danish Negro Slave Trade, 1733-1807. An Interim Survey Relating in Particular to its Volume, Structure, Profitability and Abolition." *Revue française d'histoire d'outre mer* 62 (226-27) (1975): 196-220.

——. "Negro Slavery and Christianity: On Erik Pontoppidan's Preface to L. F. Roemer, *Tilforladelig Efterretning om Kysten Guinea* (A True Account of the Coast of Guinea), 1760." *Transactions of the Historical Society of Ghana* 15 (1974): 85-102.

——. "The Economic Considerations behind the Danish Abolition of the Negro Slave Trade." In *The Uncommon Market: Essays in the Economic History of the Atlantic Slave Trade*, edited by Henry A. Gemery and Jan S. Hogendorn. New York: Academic Press, 1979.

——. "Slave Demography in the Danish West Indies and the Abolition of the Danish Slave Trade." In *The Abolition of the Atlantic Slave Trade*, edited by David Eltis and James Walvin. Madison: University of Wisconsin Press, 1981.

GURNEY, J. J. *A Winter in the West Indies*. London: John Murray, 1840.

HAAGENSEN, Richard. *Beskrivelse over Eylandet St. Croix i America i Vestindien*. Copenhagen: Lillies Enke, 1758.

HALL, Gwendolyn Midlo. *Social Control in Slave Plantation Societies: A Comparison of St. Domingue and Cuba*. Baltimore: Johns Hopkins University Press, 1971.

HALL, Neville A. T. "Anna Heegaard – Enigma." *Caribbean Quarterly* 22 (1976):62-73.

——. "Slave Laws of the Danish Virgin Islands in the Later Eighteenth Century." *Annals of the New York Academy of Sciences* 292 (1977): 174-186.

——. "Establishing a Public Elementary School System for Slaves in the Danish Virgin Islands, 1732-1846." *Caribbean Journal of Education* 6 (1979): 1-45.

——— . Translation with introduction and notes, *Forslag til Ordning af Vestindiske Forfatningsforhold Angaaende Negerne med Mere* (A Proposal for Regulating the Situation of Negroes in the West Indies, etc., Anon., 1826). St. Thomas: Bureau of Libraries, Museums and Archaeological Services: Department of Conservation and Cultural Affairs, Occasional Paper No. 5, 1979.

——— . "The 1816 Freedman Petition in the Danish West Indies: Its Background and Consequences." *Boletin de Estudios Latino-americanos y del Caribe* 29 (1980): 55-73.

——— . "Slaves Use of Their 'Free' Time in the Danish Virgin Islands in the Later Eighteenth and Early Nineteenth Century." *Journal of Caribbean History* 13 (1980): 21-43.

——— . "Slavery in Three West Indian Towns: Christiansted, Fredericksted and Charlotte Amalie in the Late Eighteenth and Early Nineteenth Century." In *Trade, Government and Society in Caribbean History 1700-1920*, edited by B. W. Higman. Kingston: Heinemann Educational Books, 1983.

——— . Translation with an introduction, "Louis Rothe's 1846 Report on Education in Post-emancipation Antigua." *Caribbean Journal of Education* 10 (1983): 55-62.

——— . "The Victor Vanquished: Emancipation in St. Croix; Its Antecedents and Immediate Aftermath." *Nieuwe West-Indische Gids* 58 (1984): 3-36.

——— . Review of David Eltis and James Walvin (eds), *The Abolition of the Atlantic Slave Trade* in *Immigrants and Minorities* 3 (1984): 94-96.

——— . "Maritime Maroons: *Grand Marronage* from the Danish West Indies." *William and Mary Quarterly* 42 (1985): 476-498.

——— . *The Danish West Indies: Empire Without Dominion, 1671-1848*. Division of Libraries, Museums and Archaeological Services, U.S. Virgin Islands, Occasional Paper No. 8, 1985.

——— . Review of David Barry Gaspar, *Bondmen and Rebels* in *Journal of Economic History* 46 (1986): 1054-1056.

——— . Review of Karen Fog Olwig, *Cultural Adaptation and Resistance on St. John* in *Hispanic American Historical Review* 67 (1987): 147-48.

——— . "Slaves and the Law in the Towns of St. Croix 1802-1807." *Slavery & Abolition* 8 (1987): 147-65.

——— . "Apollo Miller, Freedman: His Life and Times." *Journal of Caribbean History* 23 (2) (1989): 196-213.

HANDLER, Jerome S. *The Unappropriated People: Freedmen in the Slave Society of Barbados*. Baltimore: Johns Hopkins University Press, 1974.

HANDLER, Jerome S. and Frederick W. Lange. *Plantation Slavery in Barbados: An Archaeological and Historical Investigation*. Cambridge: Harvard University Press, 1978.

HANSEN, Thorkild. *Slavernes Kyst*. Copenhagen: Gyldendal, 1967.

——— . *Slavernes Øer*. Copenhagen: Gyldendal, 1970.

HARRIS, Marvin. *Patterns of Race in the Americas*. New York: Walker, 1964.

HAY, Douglas. "Property, Authority and the Criminal Law." In *Albion's Fatal Tree* by Douglas Hay et. al. New York: Pantheon Books, 1975.

HERSKOVITS, Melville J. *The Myth of the Negro Past*. Gloucester, Mass.: Peter Smith, 1970. First published 1941.

HEUMAN, Gad J. *Between Black and White: Race, Politics, and the Free Coloreds in Jamaica, 1792-1865*. Westport, Conn.: Greenwood Press, 1981.

——— . (ed.) *Out of the House of Bondage: Runaways, Resistance and Marronage in Africa and the New World*. London: Frank Cass, 1986.

HIGMAN, B. W. *Slave Populations of the British Caribbean, 1807-1834*. Baltimore: Johns Hopkins University Press, 1984.

HOLTEN, C. H. "Af en gammel Hofmands Mindeblade (Konferensraad Carl Henrik Holtens Optegnelser)." In vol. 11, *Memoirer og Breve*, edited J. Clausen and P. F. Rist. Copenhagen: Gyldendal, 1909.

JENSEN, Hans. *De danske Stænderforsamlingers Historie 1830-48*. Copenhagen: Schultz, 1931-34, 2 vols.

JOHANSEN, Hans Christian. "Slave Demography of the Danish West Indian Islands." *Scandinavian Economic History Review* 29 (1981): 1-20.

——."The Reality behind the Demographic Arguments to Abolish the Danish Slave Trade." In *The Abolition of the Atlantic Slave Trade*, edited by David Eltis and James Walvin. Madison: University of Wisconsin Press, 1981.

KARASCH, Mary C. *Slave Life in Rio de Janeiro 1808-1850*. Princeton: Princeton University Press, 1987.

KARRAS, Ruth Mazo. *Slavery and Society in Medieval Scandinavia*. New Haven: Yale University Press 1988.

KIRSTEIN, E. "Udtog af Forestilling en til Kongen angaaende Negerhandelens Afskaffelse." *Minerva* (April 1792): 43-86.

KLEIN, Herbert S. *African Slavery in Latin America and the Caribbean*. New York: Oxford University Press, 1986.

KLINGBERG, Frank Joseph. *The Anti-Slavery Movement in England: A Study in English Humanitarianism*. Hampden, Conn.: Archon Books, 1968. First published New Haven: Yale University Press, 1926.

KNIGHT, Franklin W. *Slave Society in Cuba During the Nineteenth Century*. Madison: University of Wisconsin Press, 1970.

——. *The Caribbean: The Genesis of a Fragmented Nationalism*. New York: Oxford University Press, 1978.

LABAT, Jean-Baptiste. *Nouveaux Voyages Faits aux Isles de l'Amérique*. Fort de France: Horizons Caraï, 1972. First published 1742.

LAMUR, Humphrey E. *The Production of Sugar and the Reproduction of Slaves at Vossenburg, Suriname 1705-1863*. Amsterdam: Amsterdam Centre for Caribbean Studies, 1987.

LARSEN, Jens. *Virgin Islands Story*. Philadelphia: Fortress Press, 1950.

LARSEN, Kay. *Dansk Vestindien 1666-1917*. Copenhagen: C. A. Reitzel, 1928.

——. *Guvernører, Residenter, Kommandanter og Chefer. Samt enkelte andre fremtrædende Personer i de tidligere danske Tropekolonier*. Copenhagen: Arthur Jensens Forlag, 1940.

LAURING, Palle. *A History of the Kingdom of Denmark*. Copenhagen: Høst and Søn, 1973.

LAWAETZ, Herman. *Brødremenighedens Mission i Dansk-Vestindien 1769-1848*. Copenhagen: Otto B. Wroblewski, 1902.

——. *Peter v. Scholten. Vestindiske Tidsbilleder fra den sidste Generalguvernørs Dage*. Copenhagen: Gyldendal, 1940.

LEWIS, Gordon K. *The Virgin Islands: A Caribbean Lilliput*. Evanston: Northwestern University Press, 1972.

LEWISOHN, Florence. *St Croix Under Seven Flags*. Hollywood, Florida: The Dukane Press, 1970.

LOMBARDI, John V. *The Decline and Abolition of Negro Slavery in Venezuela 1820-1834*. Westport, Conn.: Greenwood Publishing Corp., 1971.

——. "Comparative Slave Systems in the Americas: A Critical Review." In *New Approaches to Latin American History*, edited by Richard Graham and Peter H. Smith. Austin: University of Texas Press, 1974.

LOSE, E. V. "Kort Udsigt over den danske-lutherske Missions Historie paa St. Croix, St. Thomas og St. Jan." *Nordisk Missions-Tidsskrift* 1 (1890): 1-37.

LOVEJOY, Paul E. "The Volume of the Atlantic Slave Trade: A Synthesis." *Journal of African History* 23 (1982): 473-501.

MACPHERSON, John. *Caribbean Lands: A Geography of the West Indies*. Kingston: Longman, 1973. Third edition.

MALINOWSKI, Bronislaw. "Introduction" in *Methods of Study of Culture Contact in Africa*. London: Oxford University Press for the Institute of African Languages and Cultures, 1938.

MARSH, Clifton. *A Socio-Historical Analysis of the Emancipation of 1848 and the Labor Revolts of 1878 in the Danish West Indies*. St. Thomas: Caribbean Research Institute, 1981.

MATTOSO, Katia M. de Quierós. *To Be a Slave in Brazil 1550-1880*. New Brunswick: Rutgers University Press, 1986.

MILLETTE, James. *The Genesis of Crown Colony Government: Trinidad, 1783-1810*. Curepe, Trinidad: Moko Enterprises, 1970.

MINTZ, Sidney W. and Douglas Hall. *The Origins of the Jamaican Internal Marketing System*. Yale University Publications in Anthropology, no. 57. New Haven: Yale University Press, 1960.

MINTZ, Sidney W. and Richard Price. *An Anthropological Approach to the Afro-American Past: A Caribbean Perspective*. Philadelphia: Institute for the Study of Human Issues, 1976.

MOORE, R. I. (ed.). *The Hamlyn Historical Atlas*. London: Hamlyn, 1981.

MORALES-CARRION, Arturo. *Albores Históricos del Capitalismo en Puerto Rico*. Rio Piedras: Editorial Universitaria, Universidad de Puerto Rico, 1974.

MORENO FRAGINALS, Manuel. *El Ingenio: Complejo Económico Social Cubano del Azúcar*. Havana: Editorial de Ciencias Sociales, 1964.

MORRISSEY, Marietta. *Slave Women in the New World: Gender Stratification in the Caribbean*. Lawrence: University Press of Kansas, 1989.

MURDOCK, George P. *Africa: Its Peoples and Their Culture History*. New York: McGraw-Hill, 1959.

MURPHY, Patricia Shaubah. *The Moravian Mission to the African Slaves of the Danish West Indies 1732-1828*. St. Thomas: Caribbean Research Institute, College of the Virgin Islands, 1969.

NICHOLLS, David. *From Dessalines to Duvalier: Race, Colour and National Independence in Haiti*. Cambridge: Cambridge University Press, 1979.

NISSEN, Johan Peter. *Reminiscences of a 46 years' residence in the Island of St. Thomas, in the West Indies*. Nazareth, Pa.: Senseman and Co., printer, 1838.

ØRSTED, A. S. "Beholdes Herredømmet over en vestindisk Slave, naar han betræder dansk-europæisk Grund." *Arkiv for Retsvidenskaben og dens Anvendelse* 1 (1824): 459-85.

ØRSTED, A. S. (ed.). *Collegial-Tidende for Danmark 1834*. Copenhagen, 1840.

OLDENDORP, C. G. A. *Geschichte der Mission der Evangelischen Brüder auf den caraibischen Inseln S. Thomas, S. Croix und S. Jan*. Edited Johann Jakob Bossard. Barby, Germany, 1777. English edition and translation Arnold R. Highfield and Vladimir Barac, *History of the Mission of the Evangelical Brethren on the Caribbean Islands of St. Thomas, St. Croix, and St. John*. Ann Arbor : Karoma Publishers Inc., 1987.

OLSEN, Gunnar. *Den unge enevælde 1660-1721*. Vol. 8, *Danmarks Historie*, edited John Danstrup and Hal Koch. Copenhagen: Politikens Forlag, 1964.

OLWIG, Karen Fog. "Finding a Place for the Slave Family: Historical Anthropological Perspectives." *Folk* 23 (1981): 345-58.

——. *Cultural Adaptation and Resistance on St. John: Three Centuries of Afro-Caribbean Life.* Gainesville: University of Florida Press, 1985.

OXHOLM, P. L. *De Danske Vestindiske öers Tilstand.* Copenhagen: Johan Frederik Schultz, 1797.

——. "Nogle Anmærkninger over en Afhandling om Negerhandelens Ophævelse udi Maanedskrift Minerva af Februarii 1805." *Minerva* 2 (1806), special issue.

PANNET, Pierre J. *Report on the Execrable Conspiracy Carried Out by the Amina Negroes on the Danish Island of St. Jan in America 1733.* Translated and edited by Aimery P. Caron and Arnold R. Highfield, St. Croix: Antilles Press, 1984.

PARRY, J. H. and P. M. Sherlock. *A Short History of the West Indies.* London: Macmillan, 1956.

PATTERSON, Orlando. *Slavery and Social Death: A Comparative Study.* Cambridge, Mass.: Harvard University Press, 1982.

——. "Slavery: The Underside of Freedom." *Slavery & Abolition* 5 (1984): 87-104.

PETERSEN, Bernhard Von. *En Historisk beretning om de danske vestindiske øer St. Croix, St. Thomas og St. Jan.* Copenhagen: Stinck, 1855.

PRICE, Richard (ed.). *Maroon Societies: Rebel Slave Communities in the Americas.* New York: Anchor Books, 1973.

PROSCH, Victor. "Om Slaveemancipationen paa de dansk-vestindiske Øer." *Dansk Tidsskrift* 2 (1848): 385-431.

QUINNEY, Richard. *Critique of the Legal Order.* Boston: Little, Brown, and Co., 1973.

RAHBEK, K. L. "Om Negerhandelens Ophævelse i Hensyn til de danske vestindiske Øer." *Minerva* 1 (1805): 189-240.

RAMLØV, Preben. *Massa Peter.* Copenhagen: Gyldendal, 1967.

——. *Brødrene og Slaverne.* Copenhagen: Kristeligt Dagblads Forlag, 1968.

RICHARDSON, Ronald Kent. *Moral Imperium: Afro-Caribbeans and the Transformation of British Rule, 1776-1838.* Westport, Conn.: Greenwood Press, 1987.

SCARANO, Francisco A. *Sugar and Slavery in Puerto Rico.* Madison: University of Wisconsin Press, 1984.

SCHMIDT, I. C. "Blandede Anmærkninger, samlede paa og over Ejlandet St. Croix i Amerika 1788." *Samleren* 2 (1788): 199-260.

SCHOELCHER, Victor. *Colonies étrangères et Haïti: résultats de l'émancipation anglaise.* Paris: Pagnerre, 1843. 2 vols.

SCHOU, J. H., ed. *Chronologisk Register over de Kongelige Forordninger og Aabne Breve.* 1793-1810, 1814. Copenhagen: Gyldendal, 1848.

SCHULER, Monica, "Akan Slave Rebellions in the British Caribbean." *Savacou* 1 (1970): 8-31.

SHERIDAN, Richard B. "The Rise of a Colonial Gentry: A Case Study of Antigua." *Economic History Review* 13 (1960-61): 342-57.

——. "Africa and the Caribbean in the Atlantic Slave Trade." *American Historical Review* 77 (1972): 15-35.

——. *Doctors and Slaves: A Medical and Demographic History of Slavery in the British West Indies, 1680-1834.* Cambridge: Cambridge University Press, 1985.

SKOVMAND, Roar. *Folkestyrets fødsel 1830-1870.* Vol. 11, *Danmarks Historie,* edited by John Danstrup and Hal Koch. Copenhagen: Politikens Forlag, 1964.

SKUBBELTRANG, Fridlev. "Dansk Vestindien 1848-1880." In Vol. 3 *Vore Gamle Tropekolonier,* edited by Johannes Brøndsted. Copenhagen: Fremad, 1967.

SMITH, James. *The Winter of 1840 in St. Croix, with an excursion to Tortola and St. Thomas.* New York: the author, 1840.

SPINGARN, Lawrence P. "Slavery in the Danish West Indies." *The American-Scandinavian Review* 45 (1957): 35-43.

SVEISTRUP, P. P. "Bidrag til de tidligere dansk-vestindiske øers Økonomiske Historie, med særligt Henblik paa Sukkerproduction og Sukkerhandel." *Nationaløkonomisk Tidsskrift for Samfundsspørgsmaal, Økonomi og Handel* 80 (1942):1-120.

——. "Det Kongelige Danske octroyerede Vestindiske Handelsselskab 1778-85." *Historisk Tidsskrift* 10 (6) (1943): 385-427.

TANNENBAUM, Frank. *Slave and Citizen: The Negro in the Americas.* New York: Vintage Books, 1946.

TRIER, C. A. "Det danske-vestindiske negerindførelsforbud af 1792." *Historisk Tidsskrift* 5 (1904-1905): 405-508.

TURNER, Mary. *Slaves and Missionaries: The Disintegration of Jamaican Slave Society 1787-1834.* Urbana: University of Illinois Press, 1982.

TYSON, George F. *The Enighed Estate and Ruin on St. John, U.S.V.I.: An Historical Survey.* Island Resources Foundation, for the Department of Conservation and Cultural Affairs, Government of the U.S. Virgin Islands, 1976.

VAN DE VOORT, J. P. *De Westindische Plantages van 1720 tot 1795: Financien en Handel.* Eindhoven: De Witte, 1973.

VIBÆK, Jens. *Dansk Vestindien 1755-1848.* Vol. 2, *Vore Gamle Tropekolonier,* edited by Johannes Brøndsted. Copenhagen: Fremad, 1966.

——. *Reform og Fallit 1784-1830.* Vol. 10, *Danmarks Historie,* edited by John Danstrup and Hal Koch. Copenhagen: Politikens Forlag, 1964.

VON SCHOLTEN, Peter. *Most Submissive Report Proposing an Improved and More Distinct Organization of Your Majesty's Free Coloured Subjects in the West India Colonies.* Copenhagen: 1830.

——. *Plan for an Improved and More Distinct Organization for the Free Coloured Inhabitants of the Danish West India Islands: St. Croix, St. Thomas and St. John's.* Christiansted, St. Croix: 1831.

WADE, Richard C. *Slavery in the Cities: The South 1820-1860.* New York: Oxford University Press, 1964.

WALVIN, James. *Black and White: The Negro and English Society 1555-1945.* London: Allen Lane, 1973.

WATTS, David. *The West Indies: Patterns of Development, Culture and Environmental Change Since 1492.* Cambridge: Cambridge University Press, 1987.

WEED, Thurlow. *Letters from Europe and the West Indies 1843-1852.* Albany: Weed, Parsons and Co., 1866.

WEST, Hans. *Tiltrædelsestale holden da Skolen i Christianstæd paa St. Croix blev aabnet den 8de October 1789.* Christiansted, St. Croix: Daniel Thebou, 1789.

——. "Beretning om det danske Eilande St. Croix i Vestindien, fra Juniimaaned 1789 til Juniimaaneds Udgang 1790." *Iris* 3 (1791): 1-88.

——. *Bidrag til Beskrivelse over Ste. Croix, med en kort udsigt over St. Thomas, St. Jean, Tortola, Spanishtown og Crabeneiland.* Copenhagen: Fridrik Wilhelm Thiele, 1793.

WESTERGAARD, Waldemar. *The Danish West Indies under Company Rule (1671-1754), with a supplementary chapter, 1755-1917.* New York: Macmillan, 1917.

——. "Account of the Negro Rebellion on St. Croix, Danish West Indies, 1759." *Journal of Negro History* 11 (1926): 50-61.

WILKS, Ivor. *Asante in the Nineteenth Century: The Structure and Evolution of a Political Order.* Cambridge: Cambridge University Press, 1975.

WILSON, Peter. *Crab Antics: The Social Anthropology of English Speaking Negro Societies of the Caribbean.* New Haven: Yale University Press, 1973.

WOOD, Peter H. *Black Majority: Negroes in Colonial South Carolina from 1670 through the Stono Rebellion*. New York: Knopf, 1974.
WRIGHT, Richardson. *Revels in Jamaica 1682-1838*. New York: Dodd, Mead and Co., 1937.

3. Newspapers and Journals

Berlingske Tidende (Copenhagen).
Dansk Vestindisk Regerings Avis (Christiansted, St. Croix).
Fædrelandet (Copenhagen).
Jamaica Courant (Kingston, Jamaica).
Kjøbenhavnsposten (Copenhagen).
Kiøbenhavnske Lærde Efterretninger (Copenhagen).
Oeconomisk Journal (Copenhagen).
Royal Danish American Gazette (Christiansted, St. Croix).
Royal Gazette (Kingston, Jamaica).
Royal St. Croix Gazette (Christiansted, St. Croix).
St. Croix Gazette (Christiansted, St. Croix).
St. Thomæ Tidende (Charlotte Amalie, St. Thomas).

4. Dissertations and Unpublished Papers

BAA, Enid M. "The Brandenburgers at St. Thomas." A paper presented at the Tenth Annual Conference of the Association of Caribbean Historians, St. Thomas, 1978.
BENTZEN, Grethe. *Debatten om det dansk-vestindiske Negerslaveri 1833-48 med særligt Henblik på de igennem Tidsskriftpressen og stænderdebatter udtrykte holdninger.* Cand. mag. dissertation, Aarhus Universitet, 1976.
CHRISTENSEN, Jorgen Bach, *Kolonisamfundet på St. Croix i sidste halvdel af det 18. århundrede, med særligt Henblik på aristokratiet blandt plantageejerne.* Cand. mag. dissertation, Aarhus Universitet, 1978.
DUNCKER, Sheila. *The Free Coloured and Their Struggle for Civil Rights in Jamaica.* M.A. dissertation, University of London, 1960.
GARRIGUS, John D. *A Struggle for Respect: The Free Coloreds of Pre-Revolutionary Saint Domingue, 1760-69.* Ph.D. dissertation, Johns Hopkins University, 1988.
GOSLINGA, Cornelius. "The Fall of the Dutch West India Company." A paper presented at the Eleventh Annual Conference of the Association of Caribbean Historians, Curacao, 1979.
HALL, Neville A. T. "The Post-Emancipation Court Martial in Frederiksted, St. Croix, July-August 1848: An Account and an Analysis." A paper presented at the Thirteenth Annual Conference of the Association of Caribbean Historians, Guadeloupe, 1981.
—— . "Apollo Miller, Freedman: His Reconstructed Life and Times." Seminar paper, Department of History, University of the West Indies, Mona, 1985.
OLWIG, Karen Fog. *Households, Exchange and Social Reproduction: The Development of a Caribbean Society.* Ph.D. dissertation, University of Minnesota, 1977.
POPE, Pauline Holman. *Cruzan Slavery: An Ethnohistorical Study of Differential Responses to Slavery in the Danish West Indies.* Ph.D. dissertation, University of California at Davis, 1969.

Index